CRITICAL ACCLAIM FOR THIS VOLUME

'This landmark collection shows the important role of feminist scholarship in rethinking post-nationalist identity in Europe – a problematic from which US feminists have much to learn. In this way and others these essays expand the horizons of the common feminist heritage of international feminisms. The introductory essay alone is worth the purchase of the volume for its brilliant analysis of the strengths and limitations of different focuses and styles of thinking in the US, Northern, and Southern Europe. This is a fine teaching text.'

*Sandra Harding, Graduate School of Education
and Information Studies, UCLA*

'*Thinking Differently* represents a crucial step towards a truly transnational perspective in European Women's Studies. As a prominent result of several years of Community-funded European Women's Studies networking, this highly ambitious book aims at displacing the Anglo-American outlook that often has been confounded with transnationalism in favour of sophisticated analyses grounded in feminist scholarship based on in-depth knowledge of national and regional differences as well as on balanced insight into pan-European processes of change. This approach allows the authors, a multinational group of distinguished feminist scholars from Southern, Eastern, Northern and Western parts of Europe, to identify important new agendas for European Women's Studies. They articulate a range of highly important questions – from shifting meanings of the single woman and the specific European histories of racism to the semantics of sex/gender in different European languages. This advanced textbook is a must for researchers, teachers, students, politicians and others, interested in European Women's Studies and gender issues in Europe.'

*Nina Lykke, Department of Gender Studies,
Linköping University, Sweden*

D0145221

THINKING DIFFERENTLY

A Reader in European Women's Studies

EDITED BY GABRIELE GRIFFIN AND ROSI BRAIDOTTI

(ATHENA)

ZED BOOKS
London & New York

In Memoriam: Zarana Papic, 1949–2002

Thinking Differently was first published in 2002 by
Zed Books Ltd, 7 Cynthia Street, London N1 9JF, UK,
and Room 400, 175 Fifth Avenue, New York, NY 10010, USA

This book has been published in the context of the European Thematic Network
of Women's Studies, ATHENA, with the financial support of the Socrates/Erasmus
programme for Thematic Networks of the European Commission

Designed and typeset in Monotype Bembo by Illuminati, Grosmont
Cover designed by Andrew Corbett
Printed and bound in Great Britain by Bookcraft, Midsomer Norton

Distributed in the USA exclusively by Palgrave, a division of
St Martin's Press, LLC, 175 Fifth Avenue, New York, NY 10010

A catalogue record for this book is available from the British Library

Library of Congress Cataloging-in-Publication Data applied for

ISBN 1 84277 002 0 (Hb)
ISBN 1 84277 003 9 (Pb)

Contents

Introduction: Configuring European Women's Studies

GABRIELE GRIFFIN AND ROSI BRAIDOTTI

A Game

Here is a game, for you, the reader. It has two elements. Part one: write down – without looking them up – the names of five American feminists; five British feminists; and five feminists who are German, Italian, Spanish, Slovenian, Greek, Hungarian, Portuguese, Finnish, and Belgian. How did you get on? The likelihood, since you are not a beginner in Women's or Gender Studies, is that you could manage American and British, and possibly those relating to your own country of origin, but beyond that? How many Slovenian or Hungarian or Portuguese feminists can you name if you are not from one of those countries? Two, one, none? Or actually five? If you were able to name five feminists for all of the countries listed above we want to hear from you, because you would be the most knowledgeable European feminist we have come across. It is more probable, however, that you faltered and possibly were not able to name a single Greek or Finnish feminist, for example. If so, this is *not* to your discredit; it tells us something about the circulation of Women's Studies knowledge in Europe.

Now to part 2. Do you have on your bookshelves – providing you can afford to buy, or are able to borrow, books – three (we are getting more modest now) books by American feminists, British feminists, German feminists, Italian feminists, Spanish feminists, Slovenian feminists, Greek feminists, Hungarian feminists, Portuguese feminists, Finnish feminists, or Belgian feminists? Check it out! What did you find? How many books by Greek feminists do you harbour on your shelves? How many Italian ones? How many by Slovenians? Again, the likelihood is that whilst you will have quite a few texts by American, British, and possibly French feminists, and maybe also books by feminists from your own country of origin, or from the country in which you now live, it is unlikely that all the countries named above are equally represented, and some will not be represented at all. Again, this says something about both the production and the circulation of Women's Studies knowledge in Europe.

It was with an understanding of these gaps in our knowledges and on our bookshelves that *Thinking Differently: A Reader in European Women's Studies* was first conceived.

European and Anglo-American Women's Studies

Thinking Differently: A Reader in European Women's Studies is the product of a research process which began properly in 1997[1] when DG XXII of the European Union, the directorate general with special responsibility for education and training, awarded funding to ATHENA, the Thematic Network of women from all over Europe already involved in teaching Women's and/or Gender Studies, or seeking to establish Women's Studies as an academic discipline in their country. One of the projects which the members of ATHENA decided to work on was a European Women's Studies textbook. The reasons for this were many, some already demonstrated through 'the game' above. For one thing, it was felt by many women working in Women's Studies in Europe that the discursive flow in Women's Studies, the migration of knowledge, occurred along very distinctive and one-way lines, from West to East, from the Anglo-American alliance to (the rest of) Europe. Internationally, the production and circulation of feminist knowledge was dominated, and, one might argue, continues to be dominated, by the United States and the United Kingdom.[2] This means that whilst the work of many American and British feminist authors is the object of widespread dissemination, feminists from (other) European countries struggle to get their work known. This is not to suggest that some European countries do not have well-established Women's Studies courses and research centres. The Nordic countries spring to mind here. However, their local success has not received the international resonance that it deserves. The point is that, in the early years of the third millennium, we still witness a de facto domination of Northern Europe, the UK and the USA in the making of the curricula and the teaching material in Women's Studies.

One role that this volume fulfils, then, is to provide a platform for a series of European feminists, not all of whose voices are commonly heard outside of their home countries. It is therefore a volume written by European feminists for feminists and others interested in Women's Studies issues both within Europe and in the wider world. It is part of an attempt to broaden a certain common heritage of feminist work. That heritage, a sort of general internationalized feminist culture, has pervaded Women's Studies and has filled the bookshelves of at least the first generation of academic feminists in Europe. Let us try another game here and ask: who does *not* have Simone de Beauvoir's

The Second Sex, and Kate Millett's *Sexual Politics* on her bookshelf? Or Germaine Greer's *The Female Eunuch*? Or Adrienne Rich's and Audre Lorde's poetry? These can be considered as foundational texts that are part of the feminist canon. As such they constitute, in a multitude of translations, the grounds for a common world of academic and non-academic feminists. This common heritage and intellectual genealogy create also a certain intellectual and political wealth. They constitute a great advantage, which we are not likely to want to disperse. What is therefore at stake in the realization that English-language feminism has a hegemonic hold over Women's and Gender Studies is, rather, the desire to broaden this common heritage, insert more diversity into it, and move it along the road of a two-way exchange with a number of 'minority' languages and cultures within the kaleidoscope of Europe.

In working to broaden our feminist heritage, we build upon a history of European feminist work. Since the start of the European Union's cultural and educational exchanges in the late 1980s, academic feminists in Europe have seized the opportunity offered by community funds to explore alternatives to the Anglo-American domination of the Women's Studies and gender curricula. Although these initiatives often took the form of reflections on education and on curriculum development, they inevitably raised larger historical, cultural and political issues. One simple reason, for example, why courses on European feminist traditions cannot be taught is that some of the fundamental research on the matter is just not available. And without the groundwork of archive and documentation of the different political and cultural traditions, it is almost impossible to devise teaching materials that do justice to the local perspectives. Significantly, the membership of the ATHENA network which has supported the drafting of this volume also includes a significant number of women's libraries and documentation centres, geographically located in the different areas of Europe.[3]

There are perhaps three main, in part historically determined, reasons why the United States and the United Kingdom have gained such prominence in Women's Studies. The first of these is that the institutionalization of Women's Studies as an academic discipline, and hence academic publishing in the field, occurred earlier and to a greater extent in the USA and the UK than in most European countries. The history of the establishment of Women's Studies in Europe itself was first extensively documented as early as 1989 in a study funded by the European Commission. It was carried out by the independent feminist journal *Les Cahiers du Grif* and it resulted in the creation of the first European data bank of courses in Women's Studies, also known as the GRACE project. This project received further impetus through the EU-funded SIGMA evaluation of Women's Studies co-operation projects in Europe, which re-sulted in a Synthesis Report on Women's Studies (1995). This revealed that whereas Women's Studies as a named degree route at undergraduate and/or postgraduate level was well established by 1995 in countries such as the United Kingdom and Finland, for example, it was much less developed in countries such as Germany, Spain, Italy and France, where one might get individual researchers and some research centres working on Women's Studies-related topics but where there were no, or hardly any, named degree routes in Women's Studies. This situation has, to some extent, changed since 1995; whereas courses in Women's Studies in the UK have experienced difficulties in recruiting students and some courses have, in consequence, either closed or been integrated into the teaching of traditional disciplines in the social sciences and humanities, Women's Studies in other countries such as the Netherlands and Sweden is buoyant, and is growing in countries such as Germany, Spain and Portugal. These shifts notwithstanding, it remains the case that the early institutionalization of Women's Studies in the United States, where it occurred from the 1970s, and in the UK, where this happened from the early 1980s, led to an active feminist knowledge production which found its ready dissemination in European countries as they began to develop their own courses in Women's Studies.

The second reason why these two countries gained such prominence in Women's Studies in European countries – and this may be a contentious point – is the philosophical tradition which informs that work. Grounded in empiricism and a certain anti-intellectualism or resistance to abstraction and theory, English as a medium and as a practice had a certain appeal for Women's Studies in that its groundedness and empiricism aligned it with one of Women's Studies' key postulates, namely the importance of experience as a source of knowledge and of theorizing. Many early works in Women's Studies that had a wide circulation were 'bestsellers' because they related practice and theory, because they offered empirical findings to underpin their theoretical stance. What made Adrienne Rich's work so powerful, for example, was the conjunction between personal experience and theorizing that it presented. In addition feminist writers such as Rich, or for that matter de Beauvoir, were 'generalists', in that they took on the great intellectual issues and challenges of their day, independent of any institutional affiliation. They were not academic in the strict – and sterile – sense of the term. We think that this is an important element in our intellectual and political tradition, and continue to draw inspiration from it.

This factor, however, points to another important issue, namely the extent to which different understandings of both the social function and the social status of 'the intellectual' affect the role that feminists can play in the institutions of their respective countries. Here, too, the more pragmatic tradition of England and of Northern European cultures clashes with the more flamboyant tradition of Southern and Eastern Europe, where the mystique of the intellectual did not fail to influence and to impact negatively upon women's access to the means of intellectual production. In turn, the universities in the diverse European countries adopted very different stances to the sacred monsters of culture: met with institutional diffidence in the North, they were venerated in the South or to the East. This major cultural difference also affects another extremely important dividing line: that between the inside and the outside of the institutions. Our experience of the institutionalization processes of Women's Studies in Europe has shown that, in cultures where the actual degree of institutional visibility is low – especially in Southern and Eastern Europe – Women's Studies mostly situated itself outside the university, or in a very critical position vis-à-vis the institution. We encountered this as a problem in our work, in so far as groups that reject institutional practices cannot easily be accounted for, and de facto fall into a form of marginality, which may be chosen or imposed.

Clearly, part of the appeal of a feminist scholarship that combined the personal with the political was the rights-oriented stance of the women's movement of the late 1960s and the 1970s. As women were campaigning outside of institutions for women's rights to equal or fair wages, abortion on demand, and so on, so inside academic institutions much of the Women's Studies writing in the English language mirrored those demands by furnishing the personal and empirical evidence, as well as explanations, for the need for change women were expressing. Part of these demands was the demand to make higher education accessible to women, and to include women and their knowledges in higher-education curricula. Much of the Women's Studies writing in English, especially of the 1970s and early 1980s, responded to these demands, which, in any event, coincided with the empiricist, deductive tradition of thinking that informed academic work in English. The equivalent response in the South was a major investment of the non-institutionalized groups and thus an impressive growth of autonomous or radical women's centres, which produced a great deal of knowledge and of publications that are not necessarily conventionally academic. It is not surprising therefore that the concept of *écriture féminine*, for example, was generated by women living in France with Southern and Eastern backgrounds, rather than in the UK or the USA. The stylistic and semantic divergences referred to here are to some extent reflected in this book, in which an empiricist tradition, typical for Northern Europe and found in chapters such as Tuula Gordon's (Chapter 2), is juxtaposed with a more abstracted form of writing typically encountered in Southern and Eastern countries.

In the 1970s and 1980s a happy coincidence emerged between English pragmatism and down-to-earthness and the empirical urge to document women's ways of knowing and to legitimate women's experience. It is one, however, with its very own and very particular drawbacks in that the language of the academy as practised in the English-speaking world is quite different from the language of the academy as practised in many European countries. *It coincides* with the structure of the university and the role it plays in the different European cultures. Throughout Continental Europe, the ivory-tower mentality, as well as mono-disciplinarity and the enormous power of disciplines, have created great obstacles to the development and the integration of Women's Studies. Continental universities are supposed to represent and even embody 'high culture', and to be the guardians of canonical, mainstream scientific knowledge complete with its own codes and discourses. It is difficult to imagine the full implications of these differences: in English, unlike for example in Germany or Greece, there is no distinction between 'demotic' English and a high cultural/academic form of the language. 'Plain English' is a term of praise in the UK, and writers are exhorted to write in 'plain English' rather than in a 'highfalutin' version which lays one open to ridicule. Sentences, writers are encouraged, should be short and in the active; dependent clauses are to be kept to a minimum. Significantly, the spell-check and grammar-check software programs issued by the Anglo-American computer giants dominating the market have as an indication of a problem to be addressed 'long sentence' as a category that comes up almost invariably when one writes anything that is more than two lines long. This contrasts significantly with the academic tradition in Germany, for example, where long sentences with multiple dependent clauses and a great deal of vocabulary of Greek and Latin derivation is considered an index of erudition and complexity of thought. In the UK, on the other hand, the term 'long word' is applied with derision to people who use complex words like 'terminology' (a joke question often asked in the context of 'long words' being derided is, 'What's that when it's at home?') The 'long word', viewed as foreign and other (presumably in recognition of its likely derivation from a Greek or Latin source), is pooh-poohed, and so is the 'long sentence'.

If, as has been consistently claimed during the twentieth century, 'language fashions thought', then it is clear that the way the English language is used in an academic context has a particular impact on how thought operates in English-speaking countries, compared to the impact the German, French or Swedish languages might have in the same context. English, on an international scale, has thus the effect of homogenizing the linguistic framework within which we operate, but at the same time it denies, even denigrates, and is ignorant of, the dimensions brought into perception by the use of other languages with different conventions of usage and philosophical traditions behind them. In the same way, therefore, that the debates of the 1980s within Women's Studies about differences among women and the need to recognize, value and articulate those differences[4] resulted in a much more highly differentiated understanding and acceptance of diverse women's positions, so we are, with this textbook, making a plea for the recognition and acceptance of the diversity of feminist work within Europe, as part of our drive to further the understanding of how women in Europe might think, argue and view feminist issues differently from their Anglo-American counterparts.

The third and very obvious reason why the US and the UK gained such prominence in Women's Studies in European countries was that – despite, or possibly because of, its homogenizing potential – English was and remains the global lingua franca, which, particularly with the establishment of the World Wide Web, has become *the* language of communication in international contexts, especially in situations where several people from diverse countries come together. English is thus without doubt the language of neo-imperialism, and as such has a market space much wider than that of any other language. From a publisher's point of view, therefore, circulation in English is likely to lead to much larger sales than circulation in any other language. This has clearly privileged those in Women's Studies publishing in the English language. If it is to reach an international market, work originally written in any other language has to be translated into English. That process alone costs money and therefore does not encourage publishers to engage in it. Significantly also, whereas in countries which do not speak a 'global' language – such as Hungary, Italy, Germany, the Netherlands, Sweden or France – there is a well-established and ready tradition of translating work from other languages into the language spoken in the given country, this is not the case in the UK, and also not as widely established in the USA, though it is more common in the latter than in the former. Few readers in the UK routinely keep up with the literatures, even in translation, of other countries, for example. Whilst some of the 'star' authors of literary production such as Isabel Allende and Christa Wolf may have their work translated into English for a UK market, when it comes to academic writing this happens to a much lesser extent. In consequence, little is known of the work of European feminist writers in the UK and the USA. And yet it is quite clear that even in countries where Women's Studies is not institutionalized to an extensive degree, much feminist work is conducted from which English-speaking feminists could benefit.

This became very clear in the discussions of the ATHENA members at the stage when this book was being conceptualized. Starting from the position that (a) work by European feminists is, on the whole, little known outside their country of origin; and that (b) there is a specific European dimension to Women's Studies, a group of feminist academics from the various European countries – whose core consisted of Eva Bahovec (Ljubljana, Slovenia), Liana Borghi (Florence, Italy), Rosi Braidotti (Utrecht, Netherlands), Marina Calloni (Milan, Italy), Jalna Hanmer (Sunderland, UK), Gabriele Griffin (Hull, UK), Serena Sapegno (Rome, Italy) and Harriet Silius (Abo, Finland)[5] – spent a considerable amount of time discussing what the contemporary key concerns in Women's Studies are, and their specific European dimension. During these discussions three things became clear:

- there are issues central to Women's Studies, such as that of sexual identity, where it is difficult to identify a specific European dimension, though there are plenty of European feminist scholars working on these issues;
- there are key areas of Women's Studies that very clearly have specific European dimensions;
- a distinction needs to be made between *a* European dimension which is pan-European, and European dimensions that reflect the diversity of positions within Europe.

In our discussions we initially identified a number of concerns under key Women's Studies headings where we saw specific European dimensions emerging. They included: (a) sex/gender; (b) identity/difference; (c) race/ethnicity; and, (d) sexuality/sexual violence and the family. These discussions were, of course, driven by our subject expertise, which came from the social sciences, philosophy and the humanities (history, literature), thus mirroring the disciplinary bases from which Women's Studies itself has emerged. Under each of these headings we discussed a whole range of concerns. Through this long and very productive discussion – which taught us much both about diversity within European countries and about the possibilities for a pan-European vision – we arrived at the final selection of topics and issues discussed in this volume. In analysing both the European and the Women's Studies angles around race and ethnicity that have dominated the late twentieth century and early twenty-first century, for instance, we began to focus on the varieties of nomadic subjects and migration patterns that have become prominent in Europe. We also discussed the impact of the crisis of the welfare state on women, and the issue of single women as a newly rising and significant cohort in Europe. In the discussions on these three topics alone it emerged that

- migration is a highly contentious subject with a long history in Europe quite unlike that of the USA, for instance, but it is also one that affects diverse European countries very differently;
- since the welfare state was differentially developed in diverse European countries (more sustainedly in the North of Europe than in the south, for example), its crisis meant different things in different European countries, though all recognize the issue of welfare as key for women in contemporary society;
- the single woman – as an older woman, a woman who is divorced or unmarried, or a lesbian – is an issue in every European country, but whereas in the UK the debates focus predominantly on lone mothers (and older women, for instance, are consummately ignored), in the Southern European countries, the debates are about the single women in their twenties and thirties who still live at home, an issue not at all prominent in most of the Northern European countries where the concern with 'older' children often centres on the tension between what the parents are expected to offer by way of financial support, and what the state should pay for.

Our debates as a matter of course also raised the question of what we actually mean by Europe.

What is 'Europe'?

Europe as an idea, an ideal, and a geopolitical reality has had varying contours throughout history. At the turn of the twenty-first century, its meaning remains in flux as changing political realities require a continual and critical interrogation of the term, mediated by context. Europe is unique in several ways. It takes its name from a woman, Europa, the daughter of the legendary king of Tyre and sister of Cadmus, who was beloved by Zeus, 'the father of gods and men' as Homer would have it. Europa was carried away by Zeus in the form of a bull to Crete, where she bore him three sons. This link to Greece, the country that is also credited with being 'the cradle of European civiliza- tion', associates Europe with seductive femininity and a specific locale. One might argue that seductive femininity is what Europe has struggled with ever since, presenting a desirable and desired ideal but at the same time not having quite the masculine identity that, in the imaginary, characterizes the USA, for instance, and its pioneer and 'go West' mentality, or that applies to the countries described as 'tiger economies'. Hence possibly its wild assertions of butchness through butchery, the instigation of colonial empires generated through force, and the world wars. But the migrant status of the mythical Europa, being removed to Crete from Tyre, and the shift in domicile she experienced, point to a second of the features that make Europe unique: its shifting boundaries; its geopolitical permeability; the fact, ultimately, that it is not a self-contained continent but a geopolitical formation that is in concrete and immediate proximity to spaces that are not designated 'European' and indeed, at different historical moments, has included or excluded spaces and peoples on its borders in a continually shifting structure of alliances and disaffiliations.

On the northern and western side the geographical space that is under- stood to be Europe is bounded by the Atlantic Ocean; on its southern side it has the Mediterranean Sea as a 'natural' boundary. It is its eastern side that has provided the source of most flux since the mid-twentieth century, as it is here that occident and orient meet, and that questions of affiliation are now most strongly raised as countries which were formerly part of the Eastern bloc are invited or proffer themselves to join the European Union. The project of the European Union,[6] in its earlier incarnations a series of strategic alliances between various nation-states in Europe, has increasingly become an attempt to move beyond the very notion of European nation-states. This history itself is indeed the most obvious example of the phenomenon of the shifting identity of Europe. And, this, finally, is another very particular difference between Europe and other superpowers/continents: Europe consists of a number of nation-states, each with its own language/s and culture/s, often radically different from each other, and in themselves subject to greater or lesser historically determined instability, fuelled both by inter- and intra-state conflicts and alliances. The internal diversity, the polylinguism and the multi- culturalism of what is homogenizingly called 'Europe' is one of the greatest challenges facing any pan-European alliance at the beginning of the twenty- first century.

The European Union is not identical with Europe, of course. Europe's geographical contours encompass more and different spaces than does the European Union. The latter is a geopolitical formation, determined by political and economic forces and intent upon creating a union which can hold its own politically, economically and militarily against, and in collaboration on an equal footing with, other, so-called superpowers such as Russia, the USA, and Japan. As an entity the European Union has grown out of a number of crucial historical factors. The first is the decision taken in the aftermath of fascism and the Second World War (truly a European civil war), by the Allied forces but also by anti-fascist political forces within Europe, to put an end to certain kinds of European nationalism. The second is the decision to streamline the reconstruction of the war-torn European economy in the face of the so-called Cold War which divided the communist Eastern bloc from the capitalist West.

On both counts, the project of federation dealt a historic blow to European nationalisms and forced upon the individual European countries (one thinks of Finland as an example) the necessity to rethink their identity in the post-Yalta world order. In this respect, the project of European federation is linked to the political and moral bankruptcy of European nationalism as manifested in the events of World War II and more specifically in the Holocaust perpetuated against the Jewish and Romany populations, as well as the persecution of Communists, homosexuals and other so-called undesirables. At the same time, however, it was also a concerted effort to reinscribe a new European identity within the 'Western bloc' as part of the drive to make Europe a major player in the globalization process.

The European Council established in 1949 in London initially consisted of France, Italy, the Netherlands, Great Britain, Norway, Denmark and Sweden, Greece and Turkey. These were joined by Ireland in 1950, the German Federal Republic in 1951, Austria in 1956, Switzerland in 1962, and Malta in 1965. This development both indicates the drive towards expansion and growth which has characterized the changing political, economic and military alliances of the various European countries over time and delineates the continually changing definitions of what is and what is not European. Not included in the European Council, for example, were the countries on the eastern borders such as Hungary, Poland and Yugoslavia, which had become signatories to the COMECON (1949), the Council for Mutual Economic Aid established under Soviet leadership. Europe in the post-World War II era has featured as a changing political alliance, set against 'the East', as a configuration of capitalist forces confronting communism.

As an ideal, Europe embodies the notion of Enlightenment, democracy and the free flow of capital. As a reality, it struggles to adjust to the critiques of the Enlightenment that have dominated European thinking since the early twentieth century; to come to terms with its imperialist and fascist histories, its treatment of women and migrants, which are an antidote to the notion of democracy; and to confront uneasily the impact of the so-called free flow of capital, which questions the meaning of the local – if we can call Europe that – in the face of the global. Both the ideal and the idea of Europe are hotly contested within Europe itself. This becomes evident in debates about which countries to consider for admission to the European Union. Whenever issues around the violation of human rights are invoked, as is the case regarding Turkey, for example, which – though it was in the Council of Europe – has not been admitted to the European Union, there is an implicit appeal to the ideal of Europe as a supranational entity that subscribes to certain ideological positions. When the idea of Europe as a supranational entity is materialized through, for instance, the introduction of monetary union, opposition occurs in the form of an assertion of national identity as being the supreme desideratum for nation-states within Europe. Great Britain is one of the examples here. The Norwegian older statesman of Peace Studies, Johann Galtung, maintains that it is the countries with a 'broken' history such as Germany and France – that is, countries which went through periods of fascist rule or dictatorship – that are keenest to establish a United Europe because it is through that process that they can acquire a new and unblemished identity. In contrast, those countries such as Great Britain that sustained democracies are least likely to want to be subsumed in a United Europe because they remain in an unproblematic relation to their own history. For them, becoming part of a United Europe would constitute the 'broken' history which they might then find difficult to come to terms with. A more charitable and less Euro-sceptic version of the same point would be the recognition of the anti-fascist historical roots of the project of the European Union, and its inbuilt critique of the very notion of European nation-states. This critique is all the more necessary since the post-colonial world order and the process of the transnational economy with the complex effects of globalization open a new chapter in the history of the decline of European nation-states as principles of economic and political organization. The coming of the electronic frontier and the information superhighways accelerates even further the process of dematerialization of the nation-state.

This decline, far from being greeted everywhere as a step forward, has also generated a wave of nostalgia, which is one of the key features of contemporary politics. The nostalgic political discourse can be clearly noted in discussions about European citizenship and immigration. The project of European unification has in fact triggered a wave of reactions that are simultaneously anti-European and racist. As Stuart Hall put it, the great resistance against European union, as well as the American suspicion of it, is a defensive response to a process of effective overcoming of the very idea and reality of European nation-states. The short-range effect of this is nationalistic paranoia and xenophobic fears. This is the form taken by contemporary 'European cultural racism'. It coincides with the resurgence of micro-nationalisms at all levels in Europe today. The unification of Europe today coexists with the closing down of its borders; the coming of a common European citizenship and a common currency with increasing internal fragmentation and regionalism; a new, allegedly post-nationalist identity with the return of

xenophobia, racism and anti-Semitism. To deal with the various types of
nostalgic identity-claims that are proliferating across Europe today, we need
to develop a post-nationalist sense of European identity. However, it is clear
that to date we have not only failed to develop adequate, positive representations of the new trans-European condition that we are inhabiting on this
continent, but also appropriate value systems which would enable us to
sustain a post-nationalist identity in Europe. There is a shortage here on the
part of the social and ethical imaginary, which both feeds upon and supports
the political timidity and the resistances that are being moved against the
European political project. A key implication of this line of argument is that
the European political project, as expressed through the European Union, is
in process, and will require enormous shifts in socio-cultural, political and
ethical thinking.

Feminist scholarship can play an important role here because gender as a
tool stresses the crucial importance of dis-identification from dominant norms
of identity as a step towards the redefinition of the role between, but also
within, the sexes. Since the subject of feminism is not Woman as the complementary of Man and as his specular other, but rather a multilayered and
complex subject that has taken her distance from the institution of femininity,
she is the subject of quite an-other story, a subject-in-process, who can figure
as an example of the kind of transformation Europe, in its shift from an
identity built around nation-states to a post-nationalist identity, has to under-
go. Second, feminist theory stresses the importance of the everyday and the
here and now – both key spaces within which change has to be generated
and sustained. For feminists in Europe this also means that we need to engage
with feminist issues as they affect us in our European situatedness, and in our
changing understanding of Europe. Feminist research, then, offers significant
instruments for thinking about the 'new' Europe, including resisting – in
proper feminist tradition – the notion of a hegemonic dream of Europe, a
'Fortress Europe'.

In this volume Europe and the European Union in many respects take
quite concrete shape. The contributors come from or reside in countries that
are part of the geographical space known as Europe, namely from the United
Kingdom, France, Germany, Italy, Spain, Norway, Finland, Slovenia, Hungary
and the Netherlands. Second, they all write about European phenomena. As
stated above, the key issue in putting this volume together was the question,
'what is the specifically European dimension of Women's Studies?' Third, and
with the exception of the final section of the book, which features case
studies of individual European countries, all the chapters take a pan-European
view. This approach *as such* moves beyond and even challenges not only
classical nationalism but also the standard way of doing comparative work.
Thus, rather than addressing issues and concerns in Women's Studies within
individual nation-states, the chapters seek to explore – in comparative form –

issues that impact on a number of European countries and thus give these issues their specific European dimension. This dimension is in part determined by Europe's geopolitical and socio-economic history, which is not only the history of Europe itself and in itself but also of Europe's relations with others such as the United States and the so-called Eastern bloc.

Women's Studies: The European Dimension

In discussing the areas we wanted to cover in this volume, we were driven and constrained by several issues:

• the question of which topics had a specific European dimension;
• the range of contributors available, both in terms of representation of European countries and in terms of subject expertise;
• current concerns in Women's Studies;
• the obvious limits of a single volume of text, which mean that it is not possible to cover everything.

We therefore, and after much discussion, chose to focus on the following themes, which figure as section headings within this volume:

1 Women as social and political entities.
2 Culture and signification.
3 Identity, subjectivity and difference.
4 Race and ethnicity.
5 Violence against women: European perspectives.
6 Sex/gender terminology and its implications.
7 The rises and falls of the women's movements in Europe.

The first five sections all contain three chapters on the section topic. The sixth offers a critical account of the divergent linguisic and political uses of the terms 'sex' and 'gender' in a number of European countries, pointing to the issue of the transferability of concepts and knowledges within Europe. The seventh section provides a series of case studies of the rises and falls of the women's movements in eight European countries to highlight both similarities and differences among these.

In addressing the themes, contributors were asked to write from a comparative European perspective, focusing in the main on the 'Europe' of the twentieth and twenty-first centuries. This decision was informed by a recognition that women's participation en masse in public life is predominantly a twentieth-century phenomenon in Europe, if one takes as one of its indicators women's ability to vote.

Women as Social and Political Entities

One of the first, and in a European context perhaps most obvious, issue we discussed was the crisis, indeed the demise, of the European welfare state in the late twentieth century and its wide-ranging impact on women. It was very clear, as Harriet Silius's opening chapter of Part I, 'Feminist Perspectives on the European Welfare State', demonstrates, that the decline of the welfare state mainly, in fact predominantly, impacts on women, as they lose out on benefits and are expected to take on the roles shed by cash-strapped nation-states. The rise of voluntary organizations, the new emphasis on and recognition of women as carers, are all effects of the gradual strangulation of welfare provision both in Eastern and such as we have known it in Western Europe, most prominently since the end of the Second World War. Given the history of the emergence of European welfare states, the death of the welfare state has a specific European meaning for women, not only because the welfare from which many Europeans have benefited has been specifically European in its manifestation but also because it is European feminist research which has addressed most extensively the implications of the demise of the welfare state for women. Silius's chapter focuses on that research in order to highlight how the meaning of the welfare state, both historically and contemporaneously, shifts within Europe depending on which analytical model you use, and what the gendered implications of the different models are.

The demise of the welfare state has gone hand in hand with another phenomenon, which has been the subject of many and various debates in Europe – the emergence of the single female. States' ability to shed welfare tasks or disperse them into 'the community' depends on the idea of particular social formations being in place which can absorb these tasks. However, current evidence suggests that things may not be straightforward here. The general rise in life expectancy, for example, means that at the older end of the age scale the population is predominantly female (the majority of over 74-year-olds are women) and that these women frequently live on their own if their (male) partners have died, or if they have never married or cohabited. Who will care for these women, who are in fact, in many welfare models, expected to be carers rather than to be cared for? Increases in divorce rates mean that more women are newly single in their thirties and forties, and rising employment rates and financial independence among women means that more women choose to remain single. In Britain the single female is discussed in two different guises: as the 'lone mother' – again, a case of someone who needs support rather than to be called upon to support – and the 'city single', the single career woman who does not want family ties or is unable to establish them. In Italy and Spain, in contrast, public discussions about the single female focus on women in their twenties and thirties who are unwilling to 'leave the nest' and continue to live with, and be a burden on, their parents. In addition, many Northern European countries have, due to the increasing public visibility of lesbians, had to rethink their definitions of the single woman as they have sought to refine notions of cohabitation to include same-sex partners, for example. Whatever form the public debate takes, there is a rising tide of interest in the single female in Europe and it is for this reason that we have included Tuula Gordon's chapter on 'Single Women' here. Gordon discusses a range of research on the phenomenon of the single female, exploring various definitions of the term and how women who are single themselves perceive their single-ness. Gordon's chapter sheds light on the issue of the single female, revealing a vital discrepancy between certain culturally endorsed ideals of social structures such as 'the family' and the reality which women in the Europe of today face.

As indicated above, in the UK the issue of the single female is tied strongly to notions of reproduction – that is, the issue of the 'lone mother'. As soon as that issue is linked to concerns about welfare – in Britain this takes the form of accusing lone mothers of sponging off the state, of deliberately getting pregnant as a way of drawing benefits – it becomes an issue about the nature and status of women as citizens and participants in the public arena. It is this that links Gordon's chapter with that of Marina Calloni on 'Women's Human Rights, Equal Opportunities and Biopolitics in Europe'. However, where Gordon's chapter focuses very much on the here and now, Calloni's chapter takes a historical overview of the emergence of women as citizens with rights in Europe, tracing the exclusion of women from rights that were meant to be 'universal' to the establishment of the notion of specific women's human rights, a phenomenon that began to take shape in the late twentieth century. Since the question of rights, and of women's human rights, has recently, *inter alia*, focused strongly on issues arising from advances in biotechnology, Calloni charts the move from women's fight for equality to women's rights in terms of difference within the context of the notion of woman as citizen. One of the key issues in this context, in European terms, has been the impact of European legislation on individual member states. Where human rights and equal opportunities were historically issues for individual nation-states, the formation of the European Union and its various previous configurations has superseded that individual-nation-based focus in favour of greater homogenization across Europe. To date, however, there has been no recognition of reproductive rights as women's human rights. As women grapple with the implications of the new gene and biotechnologies for their relations with their bodies and with reproduction, the challenge for many women is to secure reproductive rights as women's human rights.

Culture and Signification

One of the issues that emerges in the interface between nation-states and Europe – and the area of reproductive rights and regulations is an excellent example of this – is the diversity among the nation-states that make up the geographical space described as 'Europe'. The nation-states' diverse histories and cultures articulate themselves not only in different national legislative frameworks, affecting women and men differently, but also in the ways in which spaces – both actual and symbolic – within nation-states have traditionally been allocated to women and men. The genderization of space was already evident in Calloni's discussion of citizenship, which outlined the allocation of certain symbolic spaces – such as that of the public sphere of citizenship – to men, and the exclusion of women from that space.

In our discussions of the European dimension in Women's Studies issues, extended debates took place about women's participation in the public sphere and the ways in which links between culture and politics take specific forms within the European context. It is for this reason that we decided to include a section on 'Culture and Signification' as Part II of this volume – pathbreaking within Women's Studies because a number of the issues addressed are quite unfamiliar to Anglo-American feminists, whose ideas of 'culture', 'signification' (and, indeed, 'politics') are derived, on the one hand, from Cultural Studies as it has been developed predominantly in the UK and, on the other, from a history of reading culture in terms of specific embodied forms such as film, (news) media, popular cultural forms, and so on. This is *not* how 'culture' figures here, and it is one of the contexts where intra-European differences (i.e. differences between, in particular, Southern and Eastern European feminist political cultures and Northern European ones) and differences between Anglo-American and certain European forms of feminist political engagement become most obvious. For the idea of 'passion in politics' is quite foreign to Northern European and Anglo-American notions of politics, and the concept of a 'political culture' is not generally used in those places. Politics still purports to carry with it an Enlightenment model of the subject as a sovereign, rational being whose interactions in the political sphere are based on rational calculation rather than passionately held – that is, emotionally invested – beliefs and considerations. Indeed, the notion that emotions might govern one's politics, or that emotions and emotionally invested social structures should be taken into consideration in the public and political spheres, is quite anathema to North European and Anglo-American feminists, whose political beliefs are based on certain rationally defensible principles. Since it is the Eastern European and Southern European countries to whom passion in politics is most meaningful, one may speculate whether or not this disposition is associated with intensely patriarchal, Catholic nation-states that have experienced fascist and other forms of dictatorship or absolutist regimes. Without doubt, there is a correlation between the kind of states we as feminists are in and what political cultures we adhere to.

The section on 'Culture and Signification' then does three things: it investigates the interrelationship between the space that is Europe and women's culture through Liana Borghi's chapter on 'Space and Women's Culture'; it analyses the cartography of emotions and ideals of passion associated with specific European histories of thought and cultural traditions as they impact on the construction of women in European culture, in Elena Pulcini and Luisa Passerini's chapter on 'European Feminine Identity and the Idea of Passion in Politics'; and, finally, it demonstrates the significance of psycho-analytic ideas, themselves a specifically European heritage, and their trans-formation into feminist political investments in the specific contexts of Italian and French politics, in Serena Sapegno's chapter on 'Psychoanalysis and Feminism'.

Whilst all the authors in this section are Italian, a national unity unusual for this volume, they do not take a nation-state-based view of their subjects but, rather, argue from perspectives informed not only by the diverse Euro-pean traditions that make up 'European culture' but also, particularly in the case of Borghi and Sapegno, by an articulated acknowledgement of the inter-relation between Europe and its Western others, and, in the case of Pulcini and Passerini, through an examination of the use of European traditions of thought as a tool for differentiating Europe from its Eastern others. What emerges in these chapters, as much as in the others in this volume, is that Europe is not merely about the interface between the individual nation-states and their cultures that inhabit the geographical space decribed as Europe. Europe is also a formation which has articulated its varying identities in relation to other Eastern as well as Western neighbours, both immediate and distant.

Borghi's chapter provides a wide-ranging overview, historically and Euro-geographically, of women's places within European cultures, their absence from certain traditions, and their attempts to carve out spaces for themselves through phenomena such as the salon. Borghi charts a history of women-only spaces which have been critical to the development of women's culture in Europe, and argues that women's European-ness and ability to operate at local, national and international levels has been strongly fostered through those spaces. Borghi references a tradition of feminist archaeological projects, the (re-)discovery of forgotten women's cultural activities and products, which has been one of the key feminist concerns, in particular from the 1970s onwards. She demonstrates the importance of female networks for women's socio-cultural integration and socio-economic survival, and highlights the important role that European metropolises have played at different points in history in providing for women, both from within Europe and from without, the location for their networking. Not only did European women migrate within Europe in order to find a place of their own, but women from the United States and elsewhere migrated to Europe in the hope of establishing a space for their cultural practice and to live their sense of self, including their sexual self.

Pulcini and Passerini focus on the construction of femininity and its relationship to the idea of Europe through analysing the ways in which emo-tionality has historically been attributed to women, how women have been culturally tied to ideas/ideals of love in certain key cultural forms that also link emotion to the idea of Europe, and how the triangulation of women, emotion and Europe has acted to configure Europe in opposition to the orient. In particular they focus on the historically varying conception of love in relation to femininity in various European cultural configurations, ranging from Platonic and Aristotelian concepts of femininity and love, to the notion of courtly love, to the (re)invention of love and femininity in the works of psychoanalytic writers such as Sigmund Freud and C.G. Jung. They then show how the work of women thinkers and writers such as Simone Weil, Ursula Hirschmann and Margaret Storm Jameson dealt with love in their idea of Europe through the notion of the emotional basis of Europe as *an active memory of emotions*. This is particularly pertinent in the context of the Holocaust, which Borghi also references.

Sapegno takes up the issue of the role in psychoanalysis, itself of course a quintessentially European phenomenon, in her analysis of passion in European politics. She details the role psychoanalytic theory has played in the development of feminist politics and feminist political practice in Italy and in France, articulating the very different direction and meanings some of the feminist liberation practices such as consciousness-raising – shared around the world beyond Europe – took in the Italian and French contexts where those practices were linked into a politics derived from an engagement with psychoanalytic ideas. These required an understanding of familial structures and their symbolic functions in power relations among women. Sapegno analyses how Italian and French feminist practices and psychoanalytic theories informed each other so as to generate a very different feminist theoretical trajectory and preoccupation in Italy and France than in the Anglo-American world, where the emphasis was less on sexual difference and more on equality and social reform. The latter occurred despite the fact that a number of British writers, such as Teresa Brennan and Juliet Mitchell, contributed important texts to the development of psychoanalytic feminism. In describing the feminist political developments that took place in Italy and France from the late 1960s onwards, Sapegno speaks of a feminist politics of the unconscious, based on a psychoanalytically informed theory of sexual difference, which determined the feminist political agenda in these countries and differentiated their articulation of a feminist politics in ways that were radically different from those of both other European countries and other countries beyond Europe. Her arguments relate very clearly to the case studies of the rises and falls of the feminist/women's movements in Europe which constitute Part VII of this book, in that they show clearly how very different, including in terms of time frames, feminist movements have operated in Europe. That diversity is one of the other major ways in which Europe is distinguished from other continents and superpowers.

Identity, Subjectivity and Difference

Part III focuses on 'Identity, Subjectivity and Difference' and deals with a topic that extends the discussion of how difference has featured in European feminism already addressed by Sapegno in Part II. This section starts with two chapters which – in different ways – address one significant difference distinguishing Europe from the United States, namely the history of recent wars on its own soil and in regions immediately proximate to the European Community.[7] Not only has Europe seen such wars but they have also had highly gendered agendas, as Part VII, too, will make clear. Part III then concludes with a chapter by Rosi Braidotti on the concept of difference.

One of the major issues facing Europe today is the emerging nationalisms in the former Eastern bloc countries, the establishment of new patriarchies there, and the consequences this has for women. Feminists in Europe today have to engage with the wars that occur on Europe's eastern borders, their gendered meanings, and their implications for women throughout the EU and worldwide (these implications include issues of trafficking in women, various forms of forced migration, war rape and other similar gendered offences against women).

Zarana Papic, in her chapter on 'Europe after 1989', takes up the theme of nation-building processes in the post-communist countries and argues that one of the gender-specific legacies of the patriarchal communist states is the disappearance of women from the public sphere after 1989 because the countries in question created equality through effecting legal changes – which proved to be temporary – but without making any inroads in the underlying cultural formations that maintained women as subordinate to men. At the same time the imbrication of women in ideals of national identity has generated a gendered trap for women, in which their seeming idealization as carriers of national identity, history and tradition has bound them into subservient roles to states which exercise extreme forms of exploitation over them. The consequence, Papic states, is that women have become economically, socially and politically disempowered in these post-communist societies, and that the question, 'Whose Europe after 1989?' – that is, women's or men's or does it belong to both – at present suggests that a certain version of Europe belongs to men, men cowed by patriarchal structures in which they, not quite as much as women but also to a considerable extent, are objects of nationalist discourses that are destructive of their position as subjects and agents.

Svetlana Slapšak's chapter, 'Identities under Threat on the Eastern Borders', begins by highlighting the ways in which the so-called Eastern bloc is, in fact, a disparate grouping of countries to which the appellation 'socialist' used to apply in varying degrees but whose social, economic and cultural positions varied tremendously. Slapšak details the ways in which women's participation in the public and political arena has significantly decreased after 1989, and that women's identity has been threatened by the erosion of their rights in the social and health fields. The revisioning of women's roles within Eastern bloc countries has, Slapšak argues, also impacted in the cultural fields where women, in certain emerging filmic figurations, are now recast as collaborators with communist dictatorships within a newly established patriarchal – as opposed to anti-communist – framework. Women's bodies as carriers of their identity and of national(ist) ideologies have increasingly become the object of attack as the societies in transition on the Eastern borders struggle to find for themselves identities which allow them to negotiate the move from socialist communist state-planned economies to supposedly democratic, capitalist, free-market societies. Slapšak analyses how this search for new national identities ties in with historical relations to past empires, mainly of the East, such as the Ottoman or the Austro-Hungarian empires, leading to a perception of the eastern borders as spaces of liminality between East and West, between oriental and occidental cultures and traditions. Within these spaces, women's bodies figured as the carriers of national culture, embodying the very liminality experienced by the states themselves. This figuration, at a cultural level, argues Slapšak, forced women into the position of the 'native', a position which in the early twenty-first century, opens up opportunities for fruitful exchanges with Third World, rather than First World, feminists, with whom women on the eastern borders in some respects have more in common than with the occidental feminists who sometimes have been rightfully accused of adopting a missionizing and exploitative position towards East European women.

Rosi Braidotti's chapter, 'Identity, Subjectivity and Difference: A Critical Genealogy', moves away from the concerns of war to explore the European dimensions of the concept of 'difference' in an attempt to redress the rather critical reception of some 'continental' European feminist theory within Anglo-American feminism. Braidotti argues that an understanding of 'continental' European feminist theories of sexual difference as embodied in the writings of Luce Irigaray, for instance, depend on a proper appreciation of the latter's imbrication in the genealogy of late-nineteenth- and twentieth-century critical European theories of the subject, in particular those of Marx, Freud and Nietzsche. Braidotti's chapter therefore traces the philosophical and political genealogy of the term 'difference' as it has been formulated and politically functioned in pre- and post- World War II Europe, embedding its changing significance in the evacuation, under the Nazis, of critical theory from Europe and the reintroduction of those theories, albeit in changing forms, after World War II. Braidotti locates a critical break with the subject of classical humanism and liberal individualism in the radical movements of 1968, and argues that the female feminist subject, as envisaged in French feminist work such as that of Irigaray, emerged from that point of political rupture. She contrasts theories of sexual difference that reconnect the agency required of politics with a respect for the affective, libidinal structures of subjectivity as present in 'continental' European feminist theory with theories of differences as they figure in Anglo-American feminist theory, for instance the work of Judith Butler.

Braidotti's chapter thus analyses the historical conditions that have promoted the emergence of very different theories of (sexual) difference in certain European as opposed to Anglo-American feminist and philosophical traditions.

Race and Ethnicity

Issues of 'difference', as well as the nationalist discourses and their gendered subtexts which have emerged in the Eastern European countries in response to the demise of communism, connect powerfully with a long European history of particular forms of hierarchized engagements with issues of race and ethnicity. These issues figure very differently in the social realities and in the imaginary of Europe than they do elsewhere, not least because European countries which had colonial empires tended – until the twentieth century – not to bring their colonial subjects back to Europe. This did not prevent them from developing complex pseudoscientific theories of race that not only helped to justify the establishment of the colonial empires on the basis of the supposed biological inferiority of other races, but that also impacted directly on the formation of the nation-states in Europe themselves. The contemporary ethnic wars on Europe's eastern borders thus have long and well-established precedents, and a previous catastrophic culmination in the genocidal anti-Semitism and fascism that led to the Holocaust. In Europe, then, race and ethnicity have their own particular histories and manifestations as concepts and realities which have been acted upon with usually devastating consequences. Race and ethnicity in Europe are thus not only about the 'visibly other', as black American and subaltern feminist perspectives often imply, but are further, and intensely problematically, about the active othering of those who are not 'visibly other'; about the 'stranger in our midst' whom we cannot, in fact, discern as a stranger unless we brand her as such through, for example, a yellow star to signify her Jewish identity, as occurred under the Nazi regime. The construction of the neighbour as stranger – more than that, and consequently, as enemy – is one of the most historically long-standing and searing incursions into European civil society. Its recent manifestation during the Balkan wars that began in the 1990s is a reminder of an underlying and powerfully European legacy of racism and ethnically motivated oppression which we have been unable to eradicate and which haunts all European countries in diverse forms. It is for this reason that the idea of the European Union as an entity designed to move beyond the nation-state and its nationalist agendas is so important.

The first chapter in Part IV, Liliane Kandel's 'Feminism and Anti-Semitism', engages with this legacy in a particular way, analysing the complex relationship between feminism and anti-Semitism. One of the recurrent issues in Europe's history of racially and ethnically motivated forms of oppression is the role of women within it, both (as is indicated in the chapters of the previous section) in terms of their iconic and actual roles within these oppressive regimes, and in terms of their resistance to such forms of oppression. Kandel takes both a historicizing and a contemporary view in considering how feminists in Europe prior to and contemporaneous with the Nazi period, and after World War II, related to issues of anti-Semitism. She details some of the complex and contradictory positions adopted by feminists at various times which simultaneously entailed a resistance to certain forms of oppression such as patriarchy and a tacit or actual approval of other forms of oppression such as anti-Semitism. Kandel outlines how particular foci in historiography have served to draw attention away from, or deny, the Holocaust and its impact on Jewish women, and the problems Jewish feminist scholars have in articulating their views. Kandel raises the question why certain feminist theories may not be capable of dealing with specific historical phenomena such as the Shoah, and suggests that in asking such questions we shall advance our understanding both of that event and of feminist theory. Describing Nazi anti-Semitism as a 'racism of extermination' which should be differentiated from other forms of discrimination or exploitation, Kandel argues for a feminist revisioning of our understanding of anti-Semitism.

Sandra Ponzanesi, in 'Diasporic Subjects and Migration', takes the issue of race, ethnicity and regulatory regimes in a somewhat different direction. In so doing she makes a clear distinction between the migrant as material subject driven to migration by force and necessity (whether these be economic, or due to war, or other forms of violence) and the nomadic subject who chooses to migrate as part of the general global social and economic trend towards mobility. Ponzanesi articulates the differences between the American 'melting pot' model of integration of migrants and the various European models of dealing with immigrants. She then analyses the ways in which Rosi Braidotti and Avtar Brah, two feminists writing within the European context, as well as Paul Gilroy, a second-generation migrant to the UK, have taken up the issue of diaspora in a European context by articulating new ways of thinking about the interrelation between diaspora, migration and gender, pertinent to the particularities that attach to Europe as a diasporic space, to borrow a term from Brah's work.

Where Ponzanesi seeks to elaborate the distinctive models of migration, integration and transformation that have characterized European responses to the issue of migration, Gabriele Griffin and Rosi Braidotti, in 'Whiteness and European Situatedness', engage with a further issue that arises in the vexed context of race and ethnicity as figured in Europe, namely the meanings of 'whiteness' within contemporary Europe. This issue is closely associated with the history of racist and ethnicist ideologies that have served to make visible those not necessarily distinguished by their skin colour from their neighbours but by cultural attributions of differences that have served to perpetuate specific racialized hierarchies. Where in conventional Anglo-American discourses and feminist critiques of whiteness, colour is reinscribed as a binary paradigm for racialized divisions, this chapter argues that the European imaginary has a long-standing and complex relation to the critique of whiteness that is determined not only by matters of skin colour but by other kinds of attributions of difference. Conceptualizations of whiteness are here historically linked to nationalist ideologies and eugenic policies of 'pure races', replayed from the 1990s in the inter-ethnic wars in the Balkan states. Two key issues in this context are, on the one hand, the iconic representation of women within nationalist discourses as breeding vessels for pure national identities – a position that simultaneously lays women open to sexual violation as a means of soiling and destroying that purity, as was seen in the sexual atrocities, rapes and forced pregnancies to which women were subjected during the Balkan wars – and, on the other, feminist resistances to the ideological positions detailed above and the resultant crimes against women. Griffin and Braidotti's chapter seeks to complicate the critiques on whiteness as they are currently available, by analysing their limited applicability to the European situation, and by asserting the need for a more complex understanding of the notion of whiteness as a problematic category which has gender implications.

Violence against Women: European Perspectives

The violations experienced by women as a consequence of the ways in which nationalist and patriarchal discourses construct their roles is further explored in Part V, where violence against women is the key issue. Here Carol Hagemann-White's chapter on 'Violence against Women in the European Context' provides an overview of how violence against women has figured in Europe, what the emerging overarching perspective on the issue is, and the prevalence and nature of violence against women in the various European countries. In so doing, Hagemann-White is concerned to show that very real differences exist for women in different European regions in facing and confronting violence. These differences are related as much to cultural differences as to the relative economic wealth and political stability of the region in question. Rather than viewing violence against women as an undifferentiated phenomenon, Hagemann-White argues for a realistic assessment of the experiences of women from diverse regions as a way of addressing the problem of violence against women.

Rather like Gordon's chapter on 'Single Women' in Part I, Hagemann-White's chapter provides evaluative details of various surveys and empirical research undertaken to establish the prevalence and nature of violence exercised against women. The chapter shows how European legislation has influenced individual member countries of the European community to adopt measures to combat violence against women. It thus shows what role the European Union can have in intervening in and transforming gendered scenarios that work to the detriment of women. Hagemann-White also makes the point that sexual and domestic violence is treated more as a matter of gender relations and of human rights in Europe than it is in North America, where the focus is very much on the family.

In one particular context, however, as Lisa Price's chapter on 'Sexual Violence and Ethnic Cleansing: Attacking the Family' makes clear, the family is one of the key social formations implicated in sexual and other forms of violence, namely in the context of ethnic cleansing. Price's chapter vividly demonstrates the ways in which sexual violence was used in the Balkan wars to undermine the social fabric of enemy cultures by disintegrating their basic social unit, the family, through various forms of sexual and other physical and violent attacks on family members, most particularly, but not exclusively, women, in order to destroy associated value systems and render them not so much dysfunctional as non-functional. The chapter makes clear that such a mode of attack is possible only in societies that invest particular values in the family and in women, making them the bearers of patriarchal honour, family honour and national identity. Price painfully describes how women were raped, and how family members were made to watch their rapes and other violations, as part of destroying both the individuals and the community as a whole. The occurrences in Bosnia and other parts of the Balkans raise the spectre of the Holocaust, of ethnic persecution in the context of 'no visible difference', where the neighbour, indeed family members, are constructed as enemies in a corrosive policy of internal social meltdown, supposedly designed to effect 'ethnic cleansing' but storing up nationalist sentiments and reprisals for the future. The inter-ethnic wars in the Balkans of the 1990s reached new depths of inhuman treatment between diverse ethnic groups, intended to erase the cohesion of these groups at the most basic level of social unit, and also to raise the perhaps even more crippling reality of the assumed powerlessness of other states to intervene. Where the occurrence of the Holocaust was premissed on a 'we didn't know what was going on' position (now largely debunked as a failure of political and moral will), here the whole world knew what was going on but continued to allow it to happen. A new indifference to evil made itself felt, an indifference already noticeable during the Gulf War of the 1980s, and replayed here even more problematically. Such wars, on European territory, are nothing new. Yet, not only do they differentiate Europe from other continents in their juxtaposition with the advanced capitalist context, free-market economies, and democratic nation-states in whose proximity they occur; they also must raise serious concerns for the future of Europe and the situation of women within it.

Jalna Hanmer takes this line forward in her chapter on 'Violence, Militarism and War', in which she argues that the rise of the recognition of domestic violence in Europe, from the 1970s onwards, and feminists' battle against that violence, need to give way to a reviewing of sexualized violence as it occurs in the public rather than the domestic context and as it is linked to what she describes as 'badly lived heterosexuality', the coincidence of certain notions of masculinity and femininity with social formations in which strongly male-dominated structures such as the military exist in close proximity to civilian communities, ready to exploit the women within those communities. Hanmer demonstrates how the changes to the contours of Europe in the wake of 1989 have created the need to consider and combat violence against women not only in relatively stable societies but also, and at least as importantly, in unstable societies where women in much larger numbers are exposed to much greater threats of violence and violation than in many stable societies. Since the Second World War, Western European countries have tended to understand themselves as non-militarized, stable societies, even where, as in the case of the UK, such visions of self were plainly contradicted by the war in Northern Ireland. Hanmer argues that this self-understanding has failed to account for the ways in which the stationing of military personnel impacts on local civil communities, and specifically on the women within these. Second, the Balkan wars from the 1990s onwards have demonstrated the fragility of that self-understanding, as the threat of destabilization of certain Western European regions through geographical proximity to countries descending into war, as much as through participation in various forms of militarized activities within those countries, has impacted on neighbouring states through factors such as new migrations within the European region. This situation demands a new understanding of Europe for the twenty-first century as a space in which stable and unstable societies coexist, and here violence against women therefore needs to be reviewed.

Sex/Gender Terminology and Its Implications

Rosi Braidotti's chapter on 'The Uses and Abuses of the Sex/Gender Distinction in European Feminist Practices' addresses one of the fundamental issues for feminism in Europe: the meaning and significance of the terms 'sex' and 'gender' within the different cultural communities that constitute Europe. As is clear from the case studies used here, and as is clear from how sex and gender have been talked about in a whole range of feminist works, the meanings of these terms are both culturally specific and have changed over time. Not only is it the case that the terms are not always separate in every European language; every language also attaches its own meanings to them. One of the difficulties Europe faces in homogenizing its communities under one European hat is that the imposition of English as the lingua franca ignores the linguistic, conceptual and semantic diversities which inform individual cultures within Europe. And yet, when Europeans from these diverse backgrounds meet, it is always immediately apparent that they do not mean the same thing, even when they use the same English word. 'Sex' and 'gender' are particularly useful examples of this problematic. The terms were problematized in the English language particularly during the 1990s, mainly

due to the good offices of American postmodernist feminist thinkers such as
Judith Butler, whose ground-breaking work on the constructedness of sex as
well as of gender finally led to an explosion of the notion that sex = biology
and that gender = culture. The evaporation of these equations was paralleled
by the substitution of the word 'gender' for 'women' in European countries
such as the Nordic ones, driven by an equality agenda which, once directed
at the inclusion of women, now came to signal parity for men and women.
That equality/parity agenda has been adopted by international agencies such
as the United Nations and the World Bank, a move that, on the one hand,
has enhanced what is described as 'gender mainstreaming' and, on the other,
has re-invisibilized women as material entities who continue to carry the
burden of unequal treatment and conditions in virtually every sphere of life.
'Sex' and 'gender' as terms, though much contested, must be understood as
having significant implications in women's lives. To understand this within a
European context it is necessary to grasp how the sex/gender distinction is
used in a variety of European cultures/countries/languages. This is the purpose
of the case studies included here.

The Rises and Falls of the Women's Movements in Europe

One of the distinguishing features of Europe is that it has experienced, within
its geographical parameters, a very diverse range of forms and experiences of
women's movements, both historically and in terms of academic manifestation
in the form of the institutionalization of Women's Studies as a subject. What
these movements and, indeed, the subject of Women's Studies have in
common, is the desire for a transformation of society that will end women's
oppression, disadvantage and second-class citizen status within society. The
various countries presented in Part VII in terms of case studies indicate how
very differently women in diverse regions in Europe have moved in order to
work towards such a transformation. The selection of the countries represented was dictated by several concerns, a very banal but nevertheless important one of which was limited space.[8] More importantly, we wanted to include
brief case studies from diverse regions of Europe – that is, from the Scandinavian countries, from Central Europe, from Southern Europe and from
Eastern Europe. Hence the choice of Denmark, Norway, France, Germany,
Italy, Spain, Hungary and post-1989 Slovenia. What this choice shows is how
feminists in countries with relatively stable and continuing kinds of governance, such as Norway, have developed certain methods of arguing for and
advancing the case of women, relative to countries such as Spain and Hungary where changes in political regime have also led to very different opportunities for progressing women's emancipation. One important point in several
of the case histories is the role that individual women played in advancing
women's rights and changing perceptions of women's needs and roles.[9] It is

easy to dismiss stories of the individual, courageous woman, but what these narratives indicate is both the possibility of political influence in the production of social change – that is, women's agency – and the opportunities for bottom-up approaches to effecting such change. The latter, of course, fuels all revolutionary movements, but is a salutary reminder in a time when many women feel, or continue to feel, that their opportunities for influence are diminishing, not least in the weakening Western democracies, where voter apathy is becoming an increasing concern.

Conclusions

Both the European Union and European Women's Studies are projects of becoming, in process. In some respects, and for obvious reasons, similar questions and issues are raised by both formations. There is the question of what is specifically European, and, even more, how should that question be asked? Or, in the name of what agenda should that question be asked? We raise it here in an attempt to break through some of the silences that exist – for all the reasons detailed above – around European feminist scholarship. We also raise it to encourage debate between that scholarship and the work that goes on in other countries and other continents. Lastly, we raise it because there are many feminist issues with specifically European inflections which need to be articulated and addressed. These include some of the key political issues of our day, such as the impact of the decline of the welfare state in Europe on women; migration; racism, and how as Europeans we handle notions of difference; the material and ideological implications of moving from nation-states to a Europe that seeks to transcend that specificity; women's citizenship in Europe; how we deal with the violence large numbers of women in Europe continue to experience every day of their lives in both the societies in transition and in currently more stable societies. There are also many other issues which we have not been able to begin to address in this volume, not least the impact of globalization and of the new (bio)technologies in Europe. These are projects for the future, part of the plans for continuing feminist research collaborations which must be one of the aims of feminist scholars in Europe, to give their work both a platform and a structure for generating, exchanging and promoting European feminist research.

Notes

1. The Thematic Network that formed the backdrop to this textbook had its antecedents in a variety of prior European, funded activities promoting student and staff exchanges (see the 'Introduction' by Braidotti and Vonk in *The Making of European Women's Studies* (Braidotti and Vonk 2000); and also J. Hanmer in the same volume).

2. Judith Butler's work, for instance, is known and read in even the most materially

deprived of European countries, whereas the work of women from those countries themselves remains virtually unknown outside their own land.

3. Of special relevance are the following: the Nordic Women's Library at NIKK, in Oslo; the IIAV – International Archive of the Women's Movement, in Amsterdam; and the Italian Women's Library, in Bologna.

4. This debate was implicated in the establishment of standpoint theory (Harding 1986) and whilst standpoint theory itself has been the object of considerable criticism, its plea for understanding the situatedness of knowledge has had an abiding impact on Women's Studies and beyond.

5. This group was intermittently joined by many other feminists who periodically helped develop the shape and content of this volume and provided valuable advice and contacts. Among these we would particularly like to mention, and thank, Ingebjørg Strøno of the Norges Forskningsråd (Oslo, Norway), Kirsti Lempiänen (Finland), Britt-Marie Thurén (Umeå University, Sweden), and Marguerita Birriel (Granada University, Spain).

6. The term 'European Union' was agreed in the Maastricht Treaty of 7 February 1992.

7. This statement remains true despite the attacks on the World Trade Center and the Pentagon on 11 September 2001.

8. For those who want to read more extensively on the topic there is, for instance, Monica Threlfall's volume *Mapping the Women's Movement* (1996).

9. In some ways this reflects conventional – and now, not least by feminist histo-riography, much contested – historical story-telling in which the exceptional individual is both made a key catalyst in achieving change, and presented as representative of movements at a given point in time.

References

Braidotti, Rosi and Esther Vonk, eds (2000) *The Making of European Women's Studies*, Vol. 1. Utrecht: University of Utrecht.

Braidotti, Rosi, Esther Vonk and Sonja van Wichelen, eds (2000) *The Making of European Women's Studies*, Vol. 2. Utrecht: University of Utrecht.

Braidotti, Rosi, Ilse Lazaroms, Esther Vonk, eds (2001) *The Making of European Women's Studies*, Vol. 3. Utrecht: University of Utrecht.

Harding, S. (1986) *The Science Question in Feminism*. Milton Keynes: Open University Press.

SIGMA European Universities Network (1995) *Women's Studies: National Reports*. Coimbra, Portugal: Coimbra Group.

Threlfall, M., ed. (1996) *Mapping the Women's Movement*. London: Verso.

PART I

Women as Social and Political Entities

1

Feminist Perspectives on the European Welfare State

HARRIET SILIUS

This chapter raises the question of why welfare states are of interest to feminists. Second, it analyses some important feminist contributions to welfare state research. This is followed by an investigation of the results of feminist comparisons of different European welfare systems. Finally, the chapter considers the Europeanness of contemporary research, as well as the transformation of welfare states under the impact of globalization.

European welfare state research has a strong Northwest European bias. One reason for this is that welfare states are regarded as more comprehensive in Northern Europe than in the South. The same is true regarding the degree of state intervention. European welfare state research has traditionally been even more a phenomenon of the northwest than the welfare systems themselves. This is partly due to the political East–West splits in Europe, which prevented Western scholars from studying Eastern welfare systems during the Communist era, and Eastern scholars from studying Western systems. This Western-centredness is also partly due to Anglo-American influences which have been particularly strong in the social sciences of Western Europe. In most mainstream research this bias is not problematized. I shall comment on this issue at greater length at the end of the chapter. In examining the geopolitical specificity of European welfare state research – that is, its Northwestern-centredness – the chapter will ask which aspects are of interest to feminists, and why a focus on Scandinavia can be illustrative of the current state of the art of this type of research.

A broad definition of the welfare state includes a focus on education, health, housing, means of subsistence, social security and other measures for guaranteeing the well-being of people. A narrow definition would focus on social rights in the case of sickness, childbirth, unemployment and poverty, for instance. Welfare states intervene between (labour) markets and private lives, between paid work and care. In general terms, welfare states are more important to women than to men, simply because women are poorer, as official statistics verify. Feminist discussions of welfare states are important because they can offer perspectives which are neglected in mainstream research. One such perspective is how bodily and sexual rights can be included in the concept of welfare.

Histories of the Welfare State

Many West European countries, in contrast to, for example, the United States, have a long tradition of elaborate state welfare provision. In most countries the roots of the welfare state can be traced back to the nineteenth century. Social changes such as urbanization, industrialization and reshaped gender relations produced what we have since come to describe as 'social problems'. Migration to urban areas for industrial work brought bad working and housing conditions, poverty and health problems. Prostitution, on women's initiative, became one of the issues for public debate in the nineteenth century.

When Europe was urbanized – which took over a century, due to considerable unevenness in the speed of the process in different countries, and the differences in emphases – gender relations also changed. Families no longer worked together (with more or less gendered tasks) on the land, but in workplaces separated from the home. As child labour was increasingly forbidden and wages gradually rose, the phenomenon of the male breadwinner developed. Large numbers of women, mainly married, found themselves outside the labour market at home with their children. The nineteenth century also saw the rise of the discourse on the nuclear family – a family with a breadwinning husband and a housewife occupied with caring and the household. The ideology of the nuclear family was well suited for urban, bourgeois ideals and conditions.

When describing the history of the welfare state, mainstream research has usually focused on the problems of the waged worker. He was underpaid, laboured in bad working conditions, was under constant threat of unemployment or of earning insufficient for his own or his family's living because of sickness, accident or old age. The changing social conditions of the breadwinner and transformations of the welfare state have thus mainly been analysed from the point of view of the assumed male worker. Social and political movements of the nineteenth century, especially the labour movement, occupy a privileged position in the discourse concerned with the creation of the welfare state, which is regarded as being rooted historically in a deal between male workers and the patriarchal employers or government. The key issue here is that of class, and the parties involved are the interest groups of the labour market and public politics. Mainstream Scandinavian welfare state historians in particular embrace this corporatist vision, while other scholars ascribe agency to a wider range of social actors, for example philanthropic associations, political parties, and prominent, individual political actors. West European countries, so the story goes, gradually improved working and social conditions through benefits and insurance because they had an interest in a healthy population, societal peace and, in some cases, in uniting different groups into one nation. Thus improving welfare systems often went hand in hand with the building of nation-states, and so did welfare state research. Strong national interests still inform many studies. One version of comparative welfare state research is thus designed to show how things are better in the scholar's home country; another does the opposite, featuring a country where things are better.

From the 1970s onwards feminist scholars who had trained in the mainstream tradition began to ask questions such as: did working-class women not work in factories? Did women not do both paid and unpaid work in the home? Is work only work if it is paid? Who were the first 'social workers' to draw attention to social problems? What about the women's movement of the nineteenth century: did it not concern itself with these issues? Is the history of the welfare state a narrative preoccupied solely with the position and actions of men? The feminist critique of the welfare state research revealed the gender blindness and gendered presuppositions of the mainstream view, and pointed out that the focus on the male breadwinner provided a one-sided representation of the origins of the welfare state. For a long time, welfare state scholarship – including feminist scholarship – showed only a paternalistic history. Feminist research found that large numbers of women did work in factories as well as in the home, some doing laundry, sewing or cleaning for pay; others engaged in the same jobs for their family without pay. And they found ample evidence that from early on women worked to solve social problems. Women's involvement in philanthropic work, on both discursive and practical levels, could in many cases be considered as the first form of welfare. The temperance movement, as well as religious movements, engaged many women in social questions as their primary activity. Activists of the women's movement were preoccupied with the rights of women, children and families. They were interested in poverty, sickness, illiteracy, malnutrition, and bad housing. Women felt that the public arena was closed to them because they did not have the formal rights to influence politics. Due to a lack of education most women were not able to improve their own conditions. Thus women's suffrage and their right to education became important issues for the first wave of the women's movement. Women's lack of an adequate income and men's anonymous urban lives made prostitution a specific target for first-wave feminists. While the paternalistic roots of welfare state history are well documented, its maternalistic roots remain largely unknown. Already at the beginning of the twentieth century, however, countries like Italy, France, Germany, Britain, the Netherlands and Scandinavia were directing welfare schemes particularly at women as mothers (Bock and Thane 1991). Studies analysing the implications for women of these early reforms have only recently become a significant presence. Feminists interested in this area have hitherto been forced to search for knowledge of women's welfare state history in accounts of, for example, prominent first-wave feminists or early-twentieth-century women politicians. The picture emerging from these studies is that women were both the designers and the recipients of early welfare state policies.

The Myrdal Model

Alva Myrdal may serve as an example of an influential female politician who shaped ideas about the welfare state in Western Europe. Alva Myrdal (1902–1986) was a Swedish social scientist and reformer, a Social Democrat and cabinet member. Together with her husband, the economist Gunnar Myrdal, from the 1930s onwards Alva took an active interest in the life of women. They introduced the notion of the 'people's home' or 'folk home'. While Gunnar was interested in the world economy – the 'big life' – Alva was interested in the 'small life', as Swedish historian Yvonne Hirdman (1989) puts it. Alva Myrdal's project was a most ambitious one: the state/government would take care of all its citizens from the cradle to the grave by facilitating everyday life and by anticipating risks that might occur. The woman that Alva Myrdal originally had in mind was the caregiver living in an urban area. She needed a modern flat with specially designed spaces (kitchen, bathroom), so that her work could be performed as fast and efficiently as possible. She needed day-to-day services for the care of her children and elderly relatives, and as a consumer of household goods. In the case of unemployment, illness or accidents, she needed special help to cope with such unforeseen situations. Through the eager work of many (women) activists, Alva Myrdal's social engineering of the modern housewife gradually turned into the modern Swedish welfare state, which took shape from the 1960s onwards. Her ideas spread to the other Scandinavian countries Denmark and Norway, and later also to Finland and Iceland.[1] The Scandinavian welfare state model, often presented as a flagship of European welfare provision, is known for its comprehensiveness and is regarded by many as the most advanced model of its kind. It became the focus of interest for feminists in the 1980s. Did Alva Myrdal's preoccupation with the 'small life' have implications throughout Scandinavia and beyond, even on a transnational level? Was it woman-friendly? Was it advanced?

Are European Welfare States Still Patriarchal?

The modern welfare states in Western Europe are predominantly post-Second World War phenomena. The war devastated large parts of Europe (Sweden was one remarkable exception). Many Europeans had to restart life in new places because their homes were either destroyed during the war or they were located in the 'wrong' place. Citizens were given rights to housing, maintenance, education and employment. At the end of the war most European women had finally achieved basic political and economic rights, such as the vote and the right to own property. The European countries did not all follow the same model of social reform. Neither did reforms occur at the same time, nor did they affect all groups of citizens in the same way. Nevertheless, reforms were introduced everywhere. Social rights were expanded, diversified and developed both quantitatively and qualitatively until the end of the twentieth century. Even then, remarkable gaps in the systems could still be found. Women's bodily rights – for example, to be protected from violence in their own home – remained a problem, including in Scandinavia (Siim 2000). The 1990s began a new era. In response to economic recession and justified by a neoliberal ideology, cuts were introduced and benefits were targeted differentially during this period – for example, in Finland.

Early mainstream research, especially that written in English, saw the British Beveridgean welfare state model (named after Lord Beveridge, its main architect after the Second World War) as the typical example of a modern welfare state. British feminists like Elizabeth Wilson (1977), evaluating women's conditions under the welfare state, concluded that this state was patriarchal (although she did not herself use the word 'patriarchal'), gendered, and served men's interests better than women's. But what about the Scandinavian welfare state, with its strong emphasis on equality? Could that be regarded as more women-friendly?

One of the theoretical contributions of feminist research to knowledge is the concept of patriarchy, which was widely used in the 1970s and 1980s to describe modern society and women's oppression. Welfare state scholars also found the concept useful when analysing why women's conditions were different from men's. When analysing Scandinavia, Helga Hernes (1987) in Norway concluded that women had moved from a private dependence, under their husbands and fathers, into a public dependence with the state as the new, less visible, patriarch. But she also saw that women's conditions varied according to their relation to the welfare state. The situation was different if the woman was a recipient of welfare, a professional welfare worker, or a citizen with universal rights. These positions are, of course, not necessarily mutually exclusive. However, in general it is true to say that women's relation to the welfare state depended on their position in society at large. Feminists of today argue, further, that gender is intertwined with, for example, class, 'race' and ethnicity, and that a complex web of identity categories determines an individual's position both in society and in relation to the welfare state.

Helga Hernes's thesis about the potential of the Scandinavian welfare state to develop into a woman-friendly one resulted in an engaged debate among feminist scholars (see, e.g., Anttonen 1994). Although there is no answer to the question of the woman-friendliness of a welfare state because of the heterogeneity of the category woman, for example, the issue of the gendered consequences of welfare state policies remains an important one, both theoretically and empirically. Since elaborate systems providing social services especially to women are found in the Scandinavian countries, they continue to be of particular interest to feminist researchers. Scandinavian state-centredness is, however, not a guarantee for best quality in all cases. Many areas of welfare policy are more elaborate in Germany or in the Netherlands, for example, especially regarding monetary transfers and labour market insurance. The private and voluntary sectors may be more developed in the UK.

Feminist Contributions to Welfare State Research

In the nineteenth century, feminist movements across Europe reformulated the questions of motherhood and independence – the so-called Wollstone-craftian dilemma from the eighteenth century – in several ways. From a welfare perspective these questions remain crucial. The right to financially supported motherhood – the maternalistic strand of feminist welfare state thinking – meant a continuous struggle for maternal care and paid maternity leave. Feminist politics throughout the twentieth century implied a need to work to improve conditions for mothers. Maternalist politics was – for different reasons, however – never the first priority of all women. Motherhood has not constituted a major problem for well-off women, for example. Therefore the improvement of the material conditions of motherhood has traditionally engaged feminist politicians preoccupied with social problems such as poverty more than politicians with other priorities. In recent times many feminists have argued against paid motherhood, for example in the form of a care allowance, because they see it as a way of keeping women economically dependent on both individual men and the welfare state.

In the 1980s a substantial body of feminist research focused on women's caring work. Underlying this concern, with early contributions in the UK and Norway, was an interest in everyday (and everynight) life and in the work of 'ordinary' women. These 'ordinary' women could be working-class women, farmers, housewives, unemployed, and so on. From the very beginning, the recognition of divisions among women formed an integral part of the Scandinavian feminist social sciences. The divisions were conceptualized from the 1960s onwards as class-based and sometimes implicitly included 'race' or ethnicity, although these concepts were not used explicitly at the time. The research on caring work by feminist scholars had several important results, three of which I shall mention here. First, conceptualizations of care as work implying taking care of, among others, children, the elderly and the sick, as well as management of the household, described women's caring work in a more precise way. It stressed that caring was work. It emphasized that caring work requires among other things emotional, bodily and intellectual effort. It also demands the performance of several tasks simultaneously and a flexible time perspective – that is, the ability to reprioritize current tasks according to their urgency and the capacity to evaluate the future consequences of one's actions. Kari Wærness introduced this Scandinavian conceptualization of care as early as 1978. The understanding of care as both paid and unpaid work, and as an important feature of both families and many occupations, facilitated a deeper understanding, on the one hand, of women as care-givers and, on the other hand, of the content of work of professional care-givers such as nurses. It also helped to create an understanding of the conditions of women with caring responsibilities in the professions and in leadership positions (Silius 1992). Further, it raised an interest in the emergence, work, client relations, and so forth, of different welfare professions. It is important to note that this expanded understanding of care to include paid professional work extended the meaning of care as it was commonly used in the English language. It opened the way for analyses of the history of the caring/nursing professions (including midwives). In these studies feminist scholars also found that women were significant as women-friendly activists and shapers of the early welfare state. In sum, new fields of research were created and old fields benefited from these feminist contributions.

The second important contribution of feminist scholarship on care is the discussion of paid versus unpaid work. In debates about women's oppression in patriarchal systems in the 1970s, care and work were understood as repro-duction and production. Empirical studies in the next decade showed the complexity and multiplicity both of unpaid caring work in the home and of paid caring work in institutions. The empirical results laid the ground for theoretical contributions to feminist economics by focusing on the relation between paid and unpaid work. The debate also had consequences for new understandings of the concepts 'private' (connected to care, the unpaid and in the home) and 'public' (also connected to care, but in this case paid and institutionalized). Space thus became an important key to understanding women's conditions.

The third feminist contribution deriving from the debate on care was the discussion of time. Mainstream research used to understand time as either paid working time at the workplace in the public sphere or leisure at home in the private sphere. Feminist research concluded that this dichotomy held true neither for women care-givers working at home, nor for women in paid work with caring responsibilities. The first group of women did not have leisure, and the second often regarded their working time as their untied or free time compared to the tied or unfree time at home. The gendered specifi-city of time arrangements may be one of the biggest inequalities between women and men in twenty-first-century Europe.

Feminist scholarship on caring made it obvious that a prerequisite for the modern welfare state was women's unpaid caring. In her 1978 article Kari Wærness called women's work at home 'the invisible welfare state'. Later many feminist researchers concluded that the 'advanced' Swedish, or Scandinavian, welfare state relied on undervalued female labour. It was based on a hidden gender compromise, known early in the discussions as 'a gender contract', according to which women were entitled to paid work so long as they continued to take the main responsibility for the care of others. The concept of the 'contract' was originally used for either historical analyses or systems approaches. It is unusual in today's feminist research because of its inclination to universalize women and to neglect agency. The same idea, however, continues to live in concepts such as gender model or gender regime. These concepts will be discussed in the next section.

In general, criticism of feminist caring research has focused on the latter's tendency to essentialize women or universalize the category woman. It is claimed that such research has hidden the differences among women and grouped together women with very different interests, as well as neglected the political risks of appraising care, for example by demanding strong support for motherhood, which many have considered to be a traditional feminine trap.

Another type of criticism of this research concerns the preoccupation with the state in welfare state research. As the name of this type of research suggests, much more interest has been devoted to state initiatives and arrangements than to other actors' involvement in people's well-being. The importance of families, civil society, the 'third' sector, voluntary organizations, churches, and so on, has largely been neglected. Feminist scholars looking in detail into the well-being of individuals and families usually find that their welfare is a complicated mix. It relies on state systems, family arrangements and civil society organizations. A grandmother might take care of a grandchild, ask for a doctor in the public health system if she becomes ill, and have the responsibility for transportation of schoolchildren to a church after-school club. She might also turn to the private, commercial, sector when looking for a doctor. Some families employ nannies in their homes. Non-governmental organizations run homes for the elderly. These are just a few examples of the complicated mix in individual cases.

A third strand of feminist criticism is related to the quite positive view held of the state, especially in Scandinavian feminist welfare state research. This positive general view raises many questions. Why should state daycare be better than daycare by the child's mother or grandmother? Why choose education in a mainstream state daycare centre rather than in a centre operated by a voluntary organization, with a specific, alternative educational scheme? Are not state control and interference always part of state intervention? One answer to these questions that Scandinavian feminists offer is that state arrangements guarantee democratic control (e.g. through municipal bodies) which is often not the case in private-sector arrangements. This does not make sense in all cases that are not run by the state, however. One such case is the services provided by voluntary organizations; another is parent-run daycare centres. A further problematic presupposition is that feminist interests are represented in decision-making bodies, which is not the case everywhere. The positive view of the state, which is held by many feminists in the West, has not been shared by women in postcommunist countries, who, for reasons very different from those mentioned above, have been hostile towards state intervention (Dahlerup 1994).

Grounds for Comparison of European Welfare States

The growing interest in analyses of different West European welfare states from a feminist point of view has led to two conclusions, about which feminists remain in agreement. First, all welfare states are deeply rooted in masculine norms and, second, waged work plays a crucial role in the outcomes of welfare systems for individuals. As waged work is distributed in a highly gendered way, the outcomes vary accordingly. Feminist studies have also long since pointed to differences among women. Some women stay out of the labour market for a considerable period of their so-called working life; many work part-time; others are self-employed, farmers or small entrepreneurs. All these groups are 'abnormal' compared to the stereotypical welfare state citizen, the male industrial worker or civil servant.

In-depth analyses of different welfare states, especially in Scandinavia, turned the focus from individual countries to their comparison. Feminist scholars knew from experience that there were considerable differences among systems. For example, during the 1990s the periods of maternity leave awarded in individual European countries ranged from a couple of months to over a year, depending on the country. Even in the supposedly homogenous Scandinavian welfare systems, differences were found. These differences called for more detailed studies of various aspects of relevance to women's lives. Welfare states differed in the degree to which they provided for citizens or residents lacking a history of waged work. One question was whether or not universal rights to welfare existed. Another important issue was whether the welfare state system was based on an ideology of a government's right to intervene in the lives of the needy, of welfare recipients, or on an ideology of state responsibility to offer social services to anybody, to consumers. Anneli Anttonen (1994) termed the first group of countries social insurance states and the second, the Scandinavian countries, social service states. The Scandinavian welfare states have also been characterized as countries of gender equality, low income differentials, full employment, tax-financed welfare systems, and high labour market participation among women.

Among social scientists analysing welfare states the models developed by Gøsta Esping-Andersen (1990) have been widely used, including by feminists. He distinguishes three different systems of welfare state: (1) the social-democratic model, built on universal social rights; (2) the conservative model, built on compulsory labour market insurance; and (3) the liberal model, built on means-tested benefits. The basis for entitlements in his model is social citizenship, waged work, or social needs. Public social insurance and social services for all (citizens, residents) are characteristics of Esping-Andersen's social-democratic regime. Equality of income distribution, meaning transfers from the well-off to the worse-off, is another basic principle. Waged work is taken into account, however. High income results in higher levels of benefits, at least up to a certain point. The Scandinavian countries, especially Sweden and Denmark, are examples of the social-democratic model, but Esping-Andersen also included the Netherlands. Usually all Scandinavian countries are included in this model, for two reasons. One is that they do resemble each other, in spite of differences. The second is the wide, popular acceptance of the model. Many welfare state scholars have questioned whether it is appropriate to call the model social-democratic[2] and prefer to use the more neutral term 'Scandinavian model'.

The conservative regime is built on a strong wage-worker model with the aim of assuring the income level of the earner. The family is the unit for entitlements, and married non-employed women are insured through their husbands. Motherhood can also be the basis for entitlements. Esping-Andersen gave Austria, France, Germany and Italy as examples of the conservative regime.

Typical of the liberal regime are means-tested benefits, a low level of income transfer, and a limited public social insurance system. The target of the system is those in need, the poor. Esping-Andersen's examples are the USA, Canada and Australia. Most scholars include the UK in the liberal regime, although historically and still today it resembles many European societies more than the USA.

Esping-Andersen's model, which largely ignores the Mediterranean countries, has been very influential in cross-national comparisons of West European countries. It does not take gender into account – as many feminist scholars have argued since it was presented. It has, however, inspired feminist scholars to develop models by paying attention to gender relations. Jane Lewis and Ilona Ostner (1994) suggest that the majority of modern welfare states might be categorized as male breadwinner models. They argue that this basic model had been modified in different modes and to different degrees into either strong, moderate or weak male breadwinner models. They conclude that Britain and Germany were examples of the strong breadwinner model, France of the moderate, and the Scandinavian countries of the weak model. Other scholars argue that the male breadwinner model does not differentiate enough between different groups of women. Arnlaug Leira (1989), for example, when studying Norwegian childcare, concluded that Norway re-sembled Britain and several other continental countries more than Sweden or Denmark. Scandinavian feminists, although preserving their positive general view, have widely acknowledged that the roots of the Scandinavian welfare states were anchored in male interests. Thus the patriarchal, paternalist, male or masculinist nature of the welfare state is today a common point of departure for many feminist European analyses.

Esping-Andersen has recently modified the characteristics of his three regimes, partly in response to feminist criticism. He now stresses minimum benefits and a high occurrence of private insurance as typical of liberal regimes, familism and income-based benefits as typical of conservative regimes, and universalness and low occurrence of private insurance as typical of the social-democratic regimes. Central to the universal service system are daycare and care of the elderly.

An ambitious effort to include gender relations in analytical comparisons of West European welfare states has been made by Diane Sainsbury (1999). As a tool she offers three different gender policy regimes, conceived of as a given organization of gender relations associated with a specific policy logic. Central to the organization of gender relations are principles and norms that prescribe the tasks, obligations and rights of women and men. Sainsbury distinguishes her gender policy regimes on the basis of actual or preferred gender ideology, principles of entitlement, and policy constructions. The regimes are labelled according to gender ideology. These gender policy regimes are (1) the male breadwinner regime, (2) the separate roles regime, and (3) the individual earner–carer regime.

The male breadwinner regime is based on a strict division of labour between women and men. It assigns different tasks and obligations to women and men, resulting in unequal entitlements in social provision. Being married and having a family carries advantages over unmarried persons with family or single ones without family. Men as family providers have entitlements based on the principle of maintenance – that is, they receive social and tax benefits corresponding to family responsibilities. Marriage is the celebrated family form and married women have entitlements in their role as wives. Married women have a weak labour market position; their prime obligation is to care for their husband and children in the form of unpaid work. In this regime, according to Sainsbury, unmarried mothers and divorced women fall outside the regular policies.

The ideology of separate gender roles emphasizes the differences between women and men. This regime allocates social rights on the basis of these differences. It underlines a strict division of labour, but, unlike the bread-winner model, it attaches weight both to maintenance and to care. Consequently social and tax benefits are conferred on both male family providers and female care-givers. The principle of care erodes the importance of marriage for women. Care-givers in the home receive a paid component. However, the principle of maintenance privileges men in the labour market, for instance in employment and wage policies.

According to Sainsbury, the ideology of the individual earner–carer regime differs fundamentally from the other two in that the preferred relations between women and men are shared roles and obligations, leading to equal rights.

Women and men have entitlements as earners and carers, and policies aim to enable women to become workers and men to become carers. Social rights attach to the individual. Separate taxation of married persons treats husbands and wives equally. The financial costs of children are shared through public provision of services. Instead of focusing on men as family providers or women as carers, the focus is on parents. There is a strong state involvement in the care of children, the sick and the disabled, and the frail elderly through provision of services and payments to carers. For Sainsbury the elimination of marriage as a basis for entitlement is the crucial element of this regime.

From the point of view of women, instead of from that of (male) gender ideologies, Sainsbury's models could be called the marriage model, the caring model and the individual model. She also draws attention to four underlying dimensions of her scheme. The first is whether social rights are familialized or individualized. The second is whether both women and men are entitled to both work-related and care-related benefits or not. The third dimension is the scope of state responsibility for caring. At one extreme, care is a family re-sponsibility and unpaid work. At the other, state responsibility manifests itself through provision of services and payments to carers in the home. Provision of services enables women's employment and provides the scope to change the division of labour, while payment to carers in the home reinforces tradi-tional roles, according to Sainsbury. Her final dimension is women's and men's equal access to work.

In her empirical work on Scandinavia (not including Iceland), in response to Esping-Andersen's characterization, Sainsbury studied the differences among the Scandinavian countries, mainly on the basis of data from the 1980s. She labelled Norway a country that privileges men as providers and women as care-givers; Finland as a country of mothers as workers and carers; Denmark as a site of the decline of men's rights as providers and the rise of women's rights as workers; and, finally, Sweden as transforming gender differentiation into social rights.

Diane Sainsbury's 1999 book includes several comparisons of countries made by different authors and also analysed by her. These studies show very mixed results and give examples of different groupings of countries. A study of the economic well-being and of policies towards lone mothers in ten countries suggested that group 1 consisted of Belgium, Denmark, Finland, Luxembourg, Sweden (and Norway); group 2 of France and Germany; group 3 of Austria (and the USA); group 4 of Ireland; group 5 of the Netherlands; and group 6 of the UK (and Australia and Canada). This ranking of countries, with 1 for the best and 6 for the worst case, was based on whether lone mothers were predominantly working or not and whether their poverty rate was below or above the average rate. Looking at social care services for children in ten European countries, Sainsbury puts the UK at the bottom of the scale and Denmark at the top. If one grouped countries together on this scale, the UK would be joined by the Netherlands, Germany and Norway;

Finland and Italy would be found in the middle; while Sweden, France and Belgium would be closer to Denmark at the top. Looking at taxation, Sainsbury found that Germany was the country which most favoured the male breadwinner family, followed by Belgium, Denmark, the Netherlands and Norway; Finland, followed by Sweden and the UK, favoured dual-earner families; while France, Austria and Italy formed the group in between. Women's labour market participation, both full-time and part-time, was between 60 and 70 per cent in several European countries at the beginning of the 1990s. The rate was over 70 per cent in Sweden (85 per cent), Finland and Denmark, while Italy stood out with only 42 per cent together with Belgium (57 per cent) and the Netherlands (51 per cent) (Sainsbury 1999). According to the same statistics, women in Finland, Sweden and Denmark earn the most, while women in Italy, the UK, Germany and the Netherlands earn the least, compared to men.

Feminist work on comparisons of West European welfare states has demonstrated two aspects in addition to the genderedness of mainstream research. First, it is of utmost importance which perspective you choose as your starting point. Is it, for example, the perspective of the single non-white woman with a permanent job, caring for an aunt, or the perspective of the divorced mother from Lapland with three small children occasionally working part-time? Second, the grouping of countries depends on which elements of the welfare state policies you regard as important. Genderedness is not only an inherent aspect of welfare states; present-day welfare states also continue to shape gender relations.

No comparisons pay equal attention to all European countries. We know much more about the UK, Germany, France, Italy and Sweden, including in the pre-EU period, than we do of Greece, Spain or Portugal. In the huge body of Scandinavian contributions, Finland used to be missing and Iceland[3] continues to be a blank spot. It is easy to see that the length of a country's membership of the EU affects the amount of comparative work on a specific country or, as in the Swedish case, its specific features. Could size and peripherality have an impact even today?

European welfare state research is focused on members of the European Union. Most of these studies, which often label themselves European, are not European in a geographical sense, because in addition to the South, Central and Eastern Europe are usually omitted. Joanna Regulska (1998), among others, calls this phenomenon of neglecting women from Central and Eastern Europe 'othering'. Drude Dahlerup (1994) states that welfare state theorists, with few exceptions, have looked exclusively at the Western world. They seem to forget that the communist regimes were also extended welfare states with social security provision, public-service-like childcare, public healthcare, housing subsidies, and so on.

Most feminist scholars have demonstrated the complexity of comparative West European welfare state research, the mixed solutions of welfare state systems, and the problem of whose perspective is under scrutiny. They have raised a number of questions that are currently the focus of study, and pointed to problems which need further feminist research. In addition to this, the very scope of Europe needs to be addressed, not only because we know so little about Central, Eastern and Southern Europe, but also because comparative research, including in these countries, will raise new theoretical, methodological and empirical questions. The comparisons themselves, for example, are problematic for several reasons. On a theoretical level, the underlying assumptions are often either rather vague or based on unproblematized mainstream assumptions. To begin with, how do we conceive of the 'welfare state' when we wish to compare welfare systems? If systems are different everywhere, how can we find a method to compare them? How can we handle empirical findings, when we do not agree on the most important dimensions to be included in the comparisons? The example above, of ranking countries, raises all these questions.

Who Is a Citizen?

A classic understanding of the welfare state at the level of the citizen is based on the development of individual rights, from civil through political to social rights. The notion of social citizenship has been shown to be a fruitful analytical tool for feminist discussions of contemporary welfare state systems. It has drawn attention to the outcome of welfare state arrangements for persons who do not have a long relationship to the labour market or who dedicate their lives to unpaid caring work. But citizenship has from the very beginning had an exclusionary element. Women's struggle for citizenship, irrespective of their relations to individual men, took two centuries. But women do not enjoy full citizenship in every important aspect. Citizenship itself is conceived of and implemented in heterogeneous ways in Europe (Del Re and Heinen 1996).

Feminist researchers have pointed to the problem of bodily and sexual rights (see, for example, Lister 1997) in connection with social rights. Welfare systems protect women's bodily integrity less well than men's. Men's violence against women, they know, is a problem that was put on the agenda by feminists and is not yet solved. It is an area in urgent need of research both on national and transnational levels in order to find the most effective means to stop the violence. Trafficking in women is increasing. Recent wars in Europe, transitions in political systems, and the creation of new borders and markets, are some of the underlying reasons.

In addition, most family rights are based on the heterosexual couple. Scandinavia apart, registered partnerships among lesbians or gays are allowed at present only in the Netherlands. Even if legal partnerships are allowed, family rights might be more limited than in heterosexual relationships. Usually, lesbians and gays do not have exactly the same social rights as heterosexuals. Here, too, feminist research as well as activism is needed in order to abolish discrimination.

Feminist theorizing on citizenship has demonstrated the importance of obligations in addition to rights, of participation in political policy design and decision-making, of praxis in addition to law. The principle of individualization, practised most widely and for the longest time in Scandinavia, dissolves effectively an enforced bond between (married) women and men. Individualism is, however, not an ideal embraced by everyone everywhere. Scandinavian individualism has been strongly based on a white, heterosexual individual whose concept of family is restricted to a nuclear, one-generation family with one or two parents. This has been said to represent a false universalism in respect of 'race', the category woman (and man), heterosexuality and family.

Entitlements based on residence are one solution to the very problematic notion of citizenship in the European context. A discussion about residence versus citizenship immediately puts 'race' on the agenda, but it does not solve all problems − such as persons *sans papier*. This is one example of how the increasing feminist research on 'race' and ethnicity (see Lutz, Yuval-Davis and Phoenix 1995) brings new questions to the examination of previously neglected aspects of citizenship. Ruth Lister (1997) offers global citizenship as one way to deal with this. Her idea is to link citizenship to human rights and to develop new modes of citizenship practice by work in transnational social movements and non-governmental organizations. Lister suggests that this transnational co-operation should be guided by differentiated universalism, which embodies the creative tension between universalism and particularity or difference.

In addition to the discussion of caring, the other part of Wollstonecraft's feminist dilemma, independence, continues to be central to debates at the beginning of the twenty-first century. The discussion about sharing care responsibilities, implying that both mothers and fathers should be involved, turns the focus towards men. Feminists resisting care allowances in Norway and Sweden[4] argue that the care dilemma will never be solved without the involvement of men. Scandinavian fathers taking care of infants on paid leave from their job are the result of feminist work for shared care responsibilities. In the Scandinavian countries every man who becomes a father is entitled to spend several months at home for childcare purposes. Yet only a small minority of fathers actually make use of these possibilities. The statistics on the take-up of paternal leave periods, however, hide the cultural changes that have occurred in childcare patterns. My thesis is that at no time since men began to work separately from women and their family have so many fathers spent so much time together with their children, and never before have so many of them taken part in childcare as they do today. But feminist work is still needed for engaging men also in the care of the frail or sick elderly.

The principle of universalism and the creation of comprehensive service provision that are typical of the so-called 'advanced' or 'elaborate' Scandinavian welfare states tend to encounter problems with difference, heterogeneity and particularity. European welfare state research urgently needs the South and the East to overcome its Northwestern presuppositions.

The Swan Song of the Welfare State?

Nowhere were welfare states introduced overnight. In most countries it took at least half a century to establish their key elements. Throughout the twentieth century welfare states have continuously transformed, a process that has not stopped. An examination of the welfare states of today reveals a patchwork quilt throughout Europe, with both considerable similarities and significant differences. During the last decade, some scholars have argued that the West European welfare state has reached the end of the road, that we are witnessing its death, or that it will decompose in the near future. The reason offered for this is globalization. Globalization in this context is assumed to mean that welfare states will not be able to stand up against international market forces. In addition to actors in the economic marketplace, neoliberal ideology and deregulative policies are thought to weaken the welfare state's chances of survival. In Central and Eastern Europe a dismantling of the welfare state has already taken place, partly because of neoliberal ideology and partly because of lack of money in the public sector.

Comprehensive, high-quality welfare systems cost money. This money depends on contributions in the form of taxes and fees. You need people to pay the contributions and taxes out of their income, property or capital – in other words, a high labour market participation rate. Many countries' labour market policies therefore aim at full employment. The degree to which this is achieved varies because some countries have better conditions than others. Another way to finance a welfare system is via companies that make general contributions, in addition to those covering their own employees. But countries with high taxation and a tax-based welfare system – for example, Denmark, Finland and Sweden – under attack from all directions are working towards a harmonization of their tax systems in order to unify market conditions.

One example of a welfare system based on high taxes is Finland. When the economic recession of the 1990s hit the country, with resulting high unemployment, benefit levels were cut. The labour force in the education, health and social work sectors was reduced. A vast majority of the people, however, stood by the basic ideas of the system. One important reason for this was probably that a comprehensive system which is used by a large part of the population gives opportunities to develop a system of high quality. It means that public services are used also by those who are well educated and well off. A symptomatic example is Finnish daycare. Well-educated women commonly use daycare institutions even more widely than women with less education, who more often take the option of staying at home on a care allowance.

With the population of Europe ageing and global trends affecting markets and policies the question is, who sets the political agenda? What transformations are needed and in which part of the system? Whose perspective is the most important? Fortunately, many social movements of the twenty-first century are transnational to a considerably higher degree than before. This is facilitated by the ease of moving to different markets, including informational, ideological, as well as economic markets. Women's activism, in different arenas, for various feminist causes, is likely to be crucial in the future.

Notes

1. The languages of the Scandinavian countries Denmark, Iceland, Norway and Sweden have common roots. In Finland the majority of the people speak Finnish, a Finno-Ugrian, non-Scandinavian language, differing from many European languages. Geographically Finland is much closer to Scandinavia than Iceland and culturally these five countries, which are also called the Nordic countries, share large parts of their history as well as their socio-cultural heritage. In spite of 'Nordic' being a more accurate term, in this chapter I use 'Scandinavian' for all five Nordic countries. This is because the term 'Scandinavian' is so commonly used in the context of welfare state research.

2. The discussion concerns mainly three questions. All Scandinavian countries cannot be labelled social democratic. It depends on which time period you study if social democracy is an appropriate characterization. To name a model social democratic gives credit to a male labour movement, while it neglects other agents, especially the women's movement.

3. Iceland is not a member of the EU. Norway, also a non-member, has, however, more often been included in European comparisons.

4. Care allowance is a payment made to a parent taking care of the child(ren) at home. It was introduced in 1984 in Finland. Feminist resistance stopped its permanent introduction in Sweden, but not in Norway.

References

Anttonen, Anneli (1994) 'Hyvinvointivaltion naisystävälliset kasvot' [The woman-friendly faces of the welfare state], in Anneli Anttonen, Lea Henriksson and Ritva Nätkin, eds, *Naisten hyvinvointivaltio* [Women's Welfare State]. Tampere: Vasta Paino, pp. 203–26.

Bock, Gisela and Pat Thane, eds (1991) *Maternity and Gender Policies: Women and the Rise of European Welfare States 1880s–1950s.* London: Routledge.

Dahlerup, Drude (1994) 'Learning to Live with the State: State, Market, and Civil Society: Women's Need for State Intervention in East and West', *Women's Studies International Forum* 17, pp. 117–27.

Del Re, Alisa and Jacqueline Heinen, eds (1996) *Quelle citoyenneté pour les femmes? La crise des États-providence et de la représentation politique en Europe.* Paris: L'Harmattan.

Esping-Andersen, Gøsta (1990) *The Three Worlds of Welfare Capitalism.* Cambridge: Polity Press.

Hernes, Helga (1987) *Welfare State and Women Power: Essays in State Feminism*. Oslo: Norwegian University Press.

Hirdman, Yvonne (1989) *Att lägga livet till rätta. Studier av svensk folkhemspolitik* [To Arrange Life: Studies in the Politics of the People's Home in Sweden]. Stockholm, Carlssons.

Leira, Arnlaug (1989) *Models of Motherhood. Welfare State Policies and Everyday Practices: the Scandinavian Experience*. Oslo: Institute of Social Research.

Lewis, Jane and Ilona Ostner (1994) 'Gender and the Evolution of European Social Policies.' ZE–S Arbeitspapier 4/94. Bremen: University of Bremen, Centre for Social Policy Research.

Lister, Ruth (1997) *Citizenship: Feminist Perspectives*. London: Macmillan.

Lutz, Helma, Nira Yuval-Davis and Ann Phoenix (1995) *Crossfires: Nationalism, Racism and Gender in Europe*. London: Pluto Press.

Regulska, Joanna (1998) 'The New "Other" European Woman', in Virgínia Ferreira, Teresa Tvares and Sílvia Portugal, eds, *Shifting Bonds, Shifting Bounds: Women, Mobility and Citizenship in Europe*. Oeiras: Celta, pp. 41–57.

Sainsbury, Diane, ed. (1999) *Gender and Welfare State Regimes*. Oxford: Oxford University Press.

Siim, Birte (2000) *Gender and Citizenship: Politics and Agency in France, Britain and Denmark*. Cambridge: Cambridge University Press.

Silius, Harriet (1992) *Den kringgärdade kvinnligheten. Att vara kvinnlig jurist i Finland* [Contracted Femininity: The Case of Women Lawyers in Finland]. Åbo: Åbo Akademi University Press.

Wilson, Elizabeth (1977) *Women and the Welfare State*. London: Tavistock.

Wærness, Kari (1978) 'The Invisible Welfare State: Women's Work at Home', *Acta Sociologica* 21, Supplement, Special Congress Issue: The Nordic Welfare States, pp. 193–207.

2

Single Women

TUULA GORDON

Family Formations

Family patterns have become increasingly diverse in Europe, and increasing numbers of people are opting out of marriage altogether. Whilst there have been and are more single women in Northern Europe than in Southern Europe, their numbers are increasing in Southern Europe despite the family-centred image of these countries. The proportion of single women has risen in most European countries. The category 'single woman' is not static; single women are historically heterogeneous, and the representations of single women, as well as the meanings attached to them, are diverse. Nevertheless, in this chapter I argue that 'single woman' has had, and still has, ambivalent resonances as a social category. Questions are raised about the meanings of 'woman' and 'femininity' when more and more women opt out of marriage. Set against the notion of the 'married woman', the 'single woman' has been portrayed as a unitary category. Single women, however, are heterogeneous in relation to social class, age, ethnicity, sexual orientation and lifestyle. The representations of a thirty-something (white), young, single (middle-class) woman, particularly prevalent in the media in the USA and imported to Europe, render invisible elderly single women, working-class single women, single mothers, women of colour, women with disabilities, and lesbians. Yet the popularity of certain glamorous representations of single women in Europe, too, suggests that being single is an experience the meanings of which are in flux and for which new representations are being sought.

The 'family' has acquired a central place in both the political and the analytical understandings of the operation of society. Frequently concerns about the state of the family are expressed. In Britain, for example, 'family values' have been emphasized by politicians. Interconnected with these concerns are worries about the integration of people into society, and in particular the socialization and upbringing of children. 'Family' is considered a basic, often natural, unit which binds people into social networks. Therefore the well-being of families is considered crucial for the well-being of societies. Whilst the nuclear family consisting of wife and husband and their children is often the taken-for-granted image evoked by the notion of the 'family', families have not been static but are subject to social change, including organizational patterns, place in peoples' life courses and internal divisions of labour (Gittins 1985). In critical discussions 'family' has been named as a central institution in the maintenance of inequalities, through the reproduction of social class differentiation between families, and through the unequal gendered division of labour within families (Barrett and McIntosh 1982).

Patterns of family formation are more diverse than the evocations of 'the family'. Moreover, the ways in which the family is implicated in people's life courses have become increasingly heterogeneous. This is evident in the shift from the category 'unmarried' to the category 'single' when referring to women who are not married at any given time. Although the numbers of women who never marry or cohabit in marriage-type relationships have not increased to the same extent as numbers of 'unmarried' and 'single' women, more women spend longer periods in their lives as single women because they marry later, for example, or get divorced, or are single in between marriages or marriage-type relationships. Due to changes in family patterns and the increasing heterogeneity of family formations, meanings attached to, and representations of, the family have thus also become more heterogeneous.

Single Women

Defining 'single women' is increasingly difficult. Statistics based on marital status are usually compiled on the basis of the categories 'single', 'married', 'divorced' and 'widowed'. In demographic research the category of 'never-married' is used. 'Single' also overlaps with 'unmarried'. However, already in 1981 Peter Stein had suggested that it is not useful to define 'single' as interchangeable with 'unmarried'. People's life courses in Europe and America are increasingly complex, and less likely to fit the pattern of getting married and staying married (as the term 'never-married' implies). Singles include, for example, women who are divorced. Nor is it useful to categorize all those who are not married as 'single'. Cohabitation has increased and, particularly in the Nordic countries, the legal position of a cohabiting couple with children has been brought close to the position of a similar married couple.

Stein constructs a typology of singles on the basis of elements of permanence and choice. 'Voluntary temporary' singles include young people who are not married, divorced people who are postponing remarriage, and people who have never been married but are not actively seeking marital status. 'Voluntary stable singles' include those who have chosen to be single, and those unmarried and divorced people who are not actively seeking marriage. 'Involuntary temporary singles' include single people actively seeking marriage, and divorced people wishing to remarry. 'Involuntary stable singles' include people who are divorced, widowed and those who never married but wished to do so – common to them is that they have come to consider singlehood as likely to be a permanent situation.

When I conducted a study on single women in the early 1990s (Gordon 1994a), I used Stein's four categories. My main concern was to distinguish between voluntary temporary singles still hoping to form partnerships and those who had chosen to be single and planned to stay so. Many of these women, whose ages ranged from 35 to 68 (although the majority of these were under 50), had resolved, with some temporary or more permanent regret, to accept or to cherish their single status, and hence they can be characterized as voluntary singles. Only a minority of them had made a conscious decision not to marry or cohabit, often at an early age.

A more typical pattern was that many young women had postponed marriage for various reasons – 'not till I have finished this course', 'not till I have that career', 'not this person' and so on. When these women reached their early thirties, they realized that many of their friends, partners, colleagues, relatives and neighbours had married or formed partnerships. At this stage most of the women accepted their single status, although many of them with varying degrees of regret and puzzlement. Other women were actively seeking a partner. I did not include cohabiting women in the study, although technically they are single. Similarly, whilst technically in most countries lesbian women are single, lesbians as well as heterosexuals can be both voluntary and involuntary singles (permanent or temporary), and cohabiting lesbians were not included as single women in my study.

Old Maids and City Singles

In the 1950s the proportion of unmarried women was very low, both in Europe and in the USA; marriage was emphasized as the normal life course, and women who had not married were sometimes condemned and often pitied as 'old maids'. In the 1960s marital patterns began to diversify, and this diversification has continued, despite neo-conservative politics emphasizing the importance of marriage and family as the acceptable and desirable way of organizing people's lives. In my analysis I suggested that the stereotype of the 'old maid' who could not get a man has not disappeared, although it has become less prevalent. Alongside it a more modern stereotype has emerged, that of the 'city single' who does not want a man. Whilst this latter stereotype seems on the surface glamorous, it nevertheless marginalizes single women.

An exploration of the social interactions of single women demonstrated that their networks mainly consisted of members of their family of origin, their own children and other single people, mainly women. Several of them suggested that sustaining interactions with married women was difficult because of these women's ties to their families. These ties meant that meeting married women outside the family context was more difficult to organize, and the arrangements were often made on the married woman's terms. Socializing with families was complex for several reasons. Members of the family might hold an implicit stereotype of a 'city single' whereby the lives of single women were considered glamorous, and the contrast to the humdrum everyday lives in families was thought to be too great, so families were hesitant to invite single women to their homes or their parties. Single women themselves may also feel uncomfortable in familial circumstances and many of them thought that the married women they knew were subjected to too much control by their partners, and that they also subjected themselves to that control. In contrast, single women were thought to be more independent.

Independent Citizens

Independence is culturally valued, whilst dependence is generally constructed in negative terms. The young, the ill and the poor are thought of as dependent. Independent persons are in possession of their minds, bodies and life course. This 'possessive individualism' is a cornerstone of liberal ideology – and widely subjected to criticism, for example by Marxists and feminists, for ignoring the social relations of difference in the context of which such individualism operates. The status of an absolute individual is open to middle-class, white, able-bodied adult men who are constructed as universal. Individuality is more difficult to establish for those marginalized in social relations of power. Thus 'an independent woman' is an ambivalent construction, as women have been viewed more relationally than men. As an abstraction an individual is represented as gender-neutral, but as a broad field of feminist research has demonstrated, the 'individual' is gender-specific. The structures, discourses and practices centring on the individual have constructed women as the other, whilst men have provided the norm. Carole Pateman (1988), for example, has argued that the social contract which explains the formation of liberal nation-states is gendered. The social contract is a voluntary contract between men of property to handle their collective interests jointly, whilst the private sphere is characterized by possessive individualism. This social contract, Pateman suggests, was preceded by a sexual contract which relegated women to the private sphere with possessive individualism out of their reach. An interesting example of this relegation are women travellers who in the nineteenth century left Britain to go to Africa, South America or Asia. In their travels these women's social class and ethnicity compensated for their gender, and they had access to numerous privileges not available to them in Britain (Birkett 1989; Boisseau 1995). When they returned home, women travellers had to struggle to have the value of their travels recognized, for example in professional associations.

Women outside marriage and motherhood in the nineteenth century were curiosities to be pitied, and the circumstances of those who were poor were pretty dire (Anderson 1984). Participation in the labour market has improved unmarried women's position. In Finland, where industrialization took place relatively recently and rapidly, the labour of single women was necessary in factories, particularly in the textile industry (Pohls 1990). Therefore unmarried women had more opportunities to construct an independent status, and it is not coincidental that the percentage of single women has consistently been higher in Finland than, for example, in Britain. Nor did the percentage of unmarried women decrease in the 1950s in the same way as it did in many other European countries.

The increase of proportions of single women in the various European countries is due to various 'pushes' and 'pulls', suggests Stein (1981). Demographic imbalances, for example, explain pushes to singlehood, whilst feminism, expanding labour markets and increasing education have provided incentives or pulls for women to remain single. More recently, the development of New Right policies and especially neoliberal marketization has provided new 'pushes'; sustaining long-term relationships and maintaining families has become increasingly difficult. Whilst 'the family' is given renewed positive emphasis in neo-conservative politics, social policy support for families with difficulties has deteriorated in many countries. Hobson (1997) has suggested that support provided for 'solo mothers' is a litmus test of the woman-friendliness of public provision. She argues that all married mothers are potential solo mothers. Therefore state support for them has an impact on equality within families. Single motherhood is still an ambivalent choice for women, suggests Nave-Herz (1997) on the basis of her study in Germany.

Citizenship of women, and of single women, is culturally somewhat ambivalent. A citizen is a member of a nation-state, with defined rights, duties and responsibilities. T.H. Marshall (1963) conceptualized citizenship as political, legal and social. Equality in the political and legal sphere is not sufficient, unless measures are taken to address inequality in the social sphere. Citizenship rights remain formal without policies to make them widely available to everybody. Marshall's theory was mainly concerned with social class inequalities, and he largely ignored gender and ethnicity and other dimensions of difference. For citizenship to ensure social justice, the concept needs to be extended to take into account culture, sexuality and embodiment, as well as gender and ethnicity (Weeks 1996; Gordon, Holland and Lahelma 2000).

Independent Single Women

When I conducted interviews with single women in London, Helsinki and the San Francisco Bay Area, my first interviewee talked about herself in the following terms:

> I see myself as an independent person ... I see myself as a pretty strong individual. And I think I've always been pretty independent. I've always done my own thing, and that has often led to conflicts. (Greta, Britain)[1]

The women were asked to fill in association lists, and the most prevalent association for the prompt 'single woman' was independence. Therefore it seemed appropriate to explore the concept of citizenship through discussing independence. I disentangled several strands in the way in which independence was defined by single women. First, they referred to economic autonomy; it was important for the women to get by with whatever financial resources they had available. Only one of the women I interviewed was unemployed, but the emphasis on the importance of financial self-reliance expressed by the majority of the women, even when their resources were limited, suggests that unemployed single women can be particularly vulnerable to impoverishment and dependence. The second important feature of independence was being one's own care-giver. Historically, unmarried women have been important in the semi-public sphere of a range of associations. Further, they have provided care for members of their family of origin, and, increasingly, they provide social support for their relatives and friends. During periods of illness or other difficulties that support was not easily available to single women themselves.

Third, independence means being in control. This begins with practical matters: deciding what you wear, what you eat, how you spend your time. Being in control means deconstructing cultural expectations directed at women, and refusing to conform to pressures of traditional femininity.

> I have learned to say no – to different things that I don't want to do, and I just don't. And I feel that my independence is increasing all the time – little by little. (Minna, Finland)

Large proportions of women with disabilities are single. Being in control is a particularly pertinent concern for those who need assistance in their daily care. They have to struggle in order to establish independence (Lonsdale 1990).

Fourth, independence is emotional. As well as being able to take care of oneself and being in control in practices and processes of everyday life, self-reliance in social interaction is important.

> Basically I don't see myself living my life through someone else, which is what I did at one time. I seem to have got away from that and I'm a lot happier for it. (Tina, Britain)

Whilst emotional independence was emphasized, it was also the strand of independence most questioned by the single women.

Fifth, distinguishable from emotional independence is mental independence, a broader sense of being an individual in charge of one's own destiny.

> I don't live my life for other people… I don't live it for what people think of me… I'm not interested in being the norm 'cos that's not what I am. (Liz, Britain)

The final strand of independence is being alone. This is a modern aspect of singlehood, as spinsters in the nineteenth century were unlikely to live alone. As one-person households have increased, this suggests that many single women live alone, as did the majority of the women I interviewed. Many of them found their lives demanding, and being at home alone was a welcome relief, and not necessarily connected with loneliness.

There were also cultural differences in how being alone was experienced; for example, African-American women emphasized their social networks whilst often considering themselves the active centre of those social networks. Afro-Caribbean women in Britain also considered their (often familial) connections important. Most women were, however, determined to avoid patterns of dependency which they thought were typical for women in both heterosexual and lesbian relationships.

Despite these women's fear of dependence and their emphasis on the necessity of independence, many were nevertheless critical of independence as a cultural value.

> I am fairly independent, but part of the lifestyle I live – relationships with people are part of that. And in some way I am dependent on these relationships and on maintaining them and looking after them. (Harriet, Finland)

These single women needed their networks and made a great deal of effort to maintain them. Little is known about those single women, such as the unemployed, who are not successful in establishing and maintaining contacts with others.

Independence, then, is not necessarily defined in terms of separateness, as suggested in the concept of possessive individualism. For some women, being independent was like learning 'a new script' not characteristic of femininity. They explored a process of tensions and contradictions in assuming an independent status and constructing a lifestyle as a woman. In a sense they attempted to stretch boundaries of individuality. Important in this process was the idea and concept of interdependence. Many women said they were independent in terms of constructing their own lives, taking care of themselves and not being influenced by other people's judgements and attitudes. But emotional independence was not valued by most of them.

> I used to think that to be independent in everything was a good thing, but it's not like that in life; I mean you are almost always… I mean you're not independent

anyway. And it's not such a bad thing... For example, in relations with others. (Harriet, Finland)

I feel I'm a very people-centred person, although I'm very independent and I can keep people at a distance. I'm independent, but interdependence I long for. (Gwen, Britain)

Single women were not necessarily interested in being heroines of their own lives, even though many of them talked about married women in critical terms reminiscent of notions of absolute individuality. Their quest for inter-dependence, however, was marred by a fear of dependence, and subtle patterns of marginalization of single women. Nancy Fraser and Linda Gordon (1994) trace the genealogy of 'dependency', and suggest that with modernity the hitherto relatively neutral term 'dependency' acquired negative meanings.

Marginality

Women's relationship to the state was mediated through men in Western nation-states in the nineteenth century. They had no citizenship rights, no suffrage, and did not control property if they were married. The dominant conception of 'woman' centred on marriage and reproduction. Anderson's (1984) study of the residential situation of spinsters in Britain found that they lived in employers' households as servants, with relatives, as heads of house-holds or in institutions. This lack of autonomy caused strains for unmarried women, as Davidoff and Hall (1987) suggest. During the twentieth century women's lives diversified, but this was not a matter of steady progress. In the 1950s the proportions of unmarried women declined in Britain and Finland, for example. Marriage was central in defining women, and spinsters were pitied as old maids. Baker (1989) has analysed women's fiction from the 1950s and found that, whilst marriage was a yardstick for a good life, the subtext included a fear of autonomous women, who by their existence posed a threat to sexual difference. Increased educational opportunities, development of welfare state provisions and economic expansion had implications for the position of women. They were needed in the labour market, although the concept of 'dual roles' suggested that wifehood and motherhood were still at the very least important, if not central (Baker 1989). However, women entered the labour market in increasing numbers and many of them also stayed there after having children.

In this context, to ask whether single women are marginal and marginal-ized is somewhat problematic. Potentially the very question reinforces what it seeks to criticize. Therefore it is more useful to ask what the implications of being marginal to marriage are. Chandler suggests that there are continua of marriage along which women are placed, being 'more or less marginal to marriage, more or less connected to men' (1991: 3) so that marriage 'casts a long shadow' on all women, because they are defined in relation to men.

Second, it is important to emphasize that 'marginality' is a concept, not a personal characteristic. Marginality can be a social, material, cultural and subjective positioning, and meanings attached to it vary. Marginality is not a clearly defined, bordered place (although marginality is also spatial); nor is marginality constructed in relation to a clear centre. Just as there are multiple marginalities, so there are also multiple centres (Davies 1991). There are shifts in the relationship between centres and margins, and marginality can be simultaneous inclusion and exclusion. In a speech focusing on his own identity, Stuart Hall suggested that the latter has been dependent on being a migrant, and continues: 'Now that, in the postmodern age, you all seem to feel so dispersed, I become centred. What I've thought of as a dispersed and fragmented identity comes, paradoxically, to be the representative, modern experience!' (quoted in Morley and Chen 1996: 15). Shifting structures and changing cultures have blurred definitions of centres and margins, argue Isaac and Mercer (1996).

Though marginality remains peripheral to the broader mainstream, it has never been as productive a space as it is now. From the margins new subjects can step onto the political and cultural stage (Isaac and Mercer 1996). Because the marginal is not merely a consequence of the centre, the analysis of who the new subjects are and how they step onto the stage requires considerable deconstruction (Isaac and Mercer 1996: 451). Margins are ambivalent, and cultural production consists of meanings being 'crossed, erased, and translated' (Bhabha 1990: 4). But in the margins boundaries consistent with dominant power relations can also be maintained and policed. Marginalization maintains social categories – whilst at the same time eroding them (Gordon 2000).

Single women are a heterogeneous group; therefore it is not possible to provide any single argument about their marginality. Moreover, meanings attached to this amorphous position vary, not least because it refers to material, social, cultural and subjective positioning. However, several women also suggested that they were marginal and marginalized.

> I do [feel marginal]. I really don't know quite where I belong. Yes, I do actually, very much. I'm very much outside of things.... I'm quite frightened of being isolated, I suppose. (Lynne, Britain)

Many women I interviewed suggested that single women are marginal, but that they themselves were not. They had developed their own networks, and within these networks marginal can become central.

> I am with other people and a lot of people I know are in the same position. I think if most of my friends were couples I'd feel much more peculiar. (Betsy, Britain)

> I could see other people living in a different way... But I've just so arranged my life that I avoid [social pressures] ... you realize that most of the time you are actually just avoiding the way of life most people live... [I have] chosen the hardest way.... But ... I've arranged it so that people around me feel pretty much the same way. (Lorna, Britain)

Some women described the sidestepping into the margins as a conscious decision. Like Lorna, Greta is a member of alternative networks in London; both of them have 'sidestepped' their middle-class backgrounds to live in poor areas in low-standard housing with small incomes, whilst acknowledging that this is done from the advantage of middle-class positioning, including education.

Gender and being single intertwine with other social relations such as social class, ethnicity and sexuality, and in this process acquire shifting meanings.

> I am black first, and a woman second, and I come from humble origins … if I weren't black then I would fall in and be assimilated. But because I'm different I'm treated differently, and therefore I have to recognize that and respond to that in a positive way. And nobody's gonna pull me up when they're pushing me down. (Valerie, Britain)

A strong statement on the experience of inhabiting multiple marginalities is given by Gwen, who also suggested that she has made margins her centre, reminiscent of the theoretical suggestion of the space for new cultures being forged in the margins:

> I don't fit the stereotype really. I've always … felt like I'm in a group that is marginalized … it was like within the women's movement, being a black woman, and you know, the black women's feminist movement, being on the edge as a lesbian, and – yeah, I'm used to operating in the margins and I like it. (Gwen, Britain)

The question of marginality is particularly strong for women with disabilities. People with disabilities generally are likely to experience marginality and a sense of invisibility, but women are particularly invisible, often ignored and devalued, suggests Lonsdale (1990). Women with disabilities are heterogeneous, and the marginality of their position is partly dependent on the degree of their disability and the resources they have at their disposal. The two women with disabilities I interviewed connected their single status with their disabilities, whilst both of them suggested that they generally strove to 'take their place'. Multiple marginalities, then, are more likely to evoke a subjective sense of marginalization, whilst at the same time, among the women I interviewed, an effort to challenge marginalization or to make margins their centre was a response adopted.

Although many of the interviewed women described either themselves or single women as marginal, not all of them did so. Those women who questioned or criticized the suggestion that singles are marginal argued that if other single women suggested they were marginal, this marginality was 'in their heads'. No material or cultural characteristics seemed to unite these women who emphasized individual opportunity and responsibility; they included different ethnicities and social class positions. They were women who found it relatively easy to make contact with others, and they had strong social networks. They had experienced grave difficulties in the past, and, having struggled to alter their lives, they felt comfortable and in control. All of them emphasized individualism and resistance; challenging the idea of the marginality of single women in an interview with a researcher may be indicative of this resistance. I concluded that constructing an independent life, reaching the status of 'the individual' and obtaining full social citizenship are still areas of struggle for women. There have been considerable changes in the position of unmarried women since the nineteenth century. But the rise of neo-conservatism has curtailed the opportunities of at least some women. Single women are still marginalized in familist societies and many of them experience multiple marginalization. They also challenge marginality and develop 'outsider-within' positions.

Lone motherhood is still problematic in several ways. Concerns about children brought up in one-parent families are one recurrent strand in political worries about the 'family'. Welfare state provisions for single mothers vary (Hobson 1997; Lewis 1997), but it is clear that with marketization and the trend towards increasing income differentials, the position of a proportion of single parents, women or men, is just as likely to deteriorate as to improve. Voluntary single-parenthood is still not an easy option for most women, and lesbian women, whether single or in established relationships, have additional obstacles in constructing parenthood. Nevertheless lone mothers in May's (2001) study in Finland represented themselves, in their own (written) narratives, in much more multifaceted ways – lone motherhood was not a central defining feature for them.

Whilst neo-conservatism and marketization have influenced the lives of women, there have also been shifts in cultural representations of single women. During the early 1990s single women were needy and dangerous. A symptomatic text of this was the film *Fatal Attraction*, where a single woman after an affair with a married man pursues him and his family ruthlessly when he is no longer interested in her. An example of a similar text is the film *Single White Female*, in which a young woman slowly tries to take over her female flatmate's life, and resorts to a murderous rampage. Single women in these representations were sad, mad and bad. Since then a boom of visibility of a singles culture has taken place. It is to features of this culture that I now turn.

Shifting Representations

If single women were characterized mainly through invisibility in the 1950s, in the late 1990s and at the beginning of the twenty-first century they are highly visible in popular culture, through, for example, characters such as Ally McBeal and Bridget Jones. These representations are more diverse, multilayered and heterogeneous than the earlier 'sad, mad and bad' depictions. Whilst Ally and Bridget worry about their lives, observe themselves constantly and express frustration with their single status, the images are funnier, more light-hearted and open to a wider range of interpretations than the single female protagonists in *Fatal Attraction* and *Single White Female*. In popular culture we are more likely to encounter city singles than old maids.

A group of Women's Studies students in Finland explored representations of young single women, such as in popular writing (Arvola, Juurinen and Kokko) and Finnish literature (Rinne and Koivisto), singles' datelines in magazines and the Internet (Latikka, Länsiö, Hurnonen and Leinonen); finally, representations of single women were explored by asking university students to complete a story about a day in the life of a fictive single woman (Järvinen, Korhonen and Rajala). The analysis suggested that the cultural images included emancipatory, yet ambivalent, elements redefining what it means to be a single woman. One theme in these representations was that of the 'eternal seeker', a young single who observes herself, controls and moulds her body through exercise, sports, make-up and clothes. An exploration of lesbian dateline found only few references to looks; embodied beauty-work in cultural representations is connected with a heterosexual gender order. A second recurrent theme referred to the wildness and freedom of young women about town, thus reproducing the single woman as potentially dangerous. However, in these representations the women themselves were also subjected to danger. The third theme referred to the importance of home as a place of safety, where the young single woman can curl up in peace and quiet. But home was also ambivalent – at times it could be cold, there was no one to clean or cook for, nor anyone to curl up against.

Single Dreams

Many young men and young women in Britain envisage themselves marrying in the future, whilst even more see their futures in terms of heterosexual relationships, although some search for new kinds of scripts in their sexual relationships (Holland et al. 1998). Few young women and men today dream of being single. Many young people, however, want to postpone what they see as a dull settling down and the onerous responsibilities of bringing up children. Research has suggested that those women who put marriage off are more likely to remain single.

What will the lives of these young women be like in the future? In what ways will they be in positions similar to single women today and in what way will they be different? If margins are potentially increasingly productive places where new social and cultural formations can develop, perhaps there will be new kinds of single dreams, and increasing possibilities for single women to construct interdependent lives and satisfying sexual relations, as well opportunities for parenthood. On the other hand, the neo-conservative emphasis on family values curtails the liberalization of values, but not necessarily the diversification of people's life courses. Whilst the proportion of single women is likely to increase, I have suggested that this may not simply be because of 'pull', but also because of 'push' (Gordon 1994b).

The increase in numbers of single women with children, as well as of elderly single women, provides challenges to European societies. Certainly excessive marketization needs to be challenged and the balance between public and private responsibility must be carefully thought out. But this is not sufficient if gendered cultural representations of women in general and single women in particular are not deconstructed too.

Note

1. All names are pseudonyms.

References

Allen, Katherine R. (1989) *Single Women/Family Ties: Life Histories of Older Women*. London and New Delhi: Sage.

Anderson, Michael (1984) 'The Social Position of Spinsters in Mid-Victorian Britain', *Journal of Family History*, Winter, pp. 377–93.

Anttonen, Anneli (1997) 'The Welfare State and Social Citizenship', in Kaisa Kauppinen, and Tuula Gordon, eds, *Unresolved Dilemmas: Women, Work and the Family in the United States, Europe and the Former Soviet Union*. Aldershot: Ashgate.

Arvola, Kirsi, Rosita Juurinen, and Heidi Kokko (1999) 'Sinkun päiväkirja – Sinkkunaisen representaatiot päiväkirjoissa' [Single's Diary – Representations of Single Women in Diaries]. In *Naistutkimuskurrssi: 'Ikuisia Etsijöitä, kotikissoja vai pikku petoeläimiä? Nuorten naisten representaatiota* [Women's Studies Seminar: 'Eternal Seekers, Pussy Cats or Small Beasts? Representations of Young Single Women'], Tampere: Department of Women's Studies, University of Tampere.

Baker, Niamh (1989) *Happily Ever After? Women's Fiction in Postwar Britain 1945–60*. London: Macmillan.

Barrett, Michèle and Mary McIntosh (1982) *The Anti-Social Family*. London: Verso.

Bhabha, Homi (1990) 'Introduction: Narrating the Nation', in Homi Bhabha, ed., *Nation and Narration*. London and New York: Routledge, pp. 1–7.

Birkett, Dea (1989) *Spinsters Abroad: Victorian Lady Explorers*. Oxford: Basil Blackwell.

Boisseau, T.J. (1995) '"They Called Me *Bebe Bwana*": A Critical Cultural Study of an Imperial Feminist', *Signs*, vol. 21, no. 1, pp. 116–46.

Chandler, Joan (1991) *Women Without Husbands: An Exploration of the Margins of Marriage*. London: Macmillan.

Davidoff, Leonore and Catherine Hall (1987) *Family Fortunes: Men and Women of the English Middle Class, 1780–1850*. London: Hutchinson.

Davies, Carole Boyce (1991) 'Writing off Marginality, Minoring and Effacement', *Women's Studies International Forum* 4, 249–63.

Fraser, Nancy and Linda Gordon (1994) 'A Genealogy of *Dependency*: Tracing a Keyword of the U.S. Welfare State', *Signs* 19, pp. 309–36.

Gittins, Diana (1985) *The Family in Question: Changing Household Ideologies and Familiar Ideologies*. London: Macmillan.

Gordon, Tuula (1994a) *Single Women: On the Margins?* London: Macmillan.

Gordon, Tuula (1994b) 'Single Women and Familism: Challenge from the Margins', *European Journal of Women's Studies* 1, pp. 165–82.

Gordon, Tuula (1997) 'Inside and Outside Families', in Kaisa Kauppinen and Tuula Gordon, eds, *Unresolved Dilemmas: Women, Work and the Family in the United States, Europe and the Former Soviet Union*. Aldershot: Ashgate.

Gordon, Tuula (2000) 'Tears and Laughter in the Margins', *Nora*, vol. 8, no. 3.

Gordon, Tuula, Janet Holland and Elina Lahelma (2000) *Making Spaces: Citizenship and Difference in Schools.* London: Macmillan.

Hobson, Barbara (1997) 'Remaking the Boundaries of Women's Citizenship and the Dilemma of Dependency', in Kaisa Kauppinen and Tuula Gordon, eds, *Unresolved Dilemmas: Women, Work and the Family in the United States, Europe and the Former Soviet Union.* Aldershot: Ashgate.

Holland, Janet, Caroline Ramazanoglu, Sue Sharpe and Rachel Thomson (1998) *The Male in the Head: Young People, Heterosexuality and Power.* London: Tufnell Press.

Isaac, Julien and Kobena Mercer (1996) 'De Margin and De Centre', in David Morley and Kuan-Hsing Chen, eds, *Stuart Hall: Critical Dialogues in Cultural Studies.* London: Routledge.

Järvinen, Aino, Maria Länsiö, Lilli Hurnonen and Minna Leinonen (1999) 'Näinkö sinut löydän? – Nuori sinkkunainen kontakti-ilmoituksissa' [Is This the Way I Find You? – Young Single Woman in Contact-advertising'], in *Naistutkimuskurrssi: 'Ikuisia Etsijöitä, kotikissoja vai pikku petoeläimiä? Nuorten naisten representaatiota'* [Women's Studies Seminar: 'Eternal Seekers, Pussy Cats or Small Beasts? Representations of Young Single Women']. Tampere: Department of Women's Studies, University of Tampere.

Järvinen, Heli, Päivi Korhonen and Maarit Rajala (1999) 'Nuori, vapaa ja kykeneäivien mihin tahansa? Eläytymismenetelmätarinoita nuorista sinkkunaisista' [Young, Free and Capable of Anything?], in *Naistutkimuskurrssi: 'Ikuisia Etsijöitä, kotikissoja vai pikku petoeläimiä? Nuorten naisten representaatiota'* [Women's Studies Seminar: 'Eternal Seekers, Pussy Cats or Small Beasts? Representations of Young Single Women']. Tampere: Department of Women's Studies, University of Tampere.

Jones, Kathleen (1990) 'Citizenship in a Woman-Friendly Polity', *Signs* 41.

Lewis, Jane, ed. (1997) *Lone Mothers in European Welfare Regimes: Shifting Policy Logics.* London and Philadelphia: Jessica Kingsley.

Lonsdale, Susan (1990) *Women and Disability: The Experience of Physical Disability Among Women.* London: Macmillan.

Marshall, T.H. (1963) *Sociology at the Crossroads.* London: Heinemann.

May, Vanessa (2001) *Lone Motherhood in Finnish Women's Life Stories: Creating Meaning in a Narrative Context.* Åbo: Åbo Akademi University Printing House.

Morley, David and Kuan-Hsing Chen, eds (1996) *Stuart Hall: Critical Dialogues in Cultural Studies.* London: Routledge.

Nave-Herz, Rosemary (1996) 'Single Motherhood: An Alternative Form of Life', in Kaisa Kauppinen and Tuula Gordon, eds, *Unresolved Dilemmas: Women, Work and the Family in the United States, Europe and the Former Soviet Union.* Aldershot: Ashgate.

Pateman, Carole (1988) *The Sexual Contract.* Cambridge: Polity Press.

Pohls, Maritta (1990) 'Women's Work in Finland 1870–1940', in Päivi Setälä, ed., *The Lady with a Bow: The Story of Finnish Women.* Keuruu: Otava.

Rinne, Liisa and Mari Koivisto (1999) 'Sinkku – itsenäinen nainen vai parisuhdepyrkyri? Nuoren, naimattoman naisen esityksiä suomalaisessa kirjallisuudessa' [Single – An Independent Woman or a Small Beast? Representations of a Young, Unmarried Woman in Finnish Literature'], in *Naistutkimuskurrssi: 'Ikuisia Etsijöitä, kotikissoja vai pikku petoeläimiä? Nuorten naisten representaatiota'* [Women's Studies Seminar: 'Eternal Seekers, Pussy Cats or Small Beasts? Representations of Young Single Women']. Tampere: Department of Women's Studies, University of Tampere.

Siim, Birte (1997) 'Dilemmas of Citizenship in Denmark: Lone Mothers Between Work and Care', in Jane Lewis, ed., *Lone Mothers in European Welfare Regimes: Shifting Policy Logics.* London and Philadelphia: Jessica Kingsley.

Stein, Peter (1981) *Single Life: Unmarried Adults in Social Context.* New York: St. Martin's Press.

Weeks, Jeffrey (1996) *Invented Moralities: Sexual Values in an Age of Uncertainty.* Cambridge: Polity Press.

3

Women's Human Rights, Equal Opportunities and Biopolitics in Europe

MARINA CALLONI

In Western countries the history of the women's movement is strictly interconnected with the affirmation of universal/formal principles (as theorized by the illuminists of early modernity) and their immanent critique. That is, intellectual women, the women's movements and feminists indicated the 'ideological' limits and the origin of a 'false universalism' implicit in the notion of human rights. Indeed, the latter was based on a fundamental 'exclusion': women were excluded from citizenship and therefore from human rights. Political feminism thus arose in opposition to forms of 'patriarchal power' and as the struggle for recognition of citizenship, starting with the suffrage. It is through this struggle that the women's movement relates to the establishment, but also to the transformation, of a limited notion of the nation-state and of citizenship.

Feminism is one of the main revolutions of the nineteenth century, which has contributed to changing unfair gender relations. It challenged the fundamental dichotomy between public space and the private sphere, the basis of the division of work as well as of the practice of politics. The attempt at 'gendering' a formal determination of human and socio-political/economic rights can thus be taken as an example of women's struggles over decades, aimed at constructing a more inclusive and less discriminatory form of democracy both at national and at international level.

This chapter reconstructs the main steps and meanings of women's human rights, connecting them with the modification of the nation-state, the establishment of the European Union and the global transformation of previous socio-political orders. The chapter has four main sections, following the principal waves of Western women's movements and feminism:

1. The origin of women's critique against an exclusive notion of human rights.

2. Claims for the recognition of citizenship within political parties and the affirmation of feminism as an autonomous mass movement.
3. The application of the European Union's directives and policies to equal opportunities/treatment of women and men, which had an important impact on national legislation.
4. The internationalization of gender issues, the global struggle against gender-based violence, and the arising of new questions on life and death, related to the development of new reproductive biotechnologies and discoveries in genetics.

In my conclusions, I shall stress the new challenges that face women in Europe today. They are related not only to socio-economic issues, to claims for augmenting the representation and participation of women in the political domain, and to requests for increasing women's leadership in decision-making sectors. These new challenges are also related to a broader notion of the 'quality of life'. However, quality not only implies the improvement of social standards for a better daily life and the development of human capabilities. It also concerns an understanding of the expanding role that biotechnologies (from food to human reproduction), and their impacts on our lives, have in the form of bioethical questions about the limits of scientific research and about freedom of choice, for example. These new issues contribute to changes in the perception of one's own body, the meaning of individual/collective responsibility, and the 'socio-cultural' idea of respect for the life of human and non-human animals.

Women have thus to face the new impact that science is having on every-day life and on the development of new forms of biopolitics, including the promotion of restrictive laws in reproductive fields, from abortion to *in vitro* fertilization. Reproductive rights have not yet been recognized as part of women's human rights.

Do Human Rights Have a Sex?

The idea of women's human rights arose during the French Revolution, strictly in relation to the *Declaration of Rights of Man and Citizen* (1789), when these rights' limits in terms of women's representation were stressed. Rights were enunciated in 'another voice' and conjugated in the feminine. In the *Déclaration des Droits de la Femme et de la Citoyenne*, published in September 1791, Olympe de Gouges underlined the necessity for a National Assembly for 'women and female citizens', as well as for, among others, suffrage, and the right to education and property. Paraphrasing and integrating in seventeen articles the French Declaration, in a feminine language, de Gouges asserted, in Article 1, that: 'Woman is born free and lives equal to man in her rights. Social distinctions can be based only on the common utility.' Article 2 states:

'The purpose of any political association is the conservation of the natural and imprescriptible rights of woman and man; these rights are liberty, property, security, and especially resistance to oppression.' And in the postscripts, de Gouges argues:

> Woman, wake up; ... discover your rights. The powerful empire of nature is no longer surrounded by prejudice, fanaticism, superstition, and lies.... Marriage is the tomb of trust and love. The married woman can with impunity give bastards to her husband, and also give them the wealth which does not belong to them. The woman who is unmarried has only one feeble right; ancient and inhuman laws refuse to her for her children the right to the name and wealth of their father.

Yet de Gouges had to experience that social prejudices against women were still alive and far from being removed by male revolutionaries. Moreover, she was a member of the Girondists, a group who felt in the minority in the French Assembly with the affirmation of the Jacobins. Among other decisions, Robespierre, leader of the Jacobins, suppressed the 'Society of Republican Women' in February 1793. Olympe de Gouges – considered a woman with an 'exalted imagination' which contributed to 'her delirium for an inspiration of nature' – was arrested in July 1793 and condemned to the guillotine in November 1793. Commenting on the reasons for her capital punishment, a report announced that, 'Law has punished this conspirator for having forgotten the virtues that belong to her sex.' For the 'revolutionary' Jacobins, the law had thus persecuted a woman who had acted against nature. Yet this notion of nature was based only on social conventions.

These events induced intellectual women to reflect upon the interpretations by philosophers and politicians of the supposed female nature. Mary Wollstonecraft, a contemporary of de Gouges, wrote *A Vindication of the Rights of Woman* in 1792. In the chapter devoted to 'The prevailing opinion of a sexual character discussed', she argues that

> women are told from their infancy, and taught by the example of their mothers, that a little knowledge of human weakness, justly termed cunning, softness of temper, *outward* obedience, and a scrupulous attention to a puerile kind of propriety, will obtain for them the protection of man; and should they be beautiful, every thing else is needless, for at least twenty years of their lives.

A better education for women and changes of unjust laws were thus necessary for a radical transformation of society.

Indeed, the history of the formal affirmation of human and political rights is quite controversial (Duby and Perrot 1990–93). The *Declaration of Rights of Man and Citizen* refers in fact to two 'male' determinations, although it was intended to indicate a sort of 'neutral' universal meaning of humanity as well as a national attribute of the citizen. *Universalism* (all human beings are equal) and *citizenship* (all human beings belonging to a nation-state have rights) became thus two interrelated aspects of a more general idea of rights.

In the case of the *Declaration of Rights of Man and Citizen*, promoted and approved by the National Assembly of the 'French people', it meant that human rights had to be first applied within the borders of the French nation-state and then extended to other political communities, who were still subjected to monarchical powers. This was at least the intention of Napoleon in the early years of his military career: to 'export' the spirit of the French Revolution and the meaning of the 'rights of man and citizen'. But even though Napoleon later transformed his political action into a new form of imperialism, we can say that since their formulation human rights have implied always a double dimension: a local one and an international one, in an often very ambivalent way.

From the beginning the French *Declaration* presented various problems. Karl Marx, for instance, stressed the ideological substratum and class structure sustained by the *Declaration*: the *citoyen* was in reality the exponent of the new emerging class, the *bourgeoisie*, who wanted to affirm their economic and cultural power over the old orders (the clergy and the aristocracy). Marx indicated, therefore, the lack of presence of other social actors: the proletarians. The history of human rights is thus related to an original and inherent double contradiction: although formal universalism was aimed at, including *in theory* all human beings, *in practice* it excluded parts of the population. In consequence, women had to struggle for centuries for the recognition of their status as citizens, having rights and duties. The *Declaration of Rights of Man and Citizen* thus had a double implication for women: the initiation of struggles for their inclusion in the political domain and the struggle for their recognition as human beings at all. Many theological and cultural prejudices excluded women from the public arena. If we take as an example the Greek model of citizenship theorized by Aristotle, we note that women cannot 'by nature' participate in political activities. These were reserved for men born in Athens (on the basis of the *jus sanguinis*), who could vote/be elected, and become representatives in public offices, magistrates and soldiers.

The political and public exclusion of women from the political sphere was due to cultural–intellectual convictions, based on prejudice regarding what was considered public or private: rationality referred to the male, while emotions were considered as belonging to feminine nature. Women could not have rights because they were not recognized as having the necessary qualities to become citizens. Woman was relegated to the 'low sphere' of material needs due to her biological specificity: the faculty to procreate.

An analogous gender-based contradiction can implicitly be found in Rousseau, who was the major inspirer of the *Declaration of Rights of Man and Citizen*. Article 1 affirms that 'men are born equal and free', as Rousseau theorized, following the main ideas of the Enlightenment and considering inequality as a factor produced by society and not by nature, as asserted in the *Discourse on Inequality* and *The Social Contract*. However, in two other famous works, *La Nouvelle Héloïse* (which inspired Romanticism) and *Émile* (which became the basis of further pedagogical treatises), Rousseau indicates strictly the natural differences between the genders, reproducing cultural stereotypes about gender bias.

The issues of *formal equality* and *biological difference* remained for centuries the basis for socio-political controversies, and have shaped feminist theories and epistemologies in more recent years. They were central to the entire dispute about women and human rights and have acquired a new impetus with the increasing discussions about women's reproductive rights, bioethics and biotechnologies. Theoretical debates about women are thus always connected to the analysis or critique of a supposed feminine nature from a social, biological and political perspective, starting from the notion of difference and/or equality/parity between women and men.

One of the first defenders of parity between the 'sexes' was John Stuart Mill. With his wife, Harriet Taylor Mill (who, being a woman, at that time could not sign with her name the papers she wrote), Mill affirmed in 'The Enfranchisement of Women' (1851, later collected in the *Subjection of Women*, published in 1869) that

> Many persons think they have sufficiently justified the restrictions on women's field of action, when they have said that the pursuits from which women are excluded are *unfeminine*, and that the *proper sphere* of women is not politics or publicity, but private and domestic life. We deny the rights of any portion of the species to decide for another portion, or any individual for another individual, what is and what is not their 'proper sphere'. The proper sphere for human beings is the largest and highest which they are able to attain to. What this is, cannot be ascertained, without complete liberty of choice. (Mill and Mill 1970: 100)

For the first time a liberal intellectual and politically engaged couple stressed the internal connection between individual ethics, social justice and political liberalism – that is, respect for the individual and for the substantial principles of liberty, equality and solidarity. Women and men must share duties and rights, breaking the traditional dichotomy between public and private. Intellect and sentiments, reason and emotions are in fact interrelated and belong to both genders. Mill was also a supporter of women's suffrage. Thus in 1867 he proposed in the House of Commons an amendment to the Bill of Rights: the substitution of the word 'man' with that of 'person'. Yet his proposal failed: only 3 votes went in his favour compared to 196 against.

From the end of the nineteenth century the issue of women's right to vote became a main factor both in the feminist movement and in the engagement of women within trade unions and political parties, mostly connected to the two main political currents of that time – liberalism and Marxism. Yet in the twentieth century feminism has tried to present its actions and theories as autonomous or antithetical frameworks in respect of traditional parties and political ideologies. This has also been the case in the dispute concerning women's human rights.

Rights and Nation-States

As argued at the beginning of this chapter, since their declaration human rights and citizenship have been closely connected: rights must first be recognized and applied within the borders of a nation-state as political rights and then respected everywhere else. Being excluded, women therefore initiated their struggles to be recognized as citizens, obtaining the right to vote and to be elected. The first example of this movement were the *suffragettes* (such as the Dutch woman Etta Palm d'Aelders), who initiated a tradition of protests, mass mobilization and strikes, actions emulated in later struggles by women workers and feminists. Emmeline Pankhurst and her daughter Christabel were the most famous activists at the end of the nineteenth century in Britain, leaders of the suffragette movement, who in 1897 had already founded the National Union of Women's Suffrage Societies.

Yet the struggle for suffrage was not easy. Opposition to the right to vote for women was quite strong in Europe. For instance, some women intellectuals asserted that the vote would change the 'nature' of women, turning them into men. This argument was made by the Italian scientist Gina Lombroso (1919), who shortly after the end of the First World War wrote a pamphlet against the concession of political rights to women on the basis of bio-sociological arguments. Another kind of political argument was supported in Italy by leftist parties: women were too traditionalist and illiterate, and could easily be influenced by the Catholic Church.

The history of women's acquisition of citizenship differs considerably in the various countries of Europe for cultural/religious and political reasons. Citizenship began to be conceded to women at the beginning of the twentieth century. The first country in the world to do so was Australia in 1902; in Europe Finland was first in 1906, followed by Norway in 1913, and Denmark and Iceland in 1915. During and after the First World War other countries followed: Russia in 1917, at the time of the Soviet Revolution; Great Britain partially in 1918, fully in 1928; Germany, Austria, Czechoslovakia and Poland in 1919, after the fall of the Prussian and Habsburg empires; Hungary in 1920; Ireland in 1922; Spain in 1931 before the beginning of the civil war and Franco's dictatorship. Other countries, where women had played a crucial role not least as partisans and combatants, followed after the Second World War: France in 1944; Italy in 1946, after Fascism and in response to a popular referendum where citizens had to choose between monarchy and republic; Yugoslavia in 1946 with Tito's socialist regime; Greece in 1952. The last were Switzerland in 1971 and Lichtenstein only in 1984. Yet many (mainly Islamic) countries in the world do not yet recognize women's suffrage, and women are still underrepresented in politics in Western countries (Inter-Parliamentary Union 2001).

To avoid women's underrepresentation in institutional politics new initiatives began to be organized from the mid-twentieth century. For instance, a law on 'political parity' was recently approved in France that modified Articles 3 and 4 of the French Constitution of 1958. This case provides evidence of the impact feminist debates can have in changing institutions and laws. The debate on parity started in France in 1995 during the presidential campaign, whereafter an Observatoire de Parité was created, followed by the publication of a Manifeste pour la Parité by women politicians. Lionel Jospin, speaker of the Socialist Party and later prime minister, supported the campaign for the modification of the Constitution, introducing the principle of political parity. On 3 May 2000, the Assemblée Nationale agreed to the modification of article 3 of the French Constitution as follows: 'the law promotes the equal access of women and men to the electoral mandates and electives' functions' ('La loi favorise l'égal accès des femmes et des hommes aux mandats électoraux et fonctions électives'). The notion of 'parity between women and men' thus replaced the 'neutral' assertion of the equality between 'individuals'. In practice this means that women and men must always be represented in equal numbers as candidates in all election campaigns.

There is no doubt that women's struggles have made a substantial contribution to the transformation of a limited notion of citizenship and to the social structure of the nation-state. However, the history of rights is usually reconstructed as a process of democratization from the bottom up, where civil society induces the state to promote new kinds of rights, generating a transformation of its structure and duties. The modification of the nation-state has thus been interpreted in relation to the gradual concession of different generations of rights: civil-human, political, socio-economic, cultural and, recently, bioethical. Yet in at least two respects the history of women's citizenship does not confirm this 'linear' reconstruction. In many cases women won recognition of their socio-economic rights (as workers) before having the right to vote (as in the case of Switzerland). Furthermore, women have struggled not only for the realization of equality/parity, for example in the case of equal opportunities/treatment. Women also obtained recognition of a 'gender difference' within human rights, with regard to gender-based violence and reproductive rights (from contraception to abortion and *in vitro* fertilization). Because these rights are gender-based, they are of concern only to a specific sector of the population: women.

Distinct from the *Declaration of Rights of Man and Citizen*, the *Universal Declaration of Human Rights* – promoted by the United Nations and voted into being in New York on 10 December 1948 – introduced a gender perspective, thanks to the pressure of the Commission on the Status of Women. The words 'men and women' are used in the preamble. De Gouges's dream was realized 250 years after her declaration. The preamble affirms the 'dignity and worth of the human person, in the equal rights of men and women'. Yet this formal assertion admits indirectly the existence of forms of discrimination between genders, which can now be persecuted by law.

However, besides the affirmation of the principle of equality among human beings, the *Universal Declaration* articulates a specific notion of 'gender/sexual difference'. Article 25.2 asserts that 'motherhood and childhood are entitled to special care and assistance'. This affirmation seems quite ambivalent. Indeed, on the one hand this notion has over the years permitted the recognition of maternal leave, reproductive rights and the initiation of policies on equal opportunities; on the other, it compares women to children as a vulnerable group. Yet this aspect can be historically explained by the fact that women at that time (1948) were 'newcomers' in the domain of citizenship and therefore had to be 'protected'. However, this approach to gender issues has changed radically in the last few decades thanks to the feminist movements. While in the past the idea of quotas, positive action and positive discrimination was based on the assumption that woman was a 'weak and vulnerable' subject, nowadays the conception is of woman as an active, conscious and strong social actor, who, however, can be discriminated or harassed on the basis of the 'gender difference'.

The *Universal Declaration* opened the way for gender to become an important category in many other contexts. In 1952 the UN General Assembly subscribed to the *Convention on the Political Rights of Women*, aimed at protecting political rights and promoting actions for reaching equality at work and in education; on 7 November 1967 the *Declaration for Eliminating all Forms of Discrimination against Women* was adopted by the UN in New York. Yet a *Convention on the Elimination of all Forms of Discrimination against Women* (CEDAW) was agreed only in 1979. These measures had an impact on states, because in general when representatives vote for them, they must be implemented by national governments through the debate and promulgation of bills in parliament. Gender issues thus become 'gendered' and 'globalized'.

The European Union: From Non-discrimination/Equal Opportunities to Ethical/Biomedical Issues

The name 'European Union' (EU) was agreed by the then twelve member states with the signing of the Maastricht Treaty on 7 February 1992, extending and changing previous European associations, like the European Economic Community, the European Coal and Steel Community, and Euratom. The aim was the constitution of an economic–monetary and political union. Moreover, with the Maastricht Treaty a European citizenship was awarded to 'Every person holding the nationality of a Member State' (Article 8).

Over the years many critiques of this Treaty have been developed, because it seems more oriented to the market than to a social Europe. Since the beginning of the EU, women's organizations and lobbies have contributed strongly to attempts to change this trend. In 1976 a section of the General Directorate 'Employment and Social Affairs', of the European Commission, section VC, was specifically devoted to 'Employment, Work Relations and

Social Opportunities'. A section of the Directorate General, 'Education and Culture', DG 10, was also devoted to 'Information for Women'. Moreover, following a transformation of the structure of the previous General Directorates, a Unit devoted to 'Women and Science' was constituted in 2001 under the General Directorate 'Research'. It deals in particular with 'gender, mainstreaming and research' and the interest in considering 'gender equality in all policies' (European Commission 2000c, 2002).

Two indicators – employment and research – show the transformation of European policies, from equal opportunities to empowerment/mainstreaming. This change is due, of course, to socio-economic modifications as well as to the transformation of the feminist movement and the strong impact of gender issues on public discourse.

However, one of the main challenges of the European Union is what impact European directives will have in different countries, with their diverse traditions of gender relations, feminism and state feminism. If we take as an example the different regimes of welfare state in Europe, we can see the differential impacts of women in politics and in the promotion of more egalitarian policies between the genders. Social-democratic regimes in the Nordic countries (Bergqvist et al. 1999) have elaborated family policies based on highly articulated negotiations between women and men. In Southern European countries, where the figure of the mother has traditionally been considered more central in the family for the education of children than that of the father, in the past state policies have tended to favour mother workers. The various welfare states in Europe not only reflect specific national cultures of gender relations but also reproduce traditional forms of gender dynamics, starting with the family.

In this context an ambivalence is apparent regarding the connection and the difference between universal rights, various practices of citizenship and gender relations. The history of feminism and reproductive rights in Europe indicates this very clearly. If we take as an example the struggle for de-criminalizing abortion, different but interrelated stages of political action become apparent: first, there were protests initiated within the borders of nation-states as a form of mass mobilization; later these were generalized at the international level, even though they found their origin in the concrete biographies of women. In this case individual problems were generalized because they were affecting women in all countries of the world.

Indeed, struggles for legal abortion – which has not yet been recognized either as a European law, due to the resistance of the Irish government, or as a human right – signalled a deep transformation in both national policies and feminist practices (Stetson 2001). However, the abortion issue caused many splits in the women's movement due to disagreement from radical collectives that did not accept the intervention of the state in the life of women through norms regulating legal abortion. The introduction of the notion of freedom of choice in reproductive issues also generated a crisis in traditional liberal law and in the meaning of justice (Rhode 1989) because such laws and rights can be applied to women only and not to all human beings. At the same time, these issues opened new frontiers for the development of bioethical discussions about the meaning of life and death, mainly in relation to the increasing power of biotechnologies and discoveries in biogenetics.

Directives, policies and reports of the European Union reflect all these debates and social changes: from equal opportunities to bioethics. Indeed, if we look at the main directives issued by the European Economic Community/European Union we can see the different 'generations' of women's rights. In the 1970s European Community directives were mostly aimed at protecting women workers according to the principle of parity. The first directive (1975/117) concerned equal pay for women and men for equal work, making work legislation coherent among different member countries. It referred to Article 141 of the *Treaty of the Constituting European Community* (1957), which ratified the basic principle of the parity of remuneration and sex equality. In 1976 an analogous directive (1976/207) stated the principle of parity and equal treatment for men and women in access to work, employment, vocational training, promotion and working conditions. In 1979 a directive concerning the principle of equal treatment for men and women in social security (1979/7) was established.

In the 1980s European directives were oriented towards the protection of health, improvement of social security for woman workers, and occupational pension schemes (1986/613). In the 1990s they focused more prominently on the promotion of self-employment (1986/613), the defence of pregnant workers, and puerperae (1992/85).

The promotion of policies devoted to equal opportunities was supported by increasing positive actions and the admission of the notion of 'positive discrimination'. On the basis of the EU directive 1976/207 concerning equal treatment, the European Court of Justice issued a ruling in 1988 which affirmed the admissibility of the principle of 'positive discrimination'. Yet it was to be limited to specific circumstances and directed at justifying particular measures, aimed at reducing in effect or even at eliminating existing disparities among genders. Some years later, in 1996, an EU directive on equal opportunities stressed the importance of the principle of parity also for father workers. Indeed, it emphasized not only the obligation for employers to concede 'maternity leave' to women, but the right to 'paternity leave'. The directive affirmed the right of 'parental leave' for men and women (1996/34). This means that bills which concerned mostly women, being 'gendered', are now extended also to men. European directives such as this one have had an important political impact on national parliaments and policies (Liebert 2001), changing previous national legislation regarding women and men at the workplace and contributing to the modification of cultural stereotypes about the different attitudes towards 'caring for children' among the genders.

In the last few years, sex/gender equality has become a crucial factor for EU bodies employed in equality cases. The European Court of Justice in Luxembourg, among others, has examined an increasing number of cases related to sex discrimination and lack of equal opportunities. Many countries – as indicated by the Court's decisions – failed in applying European directives and for this reason were induced to respect and apply EU law (European Commission 2000a).

Yet until 2000 European legislation was promoted on the basis of the *European Convention of Human Rights and Fundamental Freedoms* (which referred to the *Universal Declaration of Rights*), which was supported by the Council of Europe and signed in Rome on 4 November 1950. Gender issues were mentioned in Article 12 regarding the right to have a family ('Men and women of marriageable age have the right to marry and to found a family…'), and Article 15 regarding 'discrimination' ('The enjoyment of the rights and freedoms set forth in this Convention shall be pursued without discrimination on any ground such as sex, race…').

Later, the *Treaty of the European Union* – amended by the Amsterdam Treaty on 2 October 1997 and ratified by the fifteen member states of the EU – introduced in Article 13 provisions related to the struggle against all forms of discrimination and the protection of human rights, starting from equality between men and women (Articles 2 and 3).

In 2000 a *Charter of Fundamental Rights of the European Union* was adopted by the EU and signed in Nice (18 December 2000), integrating previous conventions and provisions on human rights. An interesting aspect of this is that in this Charter the fifth generation of rights is introduced, after the recognition of civil-human, political, socio-economic and cultural rights: the bioethical. The latter rights refer mainly to biotechnologies, the environment and new discoveries in genetics.

The Charter refers to the *Convention for the Protection of Human Rights and Dignity of the Human Being with Regard to the Application of Biology and Medicine*, adopted by the Council of Europe and signed in Oviedo on 4 June 1997. Here issues of life and death acquire a gender meaning, being connected to human reproduction, from abortion to *in vitro* fertilization. For instance, Article 14 affirms that 'The use of techniques of medically assisted procreation shall not be allowed for the purpose of choosing a future child's sex, except where serious hereditary sex-related disease is to be avoided.' Article 18.1 asserts that, 'Where the law allows research on embryos *in-vitro*, it shall ensure adequate protection of the embryo.' This article is nowadays the source of many public controversies about the use of embryos or stem cells for therapeutic reasons and research. A new debate has thus started concerning, on the one hand, the freedom of scientific research and, on the other, legal restrictions that national parliaments are now promoting. This issue is very important for women because in many cases it is applied to *in vitro* fertilization, with very restrictive indications, on the basis of ethical arguments. In Italy, for instance, a bill on

IVF has been debated in parliament for many years now without resolution because of basic disagreements among parties. One article, for example – already approved by the Chamber of Deputies while still under discussion in the Senate – affirms that only married couples can be subjected to the intervention, which can be performed only under specific conditions. New forms of biopolitics regarding reproductive rights have thus been establisned in Europe.

'New bioethical rights' related to biomedicine are also mentioned in the *European Charter* in the form of a prohibition of some practices: 'the prohibition of eugenic practices, in particular those aiming at the selection of persons' and 'the prohibition of the reproductive cloning of human beings' (Article 3). However, a section is also devoted to the 'old' rights: to 'equality', the refusal of discrimination and the acceptance of 'cultural, religious and linguistic diversity'. In particular, Article 23 states that 'Equality between men and women must be ensured in all areas, including employment, work and pay. The principle of equality shall not prevent the maintenance or adoption of measures providing for specific advantages in favour of the under-represented sex'.

'Traditional' women's human rights referring to non-discrimination and equality are connected with the 'newer' one: reproductive rights, which represent a new challenge for women in this century. Equality and difference become interrelated. Yet bioethical and reproductive rights seem to collide in some aspects, as in the case of the 'priority/rights' of the fetus.

Gendering and Globalizing Women's Human Rights: The Case of Gender-based Violence

In the section devoted to 'Equal Opportunities and Non-discrimination', *The Report on the Implementation of the European Initiative for Democracy and Human Rights in 2000* (Brussels, 22 May 2001) asserts that 'The equal value of all human beings, independent from gender, race, background or sexual preference, is for most of us a self-evident fact.' This quotation underlines two different but interrelated aspects of social action and agency: on the one hand the role played by feminists, grassroots movements, NGOs, and gay and lesbian pressure groups; on the other the increasing importance that femocrats, working in administration and decision-making sectors, have in helping to promote other voices within rights debates. The language has changed: the notion of gender has substituted for the word sex, and the respect for sexual preference is clearly mentioned. However, if non-discriminatory and equal opportunity policies are no longer addressed only to women but to other human groups as well, what does women's human rights mean?

In section 5.12, devoted to women's rights, the *EU Annual Report on Human Rights* (1999) affirms that the need to emphasise women's rights is based on the fact that the realization of human rights differs. Various obstacles to the implementation of the human rights of women remain. Disadvantageous economic situations and certain cultural traditions prevailing in various countries can be mentioned here. Women and girls often suffer from specific violations of human rights in a different way than their male counterparts do. In addition, some rights and human rights violations are clearly gender-specific. Violence against women is a pertinent example. Therefore, any analysis or action in the field of human rights must not to be gender-blind. (European Union 1999)

This affirmation shows a substantial change in the conception of women's human rights, if compared with the definition given by the *Universal Declaration*, where women were mentioned in relation to motherhood, marriage and children. But other new aspects are implicitly mentioned: the figure of the girl-child, the increase of trafficking in human beings, the affirmation of new forms of slavery, and the perpetuation of traditional prejudices against women, as the recent debate on women and multiculturalism has stressed (Cohen et al. 1999). A specific notion of 'gender difference' is introduced in two different ways. Difference refers to a 'genital' distinction between women and men, which conduces not only to specific forms of discrimination/segregation but also to *violation*, as in the case of sexual violence and genital mutilation. Women's human rights are 'different' from those of men, but at the same time 'equal' in respect to the normative ideas of equality, liberty, justice and solidarity.

However, the notion of women's human rights is here mostly considered *ex negativo* – that is, in terms of violation. Indeed, specific women's human rights, as the reproductive ones should be, are not mentioned *ex positivo*. The reason for this omission is 'ideological', due to the opposition of conservatives and religious communities. EU and international documents are in fact the results of exhausting compromises precisely about controversial issues such as abortion and *in vitro* fertilization. Reproductive rights are thus not mentioned in terms of women's rights, but at most in terms of health policies. This approach has been strongly criticized by feminists, who see once again the affirmation of the woman as a victim more than as an active actor. Yet the affirmation of women's agency through gender mainstreaming and the empowerment of individuals was one of the main aims of the Beijing *Platform for Action* (United Nations 1996).

The interpretation of women's human rights quoted above refers in fact to the fourth world conference organized in Beijing by the United Nation in 1995, following the conferences held in Mexico City (1975), Copenhagen (1980) and Nairobi (1985). The Beijing conference was devoted to 'The rights of woman and the girl-child'. Although the conference was addressed to national governments (the European Union took part for the first time as a member 'state'), twenty thousand women belonging to NGOs participated as pressure groups and in forums for the development of a cross-cultural public debate and to help produce fair decisions. In the end 189 delegations subscribed to the *Beijing Declaration and Platform for Action*'s twelve priority areas: (1) women and poverty, (2) education and training of women, (3) women and health, (4) violence against women, (5) women and armed conflicts, (6) women and the economy, (7) women in power and decision-making, (8) institutional mechanisms for the advancement of women, (9) human rights of women, (10) women and the media, (11) women and the environment, (12) the girl-child.

The impact of the Beijing Conference has been decisive at national and international levels: new forms of cross-border initiatives conducted by feminists have begun and aspects of 'cosmopolitan and deliberative democracy' have been initiated. In many countries the Beijing Conference has had important consequences at the cultural, political and legal levels, as stressed by the debate on *Beijing +5*. This was the follow-up to the Beijing Conference, as discussed by the UN General Assembly in 2000, where national governments had to indicate the policies they would introduce for avoiding gender discrimination (European Commission 2000b). Yet many problems remain.

For many years, for example, feminists and grassroots movements have been engaged in struggling against sexual violence, (marital and ethnic) rape and harassment in the private sphere, public spaces and workplaces; constructing shelters and aid centres for battered and abused women; and putting pressure on MPs to promote relevant laws in parliament. Yet the crucial turning point occurred at the World Conference on Human Rights, held in Vienna in June 1993. This is a very interesting case study because the question of sexually based violence was for the first time put on the table of the negotiations of the 171 representatives of the UN member states. NGOs organized activities parallel to the UN Conference and prepared a report on 'All Human Rights for All', which became very influential for the final provisions. One of the main results was the recognition of women's rights as human rights and the necessity of promoting and protecting the rights of children and indigenous populations.

Another crucial step was the recognition of violence against women as a form of violation of human rights, which must thus be prosecuted by criminal law on the basis of national legislation. Article 18 of the *Vienna Declaration* affirms that

> The human rights of women and of the girl-child are an inalienable, integral and indivisible part of universal human rights. The full and equal participation of women in political, civil, economic, social and cultural life, at the national, regional and international levels, and the eradication of all forms of discrimination on grounds of sex are priority objectives of the international community.
>
> Gender-based violence and all forms of sexual harassment and exploitation, including those resulting from cultural prejudice and international trafficking, are incompatible with the dignity and worth of the human person, and must be eliminated. This can be achieved by legal measures and through national action and international cooperation in such fields as economic and social development, education, safe maternity and health care, and social support.

> The human rights of women should form an integral part of the United Nations human rights activities, including the promotion of all human rights instruments relating to women. The World Conference on Human Rights urges governments, institutions, intergovernmental and non-governmental organizations to intensify their efforts for the protection and promotion of human rights of women and the girl-child.

This article was made possible not only thanks to the efforts of feminist pressure groups and representatives of the UN member states but also thanks to the preparatory work developed by a woman politician, Johanna Dohnal. At that time she was the German Minister for Women's Issues (Bundes-ministerin für Frauenangelegenheiten) for the Austrian Social Democratic Party in power. As key topics for the years 1992–93 she chose the issue of 'Violence against Women', organizing also an international symposium entitled 'Test the West: Gender Democracy and Violence'. When the UN conference took place, a mass of material on gender-based violence was already elaborated and prepared for a 'world discussion'. The results were crucial for further local and international actions.

Two years later the major statements and provisions decided in Vienna were introduced in the Beijing conference. As the representatives of the UN member states signed the *Platform for Action* – although decisions were not taken unanimously – national governments had to apply the provisions sub-scribed to during the Beijing conference, promoting bills and policies. The European Union, too, has reinforced debates, promoted provisions at the European Parliament, and encouraged in all member states 'Zero tolerance against violence' campaigns. The EU has also supported research, financed networks and NGOs for their initiatives to increase awareness (such as the Daphne programme), but mostly has induced national governments to intro-duce legislation against gender-based violence and sexual harassment – and not just in the European countries, but also in many other countries, such as China. Many critiques took issue with the fact that the World Conference on Women's Rights was held in China, where there is a constant violation of human rights and where, statistics indicate, there are 50 million 'missing women'. Yet recent socio-economic transformations in China, and the legal impact of the World Conference, have induced the Chinese government to prepare legislation against violence. The commission working on this project, called the Multi-Agency Domestic Violence Networking Project – consisting of sociologists, lawyers, NGOs, women's federations and other interested social actors – is supported by European institutions, among which are the British Cultural and Education Section in China.

This example of the institutionalization of the struggle against gender-based violence in terms of women's human rights reveals the circular and complex interrelation of bottom-up and bottom-down initiatives that can be generated by gender questions. This case indicates the possibility of relating the personal in a democratic and legitimate way to local questions, national issues, European perspectives, and international provisions. Individuals, social actors and political institutions are thus interconnected to produce a more adequate notion of women's human rights and cosmopolitan democracy.

Conclusions

In this chapter I have tried to indicate how human rights, intended to be universal, were from their inception characterized by a lack. This was the exclusion of women from the domain of citizenship and 'humanity', due to cultural prejudices and a limited conception of 'reason', attributed only to the public man, the male citizen. The struggle of women for recognition of their human rights was connected with the demand for citizenship, starting with the political right to vote. Women's movements in the last two centuries have radicalized struggles to obtain not only civil and political but also socio-economic rights, thereby contributing to the transformation of the structure of the nation-state in the form of a fairer welfare state.

However, the constitutive ambivalence of the notion of women's human rights – that is, the dynamic between formal equality and gender difference – persists. This has been acknowledged both in the Universal Declaration of Human Rights and in the directives issued by the European Union. Gender difference concerns *ex negativo* the struggle against gender-based violence and discrimination, while *ex positivo* it should concern the admission of reproductive rights. However, while UN conferences and European legislation have confronted the issue of gender-based violence through the promotion of relevant legislation and policies in the last few decades, there is still a lack of recognition of reproductive rights (from abortion to *in vitro* fertilization) in terms of women's human rights. On the contrary, new forms of biopolitics are emerging not only due to the opposition of conservatives and the Catholic Church, but also due to the increasing power of biotechnologies and genetic discoveries, which create new bioethical problems. These new frontiers of the discussion about life and death will constitute challenges for women, not least for European feminists.

References

Bergqvist, Christina, et al. (1999) *Equal Democracies? Gender and Politics in the Nordic Countries*. Oslo: Scandinavian University Press.

Cohen, Joshua, Mark Howard and Martha Nussbaum, eds (1999) *Is Multiculturalism Bad for Women? Susan Moller Okin with Respondents*. Princeton: Princeton University Press.

Duby, George and Michélle Perrot, eds (1990–93) *Storia delle donne in Occidente*, 5 vols. Rome and Bari: Laterza.

European Commission – DG for Employment and Social Affairs (2000a) *Bulletin of Legal Issues in Equality* (Bulletin of the Commission's network of legal experts on the application of Community law on equal treatment between women and men), no. 3/2000. Brussels: European Commission.

European Commission (2000b) *Beijing +5. An Overview of the European Union Follow-up and Preparations*, edited by Anna Diamatopoulou (European Commissioner for Employment and Social Affairs). Brussels: European Commission.

European Commission (2000c) *Science Politics in the European Union*. Brussels: European Commission.

European Commission – The Helsinki Group on Women and Science (2002) *National Policies on Women and Science in Europe*. Brussels: European Commission.

European Parliament (2002) www.europarl.eu.int/plenary/default_en.htm.

European Union (1999) *EU Annual Report on Human Rights*. Brussels: European Commission.

Gouges, Olympe de (1791) *Déclaration des Droits de la Femme et de la Citoyenne*. Paris.

Inter-Parliamentary Union (2001) 'Women in Politics', www.ipu.org.

Liebert, Ulrike, ed. (2001) *Europeanisation, Governance of Gender (In)equalities, and Public Discourses in EU Member States*. Bern: Peter Lang.

Lombroso, Gino (1919) *Il pro e il contro. Riflessioni sul voto alle donne*. Florence: Associazione Divulgatrice Donne Italiane.

Mill, John Stuart and Harriet Taylor Mill (1970 [1869]) *Essays on Sex Equality*, edited by Alice S. Rossi. Chicago: Chicago University Press 1970.

Rhode, Deborah L. (1989) *Justice and Gender: Sex Discrimination and the Law*. Cambridge, MA: Harvard University Press.

Stetson, Dorothy, ed. (2001) *Abortion Politics, Women's Movements and the State*. Oxford: Oxford University Press.

United Nations (1996), *Platform for Action and Beijing Declaration*. New York: United Nations Department of Public Information.

United Nations Development Program (2000), *Human Development Report 2000*. New York and Oxford: Oxford University Press.

Wollstonecraft, Mary (1792), *A Vindication of the Rights of Woman, with Strictures on Political and Moral Subjects*. London: T. Fisher Unwin, 1891; republished Cambridge: Cambridge University Press, 1995.

PART II

Culture and Signification

4

Space and Women's Culture

LIANA BORGHI

Geography and Gender

Drawing on British studies of feminist geography, this chapter will examine one particular European dimension of women's culture: how the spatial concept of Europe, imagined or real, has affected concepts of identity, subjectivity and self-representation in a few given situations. 'Culture' is a complicated term, and the many definitions already given of the word have not exhausted its meanings. In a classic study, *Keywords* (1976), British critic Raymond Williams has pointed out its aesthetic, anthropological and social dimensions, which include intellectual practices and developments together with ways of life and work. Culture should therefore not be addressed as an entity, but as a complex cluster of activities in process which are not superstructural but rather constitutive of economic and political change. Lately, scholarship has focused on the interaction between culture and space, and many women geographers have viewed this field from their gendered perspective.

Feminist geography can be termed a branch of Women's Studies, and as such it owes much to Cultural Studies, a field established in England in the 1960s, which branched out from an early interest in working-class and youth cultures to media and minority studies, women's issues, immigration and postcoloniality. Spreading out to other English-speaking countries and Europe, its strong political bias and interdisciplinary methods have provided a model for Women's Studies proper. Historical specificity, the material conditions of existence and cultural production, multiculturalism, diasporas, race, gender, hetero- and homosexualities, questions of identification and identity, the re-buttal of objectivity, and the endorsement of situated knowledges have also become Women's Studies issues. In our field, knowledge and culture are considered forms of power, never neutral, always positioned along axes of simultaneous differences like gender, class, race, age and sexual orientation. Traditional hierarchies of knowledge and cultural expression are questioned accordingly; the new feminist criticism is locational.

Convinced that place and space are gendered, since thinking space and representing it are interconnected and mutually constituted activities (McDowell 1999: 7), for almost two decades Women's Studies scholars have increasingly concerned themselves with the integration of space into their analysis of cultural and social processes. Viewing geography as a key constituent of identity, and assuming that the body and the environment produce each other, feminist geographers have studied the spatial dimension of gender re/production: how men and women are constructed in space (the home, the workplace, metaphors like 'women's sphere'); how cultural patterns related to space influence the construction of gender, race, class and other social markers – hence the relationship between identity and space; the reciprocity of space, subjectivity and status and women's spatial segregation in the access to knowledge and citizenship rights (skills, education, professions and trades, welfare, suffrage, unionism…); spatial institutions and gender stratification (purdah, the harem, the hammam, the *mikvah*…); the relationship between minority culture, sexual identity, and space; the gendering of the sexual contract and of biological reproduction (Bell and Valentine 1995; McDowell 1996, 1999; Massey 1994, 1995; Rose 1993, 1995). Ethnography and geography theorize something we already know through experience: that society is structured by diverse interactive fields through which discursive and cultural practices are transmitted; that space and knowledge interact in the formation of multiple audiences and communities (During 1993).

Just as architecture has been linked to cultural trends, places and spaces are seen as marked by the cultural processes which they themselves help produce, market and institutionalize. Space is invested with the task of performing cultural and political work: political geographies produce cultural formations just as a united Europe produces its new culture and cultural locations, connected with and structured by transnational configurations of power (like multinational corporations and the Internet). The culture industry induces us to consume and overconsume products, space, images. The space of entertainment that was once located at the heart of the cities and in appointed districts now occupies, virtually, home and work spaces through television, computers, sound reproduction equipment and video games. The mass market in turn conditions what counts as culture.

But the choice of entertainers, publicity, funding, promotions is not outside the power game. Which identities confer cultural credibility is also a question of economic and political interest. Historical, cultural and imaginative boundaries are being redrawn through narrative practices (from fiction to art and the media) which sexualize and gender women in increasingly homogenized fashion. At the same time, shifting boundaries and increased mobility produce 'communities of practice' (such as feminist and interest groups, immigrant networks, emailing lists) capable of creating alternative spaces and projects. Many of the scholars engaged in the new cultural cartographies of Europe were born elsewhere and speak from the position of insider–outsiders, immigrants, exiles, temporary guests, usually as committed to the making of Europe as its more stable residents, but sometimes more attentive to patterns of inclusion and exclusion. Practices of displacement, as James Clifford (1997) has observed, also constitute cultural meanings, and in any case cultures are fluid and temporary constructions made and remade over time.

Women's Access to Culture

According to these recent theories, space is first and foremost a cultural construct that describes how we represent the positions occupied at different times by an object or a subject. These positions are relational. When thinking of women's cultural space, for instance, it can be helpful to track the construction of transnational icons that have furthered the idea of a united Europe. One of the common factors in the background of women's condition in most countries has been the difficulties they encountered when accessing culture. As we know, for centuries women have inspired (men's) 'culture', and purchased or patronized it if they had the wealth to do so, but at the same time they were discouraged both from producing it and from getting credit for their creativity. This discrimination rests on the construction of gender as we still know it: a technology (De Lauretis 1987), a regulatory performance (Judith Butler 1990), a transnational practice symptomatic of power relations like phallogocentrism and compulsory heterosexuality. For the longest time women have been associated with nature and nurture, men with culture, commerce and war; women have procreated, men created. But even the most stubborn gender construction can be resisted.

Research on this topic has in fact revealed many exceptions. Christine de Pizan, Artemisia Gentileschi, Sofonisba Anguissola and Lavinia Fontana, Madame de Staël, Angelika Kauffman, Mary Wollstonecraft, Rosa Bonheur are among the upper- or lower-class artists and writers who achieved great renown, and paid for it in the many punitive ways devised for those who overstepped the boundaries drawn for their sex. Germaine de Staël's famous fictional heroine Corinne, icon to a host of women writers and artists, is condemned to disappear, nameless and unnameable. Often indeed, as Griselda Pollock has pointed out, the artistic output of women became a disappearing oeuvre, in the sense that the reputation they had achieved died down fast, for it did not enter the canon which was mostly male. Their works were lost, and *history* ensured that they were left out of museums and textbooks (Pollock 1996). Women writers met a similar fate. Critics (e.g. Jane Spencer, Felicity Morgan) have successfully investigated the 'disappearance' of hundreds of women's novels and plays written in and around the eighteenth century, finding that they were simply kept off the literary histories for a couple of centuries. And this is not a negligible oversight. This loss of collective memory contributes to the subordination of women, observed Theodore Stanton in his 1884 *The Woman Question in Europe*, as he collected evidence of years of intense feminist struggle in various countries, aimed at toppling similar social instances of male domination. Better international networking might have positively affected nationalisms and suggested more equitable social changes. As it was, Europe was paradoxically united in keeping down its women (and other subjects).

One of the first tasks of Women's Studies everywhere has been to change this pattern of erasure by retrieving the lives and work of 'lost' cultural figures, understanding the reasons for their erasure, revising categories of value, questioning distinctions between high and low culture, and establishing a new and ever-expanding canon. In short, women have taken over the task of *placing* ourselves and our foremothers in the symbolic and real space of the world's cultural production.

An example that alters the cultural map of Europe is the case of the recently revalued Futurist women artists, ignored for decades while their male partners were pushed back up to the limelight of the Modernist scene (Bentivoglio and Zoccoli 1997). The treasure hunt for exceptions to the rule of the cultural erasure of women over the centuries has confirmed, however, that as a rule women had very limited access to Art. More than that, they had limited access to culture as subjects. Our struggle to enter male spaces has been hard and long, even though its skirmishes may have appeared quite harmless. How not to laugh, for example, at Molière casting ridicule over the *Précieuses* and *Femmes Savantes* in his famous plays? Yet he was fighting women's access to cultural and social spaces then reserved for men. Also, we may not have noticed how far-reaching certain forms of exclusion were. For centuries, in England (and in other European countries) women could not be, as science critic Donna Haraway explains, 'modest witnesses', endowed with the masculine virtues which gave men the faculty to be objective, the power to establish facts, legitimize them, turn them into science and culture (Haraway 1997: 23–4). And almost all the famous women painters were 'born' into their profession, being related to male artists who taught them the craft and protected them. Even so, they still had no access to certain resources, like the study of anatomy that was vital for would-be artists as well as healers. Tamar Garb has written a fascinating account of the battle fought by the French Union of Women Painters and Sculptors to allow members to be admitted to the École des Beaux Arts, and to exhibit, or to access the art market. Deborah Cherry has investigated the plight of Victorian women artists, their attempt to enter life-drawing classes and to break down prejudices linking femininity only to watercolours and pastels. Not surprisingly, nineteenth-century Italy became a haven for expatriate female painters and sculptors, who found there not only picturesque landscapes, ruins and the works of old masters but also cheap living and working conditions, including helpers, models, craftsmen, raw materials, and wealthy travellers interested in modern art production.

If, for lack of access to the profession, women artists were necessarily a small and often privileged minority, other women constantly occupied themselves, for necessity or leisure, with the so-called 'applied arts' like sewing, embroidery, weaving, lace and cloak making. Wonderful examples of this kind of work can now be seen in museums like the Victoria and Albert in London or the Museo del Costume in Florence, and anywhere one may find collections of old linens, church apparel, antique clothing and upholstery. It is easy to forget nowadays that needlework was one of the very few 'proper' occupations open to women in the nineteenth century, who thereby produced plain sewing or finery for themselves, their family, and for middle- and upper-class buyers. The needleworker became a cultural icon signifying domesticity, female industry, and goodness (for instance, Mimi, Puccini's heroine in the opera La Bohème). But the icon also stood for the precarious social condition of the single woman, vulnerable to moral and economic disaster in sweatshops and textile mills. In Great Britain, Chartism took up as a rallying cry for the 'condition of England', Thomas Hood's 'The Song of the Shirt' (1843), and many painters drew pathetic portraits of sewing women. The helplessness of the icon was many times contradicted by the women who fought both to enter trade unions and to gain better working conditions through strikes. A world-famous example of this is the Triangle Shirtwaist Company strike (New York, 1909), which was followed two years later by the disastrous fire now commemorated on International Women's Day. The deaths of so many workers could have been avoided by not locking the emergency exits of the factory, and by granting the women's demands for safer working space, better wages, shorter hours. It is the freedom to demonstrate, march, work and vote that we celebrate on 8 March, aware that the plight of – not only female – workers persists the world over.

The craft of needlework is still taught and practised, even though the use of machinery in the ready-to-wear market has reduced a daily activity carried out by most women to the specialized work of a shrinking minority. Most high-fashion clothing, with its gorgeous and individual finishing, is no longer made in Europe, but in other countries which all too often serve as reservoirs of cheap labour. The anonymity of the work of seamstresses and piece workers replicates the trend that has held true over the centuries. The beautiful linens exhibited at the Rothschild mansion on Cap Ferrat remain as anonymous as the hand-embroidered Chinese silk blouses, probably made by prison workers, which we can buy cheaply at street markets. They are the unmistakable sign of the widespread system of 'First World' exploitation connected with a largely ignored process of exploitative economic globalization.

It seems all too easy to forget that culture and economics are intimately connected, and that women were denied access to employment, the professions, and financial recognition for their creative work, being forever classed among the 'amateurs', the copyists, the photo colourists. The credentials for accessing the higher reaches of culture required access to (higher) education, which, as we know, has come late to most women this past century.

Cross-cultural Networks

Still, through multicultural, international and transnational feminism, women's culture has paved the way to a new Europe. The history of Eurofeminism, which is even now being written, is based on a recognition of the differences and similarities among us, and on a respect for national cultures and priorities. In our recent feminist *her*story, women's separate spaces construct identities and make change possible. Consciousness-raising groups have taught a generation of women that the personal is political; self-help groups have challenged, among other things, the dictates of official medicine; adult education classes and women's seminars have enabled women to experiment with knowledge that is empirical as well as theoretical; rape crisis centres and women's places are where culture has been made, preserved, and transmitted; women's groups have theorized identity and ethics, recasting culture along more congruent (and unorthodox) gender lines and goals. Lesbians have constructed their own geographies of desire and created distinct landscapes of socio-cultural exchanges based on sexual preference and on the performance of sexually dissident identities (Valentine 2000). Their European networks rely on the Internet as much as on personal encounters.

The foundation of a women's Europe goes back in history to the worship of the Goddess and a long tradition of separate spaces like Sappho's *thiasos*, ritual enclaves reserved for women like vestal virgins and nuns, women-only spaces of confinement like women's prisons and asylums, shared domestic and work spaces, places of learning and socialization like day schools and boarding schools, or places of encounter and cultural exchange like women's salons.

For centuries salons have been cultural centres for the intelligentsia and the rich, whose cosmopolitanism can only provide a relative model for our united Europe, and needs careful assessment in terms of privilege and exclusion. The late seventeenth and eighteenth centuries were a cosmopolitan and polyglot world of multiple connections both for the nobility and for the rising bourgeoisie. French was overtaking Latin and Italian as the language of the court, and conversation was a major international cultural activity. At the time of Louis XIV, four salons catered for the cultural needs of the French capital: Mme de Sevigné opened her doors to the nobility, Ninon de Lenclos to the libertines, Mme de Sablé to the moralists, while the encyclopedists met at Mme de Léspinasse's. In Britain, the 'bluestockings' did not all have the privileges enjoyed by Mary Wortley Montague (traveller, author and letter writer) which enabled her to travel in Europe and the Middle East, but the meeting and discussion space which they carved out for themselves was nonetheless a local counterpart of the 'salon culture' developed by the French *Précieuses* like Madeleine de Scudéry, and later widely travelled hostesses like Germaine de Staël-Necker, who even as an exile made European culture wherever she opened her rooms to guests.

One interesting type of network connecting space and culture and recurring in different historical periods with very different connotations is that of exiled women, who are usually compelled by diminished financial circumstances to live modestly, earn a living, and integrate in one or more foreign countries. The difficult adjustment to forced proletarization and loss of cultural roots following displacement is one of the recurring themes of migrants' literature. Rather unexpectedly, because wealth tends to insulate from the worst but does not always provide the antidote, we find a positive evaluation of this experience among the noblewomen who fled from their home countries during the French Revolution. Mme de Genlis, Dutch-born Isabelle de Charrière, and their friend Belle van Zuylen are examples of a multi-cultural, multilingual minority at home in several countries who wrote letters and utopian fiction upholding values of international peace and cooperation (Paquin 1994). And Mme de Staël herself, knowing full well that fear of exile prevented many from opposing Napoleon's sprawling European empire, upheld those same values even as she hastily retreated through Europe just ahead of his conquering armies.

If being a diaspora Jew can be termed a permanent exile, and a condition that predisposes one to view with some scepticism nationalist ideals rooted in the bloodline, it is worth mentioning that between the end of the eighteenth century and the end of Napoleon's rule Rahel Levin Varnhagen was one of the eight Jewesses who opened transnational cultural spaces in Berlin. The French salon model had became very fashionable and was widely exported. Varnhagen's was a humble salon where only weak tea was served, but great ideas from many countries were exchanged.

United Europe was, of course, still a vague notion at that period, quite opposed to the Romantic trend towards national formations. Giuseppe Mazzini, for many years an exile, mostly in England, constituted an exception, planning his 'Young Europe' as early as 1834, well before Carlo Cattaneo and Victor Hugo broadcast the idea at the time of the 1848 revolutions. The Italian Risorgimento (the political revival that led to unification) was partly hatched, partly aided and abetted by women of many nationalities conversing in British drawing rooms, or during the 'at home' of French residents, foreign visitors and political exiles. Princess Cristina di Belgiojoso in Paris and Emilia Peruzzi in Florence pursued both utopian and concrete political goals that helped shape Europe's nineteenth-century configuration. Bucharest-born Dora D'Istria, a lifelong expatriate, dwelled and entertained in many Western countries. One of the most learned women of her time, she published in several languages books and articles about women's rights and her utopian idea of a united Europe well above single nations (Rossi

1998). From Venice, Elena Raffalovich Comparetti, whose sister had a salon in Paris attended by important politicians at the time of the Commune, was at the centre of a group of European women of various denominations – Jews, Catholics and Protestants – interested in comparative education reform. There were many other reform networks, of course, and it is worth remembering here Elizabeth G. Fry (1780–1845), a Quaker who spent her life organizing prison reform activities throughout continental Europe.

American women travellers and expatriates in Paris and other European locations also opened their homes to gossip and ideas from all kinds of women of many nationalities, some of whom were wealthy patrons of the arts. Actress Charlotte Cushman and sculptor Harriet Hosmer in late-nineteenth-century Rome, and in the early twentieth century Gertrude Stein and Natalie Barney in Paris, Peggy Guggenheim in Venice, Mabel Dodge and Violet Trefusis in Florence are just the tip of the iceberg of transcultural women's networks.

The romanticization of exile continued to be fashionable in the new century. In fact, it became the Euro-American myth of modernist artistic production voluntarily fuelled by the process of experiencing estrangement and separation (Kaplan 1996). Although exile is not just a metaphor for a condition of the soul, or a logistic preference, but most often a disabling, enforced experience of loss and dislocation, women more often than men needed to get away from places where their creativity was kept in check by issues of propriety and social stability, or just by an uncongenial environment – Isak Dinesen (Karen Blixen) chose Africa over Denmark; Gertrude Stein chose Paris; and women from the colonies, such as Katherine Mansfield, Jean Rhys and Doris Lessing, sometimes just relocated elsewhere. Leaving home had different meanings for each of them. So, if we accept that practices of displacement such as travel, diasporic movements and exile are constitutive of cultural meanings, we must look into that extraordinary phenomenon that was Paris when it became the European capital of women's modernism just before the First World War (Benstock 1986; Hanscombe and Smyers 1987).

Much has been written about the 'women of the Left Bank', who included photographers like Berenice Abbott and Gisèle Freund; journalists like Germaine Beaumont, Janet Flanner, Solita Solano; magazine editors like Margaret Anderson and Jane Heap; sculptors like Thelma Wood; singers like Georgette LeBlanc and Ada Smith; performers like Josephine Baker; painters like Romaine Brooks and Marie Laurencin; designers like Eileen Gray and poet Mina Loy; and a crowd of writers like Djuna Barnes, Kay Boyle, Bryher (Winifred Ellerman), Colette, H.D. (Hilda Doolittle), Radclyffe Hall, Anaïs Nin, Gertrude Stein, Renée Vivien, Edith Wharton and Dolly Wilde. Their international web of close connections, the extraordinary coincidences in their meetings, helped to redesign not just the culture of Europe but world culture. Besides salons (which modernists disapproved of as old-fashioned despite Gertrude Stein's and Natalie Barney's famous gatherings) and bookshops (most famous of which were the English-language 'Shakespeare and Company' run by Sylvia Beach, and her partner Adrienne Monnier's French-language bookstore, 'La maison des amis des livres' which, for a while after 1921, were both on rue de l'Odéon), there were other forms of cultural networking that made women's culture visible, like publishing houses and journals often financed through the 'matronage' of rich women, as in the case of British author Bryher or the American poet Nancy Cunard, or the many public forms taken by women's networks. I will here mention only two forgotten examples: the London International Society of Women Painters, connected with the Women's International Exhibition of 1900, and the exhibition of Les Femmes Artistes de l'Europe, which took place in Paris at the Musée du Jeu de Paume in 1937. The latter gathered some of the most famous modernist artists, like Marie Bashkirtseff, Marie Cassat, Berthe Morrisot, Romaine Brooks, Natalia Goncharova: 550 works from fifteen countries.

By 1937 Paris had become the capital of another kind of expatriate. In the turbulent years before the Second World War and the 'relocation' of millions of German and Eastern Jews, political refugees from Nazi/Fascist regimes created new international communities united across national histories, races and cultures in the large cities of Europe – mainly Amsterdam, London and Paris. Later, Hitler's armies closed in through France, and between 1940 and 1942 the refugees who had escaped capture but were unable to meet the emigration requirements of the Vichy government crowded, in relative temporary safety, in the Côte d'Azur, the Mediterranean sanctuary of the Alpes Maritimes, one of the eight départements occupied by Italy. The painted 'autobiography' of Charlotte Salomon, who was eventually forced to leave Nice for Auschwitz with so many others, survives in the Amsterdam Jewish Museum as the testimonial of a young woman who, like Anne Frank and Etty Hillesum, made, recorded and lived the maimed cultural experience of the younger generation of early-twentieth-century European Jews wiped out by racist governments.

Not painlessly or without opposition, the Shoah has finally been assumed by European countries as an event that has left its visible imprint on our culture, hence as a structural paradigm in the unification of Europe – and as yet another caveat on how not to unite Europe through violence and terror. Feminist scholars have researched extensively the history of Jewish women in European countries, their networks and affiliations with national cultures, their manner of bonding by way of cross-cultural affinities and traditions, if not through religion. Philosophers like Simone Weil and Hannah Arendt, widely read and translated, have thus left their mark on our feminist theories and ethics.

More and more, since the term 'woman' came under fire in the 1980s for not giving adequate recognition to the differences and disparities among women, the accepted racial and religious Jewish paradigm of diaspora has been altered to include other diasporic subjects – immigrants and migrants, guest workers and refugees, postcolonials now tightly woven into the fabric of Europe – as well as citizens from European countries relocating to more suitable social habitats. The experience of difference described in so many fictional and autobiographical accounts of the new literatures continues to ride the double edge of the aestheticization of the diasporic condition as an avant-garde model and the real-life pain of its multiple alienations.

I am tempted to draw a link between this developing consciousness of white Eurocentrism within the feminist movement and the wave of Eco-feminism that established itself militantly in the 1980s as a new field that explores the connection of women to nature. Whether it contested or not the traditional equation of women with nature, ecofeminism has recently steered away from a possible mythical approach and developed instead a post-structuralist analysis according to which nature and sex are not resources to culture and gender. Observing the devaluation of indigenous cultures around the world, ecofeminists could no longer fail to notice our own daily dis-criminatory practices, and the things we ignore or fail to see from our 'First World' perspective. Women's worldwide opposition to the prevailing forms of neoliberal globalization has created a myriad of militant new affinity groups working on issues that range from racism to war, to the destruction of the environment, the biotechnologies, pharmaceutical monopolies, and sustain-able development.

The new coalition lines are taking cultural shape. We are giving keen attention to women's voices from diverse ethnic groups that help us under-stand how our social environment has changed. Algerian writer Khalida Messaudi has rightly complained of 'Western blindness' as regards Africa in general and her country in particular. European feminism must take stock and change its course. Accordingly, our cultural approach is becoming more and more multiethnic, antiracist and multicultural. We critique our traditional binary patterns of inclusion and exclusion, identity and difference; we try not to forget that bodies depend on a complicated tangle of material and discursive relations. From this perspective we look at ourselves as Others, becoming other.

I am reminded here of a Moroccan author whose writings, translated in many languages, hold up a mirror to our Western imaginary that we can't afford to ignore. Fatema Mernissi, both in her essay *Scheherezade Goes West* (2002) and in her childhood autobiography *Dreams of Trespass* (1995), addresses the spatial institution of the harem with its gender stratification, comparing her real-life experience with the European representations of harems, especially by French painters, Ingres in particular. She finds these unrecognizable. Why is it, she asks, that in the emancipated Western Europe men fantasize women's passive surrender, while in countries where women wear the veil artists portray active amazons and powerful lovers? Which revolutions can finally make men dream of free and independent women? Throughout her discussion, Mernissi analyses with shrewdly pretended innocence the negotiation of cultural spaces that she saw taking place around the time of the Second World War, in a post/colonial country kept under siege by Western modernization. In her description – obviously addressed to Europeans – of the many harems of her childhood, the *hudúd* is the cultural, imaginary, physical boundary, the limit that divides private from public, men's from women's spaces, 'true believers' from 'unbelievers', Arabs from Jews, traditionalists from modernists. It is an area of constant negotiation and cultural grafting that must be granted utmost respect so that the dialogue between different subjects and peoples, at home and abroad, may begin.

Borderlines

While looking elsewhere, we may forget that there are communication problems within the borders of Europe. Language barriers are one of our major cross-cultural problems. Although the media make it easy to learn English, our lingua franca, cultural products in minor languages find it hard to reach international audiences. In order to circulate information about women's national cultures, WISE, a European women's network, has founded a new magazine, *Feminist Europa*, aimed at redressing the cultural hegemony of English-speaking communities by reviewing literary and critical publications in languages other than English. Its varied scholarship highlights national academic traditions, local styles and key issues, engaging readers in translation, encouraging intellectual nomadism across Europe through cross-cultural comparison and transnational dialogue.

Contemporary women's literature offers a good example of how feminism has required structural changes in the way texts are written, read and produced. From thesis novels to heroic women's utopias and science fiction, from *écriture féminine* to narrative poetics, minimalist or baggy hold-all novels, we find throughout Europe a wonderfully versatile body of writing freely combining gender and genre. Following cultural trends, many writers adopt magic realism; rewrite history, classical texts and fairy-tales; invent and cast new narratives.

In our postmodern climate, styles – literary, historical, autobiographical, figurative, personal, functional, abstract – mix and match relatively freely. Different kinds of texts and performances are now recognized as constitutive of culture: popular culture, 'minor' arts and genres like horror, noir, detection and science fiction, harlequin romances, soap operas, video clips. Disciplines, genres and art forms interact, providing fertile contaminations. The very originality of cultural phenomena is in question. Now that the quill and the palimpsest are obsolete, borrowing and cloning have become easily available through technology. We seem to have moved from an economy of scarcity which treasures the rare and unique (a Vermeer, a Goya, a Fabergé egg) to a globalized economy which values an ever-increasing demand and faster

turnover of cultural commodities (from home deliveries of carpets and paintings to taped, cloned and downloaded music, images and software), induced
and satisfied by invasive publicity methods. Accordingly, cultural artefacts are
not seen as just 'objects', but as a process through which genres and different
forms of expression can be compared. They are embedded in a network of
power effects whose socio-political import requires careful study.

Just as Khalida Messaudi criticizes Europe's blindness vis-à-vis Africa, many
people criticize Eurocentric practices as shortsighted and depleting. Art critic
Thomas McEvilley, for example, indicts eurocentric art views in museum
collecting and exhibiting because they cut visitors off from the emerging
'Third World', and isolate national from global culture (McEvilley et al. 1993:
394). 'Civilization transcends geography', he explains; it is therefore necessary
to revise frameworks as social needs change, and our culture changes with
them. Geographers would not agree with his statement, and would insist
instead that civilization is very much a question of geography. As we have
seen, in the new geographic criticism, positionality is a key word exactly
because it implies that subjectivity is always relational and situational, multiple, contradictory, interactional. A subject is always positioned at the crossroads of many factors. But McEvilley's message of cultural integration cannot
be refuted. 'Roots' and 'routes' need not be in opposition in the formation of
identities (Clifford 1997; Friedman 1998).

For this same reason geographic criticism no longer considers it sufficient
to focus on gender alone when reading literary texts. It is gender 'and its
others' that we need to consider; how gender interacts with other cultural
narratives, often creating stress patterns and faultlines. Narrative space has
been described as a space of resistance; women's texts have been analysed in
terms of their disaffection from traditional narrative models. *Bildung*, the cultural and existential construction of the fictional characters, offers evidence
that identity is not just an alliance to place or property, but a question of
stakes in a power struggle. Cultural identity can be said to represent the scene
and object of political struggles, and the 'porosity of frontiers' (Mouffe 1994:
110–11). Authors and characters can also be viewed in the role of cultural
rebels practising insubordination under subordinate conditions (Stimpson 1986),
and one can draw cartographies of resistance in the art world (Rose 1997), or
track narrative energies beyond the oedipal plots of the family romance
(Friedman 1998).

For over two centuries (but who can say what we have not retrieved?)
women have recorded their organic visions of changed worlds where all individual needs are respectfully negotiated by the community. Some of these
utopias are separatist; others are not. Recently, in a socio-anthropological
study, Daphne Spain has underlined the correspondence between public and
private, and the mutual nature of maleness and femaleness, maintaining that
space integration is vital for social integration (Spain 1993). Endorsing this
tendency to veer from the concept of difference towards affinity, Linda

McDowell concludes, agreeing with Lawrence Grossberg, that it's time to move from cultural models of opposition/resistance, dominant/subaltern cultures, and binary gender divisions towards models of transformation and translation capable of creating the alliances needed for becoming a community (McDowell 1999: 221–3). This, of course, applies to a united Europe as well.

References

Bell, David and Gill Valentine (1995) 'Strategies of Performance, Sites of Resistance', in S. Pile and N. Thrift, eds, *Mapping the Subject: Geographies of Cultural Transformation.* London: Routledge, pp. 143–57.

Benstock, Shari (1986) *Women of the Left Bank: Paris 1900–1940.* Austin: University of Texas Press.

Bentivoglio, Mirella and Franca Zoccoli (1997) *Women Artists of Italian Futurism: Almost Lost to History.* New York: Midmarch Art Press.

Butler, Judith (1990) *Gender Trouble.* London: Routledge.

Clifford, James (1997) *Routes: Travel and Translation in the Late Twentieth Century.* Cambridge, MA: Harvard University Press.

De Lauretis, Teresa (1987) *Technologies of Gender.* Bloomington: Indiana University Press.

Duncan, N., ed. (1996) *Body Space: Destabilizing Geographies of Gender and Sexuality.* London: Routledge.

During, Simon, ed. (1993) *The Cultural Studies Reader.* London: Routledge.

Ferguson, Russell, William Olander, Marcia Tucker and Karen Fiss (1990) *Discourses: Conversations in Postmodern Art and Culture.* New York: New Museum of Contemporary Art/MIT Press.

Friedman, Susan Stanford (1998) *Mappings: Feminism and the Cultural Geographies of Encounter.* Princeton: Princeton University Press.

Hanscombe, Gillian and Virginia L. Smyers (1987) *Writing for Their Lives: The Modernist Woman, 1910–1940.* London: Women's Press.

Haraway, Donna J. (1997) *Modest_Witness@Second_Millennium.* London: Routledge.

Kaplan, Caren (1996) *Questions of Travel: Postmodern Discourses of Displacement.* Durham, NC and London: Duke University Press.

McDowell, Linda (1996) 'Spatializing Feminism: Geographic Perspectives', in N. Duncan, ed., *Body Space: Destabilizing Geographies of Gender and Sexuality.* London: Routledge, pp. 28–44.

McDowell, Linda (1999) *Gender, Identity, and Place: Understanding Feminist Geographies.* Minneapolis: University of Minnesota Press.

Massey, Doreen (1994) *Space, Place, and Gender.* Cambridge: Polity Press.

Massey, Doreen (1995) 'Masculinity, Dualisms, and High Technology.' *Transactions of the Institute of British Geographers* 20, pp. 487–99; reprinted in N. Duncan, ed., *Body Space: Destabilizing Geographies of Gender and Sexuality.* London: Routledge.

McEvilley, T., W. Rubin, and K. Varnedoe (1993) 'Doctor Lawyer Indian Chief: "Primitivism" in 20th Century Art', in R. Ferguson et al., eds, *Discourses: Conversations on Postmodern Art and Culture.* Boston, MA: MIT Press.

Mernissi, Fatema (1995) *Dreams of Trespass: Tales of a Harem Girlhood.* New York: Addison Wesley.

Mernissi, Fatema (2002) *Scheherezade Goes West: Different Cultures, Different Harems.* Washington DC: Washington Square Press.

Mouffe, Chantal (1994) 'For a Politics of Nomadic Identity', in George Robertson et al., eds, *Travellers' Tales: Narratives of Home and Displacement*. London: Routledge.

Paquin, Éric (1994) 'Sur les traces de Télémaque: romans féminins de l'émigration', in Joëlle Cauville and Metka Zupančič, eds, *Réécriture des mythes: l'utopie au féminin*. Amsterdam: Rodopi, pp. 35–48.

Pile, S. and N. Thrift, eds (1995) *Mapping the Subject: Geographies of Cultural Transformation*. London: Routledge.

Plant, Sadie (1996) 'The Virtual Complexity of Knowledge', in George Robertson et al., eds, *FutureNatural: Nature/Science/Culture*. London: Routledge, 203–17.

Pollock, Griselda, ed. (1996) *Generations and Geographies in the Visual Arts: Feminist Readings*. London: Routledge.

Rose, Gillian (1993) *Feminism and Geography: The Limits of Geographical Knowledge*. Minneapolis: University of Minnesota Press.

Rose, Gillian (1995) 'Making Space for the Female Subject of Feminism', in S. Pile and N. Thrift, eds, *Mapping the Subject: Geographies of Cultural Transformation*. London: Routledge, pp. 332–54.

Rose, Gillian (1997) 'Performing Inoperative Community: The Space and the Resistance of Some Community Arts Projects', in Steve Pile and Michael Keith, eds, *Geographies of Resistance*. London: Routledge, pp. 184–202.

Rossi, Luisa (1998) 'Introduction', *I bagni di mare, by Dora d'Istria* (1867, 1972). Genoa: Sapeg.

Sharp, Joanna P. (1996) 'Gendering Nationhood: A Feminist Engagement with National Identity', in N. Duncan, ed., *Body Space: Destabilizing Geographies of Gender and Sexuality*. London: Routledge, pp. 97–108.

Spain, Daphne (1993) *Gendered Spaces*. Chapel Hill: University of North Carolina Press.

Stimpson, C.R. (1986) 'Female Insubordination and the Text', in Judith Friedlander, ed., *Women in Culture and Politics: A Century of Change*. Bloomington: Indiana University Press.

Valentine, Gill (2000) *From Nowhere to Everywhere: Lesbian Geographies*. Binghamton, NY: Haworth Press; co-published as *Journal of Lesbian Studies*, vol. 4, no. 1, 2000.

Williams, R. (1976) *Keywords: A Vocabulary of Culture and Society*. London: Fontana/Croom Helm.

5

European Feminine Identity and the Idea of Passion in Politics

ELENA PULCINI AND LUISA PASSERINI

Editorial Introduction

This chapter deals with the specular relationship between two clusters of ideas: on the one hand, the ancient and persistent link between feminine identity, the idea of love and of passion; and on the other, the interconnection between that idea of love and a certain definition of Europe and of European culture. In the first section, Elena Pulcini outlines the former; in the second, Luisa Passerini goes on to examine the latter.

The approach of this chapter is historical and it deals with the very definition of Europe and of European identity; as the product of two Italian scholars, it bears the distinctive traits of the classical humanistic approach so common in Italian feminism. In the next chapter Serena Sapegno takes a similar approach in her discussion of the role played by psychoanalysis – and hence questions of desire, passion and fantasy – in the Italian women's movement.

The authors maintain that a specific idea of heterosexual love, passion and desire has been constitutive of the very notion of Europe since Antiquity and more especially since the eighteenth century. This has specific implications for women, who are the empirical referents for the kinds of discursive production of ideas about bodily love and affectivity which have been so alive in the West since classical Greece. The position of women in this debate, however, is not free from ambivalence. Women are appointed as subjects who are prone to love, emotions and affectivity. In so far as these qualities are dialectically opposed to the 'reasonable' attitude of moderation and self-control that is expected of the classical visions of the perfect citizen, affectivity and love play a major role in disqualifying women from their social and political rights. Confined to the private sphere and to the realm of the family, women are coerced into representing the sexual and emotional sides of human endeavour.

In modernity, and especially since the eighteenth century, this evolves into a discourse about passion which leads to the pathologizing of the lives of women and further restricts their entitlement to basic rights.

On the other hand, the relevance and priority that are assigned to subjectivity, love and emotions make women into the object of heterosexual male desire. This creates a notion of love as *amour courtois* or courtly love, which also empowers certain classes of women. More importantly, however, this specific attitude to women has played a role in defining European civilization since the Enlightenment, as the site where subjectivity entails the right to the exercise of emotional and sexual freedom for women.

The authors conclude by raising the question of what shifts of perspective on the issue of women/love/Europe can be introduced under the double impact of feminist research, on the one hand, and the project of the European Union, on the other.

Women, Passion and the Compulsory Bond to Affectivity

The importance of the idea of passion in the formation of feminine identity is evident even in the origins of Greek thought. Plato and Aristotle laid the groundwork for Western identity as a clear dualism which established a hierarchy of opposite terms. These would become the pivot of the whole Western tradition. The opposition between *polis* and *oikòs*, between the public life of the city and the private home, is mirrored in the opposition between reason and passion, freedom and necessity, soul and body, masculine and feminine.

Women, associated with the negative polarity – that is, the body, necessity and passion – underwent a process of devaluation and exclusion. For the orderly and rational world of the *polis*, women represent the threat of *pathos*; they incarnate the chaos and the irrationality of nature and of the emotions which are confined in the name of law and order to the private world of the *oikòs*. Women lose their right to speak – a right they kept in the tragic thought which still allows Antigone to affirm the law of feelings and of blood against the abstract commandments of the law and political order defended by Creon (in Sophocles' *Antigone*).

Philosophy and politics legitimate themselves by dispossessing women, carriers of *pathos*, of their right to speak and of their access to free citizenship. Plato's Diotima, whom Plato himself acknowledges as a repository of the knowledge of Eros (in the *Symposium*), is the symbol of a disembodied Eros. Purged of any connection with the body, this disembodied Eros becomes the instrument through which the philosopher has access to the *logos*, the eternal and immaterial truths of the spirit. Only the possession of this truth makes it possible for the city to be governed (Irigaray 1985; Cavarero 1990).

Women, supposedly devoid by nature of intellectual and rational faculties, are chained to the inferior spheres of affectivity, appetite and the body. Aristotle explicitly affirms that women are bound to be confined to the pre-linguistic and pre-political sphere of the home. There they perform reproductive activities, which are necessary to the well-being of the *polis* but are also separate from and subordinate to it, in the name of a natural hierarchy of male and female that mirrors the metaphysical opposition of form and matter (*Politics*).

It may be said that the difference between the sexes — one associated with *logos*, rationality and order; and the other identified with *pathos*, irrationality and disorder — is the basis for their inequality. This implies a woman's subordination and obedience to a man in the private sphere as well as her exclusion from public life. This inequality translates into a fatal injury to women's identity.

Several feminist studies demonstrate that the Aristotelian dichotomy and the image of the woman deriving from it persist through the Middle Ages to the modern world (Coole 1993; Elshtain 1981). A first fracture in this is brought about by Christianity, which, by reconsidering the importance of the private sphere of the *domus*, gives a new dignity to women. But the Christian predicament of a universal equality of individuals mainly concerns their spiritual and interior life, the life 'beyond the world', as Louis Dumont would say, not the life 'in the world'. It is also true that the medieval code of *amour courtois* introduces a different appreciation of the female figure, but this is still confined to the imaginary world and based on a conception of love as adultery which does not affect the institutional forms of the relationship between the sexes.

European modernity, instead, by affirming the as yet unheard-of value of the supremacy of the individual without distinction of classes, status or sex and considered in his/her social and worldly relationships, laid the philosophical, social and political grounds for the overcoming of any inequality, including inequality between the sexes. Nevertheless, European modernity actually reproduced a more subtle form of subordination and exclusion of women through the repetition of a renewed opposition between public and private, reason and passion.

Recent feminist criticism of modern liberalism, from Jean Bethke Elshtain to Carole Pateman and Seyla Benhabib, has shed light on this aspect of European modernity, demonstrating how it contradicts the relationship between the sexes in its liberal and egalitarian foundations. Starting with Hobbes, Locke and Rousseau, liberalism builds the image of a sovereign and autonomous individual able to set up rational relationships in order to pursue his own interests and establish an agreement upon which to found a free political society apparently accessible to everyone. In reality, this happens through a double operation: detachment from the passions and the exclusion of women. First of all, the individual becomes, as Michel Foucault would say, 'his own master' through the control over and removal of his emotional life; second, he forces a tacit 'sexual contract' upon women. This contract, based upon would-be natural laws and accepted by women (Pateman 1988), denies access for women to the 'social contract' and public life, confining them to the sphere of the private. The autonomous and self-sufficient self, the 'disengaged self' (Taylor 1989, and communitarians) which builds its own identity and freedom through detachment (in a Cartesian manner) from the world of desires and affections, is in reality only the male subject which erects the myth of his own self-sufficiency on the double exclusion of the passions and the female (Benhabib amd Cornell 1987). Women are left with the management of the private sphere, which once again becomes the repository of feelings, desires and values removed from the public world.

Nevertheless, the private sphere now has a new positive connotation which creates a fracture with the Aristotelian vision. The private is no longer, as Hannah Arendt (1958) has understood, a synonym for privation or 'deprivation', as it used to be in the ancient sensibility, but becomes, by virtue of the development of modern individualism, the object of an evident reappreciation. It may be enough to think of the radical transformation of the image of the family. As historians of ideas show, the family's traditional economic and social functions of the perpetuation of rank and reproduction of the division of labour lose strength and the family becomes, in modern Europe, an area of affections based on love marriages and on partners' right to free choice. The family is called upon to perform the delicate and complex task of fulfilling the individual's need for happiness (which, since the eighteenth century, has become a right, along with the right to freedom and to equality) without disturbing the public and social life governed by rational and impersonal relations (Heller 1979). Thus the articulation *homme/citoyen*, upon which the modern distinction between private and public is based, has been formulated.

For the first time in the history of European civilization the family houses affection as its fundamental core. It has also become the centre of control and regulation of the individual's emotional life. It may be said that the family becomes the privileged area of that process of the taming of the passions which Norbert Elias (1978) recognized as the peculiar feature of modern European civilization. The family is not grounded in passion, but in what might be called sentiment – that is, an emotional dimension at equal distance from passion and reason and therefore compatible with the institution and needs of society, capable of duration as well as of responding to the daily vicissitudes of the times. Eighteenth-century Europe saw the birth of a new affective code – the code of sentiment – which finds manifold representations in literature and philosophy, in sentimental novels as well as in the numerous treatises on love, happiness and friendship, upon which the 'culture of modernity' (Taylor 1989) was founded.

Women, active protagonists of the private sphere, are identified with this new affective code. Suffice it to think of Rousseau and of the female image which arises from *La Nouvelle Héloïse* or from *Émile*, an image bound to last until the contemporary age (Okin 1979). A woman as a wife and mother incarnates the two fundamental dimensions of modern sensibility: marital and maternal love. She is given new dignity in her capacity to choose freely and a new identity based on values 'different' from the male identity. But, at the same time, by virtue of her own difference, she is confined even more radically to the private sphere, where she performs an essential psychological and moral purpose, indirectly related to the public and social sphere. She becomes the carrier of the values expelled from the public world such as care, solidarity, devotion and sympathy, through which she attains a kind of power: the power of love, with which she governs the relationships inside the sphere of intimacy.

Modernity thus confers on women the dignity of a subject but builds, in its Foucauldian sense, a peculiar image of female subjectivity in which love becomes a screen for inequality. In the name of her identification with love or, rather, with sentiment, the female subject's identity undergoes two funda- mental amputations. The first consists in her exclusion from the public sphere and her reduction to indirect and ancillary functions aimed at sustaining the balance between *homme* and *citoyen* on which the liberal myth of the rational and self-sufficient (male) individual is based. The second, which recent femi- nist thought has not reflected upon enough, concerns the woman's exclusion from *pathos* and from the excesses of passion, and her identification with a sweetened and purely positive form of affectivity, which may find its arche- type in Agape more than in Eros and which also implies an embitterment of the punishment should the code be transgressed. European modernity builds an image of woman as the subject of sentiment and at the same time deprives her, with her own unconscious complicity, of two fundamental rights for the formation of identity: the right of citizenship and the right of passion, also meaning the right of excess, disorder, conflict – that is, the negative – as a vital and unrenouncable dimension of the building of the self.

Romanticism itself, in spite of its rehabilitation of some aspects of love as passion, ends up confining women to the intimate sphere, reinforcing their image as guardians of feelings and privacy (Giddens 1992). Starting from the nineteenth century, transgressions of this image are condemned morally and socially (see Tolstoy's novels). And if in the entire European tradition, starting from *amour courtois*, passion is identified with the negative value of death (De Rougemont 1939; Passerini 1998), female passion is devoid even of the symbolic strength of myth and of any nihilistic representations and becomes more and more often sickness and pathology to be treated and exorcized. Female passion becomes the object of the aseptic and apparently neutral power of medical and psychological discourses, which, through the image of the hysterical woman, deprive female *pathos* of any access to language, stigmatiz- ing it as folly (Vegetti Finzi 1992). It is significant that psychoanalysis, which springs out of the will to rehabilitate the pathologies of subjects by rebuilding their significant potential, is not able to confer upon passionate female emotions an autonomous status, and attributes an essentially negative and private connotation to female 'difference'. There is an important exception, wrongly ignored by feminist thought, represented by the psychology of Jungian origins, which attributes to the 'feminine' indisputable dignity and symbolic and psychological complexity.

Recent feminist thought has proposed a revaluation of the link between woman and affectivity upon which to base an idea of subjectivity different from that of the male subject (abstract, neutral and purely rational). Even within this very different perspective, the female inclination for caring and relationality (Gilligan 1982), the attention to others as 'concrete beings' (Benhabib, in Benhabib and Cornell 1987), the ability to keep her relationship with origins and with the mother (Cavarero 1990; Irigaray 1985; Fusini 1995), are aspects of the emotional fundamentals of female identity. This does not result in a segregation of women to the closed and sweetened world of affections, but an appreciation of the peculiarity of the female subject to reconcile freedom and dependence, rationality and affectivity, autonomy and responsibility in order to lay the grounds for a new ethics (of care) and a new subjectivity (dialogical, relational).

This perspective runs the risk of falling into essentialism and of reprocessing a certain absolutism, this time in a positive way, of women's difference, enchaining women, each individual woman, to a generalization which may sacrifice individual differences and the discordant individual's voice. This risk may be overcome if the idea of difference is understood not only as a difference *from* the other (the male subject) but also as a difference *within* – that is, a difference inside the same female subjectivity. This difference, which may never be reconciled, constitutes itself and always contests any generalization and impedes any recomposition. This idea may be thematized through the idea of passion understood, as Georges Bataille (1962) suggests, as the transgressive and chaotic dimension which leaves a permanent 'wound' in any would-be condensation of the self, opening it up to the most unconfessable truths and giving the female not only autonomy and the dignity of choice but also the courage of the negative without which there cannot be a unique and singular identity.

European Culture, the Idea of Love and Women

In the European cultural tradition, the constellation subject/love/Europe became relevant during the Enlightenment, especially in the second half of the eighteenth century. In that century, a central core of the definition of European civilization – namely, the status of European women and the attitude towards them – was given new and sometimes contrasting values. For Voltaire (1756) in *Essai sur les moeurs*, the main difference between the Orientals and the Europeans was evident in the way they treated women: giving them freedom in Europe, consigning them to slavery in the Orient. For Montesquieu (1721) in *Lettres persanes*, the freedom of European women was the ambivalent source of their impudence, which he contrasted with the modesty and chastity of Asian women, whilst acknowledging the spirit and liveliness of the European ones. This European specificity, defined on the basis of a contrast to Asia – considered to be the Other par excellence – was the basis of the claim that relations between the sexes had reached a level of civilization in Europe which was unheard of elsewhere.

Attention to and respect for women was considered to have been born with chivalry, understood as a founding institution of European political and cultural civilization. Another major contrast was thus established, that with classical antiquity, which was essential for defining a European specificity in terms of the conception of a 'modern' Europe and its sensitivity. This was understood to be born from the plurality of cultural influences which had mingled in southern France at the beginning of the second millennium, giving rise to the culture of Provence and to the particular form of love sung by the troubadours as *fin'amors*, *amor honestus*, *cortezia*. The term *amour courtois*, 'courtly love', was made successful by the French philologist Gaston Paris only as late as 1883. During the whole nineteenth century the dispute around the possible Arabic derivation of Provençal poetry and love continued, a derivation opposed by the claim for a purely European origin.

An important centre of this debate was the Coppet group around Madame Germaine de Staël. Intellectuals of various countries gathered at Coppet, a little village and castle near Geneva, where the Baroness withdrew when Napoleon exiled her from Paris for her influence on the liberal opposition. Among them were writers such as Simonde de Sismondi, author of an important *Histoire de la littérature du midi de l'Europe* which maintained that chivalry and Provençal poetry were born together, generating at the same time the cult of women and the cult of honour, while anticipating the taste for romantic poetry. Madame de Staël corresponded with François Raynouard, author of a grammar and a dictionary of Provençal (published in 1816–21), who paid particular attention to women not only as objects but as subjects of Provençal poetry, therefore as capable of giving voice to the subject speaking love (or, in the terms used by Roland Barthes, the subject of the love discourse). He observed that one of the most significant *trobairitz*, the Comtessa de Dia, spoke a different language from Sappho: what counted for the countess were the heart and the sentiments, such as tenderness, coupled with intellect, and the desire of love for love's sake. For Raynouard, the poems of the *trobairitz* expressed 'un abandon plus vif, plus passionné', a more lively and passionate abandonment, than those of the troubadours. His was an important step in the construction of a feminine loving subject, legitimated on the basis of women's closer relationship with passion – and therefore with nature – than men's. While giving women a right of citizenship in the realm of letters and emotions and at the same time the dignity of a speaking subject, this operation was not without ambivalence.

In 1810 Madame de Staël published *De l'Allemagne*, which was immediately destroyed on the orders of Napoleon; but the book was very successful when it reappeared in 1813. In this work, she ascribed much more importance to chivalry than she had in her previous writings, and praised its positive qualities, such as love and respect for women. This change is usually ascribed to her intellectual exchange with August Wilhelm von Schlegel, who played a crucial role in redefining the role of the troubadours in European culture. But Madame de Staël disagreed with him on the importance of the German *Minnesänger*, whom she did not regard as comparable with the French *trouvères* and Provençal troubadours. Schlegel could not accept the idea of the Arabic origin of Provençal poetry, precisely because he could not be persuaded that the inspiration of a poetry based on the adoration of women and their social freedom could be taken from a culture in which women were slaves. Thus, another stereotype was being reinforced, that of an Asian Other which includes women as slaves, downplaying the role that women slaves had had as poets in Moorish Spain.

These processes were accompanied by a crystallization of a concept of Europeanness which stressed the superiority of Europe in relation to the imperial and colonial experience, trying to exclude influences from the Orient. The interpretation of Provençal love as a sentiment expressed only by men, including little or no physical satisfaction, and uniquely characteristic of European civilization, came to be dominant in the second half of the nineteenth century and the first decades of the twentieth. In the course of this process of Eurocentralization, Arabic influences, as well as the importance of women as composers and performers of poetry, were negated at the same time as forms of sexuality and sensuality for purposes other than procreation were ignored. The resulting conception of Provençal love integrated the superiority of Europe over the other continents and of men as authors with a vision of women merely as objects of the discourse of love.

It is no wonder that, when Raynouard's approach to women's poetry was criticized in the 1930s, more than a century later, by another illustrious romance philologist, Alfred Jeanroy of Paris University, the criticism was done in a misogynist and Eurocentric spirit. Jeanroy was right in attacking the belief that women's poetry was more 'natural' than that of men and in demolishing the opinion that love courts headed by women had actually existed, as he did by demonstrating that they were a literary exercise developed from a *jeu de société*. But his criticism was coupled with the assertion that the *trobairitz* were slaves of tradition, incapable of finding new themes, lazy of spirit, lacking in taste, shame and decency. Jeanroy was also very sceptical of the Arabic origins of courtly love and poetry, still quoting Schlegel without dissent.

We want to argue against interpretations according to which 'putting women on a pedestal' was a shrewder form of medieval misogyny. We are convinced that insisting in this context only on the continuity of misogyny in various epochs and societies is reductive, since it ignores the fact that courtly love not only put 'women on a pedestal' but also indicated an attitude which exalted the object of love, be it woman or man, and the unfulfilled aspect of desire.

Moreover, it should not be forgotten that women had an important role in Provençal culture not only as ladies of the courts where the poems were created and sung but also as *trobairitz* – as composers and performers of the love songs. A crucial step in this direction has been the critical edition of the *trobairitz'* corpus by Angelica Rieger (1991), establishing the songs of poets such as N'Azalais de Porcairagues, Na Castelloza and the Comtessa de Dia.

In the period between the wars, the connection between Europe and love became particularly important as a way to save Europe from the impending risk of a second world war. This connection was evident, with different meanings, in works by Sigmund Freud and Carl Gustav Jung, respectively *Civilization and Its Discontents* and *Woman in Europe*. For both, the theme of the *finis Europae* was closely linked to the situation of women, the crisis of the traditional concepts of masculinity and femininity deriving from the emancipation of women, the mourning of many young men dead in the war, the increasing problems of marriage and sexuality. For Freud, women had laid the foundations of civilization 'by the claims of their love', but they had come to oppose civilization as inimical to the developments of libidinal love. For Jung, women were at the very core of the social and spiritual European crisis, and they could repair the wounds inflicted on the European psyche by the barbarity of war. These ideas were developed by Mary Esther Harding (1933) in *The Way of All Women*, but without stressing the European dimension, while both writings by Freud and Jung appealed to Eros as a hope for the future of Europe.

The connection Europe/love/subject was established most clearly by Denis de Rougemont in *L'amour et l'occident* (1939). Rougemont traced a history of the European subject from the myth of Tristan and Isolde to the present, and indicated two conceptions of love as crucial: that where love, understood as fusion, is inextricable from death, and that based on a Christian notion of the duality between lovers. The former is passion, therefore passive; the latter is action, in the form of fidelity. Rougemont criticized the illusion of happiness which leads to multiple divorces and marriages, as exemplified by the social mores of the United States and on Hollywood film. This signals a drastic change in the twentieth century: the switch of the Other – in this arena – from Asia to North America. It was now the latter which represented a point of reference, in contrast with which Europe could define itself. The American woman was now the dangerous image, at the same time close to nature and engaged in a process of active emancipation, subtracting from men the role of the subject and undermining, thanks to her involvement in work, the traditional identification between love and women. This identification was subsequently criticized and reformulated in many ways by women in the second half of the twentieth century.

Among the contributions by women as thinkers to understanding and reformulating the European heritage of love, that of Simone Weil had a particular interest for her originality and utopian strength. Simone Weil, writing in 1942 in *Cahiers du Sud* under the pseudonym Émile Novis, an anagram of her own name, interpreted the Provençal conception of love as the founding principle of an order without dogmas (*amour ordonnateur*), a love which was devoid of avidity and capable of waiting, and in which the subject's orientation towards another being required the latter's consent. According to Weil, this love had the same inspiration as love in ancient Greece: the latter chose homosexuality in the same way as the former chose adulterous love, in order to express the sentiment of impossible love, which to her was nothing other than chastity. The love of the troubadours was in the end love of God by means of a beloved human being. This type of love could awaken Europeans to the search for the spiritual dimension of life, since the roots of European spirituality are the same as those of ancient Greece. The culture of Provence had achieved, Weil thought, an idea of happiness based on order, freedom and intelligence, of harmony of different classes and equality between those who serve and those who are served. This culture was created thanks to its tolerance towards different traditions, since it combined Nordic influences with those from Arabia and Persia. But after the Albigensian crusade, with which the Catholic Church destroyed Provence, Europe never again reached the same spiritual freedom.

Among the women who contributed to a different way of formulating the original constellation Europe/love/subject, at least two should be remembered, in order for their thoughts and actions to be continued. Margaret Storm Jameson, a British essayist and writer of forty-five novels, socialist and Labour supporter, active in various left-wing and libertarian causes, envisaged what today we would call a social Europe. In 1934 she wrote in favour of a European union from the point of view of 'a little Englander in love with an England which never was but could be', who had grown to love Europe while remaining loyal to her roots. Her approach to a possible United States of Europe was based on the desire to live, the sense of local and regional pride, and the local virtues of obstinacy, defiance and sense of adventure. Her appeal to reason included social and emotional colours; her argument was that all the children of Europe should be made able to enjoy the same privileges – 'the best milk, clean air, daily baths, warmth'. According to her, a process should be started aiming at a point when all the people of Europe would enjoy the same degree of comfort and security. In 1939–40 Storm Jameson took an active interest in federalism, supporting the Federal Union and its initiatives. Her idea of European federalism included the emancipation of the colonies, which is quite remarkable in a period when European federation was often understood as implying the unification of all colonial possessions under a united Europe. At that point Storm Jameson believed that it was necessary to develop certain social services in Europe, such as communications and medicine. Storm Jameson's was an idea of Europe incorporating the moral, intellectual and emotional planes, connecting it with individual lives and their local and daily dimensions.

Ursula Hirschmann, who had to escape from Berlin in the 1930s because she was both Jewish and an active anti-Nazi, went to Italy, where she married first Eugenio Colorni and then Altiero Spinelli. She was actively engaged in the anti-Fascist resistance with the group which formulated the 1941 Manifesto di Ventotene for a united Europe based on ideals of social justice and equality. In 1975 Hirschmann founded in Brussels the association 'Femmes pour l'Europe', with an appeal to a social politics aiming for equality between women and men, better working conditions, the active participation of workers in economic and social decisions. She considered herself a 'wandering European' without a language, neither Italian in spite of having Italian children, nor German even if Germany had been her homeland.

The emotional basis of the idea of Europe is linked with something one might call an active memory of emotions. The latter is capable of re-elaborating and continuing the legacies of national cultures into an international perspective, and of reworking Marxism and its struggles against social injustice in a framework of a liberal radicalism free from the rigidity of previous ideologies. In this active memory of the past, the role of 'a city called Europe' is essential, a 'city that I have in myself'. Ursula Hirschmann seemed to be very aware of the fact that there is no real memory without an emotional basis, and that any active elaboration of ideas, whether theoretical or political, requires a high libidinal investment. For her the emotional roots find their ground not only in individual and collective memories but also in art and in local places which are the homes of the 'small': 'We can only love. Not because we are good, not because we are religious, but because it is our only way to remain in reality. Because Mörike [with his beautiful poems closed in a world as small as a nutshell] is always there and no Eichmann can take him away from us.'

The contribution of feminist theory to reformulating the constellation Europe/love/subject is in progress. In the 1970s feminists criticized romantic love as 'the pivot of women's oppression', considering 'romanticism as a cultural tool of male power to keep women from knowing their condition' – the words of Shulamith Firestone (1970) – since its false idealization concealed gender inferiority through the so-called 'pedestal treatment'. In this perspective, gender and class conspired to sustain romantic love and its deceptions. For Germaine Greer (1970), romantic love, originating in the idle adulterous fantasies of the nobility, replaced paternal coercion when the Protestant middle classes started abandoning arranged marriages in favour of free and equal unions; in that sense romantic love was a prelude to the 'establishment marriages' of modern times. Juliet Mitchell (1984) changed the territory of these polemics, observing that at the end of the sixteenth and beginning of the seventeenth century woman became the object of the romantic tale, while previously the subject of passion was man. Romance shifted from being about a sexual subject – male – to being about a woman, considered the object of love and sex. In the course of this process, romantic love shifted from oppositional, adulterous love in the Middle Ages to being part of a conformist marital love in modern times and to the massification of culture represented by popular fiction and television culture. However, these feminist scholars did not challenge the Eurocentric paradigm of courtly and romantic love: the male subject was implicitly European or Western. No explicit criticism followed that line of inquiry until the 1990s, when the question of European identity from a gender perspective began, finally, to be posed (Braidotti 1995; Passerini 2000).

References

Arendt, Hannah (1958) *The Human Condition*. Chicago: University of Chicago Press.

Barthes, R. (1979) *A Lover's Discourse: Fragments*. London: Cape.

Braidotti, R. (1995) *Soggetto nomade*. Rome: Donzelli.

Bataille, Georges (1962) *Eroticism*, trans. Mary Dalwood. London: Marion Boyars.

Benhabib, S. and D. Cornell, eds (1987) *Feminism as Critique: On the Politics of Gender*. Minneapolis: University of Minnesota Press.

Cavarero, A.(1990) *Nonostante Platone*. Roma: Editori Riuniti.

Coole, D. (1993) *Women in Political Theory*. Hemel Hempstead: Harvester Wheatsheaf.

Elias, N. (1978) *The Civilizing Process*, vol. 1, *The History of Manners*. Oxford: Blackwell.

Elshtain, J.B. (1981) *Public Man, Private Woman*. Princeton, NJ: Princeton University Press.

Firestone, S. (1970) *The Dialectics of Sex: The Case for Feminist Revolution*. New York: Morrow.

Fusini, N. (1995) *Uomini e donne. Una fratellanza inquieta*. Rome: Donzelli.

Giddens, A. (1992) *The Transformation of Intimacy*. Cambridge: Polity Press.

Gilligan, Carol (1982) *In a Different Voice: Psychological Theory and Women's Development*. Cambridge, MA: Harvard University Press.

Greer, G. (1970) *The Female Eunuch*. London: McGibbon & Kee.

Harding, M.E. (1933) *The Way of All Women*. New York: Longman.

Heller, Agnes (1979) *A Theory of Feelings*. Assen: Van Gorcum,

Hirschmann, U. (1995) *Noi senza patria*. Bologna: Il Mulino.

Irigaray, L. (1985) *Speculum of the Other Woman*, trans. Gillian Gill. Ithaca: Cornell University Press.

Jameson, M. Storm, ed. (1934) *Challenge to Death*. London: Constable.

Jameson, M. Storm (1991) 'Federalism and a New Europe', in Melville Chaning-Pearce, ed., *Federal Union: A Symposium*. London: Lothian Foundation Press.

Mitchell, J. (1984) *Women: The Longest Revolution. Essays on Feminism, Literature and Psychoanalysis*. London: Virago.

Okin, S.M. (1979) *Women in Western Political Thought*. Princeton: Princeton University Press.

Passerini, L. (1998) 'Love and Europe: Cultural Trends in the 1930s', in H. Petersen, ed., *Love and Law in Europe*. Dartmouth: Ashgate.

Passerini, L. (1999) *Europe in Love, Love in Europe: Imagination and Politics in Britain Between the Wars*. London: I.B. Tauris.

Passerini, L. (2000) 'The Last Identification: Why Some of Us would Like to Call Ourselves Europeans and What We Mean by This', in B. Strath, ed., *Europe and the Other and Europe as the Other*. Brussels: Presse Interuniversitaire Européenne/Peter Lang.

Pateman, C. (1988) *The Sexual Contract*. Cambridge: Polity Press.

Pulcini, E. (1994) 'Le pouvoir féminin entre mythe et modernité', in E. Vogel-Polski, ed., *Manuel de Ressources*. Brussels: Services Fédéraux des Affaires Scientifiques, Techniques et culturelles.

Pulcini, E. (1998) *Amour passion et amour conjugal. Rousseau et l'origine d'un conflit moderne.* Paris: Champion-Slatkine.

Pulcini, E. (2000) *Modernity, Love and Hidden Inequality*, EUI Working Papers No. 2. Florence: European University Institute, Badia Fiesolana.

Rieger, A. (1991) *Trobairitz: Der Beitrag der Frau in der altokzitanischen hoefischen Lyrik.* Tübingen: Niemeyer, Edition des Gesamtkorpus.

de Rougemont, D. (1939) *L'Amour et l'occident.* Paris: Plon.

Rousseau, Jean-Jacques (1997) *Julie, or the New Heloise.* Hanover and London: University Press of New England.

de Staël, G. (1820) *De l'Allemagne et des moeurs des Allemands.* In *Oeuvres complètes*, vol. X–XI. Paris: Treuttel et Wuertz.

Taylor, Charles (1989) *Sources of the Self: The Making of the Modern Identity.* Cambridge, MA: Harvard University Press.

Vegetti Finzi, S. ed. (1992) *Psicoanalisi al femminile.* Bari: Laterza.

Weil, S. (1960) *En quoi consiste l'inspiration occitanienne?* and *L'agonie d'une civilisation à travers un poème épique*, in *Écrits historiques et politiques.* Paris: Gallimard.

6

Psychoanalysis and Feminism: A European Phenomenon and Its Specificities

MARIA SERENA SAPEGNO

It was between France and Italy, around the fatal year of 1968, and of course within the political movements born at that moment, that psychoanalysis and feminism met officially for the first time, that is to say on a 'mass/political base', notwithstanding previous individual encounters such as those on Freud's couch (Appignanesi and Forrester 1992). The practice of 'consciousness raising' in small groups, of North American origins, expanded rapidly in a political and cultural territory largely influenced by Lacan (see Lacan 1966, 1975; Roudinesco 1990), Sartre, Foucault and, through them, Freud and Marx. Groups of women increasingly left political meetings to meet regularly in private houses and talk about their specific experiences. It was a 'starting with oneself', sharing thoughts and feelings, a radical change in point of view to make true the notion that 'the personal is the political'.

The interest in psychoanalysis, which arose subsequent to a period in which traditional political and economic tools had been applied to 'woman's estate', derived directly from the need for appropriate means to deal with the main issue emerging from the new practice – that of sexuality, the female body, how to think it and give voice to it.

As early as 1970 in France a group of women, later calling themselves MLF (Mouvement de Libération des Femmes), otherwise known as 'Psych et Po',[1] staged a public event declaring the need for the most advanced contribution of contemporary thought and stressing the importance of their theoretical work on Marx, Freud and Lacan. They strongly asserted (through the voice of the dominant figure, the psychoanalyst Antoinette Fouque) the specificity of the sexual contradiction, which was to be analysed in psychoanalytical terms – psychoanalysis being 'the only existing discourse on sexuality' – and their determination to put to the test the Lacanian concept of the Symbolic in the new political practice of a mass movement.

In 1971 in Italy *La donna clitoridea e la donna vaginale* (Lonzi 1971) challenged the psychoanalytical definition of woman's sexuality, not just inasmuch as Freud would describe the little girl as a boy with a minuscule penis (clitoris) and with an envy of the proper one, but also in in terms of Reich's radical ideas of repression and sexual liberation, seen as nothing else than a more sophisticated version of the same cancellation of woman's own sexuality. The stress both on the centrality of sexuality and pleasure, and on the cultural foundations of gender roles, is the obvious sign of an interlocution with psychoanalytic discourse and a keen sense of the disappointing contribution of women psychoanalysts to that discourse.[2]

It was certainly within French and Italian feminism, or within certain currents thereof, that the use of psychoanalysis as the fundamental intellectual structure of a political practice took place, to leave persistent and significant traces in women's thought for years to come. Some documents published in Italy in the early 1970s (*Sottosopra* 1973–76), suggest that the practice of 'consciousness raising' spread widely across the movement; yet an interest in psychoanalysis and the beginning of new political practices more concerned with criticism and the use of it influenced large sections of the women's groups in important cities such as Turin, Milan and Rome. The new 'pratica dell'inconscio' (practice of the unconscious) referred explicitly to psycho-analysis and used it, on a *political and a non-professional* level, to explore and analyse the discourses within women's groups, the relations among women, conflicts and bonds. The 'psychoanalysis' referred to was a vast and not very defined body of knowledge, in particular some of Freud's writing on women and sexuality, but also some echoes of Lacan's rereading of Freud, more a political than an academic appropriation. In some cases the connection with the particular experience of Psych et Po was direct and explicit. Several other groups focused on the use of psychoanalysis to further their understanding of women's relationships to each other, starting with those within the group itself.

The cultural interest in psychoanalysis, shifting towards the political, acquired a special character through the 'experimental' use of its categories, the need to adapt them as specific tools to answer crucial questions about the nature of femininity and female sexuality; unconscious relations with the father and the mother; motherhood and womanhood. Consequently the political focus of these groups of feminists became more and more the question of what is involved in being born and brought up 'as a woman by a woman', in a literal as well as a deeply symbolic sense, where the stress was both on the new notion of a sexed subject and on the founding importance of the mother–daughter relationship. Somewhat less importance was given to 'becoming a woman' as a social construct, a broader and more sociological concept.

It was the influence of the Lacanian interpretation of Freud on the increasing importance of the 'symbolic' over the 'material' that shaped and characterized the shift from the centrality of sexuality to that of the symbolic order and particularly the unanalysed (and altogether ignored) relationship between daughter and mother that was emerging as the dominant feature in women's group dynamics.[3] The focus on the pre-Oedipal phase enabled the revalorization of that relationship; analysing cultural archetypes provided new insights and suggestions; the attempt to construct a maternal genealogy undermined given interpretations of the symbolic order and posed fundamental questions about the formation of the female ego.

This was how, in the early 1970s, a generation of women whose political culture was mainly based on leftist politics discovered, through new political practices, the need to deal with the unconscious. The year 1974 was an epoch-making one in Europe in terms of new publications on the connection between feminism and psychoanalysis: Juliet Mitchell, Julia Kristeva and Luce Irigaray, three influential female figures, practising psychoanalysts, attempted in different ways to build a bridge between psychoanalytical knowledge and the new fundamental questions posed by the women's movement (Mitchell 1974; Kristeva 1974; Irigaray 1974).

In the introduction to her important *Psycholanalysis and Feminism* Juliet Mitchell declared her wish 'to prove that the rejection of psychoanalysis and of Freud's work is fatal to feminism', and that it would also be dangerous to take the short-cut represented by Reich's or Laing's work on sexuality and the family. Large sections of her book are given over to a discussion of the prejudices that she identifies behind the violent rejection of Freud in the United States, and the hostility to his work in the European Marxist left, by giving them an historical context. She also acknowledges the existence of groups within the women's movement that actually had been involved for some time in an attempt to transform psychoanalytic theory into a political practice, trying to raise both the general problems of patriarchal ideology and the more specific questions of women's psychology. What Mitchell attempted to do in her book was to argue for what she saw as positive in the historical phenomenon of 'psychoanalytical feminism': from the Lacanian rereading of Freud to the attempt to reconcile it with Marxist theories of society, from the opposition to American radicalism (and Reich, Laing) to the accent on theory. She was more diffident about political practice as such, which is crucially important if theory, together with the impact of the analysis of sexuality, is to become a creative if critical interpretation and modification of psychoanalysis.

Kristeva's work was also very influential in the feminist debate of the 1970s, despite her defining herself as 'not feminist', or, rather, despite her challenge to the very definition of woman: 'To believe that one "is a woman" is almost as absurd and obscurantist as to believe that one "is a man".... I therefore understand by "woman" that which cannot be represented, that which is not spoken, that which remains outside naming and ideologies.' Her approach was also based on a particular interpretation of Lacan: a rejection of any understanding of the pre-Oedipal mother as a feminine entity, seeing her, rather, as a figure that includes both feminine and masculine, and therefore places the relevance of the question of sexual difference at the point of entry into the symbolic order. It is only then that the little girl is given the choice between mother-identification, with consequent marginalization in the symbolic order, and father-identification, which will enable her to construct an identity within the symbolic order. 'Femininity', then, does not coincide with historical women (*woman as such* does not exist') but, rather, is a 'position', 'that which is marginalized by the patriarchal symbolic order', in short a patriarchal construct. But it also constitutes the possibility of the latter's subversion by the very nature of its being out of it. The accent on *power* relationships as the underlying structure, both in the use of language and in the social signification of gender roles, makes this interpretation quite popular, particularly among those women most eager to define themselves as anti-essentialist. But at the same time the splitting between 'feminine' and 'woman' poses obvious political problems.

Irigaray's *Speculum* is certainly the most controversial and radical discussion of Freud's understanding of femininity. Irigaray analyses femininity in a close reading of the texts dedicated to the subject, starting with Freud's famous lecture on the mystery of femininity, where he declares it to have always been a problem for men. Neither anatomy nor psychology can solve it. According to Irigaray, Freud therefore resorts to metaphors that privilege the visibility of difference and the actual construction of a female image by comparison with the non-mysterious identity, the male one, the visibly sexed one: she is the *lacking* one, the object of enquiry for its subject, the negative image that allows the positive to be seen. The 'speculum' of the title, then, is both an instrument to open up and investigate woman's non-visible internal sexual organs and the mirror she becomes to allow the male subject to speculate and reflect on himself. Analysing, first, Freud's earnest attempt to come to terms with his failure to understand the 'dark continent', Irigaray demonstrates that what is missing is *nothing less than a representation of femininity*; patriarchal discourse, including Freud's, places woman outside representation. She then proceeds with a deconstructive analysis of Western philosophy (from Plato to Hegel), stressing the depth of the ancient roots of this 'old dream of symmetry', and showing the 'projective' nature of 'binary thought' that condemns woman to be the other, matter, darkness, object, silence.

One of the important aspects of this work is precisely the connection established between psychoanalytic discourse and philosophy, proving that what is revealed through Freud's failure is also a philosophical lack in the constitution of the subject in Western tradition. Accordingly, what Irigaray begins to do, at the same time as she denounces it, is to propose a representation of the female subject based on her being *different* and not just complementary; this she does by using psychoanalytical instruments to try and constitute a symbolic self-representation, based on the feminine body and its metaphors, to mimic and exceed the dominant language, turning it inside out to liberate a female immaginary and subjectivity.

The same inquiry is carried on in *Ce sexe qui n'en est pas un* (1977) a collection of short articles in which Irigaray tries to deal with some of the criticism of the obscurity of her language as she poses the fundamental question of the representation of a sex that is not one but many – many erogenous zones, many women. She is still trying to invent a language for it, to find the questions to ask, to choose a strategy through the institutions, to disturb the dominant discourse. Strictly dependent on this approach is, of course, the valorization of the mother–daughter relationship as the founding site for feminine identity (= representation). To remove the symbolic cancellation of this original bond, to 'go back there' to express and symbolize the deep conflict and passion involved in it, is also the first step to practising new forms of relationships between women and to challenging the traditional psychoanalytical interpretation under the sign of Oedipus.

The impact of Irigaray's provocative argument was powerful and her expulsion from Lacan's *École freudienne* contributed to it. In France and in Italy (where her works were immediately translated) her influence was at the time relevant both in certain areas within the movement, where the critical use of psychoanalysis was already common practice, and beyond. It was precisely around crucial problems pointed out by Irigaray that the deep crisis of the political practice of many groups revolved: the role of the mother-figure in the search for identity was a decisive issue in many discussions about relationships within the collectives.

Elsewhere, in Britain and in Northern Europe, where Irigaray was not translated for quite a while (and even then only in part; for *Speculum* and *Ce sexe* took ten years), the impact of her work was much less pronounced and only touched a limited part of the movement, which hastily branded her position as *essentialist*. This is one of the origins of the distinction between Anglo-American feminism (which includes part of Northern Europe) and continental feminism that has become an asset in the understanding of feminist theories and politics.[4]

At the same time psychoanalysis itself, due to the ordeal by fire through the new practices, did not emerge unscathed, revealing its age as well as some fundamental flaws and contradictions. While Freud's theoretical works were sometimes rejected and often bitterly criticized on certain very sensitive issues – such as 'penis envy' and the construction of a woman's identity on the basis of mortification and hence the repudiation of her mother, her clitoris and often her sexuality as a whole – his clinical cases were, on the contrary, read with a new interest. Of these, perhaps the most discussed case was that of Dora (Melandri 1974; Cixous 1976; Rose 1978).

The story of Dora's therapy, in Freud's words, attracted much attention from early on for a variety of reasons, not least the quality of Freud's writing and mode of thinking. The writings allow the reader to examine Freud's notes and considerations and form an opinion largely independent of Freud's own, which is exactly what happened. Dora was the first woman to teach Freud in the 'talking cure': while he struggled to decipher the symptoms through which her hysterical body spoke, she talked, telling him her dreams, and stubbornly resisted his interpretations, until the moment when she walked out on him. In his afterthoughts Freud admitted the limitations of his interpretation and considered the possibility of having overlooked Dora's strong homosexual drives.

In an article of 1974, contemporary with the prodigious growth of interest in psychoanalysis within the women's movement, Melandri notes that the case of Dora is where the interpretation based on the Oedipus complex starts to crack, and indeed is unmasked or turned upside down, indicating to Freud, who could not read it, the central role of the mother as a permanent rather than temporary love object. The crucial proposition then immediately becomes political: is the compulsory shift from the mother to the father (as the main love object) what really lies behind that eloquent silence of women's bodies that is called frigidity?

Cixous is also struck by the power of love for women in Dora, 'who could not bear family and society to be founded upon the cancellation of women's bodies, upon despised, rejected, humiliated bodies'. She redefines the hysterical woman as the prototype of woman's strength, of woman's *desire*, and not just somebody whose body speaks.

When Jacqueline Rose intervened in 1978 again in Dora's case, she referred explicitly to the meaning of reopening it, after so much had happened and to

> an urgency ... that of the present dialogue between psychoanalysis and feminism ... which constantly slides away from the point of a possible encounter; psychoanalysis attempting to delimit ... femininity ... within a theory of sexuality which constantly places and displaces the concept of sexual difference, feminism starting precisely from that difference which it then addresses to psychoanalysis as a demand, the demand for a theory of its construction. (Rose 1978)

Rose is concerned here mainly with the relevance, for contemporary feminists, of the various political interpretations of Dora's case inasmuch as they help clarify some of the fundamental issues relating to the general problem of the feminine within psychoanalysis. The central question is that of the pre-Oedipal attachment between mother and girl child. Rose claims that Kristeva and Irigaray place the maternal body outside of repression, as a site of resistance, with all the consequences for their concepts of woman's sexuality and language. Criticizing both the idea of 'an unmediated relation between body and language' and the concept of the 'feminine as outside discourse', Rose's argument concludes with the problem of *representation* – woman as representation; following Lacan she focuses the issue of the feminine on the *question* of desire.

Rose's article, which appeared in the British feminist journal *m/f*, was published in the midst of a lengthy and lively international debate that took place in the European women's movement around what came to be defined as the 'theory of sexual difference'.[5] The journal *m/f* represented a specific viewpoint in this context (largely orthodox Lacanian). Its hostility to a given sexual difference was based on the notion that it was a 'wrong' interpretation of the alliance between psychoanalytical thought and feminism[6] – rather than, as was the case for a large number of women in Britain and in Northern Europe, a more general rejection of psychoanalysis as such. The fundamental preoccupation for this position was to affirm the 'constructed' nature of sexual difference, as opposed to any 'pre-given unity of women', a notion which henceforth was branded with the derogatory term 'essentialism'. The term became widely used, and has often been the source of deep confusion and ambiguity. Generally it is used to attack the emphasis placed on the bodily self, a concept that offers no liberating potential for women.[7]

It was in the 1980s that the differences among interpretations and uses of psychoanalytical categories, along with other political disjunctions, manifested themselves more clearly in various new political practices and in new theories. But it was largely due to the importance attributed to *representation* or to the lack of it, as well to the theoretical relevance of the Lacanian version of Freudianism, with its insistence on language, both in negative and in positive terms (within the general context of poststructuralism), that attention and work were dedicated to linguistics and semiotics. Indeed, in the 1970s *l'écriture féminine* was considered the privileged site of the conjunction of 'text, philosophy and body' (Cixous, but also Kristeva), a site where the feminine subject can finally represent itself, forcing the structures of language to express the inexpressible.

In the same conceptual area, Luisa Muraro's *Maglia o uncinetto* (Muraro 1981), using Lacan to analyse the main figures of speech and signification in their connection to or disconnection from the body, takes particular issue with Kristeva's conception of the constitution of the speaking subject and argues in favour of a deconstruction of language to reveal what implications it has for the body. There is an affinity here to parts of Irigaray's *Ethique de la différence sexuelle* (1984) and *Parler n'est jamais neutre* (1985), when Muraro states that sexual difference is probably 'the imperative problem for our time to think about', and proceeds to reread some philosophical texts in order to redefine, from this particular angle, the fundamental categories of a new epoch: space/time, dwelling places, container and contents of identity. The extenuation of the philosophical categories and concepts of passion is meant to reveal the negation of woman in order to signify the male subject as neutral and universal, the positioning of the female body outside of symbolic representation, but not outside of language, where the traces of it are to be discovered. In the 1980s, thanks mostly to the focus on *representation* as a central issue and partly due to Irigaray's influence, a very important bridge was constructed between psychoanalysis and philosophy, stressing the need to research the very foundations of the feminine process of identity in the misty and ambivalent ground between the unconscious and the epistemological, both for the individual woman and for the social understanding of her. This was quite distinct from the *sex/gender* opposition popular in the Anglo-American intellectual arena.

By the mid-1980s some sexual difference theory had become more widely known internationally – Irigaray through translation, Cixous through her playwriting for the theatre. This resulted in a belated response, mostly among academics. Toril Moi's successful book *Sexual/Textual Politics: Feminist Literary Theory* (1985) is a very good example of the mixed reception of this current of political thought in the so-called Anglo-American arena. A Norwegian, at the time teaching French in England, Moi stresses in her very title the importance of a political reading of texts, and also the disciplinary, academic point of view. Interesting, clear and full of theoretical passion, the book is divided into two parts, one dedicated to Anglo-American feminist criticism and the second, clearly the new and challenging part, to French feminist theory. While Kristeva is warmly accepted by virtue of her denial of the existence of men and women as such, in favour of viewing them only as patriarchal constructs, both Cixous and Irigaray are considered irredeemably 'essentialist'. Although Moi accepts, along with the use of Lacanian psychoanalysis, the possibility that 'One way of disrupting patriarchal logic in this way is through mimeticism, or the mimicry of male discourse', she strongly rejects Irigaray's work on the symbolic starting from the representation of woman's body, and warns her that women's oppression is not just a matter of philosophy.

This is an old warning. It confirms that some divisions are deeply rooted and reveal an important *différence* to be taken into account. Feminism based on psychoanalysis has often meant a stress on the relationship between women (including the idea of 'a common world of women') a symbolic investment in women; an attribution of value to the mother, to a feminine authority; the construction of a tradition, of a feminine *genealogy*; and consequently a rejection of emancipation inasmuch as it confirms the patriarchal symbolic order. This, it is contended, has meant that it has often been necessary to consider irrelevant the general state of things material and social conditions, with a loss in political perspective, and also that ambivalences and contradictions among women or towards motherhood, or the reality of bodies and sexuality, have been left 'out of the field of vision'. On the other hand, it has been remarked that to stress too much the constructed nature of 'woman' leads to the loss of the political subject and to the removal of the bodily foundation of feminine identity. In the end it leaves ideology as the only ground upon which to operate.

These differences and oppositions are, of course, present throughout the women's movement and represent the coexistence of various political and philosophical traditions in Western culture. At the same time, it is certainly possible to draw a few general lines cutting across the entire range of opinions, lines that may help to make manifest some great original divisions that constitute the fundamental points of departure. In the Anglo-American world the rejection of psychoanalysis and the stress on individual rights set the feminist agenda in terms of political actions directed towards self-determination and strong individual and social identities; the focus was on oppression and how to fight it through social reform and the building of independent social spaces. In continental Europe, however, where the philosophical tradition met up with the psychoanalytical one, the road was open to a politics of the unconscious and to theories of the subject, the focus being on desire, on the text and on the overwhelming power of the symbolic. This is what could be read behind the simplistic opposition *theory of sexual difference/essentialism.*

Towards the end of the 1980s, though, it became clear that this specific form of the opposition was part of a more general situation of stagnation, due in part to confusion and misunderstanding based often on stereotypical images. *Between Feminism and Psychoanalysis* (Brennan 1989) is a collection of essays based on a series of Cambridge seminars, written by academic women teaching in Britain or in the United States (with the exception of Irigaray and Braidotti) and concentrating on four main issues: 'the status of the Lacanian "symbolic", sexual difference and knowledge, the bearing of essentialism on feminist politics, and the relation between psychical reality and the social.' Many of the issues previously touched upon are discussed here, this time on what may be described as more favourable ground; the volume breaks the impasse that editor Teresa Brennan acutely describes as deriving from the neglect of 'the tension between psychical and social realities'. In her introduction she points to some crucial problems that need to be clarified. These include the Lacanian position (held by Mitchell and Kristeva) on the necessity of a symbolic order outside of which there can be no sanity, where the possibility of 'a symbolic that is not patriarchal' is completeley discounted (Irigaray's main concern).[8] Another question Brennan raises is why Lacanian non-essentialism – Lacan's non-biological but also non-historical theory of femininity, whose 'relation to change was unpromising' – had been enthusiastically adopted by Marxist/feminist writers. She adds that the same debate is also 'partaking of the broad Derridean critique of metaphysics' and asserts the necessity of this 'knowledge issue' and the reformulation of the terms of sexual difference being brought together.

What is most interesting about this introduction, affording us a stimulating perspective through which to read the book, is precisely the idea of 'change' to which it aspires: 'a rethinking of fixed associations'. The argument leaves behind the old opposition between transformation in a political and social context, and a withdrawal into psychological issues and dynamics. It is the very fixity of such oppositions or associations, even, paradoxically, certain reassuring assumptions about being a feminist, that can become a prejudice so deeply rooted in the unconscious as to undermine any possibility of thinking through conceptual impasses: 'When ideas are fixed side by side, as they are when the words "essentialist, against the symbolic" are run together, their fixity makes it difficult to divorce questions about the symbolic or essentialism from the associations they have accrued' (Brennan 1989: 12). Thus the process of change, which concerns *indissolubly* the social and the psychical, implies a complex work of 'tracing and retracing contexts', a reconsideration of relations such as that between Lacanian psychoanalysis and feminism, a questioning of what has been fixed and what cancelled, as is the case for some 'wishes worth having' that have disappeared: 'the wish to know femininity, or the wish to understand what the lived experience of sexuality is about' (Brennan 1989: 13).

Among the other contributions to *Between Feminism and Psychoanalysis*, Braidotti's essay on 'The Politics of Ontological Difference' is a rich and well-argued political essay challenging 'the view that the essentialist feminist position is apolitical or even potentially reactionary'.[9] According to Braidotti, reconnecting 'the feminine to the bodily sexed reality of the female, refusing the separation of the empirical from the symbolic', is 'the epistemological basis for feminist theory and the grounds of political legitimations for feminist politics'. In analysing in detail the most important points that feminism and psychoanalysis have in common ('They both posit as a central axiom the non-coincidence of anatomical differences with the psychic representations of sexual difference') and the most relevant differences, such as 'the definition of change and how to go about achieving it' and 'the sexualization of the other, and of the subject', a particular stress is placed on the relevance of Irigaray's insistence on the necessity of working on the symbolic. It is through this complex process of claiming one's sexual difference as 'a fact' and 'also as a *sign* of a long history' that 'the *feminine* would cease to be the effect of male fantasies', and become what '"I, woman" invent, enact and empower in "our" speech, our practice, our collective quest for a redefinition of the status of all women.'

This last factor, the political reality of a mass movement as the indispensable subject for innovation, does not resound as strongly in most of the other contributions; nevertheless, what makes this book an intriguing read in general is the insight it gives into a new territory of research, an area as well connected to feminist thought as to psychoanalytical knowledge, and apparently not definable in the usual geopolitical terms. There has been a good deal of analysis, and both psychoanalysis and feminism have changed, though along different paths. Literary criticism has been a privileged ground for many, postmodern philosophy for some, psychoanalysis itself for others. Most of these writers belong to academic feminism, one of the characteristics of the so-called Anglo-American arena, as opposed to that of continental Europe, where feminist political practice has occurred almost exclusively outside of the institutions. Psychoanalysis as a theoretical framework had an early impact on continental Europe and coincided with the time of the women's movement. Irigaray was part of this phenomenon; indeed, quite a few women analysts were directly involved in feminist politics, and many more were touched indirectly through the large number of women from the movement who looked for a deeper understanding in personal therapy, not unusually becoming analysts themselves.

In the 1990s some of this work emerged, particularly in Italy, both in books written by analysts who developed their original research on the basis of their feminist experience, and through writings by individuals and groups of women who have accepted in full measure the inheritance of Irigaray's unique combination of philosophical and psychoanalytical thought, and have gone on to produce their own. Silvia Vegetti Finzi's *Il bambino della notte* of 1990 belongs in the first category. Her book explores 'maternal competence' as such (quite independently from filiation), as well as its communicational and ethical potentialities. These are illustrated through the girl-child imaginary and the mother–daughter bond, down to the symbolic forms at the roots of our civilizations, using clinical cases, and literary and mythological sources. The result is a psychoanalytical model that opens up to desires and fantasies about 'the feminine' that have hitherto been inexpressible. It reveals the impact of feminist politics on the search for new symbolic forms, for changes that have already taken place.

Furthermore, as editor of the collection *Psicoanalisi al femminile* (1992) Vegetti Finzi argues that a feminine genealogy is needed for psychoanalysis, because it has a feminine tradition with specific and important contributions, as is shown in the papers by women analysts on women analysts. She also points out that the talking therapy itself has changed through time 'from a paternal normative position to a maternal containitive one'. Situating this historical work in the context of wider research, Vegetti claims that women's contribution to analytical thought constitutes in fact 'one of the most articulate representations of femininity that Western civilization has ever produced', and that the knowledge of the unconscious can be used outside the coordinates of male culture (forcing the symbolic order).

In France the impact of the political use of psychoanalysis on its theory has been somehow more violent because of the split between Lacanians like Fouque and critical post-Lacanians like Irigaray. In 1995 Antoinette Fouque collected some of her writings and interviews in a book, *Les sexes sont deux*, polemically stressing the continuity of their research on psychoanalysis, criticizing Lacanian women analysts who still accept the existence of one libido only, the phallic one, and posing the question of a democratization of psychoanalysis. Bitterly critical of feminism as a 'phallic movement', Fouque valorizes the investment in the mother figure and insists on a 'homosexual feminine libidinal economy'.

Linked directly to Irigaray's thought and to the theory of sexual difference, and based also on a constant dialogue with her, are the various books published by Diotima (a group of women involved in long-running political/ philosophical research) and by some of the women belonging to it, particularly the dominant figure of Luisa Muraro. Her book *L'ordine simbolico della madre* (Muraro 1991) explicitly acknowledging the collective work behind it, claims the mother–daughter relationship to be the new epistemological paradigm to work upon. Discussing Kristeva's theory of the entry into the symbolic order through a *cut* from the semiotic phase of symbiotic relation to the mother, she argues that this phase is the period in which we also learn 'language' from our mother and start that *negotiation* with her upon which our symbolic independence will depend. Along with Irigaray, then, Moraro claims the importance of a new symbolic order (something of which can be experienced in the new political relationships among women) based not on a symbiotic undifferentiated relationship to the mother, but on a process of differentiation from her without denial.[10]

This shift is also the theme of a series of seminars published by Diotima in 1992: *Il cielo stellato dentro di noi. L'ordine simbolico della madre*, where the papers deal with various disciplines questioning the given symbolic order and exploring the possibility of a new one, of a new organizing authority, of a new epistemological process. A second book published by the same collective author in 1996, *La sapienza di partire da sé*, concentrates on this last theme: revolutionary feminist practice posits the subjectivity, the sexed one, as the necessary 'situation' of any process of knowledge.

The originality and creativity of the relation between psychoanalysis and feminism in Europe appear to have been strictly dependent on maintaining the original connection to the women's movement, never really becoming the enterprise of a single person. On the other hand, this very characteristic is probably behind some of its limitations, accounting for ideological rigidities and for the tendency to use labels, preventing the debate from going deeper by engaging a more interesting diversity of opinion and experience.

Notes

1. *Psychanalyse et Politics*. Analysing the different currents in the French women's movement, Claire Duchen describes the acute contradictions deriving from the 1979 decision: 'At first, *Psych et Po* was accepted as one group among many, ... in a movement which valued its diversity and multiplicity of approach.... By the end of the decade, however, actions taken by *Psych et Po* meant that there were two MLFs in France that would have nothing to do with each other. In 1979, *Psych et Po* registered the name *Mouvement de Libération des Femmes* as their own property, their commercial title ... all in all feminism = MLF = *Psych et Po* operates an unacceptable equation – particularly as *Psych et Po* call themselves anti-feminist' (Duchen 1995: 32–4).

2. Sayers (1991) and Vegetti Finzi (1992) argue the opposite.

3. Adrienne Rich was the first to give witness to this immensely significant change of perspective: *Of Woman Born* (1976) explores the relationship and the effects of it.

4. Chanter (1995) discusses the opposition, giving it depth within the context of the different philosophical traditions, and argues against the essentialist misreadings of Irigaray.

5. The definition is the beginning of a long *querelle* and of an oppositional interpretation. 'The French feminists are more convinced than their American counterparts of the difference between male and female; they are more imbued with the

notions of sexual specificity' (Marks and de Courtivron 1985: 36).

6. 'What is important is to consider how specific practices have produced sexual difference ... psychoanalysis has shown that the body has no language of its own ... it is concerned with the production of the feminine (and the masculine) through the discourse of the unconscious' (*m/f* 2, 1978: 2).

7. Cf. Braidotti (1992). An interesting analysis of the debate can be found in Fuss 1989.

8. 'She is also intervening qua analyst in a psychoanalytic debate over the symbolic, addressing the specific problem of psychical organization, of sanity' (Brennan 1989: 5).

9. Braidotti comes back to most of these problems in her important *Patterns of Dissonance* (1991), where in a general recontextualization of feminist thought within contemporary philosophy she analyses in detail most of the contributions referred to here and gives an informed and balanced political consideration of their role.

10. There are points in common here with some of the positions of German-American Jessica Benjamin (1988).

References

Alcune femministe milanesi (1974–75) 'Pratica dell'inconscio e movimento delle donne', *L'erba voglio* 5, 18–19.
Appignanesi, L. and J. Forrester (1992), *Freud's Women*. London: Weidenfeld & Nicholson.
Benjamin, J. (1988) *The Bonds of Love*. New York: Pantheon.
Braidotti, R. (1991) *Patterns of Dissonance*. Cambridge: Polity Press.
Braidotti, R. (1992), 'Essentialism', in E. Wright, ed., *Feminism and Psychoanalysis: A Critical Dictionary*. Oxford: Blackwell.
Brennan, T., ed. (1989) *Between Feminism and Psychoanalysis*. London: Routledge.
Cixous, H. (1976) *Portrait de Dora*. Paris: des femmes.
Chanter, T. (1995) *Ethics of Eros*. London: Routledge.
Diotima (1996) *La sapienza di partire da sé*. Naples: Liguori.
Diotima (1987) *Il pensiero della differenza sessuale*. Milan: La Tartaruga.
Diotima (1992) *Il cielo stellato dentro di noi. L'ordine simbolico della madre*. Milan: La Tartaruga.
Duchen, C. (1985) *Feminism in France: From May '68 to Mitterrand*. London: Routledge & Kegan Paul.
Fouque, A. (1995) *Les sexes sont deux*. Paris: des femmes.
Fuss, D. (1989) *Essentially Speaking*. New York and London: Routledge.
Irigaray, L. (1974) *Speculum de l'autre femme*. Paris: Minuit; *Speculum of the Other Woman*, trans. Gillian Gill. Ithaca: Cornell University Press, 1985.
Irigaray, L. (1977) *Ce sexe qui n'en est pas un*. Paris: Minuit; *This Sex Which Is Not One*, trans. Catherine Porter. Ithaca: Cornell University Press, 1985.
Irigaray, L. (1984) *Ethique de la différence sexuelle*. Paris: Minuit.
Kristeva, J. (1974) *Des Chinoises*. Paris: des femmes.
Libreria delle donne di Milano (1987) *Non credere di avere dei diritti*. Turin: Rosenberg & Sellier.
Lacan, J. (1966) *Ecrits*, 2 vols. Paris: Seuil.
Lacan, J. (1975) *Le Séminaire, livre XX, Encore*. Paris: Seuil.
Lonzi, C. (1971) *La donna clitoridea e la donna vaginale*. Milano: Rivolta Femminile.
Marks, E. and I. de Courtivron, eds (1985) *New French Feminisms: An Anthology*. Brighton: Harvester Press.
Melandri, L. (1974) 'Dora Freud e la violenza', in *L'erba voglio*, vol. 4, no. 16.
Mitchell, J. (1974) *Psychoanalysis and Feminism*. Harmondsworth: Penguin.

Muraro, L. (1981) *Maglia o uncinetto. Racconto linguistico-politico sulla inimicizia tra metafora e metonimia.* Milano: Feltrinelli.

Muraro, L. (1991) *L'ordine simbolico della madre.* Rome: Editori Riuniti.

Rich, A. (1976) *Of Woman Born: Motherhood as Experience and Institution.* New York: Norton.

Rose, J. (1978) '"Dora" Fragment of an Analysis', *m/f*, 2.

Roudinesco, E. (1990) *Jacques Lacan & Co.: A History of Psychoanalysis in France, 1925–1985.* Chicago: University of Chicago Press.

Sayers, J. (1991) *Mothering Psychoanalysis.* London: Hamish Hamilton.

Sottosopra (1973–76) 'Esperienze dei gruppi femministi in Italia', 1, 2, 3.

Sottosopra (1975) 'Sessualità, procreazione, maternità e aborto', fasc. spec. 'rosso'.

Vegetti Finzi, S. (1990) *Il bambino della notte.* Milan: Mondadori.

Vegetti Finzi S., ed. (1992) *Psicoanalisi al femminile.* Bari: Laterza.

Wright, E., ed. (1992) *Feminism and Psychoanalysis. A Critical Dictionary.* Oxford: Blackwell.

PART III

Identity, Subjectivity and Difference

7

Europe after 1989: Ethnic Wars, the Fascistization of Civil Society and Body Politics in Serbia

ZARANA PAPIC

This chapter deals with the specific area of representational practices in which the media production/appropriation of reality in Serbia played a decisive part in the process of the fascistization of social life and everyday practices in Serbia – before and during the wars in the former Yugoslavia. It analyses how chosen discourses of appropriation of social memory, collective trauma and the re-creation of enemy otherness in image and event can become an integral, 'self-participatory' agent in the pro-fascist construction of social reality through the very image/concept of 'reality' itself, which then becomes the lived experience of people exposed to the constant working of the image/concept.

The power over the representation of social reality can be seen as the strongest discursive instrument of a political order. Its power lies in the position of the selective legitimization/delegitimization of social memory and social 'presence': through the narration/negation of social trauma, the shiftable presence/absence of violence, the constitution/virtuality of the public sphere, and the formation of a 'collective consciousness'. The legitimizing power of this dominant discourse lies in the construction of a collective consensus as a cultural/political code of language.

The process of social and political transformation in Eastern and Central Europe since the fall of the Berlin Wall in 1989, labelled rather euphemistically 'transition', brought along with it the phenomenon of violence as an acute social and political problem, although its milder forms – both gender and ethnic – were present in all other countries of the Eastern bloc as well. The general persistence of such violence in post-communist regimes reveals its structural dependency, which allows the definition of the countries involved as societies of highly charged ethnic/racial, and sexual politics (Enloe 1993).

It would seem that in times of crisis and social transformation, the deconstruction of the previous gendered order is one of the most fundamental factors of change, and an effective instrument of the global restructuration of power. Since the most influential concept in post-communist state-building processes was that of the patriarchal nation-state, the ideology of state and ethnic nationalism (based on patriarchal principles) inevitably became the dominant building force. Various forms of hegemonistic nationalism, national separatism, chauvinist and racist exclusion or marginalization of (old and new) minority groups are, as a rule, closely connected with patriarchal, discriminatory and violent politics against women and their civil and social rights, previously 'guaranteed' under the old communist order (Papic 1994a).

The absence of women from politics in post-communist transitions reveals the damaging effects of the communist patriarchal legacy – which gave women legal rights (work, equal pay, education, divorce, abortion), but strategically prevented them from becoming active political subjects of their own destiny. The disappearance of a communist 'equality paradigm' and the rise of an old–new conservative ideology of state, nation or religion in each post-communist country was crucially based on the strategies of *retraditionalization, instrumentalization* and *naturalization* of women's identities, their social roles, and their symbolic representations.

The structural connection between ethnic and gender violence is most clearly seen in the case of former Yugoslavia. The genocidal brutality of the ethnic wars shows how ethnic hatreds have been provoked/produced in order to construct the new frontiers of enemy-otherness through the fluid and mixed lines of religion, culture, ethnicity and gender, thus reflecting the contemporary redefinition of racial hostility (Eisenstein 1996). Furthermore, ethnic nationalism, or, more precisely, *ethno-fascist nationalism*, is based on a specific gender identity/difference politics in which women are simultaneously mythologized as the nation's deepest 'essence', and instrumentalized in their 'natural' difference – as the nation's life/birth saver/producer. This means that the wars in the former Yugoslavia cannot be interpreted as a reflection of the tribal and 'eternal' barbarian mentality of its peoples, but must be seen as a contemporary phenomenon of violent, post-communist strategies of re-distribution of ethnic/gender power by defining new ethnic and sub-ethnic borders *between men*, and their respective (often militarized) elite structures (Papic 1994b).

In this context the nationalist abuse of women (Muel-Dreyfuss 1996) sheds light on the phenomenon of totalitarian ethnic nationhood as a naturalized fraternal order in which women are doubly subjugated:

1. As *insiders* they are colonized and instrumentalist in their 'natural' function as the nation's sacred 'essence' and as 'birth-machines'.
2. As *outsiders* they are reified into the target of destruction, as mediated instruments of violence against other men's national and cultural identity.

The abuse of women and their bodies in the 'pure' nation-building processes results in two interdependent forms of violence against women: highly restricted identity 'demands' (no abortion) for women insiders, and extreme violence (rape) against women outsiders.

The external destruction of a social/cultural identity system in war is the most brutal form of deconstruction, but life under the processes of malign internal mutations is, perhaps, equally disastrous because it systematically diminishes and humiliates the basic human values of decency, honesty, tolerance and individual morality; it even violates more basic assumptions, such as the concept of time (past, present and future), personal identity, or the simple Ten Commandments (love thy neighbour, thou shalt not kill, etc.). In Serbia one watched these values all disappear, only to be replaced by alien substitutes – which were taken for the 'real' thing.

Briefly, in former Yugoslavia four basic identity levels underwent extreme turmoil, under violent and (only seemingly) chaotic deconstruction/construction: self-identity, gender identity, civic/urban identity, and the identity of the other. In all four dimensions of public/private identity the following 'forces' were circularly and claustrophobically intertwined: nation, tradition and patriarchy. These forces were enacted through the following instruments or 'channels': closure, fear, exclusion, conflict, violence, revenge, extinction, displacement, disempowerment, brutality, insecurity, unpredictability, poverty.

In the case of Serbia, all four identity levels were in turmoil, not through any outside pressure, but as a result of the internal forces of nationalist and patriarchal 'aggression'. Although, on the surface, Milošević's regime continued to adhere to a strange mixture of nationalist and 'socialist' ideas and values, the decisive process is one of a peculiar retraditionalization – a tightly combined dynamics of fundamental civic disempowerment and state/nationalist/patriarchal authoritarianism which based its power on the revival/survival of the rural/feudal/collective identity that delegates/transfers a huge amount of power to the Leader – a title which (accidentally or not) in the ancient Serbian language actually has a triple meaning: the Duke/Master/Leader.

The feminist slogan 'the personal is political' became, in a development of the deepest irony, part of official, state-nationalist policy in Serbia. In Serbia's case, the axiom translates into: 'the personal *belongs* to state politics'. However, since politics in Serbia has always been identified with the national/ist cause, destiny and glory, a more precise translation might be 'the personal *is* national/ist'. In every nationalism, and particularly in that of an aggressive/ethno-fascist type, men are those who make the 'soul' and the 'engine' of the vision/interpretation of the exclusionary, war-oriented nation's 'essence'; women are systematically 'invisibilized' unless they become the much publicized victims of the enemy nation. This invisibility may appear advantageous, since at least women are not under constant pressure from nationalist slogans and advice on how to become 'real' Serbian women. But, in fact, women's 'non-presence' in the public sphere is itself the sign of a strong Serbian patriarchal culture and politics (Papic 1994b). They are not even to be talked about publicly – except in the 'natural' context of nationhood.

The nationalist revival of the patriarchal tradition post-1989 fashioned (combined with the communist patriarchal legacy) a 'new' Serbian nationalist patriarchy, very much marked by the features of Milošević's rule. One could even say that Serbian nationalist patriarchy is, to some extent, self-contradictory, since Milošević despotically subjugated *all* members of the 'female' nation. More precisely, from the beginning Milošević worked consistently to disempower all political institutions, and therefore (as shown below) all men except himself, to preclude any possibility of competition between equals.

On the other hand, the unstable social circumstances and extremely difficult living conditions in Serbia (Bolcic 1995) have activated an enormous commitment of energy by women into their mobilization for survival (Milic 1995), the hyperintensified expression of their subjugated empowerment in vital adaptation to the times of crisis, war and violence. By activating their 'natural' survival potential, women carried the heaviest burden of Serbia's social and economic crisis during the period of the UN sanctions, and therefore, willingly or not, actually played the part of Milošević's most faithful allies. The fact that his despotic charisma has been associated with certain types of women faithfully adoring him from the beginning might be read as follows: the majority of women in Serbia have, in fact, been seduced by One Man as despotic patriarch; therefore they complied with the expected, monumental epic Serbian women's destiny to be self-sacrificing mothers, dutiful daughters, unselfish mothers-in-law, open-hearted aunts, hard-working cousins, reliable neighbours, friends and supporters.

The civic void which was consistently filled with the disempowering hegemony of nationalist collective homogenization; the constant life-in-crisis conditions; the near-war situation; the economic, political and legal destruction of society in Serbia; the autocratic power structure of one man, which disempowered every other political institution and force; the mythologized total investment in Great History and Great Sacrifice – in Serbia all these resulted in a specific gender dynamics which cannot be seen as the one-dimensional oppression of women by men but as considerably more complex. This oppression has been contradictory and significantly different in its practices and discourses on the public and the private level. On the public level, both in practice and in the dominant nationalist discourse, women have been legally, economically and institutionally almost totally disempowered. But, contrary to what they might think and declare, neither have men been empowered fully on the public level. Only in the sphere of manifest *ideological* nationalist discourse have they been the dominant, ruling, militant and heroic actor-gender. For Milošević's despotic dissolution of the social/civic institutional/political fabric at the level of public practice rendered men almost as disempowered as women. They delegated and transferred all aspects of their own public power to the mysterious, unpredictable and uncontrolled power of One Man.

This structural emasculation of men's power in the public domain has made the gender power dynamics on the private level even less one-dimensional. Men's public disempowerment has made them privately power-less, more than ever before. The distribution of power on the private, every-day level has lost its traditional dichotomous character because men's power structure in everyday life has deteriorated, and almost all their means of private power over women have dissolved except within the dominant ideo-logical discourse. The increase in male violence against women is, of course, an alarming sign of how men are coping, or failing to cope, with this sudden and obviously unwanted gender egalitarianism. This gender-egalitarian soli-darity is, in fact, the result of another equality – the equality of living in a state of despotic powerlessness.

So, if we consider women's 'escape into privacy', a phenomenon visible in all other previously communist countries, in the case of Serbia their 'escape' is no escape at all, nor a nostalgic hankering after simply private rewards following on from an overly demanding prior socialist public existence. Women's case in Serbia is different. At a time of extreme existential insecurity they have been offered only one option: the traditional strategy of strength-ening by complying with the deepest, most 'natural' expectations of women – their self-identification with a re-traditionalized, basic patriarchal power structure. And as so many times before, women have taken what was, patheti-cally, offered to them – to 'save the nation' by ensuring their 'own' family survived. The private empowerment of women in this process has been, in itself, an extremely costly achievement; what is more, it has actually helped the survival of the despotic nationalist political system that caused and provoked the very crisis with which they have had to struggle.

Media-produced Reality and the Discourses of Appropriation: The Integrative Power of Fascism

Terror and repression in Serbia have been carefully planned, but they have never been systematically applied except to the media; this has left social areas in which oppositional activity simply has not been noticed by the regime. Wars in the former Yugoslavia were planned long before the first television pictures began to be broadcast in June 1991. Those pictures showed the realization of the hegemonistic Serb policy that had been articulated in the mid-1980s. It was obvious that the 'Yugoslav People's Army' would side with Milošević's genocidal ideology. Already in 1989, when Milošević went off to Gazimestan and there renewed the *Kosovo myth* and announced a 'possible war' before a million Serb men and women, war was presented to people in Serbia as 'the only option'. Like Hitler at a rally of SS units, Milošević descended from the heavens (sceptics would say landed in a helicopter) onto the holy ground of Gazimestan, in order to inform us that the time had come for new heroic battles – war.

That was a period of popular fascination with Milošević: he became a mega-phenomenon, his pictures everywhere. People became familiar with his image as the new Serb Icon. The people – the inhabitants, not necessarily Serbs – of Serbia indeed went through a phase of absolute fascination with the Leader, 'Slobo', and made possible the fascist homogenization of the collective. Everyone submitted to it: men and women, old and young, educated and uneducated. Women would repeat: 'He is so beautiful'.

Why did the majority of Serbian women side with Milošević? It is because they, too, embraced a schizophrenic role, involving an absolute separation of their private and public identities. They wished to be 'mothers of great warriors', they wished to sacrifice themselves – women readily internalize the position of victim. In patriarchal societies women are unable to imagine themselves outside this role of victim. What is more, many prominent 'democratic' members of the opposition gradually internalized some of the elements of fascism: the 'Serb holy nature' of certain territories, the heroic Kosovo past, the holy objects of the Church, the attitude of surprise as to 'why NATO is suddenly bombing us for *no reason at all*'. In other words, independent circles also lapsed into the Serbo-centric *narcissistic rhetoric* they learnt from the 'infallible' regime.

The reinvention of Serb patriarchal society was, therefore, developed at epic, political, literary, scientific, sentimental, Christian and pagan levels: people really believed that 'with Slobo' they would finally achieve a mythic, all-embracing, Serbian unity. What united the people was not so much a mythical vision of a future Serb Heaven, as the fact that this helped people confront the great issue of *fear* that had begun to take hold after 1989. Here was an almost perfect political instrumentalizaton of basic fears: the fall of the Berlin Wall, Yugoslavia's break-up, the 'void' heralded by the collapse of the hegemonistic Yugoslav nation. Milošević exploited this to the full. He sent a message to the men that they were to fight 'heroically' for the preservation of Yugoslavia, while women got the message to shut up.

The Fascist Appropriation of Social Memory, Collective Trauma and the Exclusion of Otherness

As an instrument of constructing and fuelling pre-war emotions that would finally lead to the fascist colonization of people's minds, much effort was expended to revive and evoke the Serb World War II trauma of 1941–45. Much was also done to revive the Orthodox faith among Serbs. The symbolic identification with wartime events was probably the most effective method of homogenization; this included continuous daily televisual representation of the exhumation of mass graves in Herzegovina. The intention was to encourage people once again to internalize the trauma of the Ustasha crimes. The exhumation of the bones was, in reality, preparation of the ground for new mass graves, which duly followed after 1991. Propaganda was being created that 'the Serbs are the biggest victims', who therefore have the 'right' of revenge and the 'right' to wage new wars and commit crimes. Karadzic, for example, stated that 'Serbs in Bosnia–Herzegovina have a right to preventive defence'. In other words, he amnestied *in advance* the crimes that were to come, by exploiting the traumas associated with the unearthed bones from 1941.

So there was a particular *peregrination of the trauma* (Papic 2000), just as there was a shift in time of national identity – back into the past – and a shift of responsibility for war crimes exclusively to the Croat Ustasha side, while Serb Chetniks' crimes were methodically set aside. Reality was divided schizophrenically into a virtual reality of the media and the ordinary reality of the war, with the media reality for many people becoming far stronger than anything they saw with their own eyes. This was all part of a *re-invention of the chosen trauma* at the level of *the public* political phenomenon and through state media: a carefully planned revision of the historical balance sheet. The media did a successful job in preparing people to accept war as a 'natural' and 'historic' series of events. The media consistently forged and reinforced Serb *indifference* towards the Other(s). The trauma became so internalized that Croatian and Bosnian victims could never reach the sacred status of the allegedly 'primeval', 'greatest' Serbian victims of 1941–42.

This process might even be decribed as a *fictionalization of the chosen trauma*. More than that, it was also, at the same time, a *displacement of the trauma* – *in time and in space*. This was a very sophisticated transfer of the local Bosnian-Herzegovinian drama of 1941–42 across the River Drina, to the population in Serbia, who *had never experienced* that trauma, and who were supposed to go through the 'reliving' of it in 1991.

Layers of Responsibility: Bones and Relics

The post-1989 revival of Orthodox Christianity was another aspect of these processes. The Serbian Orthodox Church once again started to teach people how to be 'good' Serb men or women. Thus it staged long Orthodox ritual processions round Serbia carrying the holy relics of Tsar Lazar, who died in the Kosovo battle of 1389. For months these relics travelled across Serbia. They were ceremonially carried along specific routes designed to ensure that the years 1389 and 1989 were symbolically fused. Here we had not only fictionalization and displacement of trauma, but a much greater political tool: *the compression/decompression of time – time fusion and confusion*. The relics 'confirmed' that to be a Serb was in fact a vocation, an invitation to become a victim, since Serbs are a 'heavenly people'. What was repeatedly written in the print media or shown on television was a 'lack of understanding for the injustice committed against the Serbs'; hence the 'Serb right' to refuse to live in peace with other nations who 'for centuries' had behaved in an evil way towards them.

In conclusion, then, for several years Serbia underwent a whole set of preparations for war: verbal and visual, emotional/psychic (even mystical) and public, horizontal and vertical, temporal and atemporal, spatial and non-spatial. All aspects were actively included in the overall fascist colonization of public and private life in Serbia. The war actually arrived late: indifference to and 'tolerance' of future genocide were in people's minds psychologically, ready for activation, as early as 1989. It was already accepted that even some 'lesser Serbs' would have to be sacrificed – those who did not *fully* belong to Greater Serbia. Those were the days and years of a specific phenomenon in Serbia, seemingly naive or rational, which I would label *turbo-fascism*.[1]

Fascism is, of course, a historical term; the histories of Mussolini's Italy and Nazi Germany are distinct from Milošević's Serbia. However, postmodernist and feminist theory speaks of 'shifting concepts' when a new epoch inherits, with some additions, concepts belonging to an earlier one; an example is the feminist notion of shifting patriarchy. In my view we should not fear the use of 'big terms' if they seem to describe accurately certain political realities. Serbian fascism had its own concentration camps, its own systematic represen-tation of violence against Others, its own cults of the family and of the leader, an explicitly patriarchal structure, a culture of indifference towards the exclu-sion of the Other, a closure of society upon itself and upon its own past; it had a taboo on empathy and on multiculturalism; powerful media acted as proponents of genocide; it incorporated a nationalist ideology; it had an epic mentality of listening to the word and obeying authority.

The prefix 'turbo' refers to the specific mixture of politics, culture, 'psychic powers' and pauperization of life in Serbia. It is still fascism in its proper sense. Like all fascisms, turbo-fascism includes and celebrates a pejorative re-naming, alienation and, finally, removal of the Other: Croats, Bosnians and Albanians. Turbo-fascism in fact demanded and basically relied on this culture of normality of fascism that had been structurally constituted well before all the killings in the wars started.

Take this example. Serbia introduced an economic ban on Slovene goods – that is, on all objects symbolizing the Slovene as the Other with whom Serbs had contacts. By an order from above and through 'populist sentiments' in the media, people were asked not to consume Slovene milk any more. This strategy discouraged people from buying an *object* because it would mean that they endorsed a *subject* – Slovenes. Slovenes, hitherto co-citizens or com-patriots, assumed the symbolic value of the 'milk' which must not be touched. This process of objectifying and excluding the Other via an object that symbolizes the whole ethnic group quickly becomes part of the 'common values' under the law of common sense. That is how people in Serbia (long before June 1991 when the war started) were taught to hate the 'Slovene body'. Without that politically constructed *aversion* towards the body of the Other, the body of the other does not become an *abject body* – and without that the massacres and murders of so many Croatians, Bosnians and Albanians would not have been possible. The integrative force of fascism is here evident; Serbs were 'united' through the demand not to invest in certain objects and therefore subjects, and the latter were simultaneously 'united' under the banner of the abjected other.

This *spatial transfer* of trauma played a significant part. Briefly, the River Drina, which divides Serbia from all the other western parts of ex-Yugoslavia, namely Bosnia and Herzegovina, played an enormous symbolic role in dividing the two realities: war and destruction stopped just west of the River Drina. That reality never entered Serbia in its full monstrosity, and so the River Drina became a symbolic border beyond which empathy no longer existed. The Serbs of Serbia had no feeling of responsibility for anything that occurred on the far west side of the Drina, since the people over there were symbolically no longer human beings; they were abjected-objectivized enemies. That made the Serb crimes in Bosnia-Herzegovina the result of a destroyed reason. There was not just a repetition but a *reinforcement,* and a continuation, of the fascist crimes of the previous two world wars. This was, in my view, a very malignant continuation of a 'reawakening of old ghosts', who are now no longer ghosts but new victims – live people suffering – and it will continue into the coming generations.

Paradoxically or not, from the late 1980s this *normality of evil* against the Other belonged to the normal everyday life of Serbia. The above-mentioned processes and changes were necessary for it to be so. It was the result of a sophisticated policy of collective amnesia which made individual consciences feel 'free' to be suspended by the collective superego. In this process 'licences to kill' were systematically issued from state television, and private and commercial television programmes. This was the dominant form of political discourse. There was even an open message from the Serbian Orthodox Church. During the 1980s Serbian institutions and individuals constructed a kind of *superconscience* that permitted oblivion and the suspension of empathy, memory and tolerance towards the Other. We are still far from an understanding that there exist a whole range of *layers of responsibility* for the crimes committed: for remaining silent, for forgetting, for hatred, for media propaganda. The responsibility for remaining silent is the most complicated of these, since silence includes both agreement and awareness of repression – but also admits shades of doubt.

Male and Female Bodies and their Representation in Serbia during the 1990s

The male body underwent a deconstruction of the peaceable and relatively urbanized identity that it had achieved under socialism. Under Tito's regime the male had always inhabited the border between the rural and the urban: he lived in a village and worked in a factory. He was a creature sufficiently hybrid to retain many epic and pagan elements that would later be transformed into the masculine ideal of the warrior under Milošević's regime.

Milošević very carefully constructed the 'Serb hero' and all his male fantasies; he permitted the highest heroism in words, particularly in his own words. In fact, Milošević as the great national Leader did not necessarily have to do much *in reality*. His powerful image and existence were sufficient. He had the help of Dobrica Cosic, a writer and 'Father of the Nation', who articulated the 'Serbian soul'. Through his words the genocidal fantasies of the collective were fulfilled. Once again, schizophrenically, the 'heroes' were *civilians* who only delivered messages of war: they did not cut throats or commit murder, but gave the orders for those things to be done. All males in Serbia were subject to a media brainwashing, in the course of which they had to identify with the Leader: the male population was gripped even more strongly with a fascination with the Leader than was the female.

Milošević's war regime was designed for patriarchal males, for whom, as in every patriarchal society, only males are subjects; women are objects (ornaments or trophies). Pertinent here is Vera Erlich's fundamental anthropological study of the pre-Second World War patriarchal family system in the Balkans (Erlich 1971), of the Dinaric patriarchal *zadruga* society, in which, for example, the eldest female has the *ritual duty* to kiss and wash the feet of the youngest male. Furthermore, there are obscure signs suggesting the homoerotic side of Milošević's regime. I recall the image conveyed by television at the start of the 1990s when the Leader visited Kosovo. In the first village he visited, we saw this ritual: the oldest villager stepped forward from a line of ceremonially assembled most-important-men – that is, the symbolic *wise man* who traditionally embodies the (male) authority of the whole community – in order to kiss Milošević's hand. This was not only homoerotic but also infantile, since the whole community was submitting symbolically to 'paternal authority'. Here we are dealing once again with the avoidance of all individual responsibility: the 'father of the nation' is responsible; we, his 'little children', did not know what we were doing, we just obeyed 'Daddy'. Male identification with the Great Leader also opens a space for molesting women. What matters is what the males from the local tavern think; women are not at all important. But there is a paradox: the Serb warriors are so humbly obedient to Big Father Milošević that they accept the female role as defined by classic patriarchal societies. They are passive, they have no right to speak, they fear the Father's anger, they submit to his desires. The warrior-volunteers played the role of the frustrated patriarchal *wives* of their ideological leaders.

The Body of the Warrior

It was mainly the poorer strata of Serbian society, the lumpenproletariat or rural poor, who gave birth to Bokan's and Arkan's volunteers, as well as to many members of the Eagles and Arkan's Tigers. These were the only ones who really did set off over the Drina to 'defend Serbdom', while the great majority, who will never be accused of the crimes committed, sat at home and enjoyed *Arkan's Travels* and the 'Balkan Cinema'. A special layer of sadists went off to terrorize, loot and murder, but only at weekends – as a kind of 'short break'. Others joined various paramilitary units and so became part of the 'great body of the army'. The body that killed, therefore, was that which fully merged into a collectivity, that which fully gave up its individuality. Its reward was that the violence it wreaked led to local public affirmation. One should not forget the role of mystifying Orthodoxy and Russophilia that provided the warriors with 'missions' – which, in other words, sanctified the body that killed. In contrast to the government that did not dare to legalize the 'heroism' of its killers, the Church rewarded them with symbolic capital.

The only 'heroes' the state legitimized were politicians or intellectuals in their political service. Arkan's men and other such death-squad volunteers until recently received no money or privileges from the state. In legal terms they were 'outsiders', invisible as a social group. Yet, through another schizophrenic splitting, they were at the centre of the Greater Serbian phantasm – the storytelling. That is why many people in Serbia could invent justifications in the form of 'We didn't take part in the war': not only because there had been no *official* recognition of these 'services' by the ethnic cleansers but also because the warriors, local heroes and killers were just a few in number compared to the majority of Serbs who watched and supported the war from their armchairs.

The Female Body under the Ruins of Milošević's Nationalist Reign

The journey into the past did not avoid the female body. It had to suffer the return to tradition and the deeper patriarchal glorification of the Serb warrior 'mentality' and the male body. Women remained silent and censored themselves so that they would not be subjected to violence. Silence became a universal norm: sons and fathers remained silent before their daughters, brothers before their sisters, women before men and other women. The sediments of the socialist emancipation of women once again worked in Milošević's favour: his wife Mira Markovic – at least in the beginning – exploited her image as a sociologist and an emancipated woman to support his cause. The rights of women in Serbia were thus suspended without their noticing. In any case, they were far too concerned with inflation and basic survival. When all other social institutions in the system fall apart, when there is no further child benefit, when men lose their jobs *en masse* or are mobilized, the burden of existence falls upon the family and on women. Women queued, secured food (kinfolk from the village played a crucial role here), cooked, looked after children and the elderly, and sometimes worked in the grey economy too. Within the family, but only in that *private zone,* women became stronger than ever – that is, they took on the Big Mother role.

What Has Happened to the Idea of Female Sexuality?

Female sexuality existed only in Serb 'neo-folk music', where it was greatly magnified. Examples of the allegedly 'happy' Serbian woman's body, a plump body acting out permanent submission and joy over its sexual accessibility, were furnished by a whole series of so-called 'turbo-folk queens' (singers). They played a mixture of Serb and oriental melodies, at first in oriental and rural settings, with belly dancers' movements (later on they were to travel and were *displaced* exclusively into urban settings but did not leave behind the belly dancers' aura). This mixture of traditional folk music, oriental influences and women singers 'giving themselves willingly' not only had the objective of arousing tavern emotions and relaxing the clientele; it also inflamed and reaffirmed pro-fascist emotions, sending a clear *sexual message* that life was beautiful, like music; that these Serbian Women, 'our women', were undoubtedly the most beautiful women in the whole world; and that sex was great and functioning even in these difficult times in Serbia.

The singers were, in a way, the representation of chosen oversexualized Serbian women (exclusively Serb, or they would hide their different ethnic origin), who alone had the right to invite and excite Serbian men through music to the fantasy of sexuality. They were there to 'comfort' men in difficult times, even the rapists, in the sense of showing them that they were still potent. Violence was wreaked solely upon the bodies of women of *other* ethnicities. Serb women were not raped 'systematically'. In the national propaganda they are presented as mothers and sisters – so they are raped only sporadically, secretly and at home.

There was a hierarchy in Serb violence against women. The greatest violence was directed against Albanian women, which is not even recorded, since they have no rights whatsoever – they are 'things' (the whole of Serb war fascism was trained in the apartheid system that Milošević's Serbs introduced against the Albanians during the 1980s). Violence against Croat and Muslim women was a matter of a warrior's 'prestige' and 'positive' self-affirmation. Violence against Serb women was usually presented as an 'excess' or hidden. Concerning the oversexualization of the female pop singers' bodies, I should add that the very fact of the empty space left on the Serbian folk scene by the disappearance of non-Serb singers also represented a kind of licence for violence against the bodies of those who were 'not there', those eliminated Others.

It is important to point out that the greatest symbolic and material politics of the destruction of the body of the Other was carried out, *much earlier*, at the end of the 1980s in the south of former Yugoslavia, with the suspension of Kosovo's autonomous rights, while the real war violence began at the start of the 1990s in the north, in Slovenia. As in all schizophrenias, reality took time to reach the centre of its virtual obsession: chronologically speaking, Kosovo was the last to be engulfed by war and Greater Serbian occupation, though Greater Serbia based itself upon the Kosovo *myth*.

Fascist Processes in Serbia

So far an attempt has been made to give an analytical overview of the cultural and political media production of reality in Serbia before and during the wars in former Yugoslavia. In fact, the intention was even wider: the aim was to trace the profile of these new societies in which the invisible social contract relied on the dominant discourse that life and politics are phenomena of 'our' 'invisible', 'soft', 'tolerable', 'small', 'innocent' fascist structures of reality and in the imagination. On the basis of the case study of Serbia, certain conclusions may be drawn to alert us to pro-fascist shifts in society. In the case of Serbia the key points in a wide register of fascist processes were:

- A nationalist/fascist discourse and order of the body, re-traditionalizing gender roles and reconstructing aggressive masculinity, were a vital symbolic precondition for the wars in ex-Yugoslavia – for strategies of the destruction, cleansing, displacing, torturing, violating of the body of the Other(s).
- The process of the deconstruction of the previous, peaceful, ex-Yugoslav ideological Communist Body and the construction of the naturalized Nationalist Body were systematically produced in Serbia.
- The exclusion of the representation of the body of the Other (nation, history, ethnicity) in the media and the systematic reinvention of enemy Otherness: the exteriorization of the other, the erasure of empathy, and the denial of tolerance. The use of Serbian media as preparatory instruments for war.
- The depersonalization of social life in favour of a violent collectivity of the nation, territory, origin, tradition and culture.
- Women were constructed as the unrepresentative Other in one's own nation, and the representative Other and the target of violence of the enemy nation. This went hand in hand with the representation of the other nation as oversexed; and with the emasculation of the 'warrior's' body into an obedient servant.
- The construction/representation of a narcissistic, self-sufficient body of the nation: the rhetoric of 'true' male Serbhood, the mythologization/ reinvention of the historical Serbian (male) body.
- The representation of a gender-dichotomized nation consisting of a naturalized gender in/compatibility: the 'virile masculine body' and the 'happy sexualized feminine body'.

'The Happy Serbian Body': Folk Queens, Wars and National Mentality

One way of analysing what happened in Serbia is to focus on a mass cultural phenomenon: the turbo-folk queens who embody the power over representation in Serbia. Women singers of the so-called 'newly composed traditional folk music' were extremely popular, whether among rural, semi-rural/

semi-urban, or urban populations. They were 'mega-media phenomena' whose images are dense with social, cultural and political strategies and meanings.

These pop-folk music personalities poignantly were the very *topos* of the cultural production of the ideological and political order. They corresponded to the dominant cultural, political and economical situation. Furthermore, they were also 'given' an active role in constructing the 'audience' in ex-Yugoslavia, or the 'nation' in post-Yugoslav Serbia. Thus they can be viewed as important symbolic powers in the cultural production of reality in Serbia.

- They functioned as homogenizing forces of Serbian 'mentality' through the cultural production of the 'happy sexualized feminine body', and the implicit 'virile male Serbian body'.
- They were the best examples of a purposeful media construction of Serbia's 'fiddling reality' while the rest of ex-Yugoslavia burnt.
- They were the focal points through which we can better read the dominant political discourse and the pro-fascist power over representation through the export of violence, fostering a culture of oblivion, the consensual exclusion of the Other, the amputation of empathy, and the normalization of fascism.

In considering the discontinuity between two periods, the 'old' socialist Yugoslavia of Tito and the 'third' Yugoslavia (Serbia and Montenegro), I shall juxtapose two folk queens with the stage names Lepa Brena and Ceca. They belong/belonged to two different social realities and dominant political atmospheres – two cosmologies, one might say. Lepa Brena became very popular in the early and mid-1970s when she was the biggest Yugoslav pop-folk star, loved by all – a Barbie of Tito's Yugoslavia. At the time she represented so-called 'newly composed folk music'. It became a very profitable industry, with a mass market, one of the few areas in which people could get rich. The singers of 'newly composed folk music' mark the beginnings of entrepreneurial activity (besides tourism) in the former socialist Yugoslavia. And although women in former Yugoslavia reached a significant level of emancipation through education and entering the professions, these women had something more: they were rich, though usually from a lower-class background, of uneducated semi-rural/semi-urban origin.

The folk queens represented and articulated very well the dominant political discourse of their day. Through Lepa Brena one can read the political reality of her time. Ethnically she was a Bosnian Muslim called Fahreta Jakic, though she took the Serbian stage name 'Lepa Brena', which means 'Beautiful Brena'. In Tito's time she did not need to conceal her ethnic identity. Instead she played an *identity–irony* game with the stereotype of the beautiful woman; all over the former Yugoslavia people would say, ironically, of a beautiful woman, 'she's as beautiful as Lepa Brena'. That identity made her famous; however, ironic gestures, melodies and words were always present in her self-presentation. Lepa Brena played the 'reincarnation' of the myth of the beautiful Serbian woman.

The idea behind the 'newly composed folk music' was to combine elements hitherto considered incompatible – rock and pop with folk. It had a ready market because it targeted the majority of the population during the former Yugoslavia's speedy process of modernization: the semi-urban, semi-rural, first generations in the cities; people in between two identities, even between two cultural histories. Lepa Brena wanted to produce this mixture of pop and folk within mainstream popular culture. She thus was a kind of fusion phenomenon, a mixture of many elements. She was a little bit plump, thereby paying respect to domestic taste, a *bricolage* of many cultural and fashion tendencies. But what made her a serious political phenomenon was the fact that she underwent many transformations, including the 'modernization' of her own body, changing from plump to slim as she followed the shifting cultural and political processes. She married a tennis player. Lepa Brena, then, was an important embodiment of former Yugoslavia, of something like a peaceful communist body on which different aspects of the rural and the urban were played out. She was like something from a fairy-tale, a blonde and benign fairy queen. Politically, she was very pro-Yugoslav; she stood for the 'Yugoslav dream'. That dream also had many dark sides but people could not or did not want to see that. We all shared a non-conscious *lethargy of confidence* in the eternity of the present state, and a narcissistic idea that, being between West and East, we were the best of all, in every respect.

The second singer I want to discuss, Svetlana Raznatovic, known as Ceca, of the 'third' Yugoslavia, became an even greater megastar than Lepa Brena. She belonged to a completely new political order of nationalism – the exclusion of the other, war, crimes and violence (she married Arkan, the war criminal). The Ceca phenomenon acted as a privileged 'carrier' of specific messages in pre-war, war and post-war Serbia: the redefinition and homogenization of national identity, the denial of trauma (memory and amnesia) in other parts of ex-Yugoslavia, as well as of fascist tendencies in Serbia.

Ceca grew up in a completely different political atmosphere. She started to be famous in the 1980s; she was already becoming a star when the crisis of the former Yugoslavia began and specifically when the wars started in Croatia, Bosnia-Herzegovina and Kosovo. A primary function of turbo-folk music was to convey a message of normality. While the rest of the former Yugoslavia burnt, Bosnia was under fire and Sarajevo was under siege, Serbia witnessed the mass production of beautiful, more or less plump, happy, sexualized Serbian women. Increasingly they were presented as oversexualized, behaving and presenting their music in an almost pornographic manner. Interestingly they were never considered pornographic women.

One explanation for this is that when the wars started, and with Serbian nationalism at full speed, the women folk queens in Serbia inevitably became political Serbians. As Serbians, in Chetnik's ideology, they were *our sisters*. As such they could not be viewed as pornographic either in public or in private. For Serbian patriarchal macho fascist narcissism, they were their *own kin* – their *sisters,* and they let them be oversexualized, in a quasi-incestuous manner. Because these women were our 'sisters', they could do whatever they liked; nevertheless their presentation was deeply problematic. The oversexualization of their bodies, the constant open sexual appeal and provocation of male erection amounted to a constant incestuous call for sexual arousal of the 'brothers'. At the same time, it functioned as an important *political message*: that all was well with Serbian men's (hetero)sexuality and that they were still functional in a common sexual sense.

Ceca conveyed a particular set of messages. In 1995 she gave a big concert in Belgrade, which started (like all other pop concerts) with much smoke and light. First she was in darkness and then she was illuminated, with more and more lights, and two things could be seen: Ceca and a big cross high above and behind her. That cross looked very much like Kazimir Malevich's 'Black Cross' on a white surface (1921–23). With this 'citation' of Malevich's cross, Ceca referred not only to Orthodoxy and religion but also to the history of modern art – and her place in it. She appeared in a tiger-skin bikini, displaying a perfect body. The reason for the minimal tiger skin became obvious at the end of the concert. She finished the concert by opening the curtain at the back of the stage to show a cage containing a tiger, a very beautiful baby tiger. The audience loved the tiger. The suggestion seemed to be that Ceca was innocently, naively playing with animals, nature and culture, how femininity can be close to beasts and so on. However, this presentation has to be seen in the following context: this beautiful baby tiger was a war mascot in Croatia, in Kraina, where the war criminal Arkan had gone in 1991 and 1992 to kill Croats. His men were very disciplined paramilitary forces (Monroe 2000). They called themselves the Tigers, and they always took this same little tiger with them. By putting the tiger on the stage at the end of her concert, Ceca conveyed the message: this is the Serbia of our 'brothers' and 'sisters'.

Ceca is a very good example of the fusion of culture and politics. Her main political message, in common with all the other women turbo-folk singers, was that it is good to forget, that everything is well, because our bodies are everything – we are the most beautiful women in the world. Ceca became an icon whom teenage girls imitated, rather as Madonna was imitated by girls in many Western countries.

In the period between 1991 and 2000 Ceca started to transform her body and her appearance very significantly. She followed the globalized Western process of shaping women's bodies. Initially plump, she presented an increasingly muscular body in later videos in line with Western body fashions. She was perfectly designed, promoting a modernized Western body. At the same time, the Serbian population underwent a great economic crisis due to inflation, sanctions, and the United Nations embargo. Serbs were not able to travel and could not afford to buy even newspapers in their own language, not to mention glossy magazines such as *Cosmopolitan*, *Vogue*, and *Elle*. In this context, Ceca came to represent contact with the outer world. She gave to the Serbian population the message of what the 'world out there' looks like since she was constantly transforming herself, and because she was one of the few who had the means to follow fashion. When Armani introduced his new collection, with a new hairstyle, Ceca's next video would show her with the Armani hairstyle. Ceca thus came to represent a particular link to the outside Western world.

Ceca married Arkan, a war criminal, national hero, killer, sadist, and secret service agent. They were a 'sexually active couple' and a realization of the Serb fairy tale: from nothing to the stars (I would add: 'and back again'). They were married in accordance with Serb epic tradition: a mass of wedding guests, Ceca dressed in the Serbian folk bridal costume, Arkan in a copy of the uniform of Vojvoda Mišic (a famous Serbian Balkan War and First World War general). Ceca's task was to bear at least three children, since she was president of Arkan's 'Third Child' Foundation. Ceca was the 'sister' who became the 'wife', permitted by her husband to be sexually provocative on stage and in the media 'for the good of the people'. Once the concert is over, however, the queen returns to her ugly fortified mansion in Dedinje (an exclusive Belgrade neighbourhood) and has no thought of wanting anyone but Arkan.

Arkan, of course, was assassinated; his funeral, like his marriage, was a major political event. Arkan's men kept a disciplined military 'royal' pose after the King's death. Ceca was calm and elegant; in her demeanour, hairstyle and dress, she acted out the famous widow role of Jacqueline Kennedy. The only thing she lacked was a small son at her side. Apart from that, she behaved in complete accord with Orthodox customs: she remained enigmatically silent; she did not weep; she withdrew from public life for a year, remaining only the president of Arkan's football team, Obilic. But, since Orthodox tradition demands of a widow that she mourn only one year, she was soon announcing her comeback.

The catastrophic drama of ex-Yugoslavia's recent history shows how the transition from one social/political system to another can turn into a human disaster, a tragedy for the civilian population. To be specific, although exceptional in its softer political, ideological, economic features compared to other, more openly totalitarian Eastern regimes of 'real socialism', and having an elaborate multi-ethnic decentralized party and state structure, ex-Yugoslavia broke down in a most brutal fashion. In the process it lost the two key characteristics of its former role: its central position in the monolithic binary East–West opposition, and its multi-ethnic and multicultural composition. The post-communist transition in ex-Yugoslavia was, therefore, not simply a dramatic but bearable crisis – involving transformation, confusion, anxiety and tension – but a phenomenon of much deeper consequence: an example of a fundamental turbulence and identity crisis within the European ideological world. The breakdown in the Balkans represents more clearly than anywhere else all the explosive potential of the 'transition' within Eastern Europe. Women's position, implication in and critical relation to the transformation have yet to be fully assessed.

Note

1. For the coining of this term I am grateful to my friend and colleague, writer Shkelzen Maliqi, from Priština.

References

Bolcic, Silvano, ed. (1995) *Drustvene promene i svakodnevni zivot: Srbija pocetkom devedesetih.* Belgrade, ISIFF.

Eisenstein, Zillah (1996) *Hatreds: Sexualized and Racialized Conflicts in the 21st Century.* New York: Routledge.

Erlich, Vera Stein (1971) *Jugoslavenska porodica u transformaciji.* Zagreb: Liber.

Enloe, Cynthia (1993) *The Morning After: Sexual Politics at the End of the Cold War.* Berkeley: University of California Press.

Milic, Andjelka (1995) 'Social Disintegration and Families under Stress: Serbia 1991–1995', *Sociologija*, vol. 37, no. 4, Belgrade.

Monroe, Alexei (2000) 'Balkan Hardcore: Pop Culture and Paramilitarism', *Central Europe Review*, vol. 2, no. 24.

Muel-Dreyfuss, Francine (1996) *Vichy et l'éternel feminin. Contribution à une sociologie politique de l'ordre des corps.* Paris: Seuil.

Papic, Zarana (1994a) 'Nationalismus, Patriarchat und Krieg', in Olga Uremovic and Gundula Oerter, eds, *Frauen zwischen Grenzen: Rassismus und Nationalismus in der feministischen Diskussion.* Frankfurt: Campus Verlag.

Papic, Zarana (1994b) 'From State Socialism to State Nationalism: The Case of Serbia in Gender Perspective', *Refuge: Canada's Periodical on Refugees*, vol. 14, no. 3.

Papic, Zarana (2000) 'The Forging of Schizophrenia', Interview conducted by Natasa Govedic and published in *Zarez* 31, Zagreb, 11 May 2000.

8

Identities under Threat
on the Eastern Borders

SVETLANA SLAPŠAK

Gender, Race, and Class in the *Other* Europe

The state frontiers between the capitalist West and the socialist East, which were symbolically challenged, and in some cases radically changed, after the fall of the Berlin Wall, contained multiple liminal markers: gender, class and race (as the main identity markers) above all others. Race markers might seem to be the least important in the context of a visible absence of race, colour and racial differences in the predominantly white European East. In fact, this 'invisibility' was related to an ideological text of racial tolerance and solidarity towards non-white groups. In the former USSR, this text was built into the federation model, with a forced Russian predominance. This fostered an inside colonial model whose traumatic traces appeared only after the dissolution of the USSR, as a more or less violent exclusion of resident Russians in the new national states. For instance, most of the resident Russians in Latvia still do not have full citizenship status. This 'socialist colonialism' had some forms close to classical colonialism, like the introduction of Vietnamese workers in Czechoslovakia after the war in Vietnam. In Yugoslavia, politics after the break with Stalin in 1948 was ideologically constructed around racial tolerance and solidarity, in the ideological text of the *Third World*, with President Tito as the first unofficial, and later official, leader of the movement of the non-aligned countries. The ideology of non-aligned politics was invented in opposition to the politics of the divided Western and Eastern blocs during the Cold War. Unfortunately, the invented model did not include reflection on democracy and human rights: the main rule of non-aligned politics was not to interfere with the internal situation of member countries.

In most of the socialist countries, including Yugoslavia, which was outside the Soviet bloc, students from Africa and Asia were present as grant beneficiaries; in the peculiar case of isolated Albania, the sole political and cultural exchange was with China. The question is how the ideological text was applied. With outbursts of racism against foreign workers in former East Germany, against Vietnamese in the Czech Republic, and against Romanies in Hungary, Romania and most of the independent states of former Yugo-slavia, it is obvious that declared principles were far from incorporated into daily life. One might also consider the reaction to the old system, and arbitrary criteria for changes of attitude and mentality, imposed by new nationalist ideologies. Paradoxically, adapting without criticism to a new set of values − in this case nationalism and racism − and the absence of an individual viewpoint were certainly among the predictable characteristics of citizens in the old system. A certain regression can be noted when the communist/socialist system (in all its varieties in Eastern Europe) and the new, nation-oriented system of education, knowledge and knowledge evalu-ation are compared. The former used to favour the power of learning and reading in the individual and the mass adoption of ideology; the latter favors 'natural' ethnic identity and its ideology. This may help our understanding of why the racist narrative was so quickly and intimately adopted in situations of inter-national tension in the new nation-states. The racist narrative is usually a cluster of oral and written (educational) memories, contemporary media manipulations, and local traditions. It often includes a lingering anti-Semitism, which has been constantly revived in Eastern Europe.

A much less researched but nevertheless convincing complex of racial markers related to gender emerges from historical anthropology, the study of Antiquity: specialists in Ancient women's studies (Greece, Rome, Ancient Mediterranean) have discussed gender constructs in Ancient texts and images in which women are construed as the other tribe/race.[1] This kind of reading of the past is still somewhat limited by a European perspective, and does not take into account possible Balkan aspects of continuity, or contingent socio-cultural gender features in the Balkan patriarchal cultures. Needless to say, the 'native' Balkan academic disciplines in the humanities did not touch the topic in a substantial way, and a debate on such issues is still far from being institutionalized. Even if not framed in concepts of continuity/discontinuity, which are not very promising for theorizing, the *longue durée* racial markers which relate to gender may help interpretation: for instance, the *longue durée* concept can be used to explain strong social, political and cultural differences running along gender lines during the war in Yugoslavia, clearly confronting male and female populations.

Class markers related to gender may serve to corroborate the above. Many analysts have noticed a traumatic gender conflict in post-socialist countries after 1989. Women were stigmatized as a part of the population most privileged by the former regime, thus responsible for the old regime's sur-vival and longevity.[2] A general backlash relating to women's rights, women's health protection, laws on pregnancy privileges and family relief measures can be observed in all the post-socialist countries. Did women really like communism more than men?[3] The history of women should not avoid such questions, because they may change the terms of the running debate within Western gender studies. Therefore, when we speak about gender markers we should be aware that they are – due to inefficient exploration of East–West, East–East, and North–South European social and cultural differences – construed in a way that might subvert the established gender studies frameworks. Gender markers reflect radical differences in the construction of the representations of social strata, and the legislative, political, cultural and media positioning of gender.

The socialist world, or the 'Soviet bloc', was far from unified. Between poverty-striken Romania, and the much wealthier Hungary and Czechoslovakia with prominent dissident cultures, there were incomparable differences. The most staunchly Soviet-linked culture, the German Democratic Republic, with its high social and cultural standing, could not compare with Bulgaria and its semi-colonial status. On the other hand, Yugoslavia and Albania, the two states that defected early on from the Soviet bloc, represented two distinct worlds: a Western lifestyle, consumerism and a degree of civil freedom in Yugoslavia, and a kind of tribal communism in Albania. In fact, very few qualities characteristic of a 'bloc' could be said to have applied to the whole of the Eastern and Central European area, although the crucial term 'socialism' was an identifier of all the states. The main epistemic problem today in researching the history of women in Eastern European socialist societies, or in theorizing the position of women in a – possibly temporarily – post-socialist world, lies therefore in the extremely dispersed, non-systematized and differentiated knowledge of both earlier and recent cultures of the area, its many languages, its semiotic and anthropological diversity. Initial contacts between Western and Eastern women after 1989, both activists and intellectuals, within the broader culture and in academia, were characterized by a certain colonial attitude and style, especially recognizable in North American women.[4] This attitude attracted, almost immediately, a kind of 'colonized' response.[5] Some debates helped overcome the initial tensions and tendency to settle for simple explanations, and the specific need for solidarity developed into highly efficient actions – as, for example, during the war in Yugoslavia. Nevertheless, overall it is the case that the study of women and women's identities in Eastern Europe has still not gelled into a particular cognitive and disciplinary framework of Women's Studies.

Women's Political and Social Identity

The most sensitive area of change affecting women's position in Eastern and Central Europe after 1989 is the socio-political. As the one-party system was generally replaced with different types of parliamentary democracy, a common feature emerged in all the newly organized political systems – a significant diminution in the number of women representatives at all levels.[6] The failure to exercise public influence so that voters might choose to elect a proportion of women greater than 35 per cent, even in the most advanced political and social settings in Europe, in the Scandinavian states, threw into relief a historic European confusion about democracy and women – how systems that totally exclude women from politics can be defined as democratic. (The historical roots of this lie in the Ancient Athenian democracy, of course, where women were denied any form of citizenship, except the role of a body-transfer of citizenship from father to son.[7]) The old socialist regimes used women as the representation of gender equality, without any democratic decision-making, voting or public debate. The new post-socialist states, for their part, still care nothing about gender representation, and make little in the way of investment towards the democratic education of the masses in this regard. The question is how to propagate an egalitarian principle without an omnipresent ideological framework and its persuasive narratives, most of them embedded in traditional rationalist, atheist and liberal European thinking since the eighteenth century. A mixture of American political correctness and EC declarations does not seem to work, especially in filling the gap vacated by the sudden and non-debatable retraction of the former ideologies. What could be construed as the celebration of two hundred years since the French Revolution received no inventive ideological injection that could have made it live longer than the initial joy of destroying and transgressing the wall, back in 1989. Instead, a package containing Western democratic and individualist values, together with a consumerist lack of sense of reality, were exported into the context of varying levels of poverty, threatened social security, and a radically distinct type of education. Thus the underrepresentation of women at every level of the political structure in the post-socialist countries remains, thirteen years after the changes started, one of the most visible and traumatizing – and least debated – problems of the new societies.

Arguably, however, women's identity in the post-socialist societies is threatened less by their underrepresentation in politics than by the diminishment of their rights in the domain of social security and health protection. This may be attributed to a certain patriarchal mentality and the consequent gender representation that was skilfully introduced over many years of social stability by all the nomenklatura. Although not openly promoted, this patriarchal mentality was in fact the easiest way of exploiting traditional views, incorporating them into the ideological texts, and consequently redistributing power, without exposing such views to unfavorable communist criticism. Communist ideology is undoubtedly women-friendly, at least in its many programmatic texts. The strategies whereby commitment is made to this ideology yet its demands avoided are an object lesson.

A good example of this process is the Yugoslav case of communist guerrillas (partisans) engaging masses of women into an open feminist movement during World War II, and then several years later abandoning them. The Yugoslav communist movement was illegal before World War II; nevertheless it existed as a movement of elites, with educated urban women the predominant, if not the only, feminine representatives. Already purged of its genuine working-class leaders by Stalin in the 1930s, this isolated group was presented with the unexpected chance of moving the masses in resistance against German, Italian, Bulgarian, Hungarian and local quisling occupation of the country in 1941. Forced to organize guerrilla actions outside the cities, in a precarious situation of constant mobility, the partisan movement began a huge propaganda exercise among the population of women – mostly uneducated rural women. Along with women's support in logistics, health care and food provision – the necessary survival strategy of any guerrilla movement – the process of 'enlightening' women about their rights and the bright communist future went on, in the most inauspicious conditions. The success was enormous. The Anti-fascist Front of Women (AFŽ), founded in 1943 as a para-communist organization, had more than one hundred times more members than the Communist Party by the end of the war. Women were instrumental in the voluntary work of reconstruction of a devastated country, in huge educational campaigns (literacy courses), in taking care of the sick, victims of war and orphans. They gained an enormous visibility in political and Party bodies, as MPs, as mothers and as widows in black in the first rows at conferences, congresses, war crimes tribunals and cultural events. All this was cut short after Tito's break with Stalin in 1948. The Yugoslav communists feared that the mass of women could turn in favor of Soviet-type communism, and challenge the Yugoslav resistance to Stalin. Many women, following internal purges in Yugoslavia, were sent, along with men, to concentration camps for Soviet sympathizers. Most of these people were kept in the camps – the most notorious situated on barren islands in the Adriatic Sea – in horrible conditions for several years, some up to fifteen years. Many did not survive torture, hunger and humiliation. AFŽ was formally kept going for a couple of years, and then silently disbanded in 1952.[8] Thereafter women would be granted only representative, symbolic roles in the communist power system. Yugoslavia's subsequent history shows the effects of such a policy over a longer timespan, with patriarchal mentalities, inculcated through media and culture, combining with a Western consumerist disposition. In any event, women in the post-socialist societies reacted openly against the backlash that affected their everyday lives. The symbolic focus of the fight-back, which took place mostly in the first years of transitional change, was abortion.[9] A good example is women's reaction in Slovenia, in the first year of independence (1991), when the proposal for a new constitution referred to the 'sanctity of life'. That language was immediately recognized as a threat to the already existing rights of women over their own bodies. Masses of women rallied and staged a symbolic siege of the parliament in Ljubljana, with all women MPs, even the conservative ones, coming out of the building to join the rally. The phrase was duly removed from the text of the constitution. Ten years later, in 2001, a group of right-wing MPs, all male, managed to press for a referendum, this time against a law that would allow women without a male partner to have IVF treatment. This highly symbolic political action provoked scattered reactions, but the question remains open as to whether or not women and liberal intellectuals are able to react in concert, after ten years of heavy Church and right-wing intervention in media and culture. The result of the referendum was a fairly convincing victory by the conservative forces: women without partners will not have the right to IVF treatment in case of sterility in Slovenia.

Another setback recorded in all the transitional societies in Eastern and Central Europe concerns women's less privileged employment status and lower wages when employed, and the significant diminishment of social services for women and children, such as kindergartens, holiday facilities, health protection, state subsidies for children.[10] The relatively slow and weak growth of union activities shows that part of the problem lies in the changed social construction and representation of the working class, but the reinstatement of patriarchy and its undeniable supremacy in public discourse may still be the main reason.

The main women's response to these transitional reversals was and still is located within alternative organizations (feminist, lesbian, humanitarian) and NGOs.[11] A fruitful coexistence with the peace movement was forged in areas recently affected by war and unrest (Yugoslavia, Russia). Initiatives for form- ing clubs, societies and circles inside or outside the mainstream male-led parties and groups have been noted all over the geographical region (political parties, clubs, business women's associations, spiritual/religious groups). In forming such groups, both alternative and mainstream, financial, intellectual and moral support from the West has been important, if not decisive. Thus the new political and social identity of women in Eastern and Central Europe cannot be constructed in the future without a dialogue with the rest of European (and global) women's identities, whatever political and social projects and solutions might open up. Common problems affecting women in all parts of Europe, and originating in transitional societies – for example, the traffic in women and immigration – offer the immediate ground for action.

New Collective Identities and Women's Culpability

One of the main strategies in constructing an anti-communist discourse with its persuasive narratives in the post-socialist societies has been to accuse women of 'collaboration' with former communist regimes. This, in fact, was done earlier, in the literature of the dissidents' circles. A good example is the literary work of Milan Kundera, a famous Czech author. His novels written in the dissident years, before he became a Western author, usually have more or less the same character pattern: namely, Stalinist agents; denouncers;

negatively represented women, figuring sometimes as overbearing mothers, sometimes as unfaithful lovers, almost always as sexually frustrated. One picturesque detail is that most of these women have dark hair... and do not shave their legs. A positive heroine, one that engages easily in a sexual relation with the hero, protects him and helps him in his plan to escape, is a silent blonde, often a nurse.[12] Sexist representations of women as a symbolic target for hidden anti-communism appeared in other developed dissident cultures, such as that in Yugoslavia. The so-called 'black wave' in Yugoslav cinematography in the 1970s had very similar stereotypical roles for women: treacherous whores (often spouses turned bad), who denounced the hero to the authorities; and, on the good side, tear-jerking mothers and silent, often terminally ill, sisters. Rape, as a symbolic representation of revenge and punishment for women, became a structural element of Yugoslav movies, although the 'black wave' was severely suppressed by the regime.[13] These representational strategies are much more patriarchal than anti-communist – but their narrative patriarchal attitudes were masked. They reappeared in a much more transparent form in the transitional context. It was easy to target Russian women who remained in the new national states as *the* gender-ethnic enemy, or Yugoslav women who defended their multi-ethnic families in the newly formed independent states and during the turmoil of war. The image of women as national traitors was so strongly rooted in propaganda in the warring national states that it remains present in Serbia even after the democratic changes. Their active pacifism is not forgotten or forgiven; their collaboration with women on other sides in the war and opposition to the regime of Slobodan Milošević even less so. A striking example is a commentary by a popular Belgrade columnist, who previously used to publish indiscriminately in the state media, fascist publications, and independent press, in a leading state-controlled daily, *Politika*, just after NATO bombing stopped, which began with these words: 'NATO generals are like Mother Theresa, compared to Serbian feminists!' He went on to argue that the greatest threat to Serbian men were Serbian women. In this case, women function as a collective screen of culpability, with a twofold function: to project onto women a collective patriarchal anger and frustration, reinforced by an inner culpability for cowardice on the part of many men during the war years, and to use this imaginary screen to hide and silence the dark side of the collective memory.[14]

The most traumatic effect of projecting culpability onto women is without doubt the mass rape that occurred in many war regions in Yugoslavia, especially in Bosnia. A cluster of patriarchal representations of the woman's body as territory and possession,[15] combined with new strategies of representation and projection of culpability in an atmosphere of proclaimed illegality and state-supported brutalization, produced this ultimate action against *all* women. Although Western media and feminist intervention put this issue in the spotlight literally while it was happening, probably saving many women from rape in the weeks and months to come, Western interpretations were often limited

to inter-ethnic trauma, even by feminists.[16] The enormous goodwill and justified rage in fact was accompanied by little or no knowledge of the background situation. A huge propaganda campaign was staged by the Serbian
media back in 1986–87, accusing Albanians of raping Serbian women. The
'beastly' character of Albanians was exposed by alleged cases of rape of older
women, children, and even animals. Although several independent international
commissions went to the region to investigate, they were unable to corroborate the stories. A law was duly introduced in the Serbian parliament, with
the support of the Albanian MPs from Kosovo, punishing a perpetrator of
rape more severely, if he was of Albanian ethnic origin. Serbian official statistics in the subsequent years showed that the number of rapes of Serbian
women perpetrated by Albanians diminished to almost zero, while during the
same period the number of rapes of Serbian women perpetrated by Serbs
grew.[17] Media propaganda manipulated rape stories, providing this usual male
war activity with a proper narrative of collective rights, revenge, and male
communities' aggressive communication through female bodies. Many wartime rapes were perpetrated against visible women, who played some role in
the pre-war community – judges, teachers, lawyers, party functionaries. Thus
many of the cases have a local and contextual prehistory, and can be understood in a general East European pattern of revenge against women. Western
feminists tended to overlook Croatian media manipulation of rape in Bosnia:
victims were presented as predominantly Muslim, thus stressing that they were
'weak' and unable to resist, like Croatian women.[18] When five Croatian women
authors dared to challenge the rape stereotypes, pointing to the fact that war
rapes were directed primarily against women, and that the ethnic element was
less motivating, they were attacked by Croatian media as 'witches', exposed to
harrassment, and accused of 'raping Croatia'.[19] Regrettably, these women were
also attacked by a number of Western feminists and intellectuals.[20] Western
media represented women in Bosnia and other warring parts of Yugoslavia as
predominantly rural, older, uneducated women, only exceptionally referring
to young, professional, self-aware women.[21]

Nation, Collective, the Body:
Limited and Liminal Identities for Women

Woman's body is certainly the main symbolic space for exercising different
concepts, and, accordingly, for creating narratives and images in most of the
cultures we know. In the area of Eastern and Central Europe and in the
Balkans this use of woman's body has at least two common features. One is
the historically recorded continuity of patriarchy from Antiquity onwards; the
other is the representation of women at the time of the forming of the new
nation-states in the nineteenth century and, in a similar way, after World War
II, and the subsequent breaking up of patriarchal communities and mentalities.

These two features are important for the specific gender identities of the area, because they differ greatly from the Western gender and cultural models used in the forming of the nation-states.

Most of the national states in the area were formed through processes of emancipation – be it through war or treaties, or both – from the colonizing powers, great empires that controlled the area from the fifteenth century onwards, like the Ottoman or Austro-Hungarian Empires, or the Roman and Byzantine Empires before them. The area was also shaped by imaginary, uto-pian 'empires' that fostered a huge cultural production: Classical Greece as the prime European example of the colonization of the past and the realization of the *ius primi possidentis* as the basic concept of any nationalism; French intellectual production (the Revolution, the inter-war years); Russian Slavic utopianism and its many colonial consequences, including the Soviet empire; the German Idealist intellectual appropriation of the native Slavic cultures, and so on. The Balkan cultural space can be defined as a space of 'floating maps' which combine political realities and imaginary projects, reflect some of the traumatic frontiers, and some of the grey liminal areas that surround them – religions, closed communities and nomadic routes; tensions between the South and the North, the Balkans and the Central Europe, the internal-ized 'civilized' West of the East and the 'savage' East of the East, the Oriental and the Mediterranean as opposed to the Middle European. Curiously enough, this complicated, multidimensional cultural and historical situation not only makes gender constructs more visible and easy to detect but also gives the impression, yet to be researched in a sustained manner, that this construct has some distinctive *universalizing* features.

Historical anthropology, oriented towards gender, and initiated by gender-interested academics and feminists, should be one of the main disciplines in which theories and research projects in this direction are tested. My own research in this context has focused on the processes through which patri-archal communities were replaced by the nation-state with citizenship-based collective identities, and the gender-construct and representation strategies that were used in these processes.[22] The working hypothesis is that patriarchal societies have a certain number of *niches* for the cultural production of women, which are not thoroughly controlled; the classic example would be oral litera-ture, but we should not underestimate healing, music, dance, crypto-ludic languages, rituals or witchcraft. Many of these niches can be interpreted in terms of *carnivalization*, as theorized in the work of Mikhail Bakhtin.[23] The secured liminality was seriously threatened by national collective ideology, which could use the upper patriarchal social narrative, but rightly considered the lower/liminal social narrative subversive and dangerous. This can be seen in the process of censoring and gendering anew the figure of the *singer of tales*, which is recorded, throughout the nineteenth century in Serbia, Bulgaria and Macedonia, as both male and female when it comes to epic songs, but exclusively female when it comes to all other oral genres. By the time the nation-states were formed, there were scarcely any traces left of this bi-sexual cultural figure, since epic poetry was one of the main textual representations of the collective, and all other genres were devaluated by institutionalized national criticism. Patriarchal niches were emptied and/or exposed to censorship, which used the upper social patriarchal narrative. Paradoxical as it may sound, women in the new Eastern and Central European nation-states, throughout the nineteenth and twentieth centuries, could rely only on the intellectual, interpretative, narrative and activist potential of Western feminism, since their own traditions were pulled out from under their feet. This forced 'native' position in their own social and cultural context could initiate new strategies, most of them liminal, in narratives and ideologies. If the mainstream national model was fixed in the presumed purity of blood and language, and a pristine (non-temporal) definition of soil, then the liminal would have been constructed around the notion of the 'poly-' – the polylingual (knowledge of languages, mixing of languages, translation), the polyethnic, the nomadic/transgressional.

Yet the relation between nation/collective identity and women/gender identity is certainly much more complicated, and far from being positioned in women's sheer creativity, subversion and innovative feminism. A national collective expanded several strategies of forcing, negotiating or compromising with women, in order to strengthen collective cohesion. The figures of the mother and the sister were used not only to accommodate women in the modified patriarchy of the nation-state but also to make women fight for, work in, and be representative of the national collective narratives. *Our* women, if the narratives succeeded, were one of the most powerful ideological, cultural and propaganda weapons in all the processes of forming nation-states in the area. From a general process of icon creation by presenting a woman's body as an abstracted sign – think of the innumerable statues, ornaments, illustrations, paintings representing the Fatherland, Justice, Victory, the Muse, Poetry, Science – where gender serves as a basic semiotic marker, because it reflects the real position of women in society, indicating exclusion and non-presence, to the immense degree of literary production on, for instance, the sacrificial East European mother, the use of woman's body was crucial in building up narratives and images of the nation-state. No wonder that some Western feminists suggested at the beginning of the transitional processes in Eastern Europe that women from the area should not reject the possibility of sharing some of the power emanating from national collective cohesion.

Women's response to such strategies of 'integration' into the bigger national picture, with the consequent loss of gender identity ('sacrifice' for the nation), was linked to Western feminism, revolutionary projects and global communication on the one side, and to exploring local women's traditions on the other. In both cases, the process could have been stopped and directed into a purely conservative adaptation to the mainstream male narratives. But there were moments and situations in which exploring the local history of women achieved some political success. The knowledge of niches dating back to patriarchal, pre-national cultures, mentioned above, was crucial in applying such strategies. For instance, the protest of Women in Black,[24] which expanded from its primary source in the Middle East and had some impact in many modern Eastern and Western cultures, could be related to the death cult and to the role of women in it in the Balkans. The crucial anthropological concept that was deployed by women activists, generally unaware of its potential, is *miasma*: the Greek term and its Latin translation, *pollutio*, denote the status of women's bodies in Ancient societies. Being polluted by birth giving, women are closer to death and its pollution. In many Ancient and later Balkan, Central European and Eastern European cultures, a dead male, even a hero, belongs to women, who, being polluted 'by nature', bear their gender marker, and are qualified *by exclusion* to deal with dead bodies – to wash them, dress them, lament over them, and play a significant part in the collective expression of sorrow. Gender-based negotiation of power in death rituals is a known phenomenon in many cultures, Ancient and modern. Women in Black in fact performed a public ritual which immediately signified death, and the specific position of women around death. Their performance was also a timely response to another big media manipulation, especially during the preparations for the Yugoslav war and on television: the presentation of women at graveyards, or in mourning, and invoking, directly or indirectly, revenge for the victims of the 'other', the ethnic enemy. Women in Black deprived these television images of authenticity and motivation, silently claiming that all the victims were useless and tragic, and that the final consequence of war was just death. The ritual fear of death made the message even more impressive, with its cultural gender-based context.

Another example is less performative, and less detectable, so was generally omitted in observation of women's activities during the Yugoslav war. A number of patriarchal attitudes were given discreet expression by women in order to overcome everyday problems emerging from the war and a state in dissolution: deceiving, convincing, tricking the authorities in a number of ways – crossing borders, avoiding the draft, smuggling goods and information, communicating with the 'enemy' across the lines. While the state media indulged in representing women-warriors, or promoted women who divorced an ethnically unsuitable husband, or devoted space to mothers and widows, many women were subverting the national ideology, on all warring sides, with their small-scale strategies. In 1992–93, when the draft presented a real threat to the male civilian population in Serbia, women not only hid would-be deserters, smuggling them over the border, but also led most of the street protests against the war and the regime, profiting from this unexpected gender visibility.

Most of the examples I have used originate from the war in Yugoslavia, as the most dramatic situation in which gender construction was played out in the transitional East European area. A further reason is that this part of the post-socialist world has been less researched by Gender Studies specialists, academics and activists. Other elements that demand a more thorough gender-based research within the Yugoslav and Balkan region are multiple colonial patterns, multilingual practices and cultural features, traces of women's culture niches, and nomadism in all of its varieties, from forced mobility to models of identity. One fascinating example of gender-based cultural differences has been present in all the former socialist countries: as part of the ideological control system in culture, all of these states had associations of artists, academics, and other specialists, which enabled the regime to react promptly to unwanted orientations; writers' and artists' associations, with their houses, resorts, clubs and restaurants, were particularly notorious. Most of these associations survived, more or less modified and adapted to the new situation. But the gender division remains almost the same: writers' associations still have a predominantly male membership, while translators' associations have a predominantly female membership. This reflects long-standing gendered cultural roles, made visible and preserved by the communist regimes. Such features should enable researchers in Gender Studies to reflect on women's history and the historicity of women's culture, and thereby to establish greater intellectual independence from the narratives of the 'universal', for which read male, culture.

With more knowledge available and shared, the necessary comparison between Eastern European and Third World women's relations to nation and nationalism will prove extremely important for further debate. Presently, liminal identities, both in the construction of gender and of alternative cultures in Eastern Europe, seem to make sense. An example is the development of a new, still less controlled space of cyber-identity: in Eastern Europe, cyber-identities present an alternative model to national-collective identity.[25] Women's identity in Eastern Europe is still a project for the future, requiring the building up of canons, history, databases and representations.

Notes

1. See Nicole Loraux, 'Sur la race des femmes et quelques-unes de leur tribus', in *Les enfants d'Athéna. Idées athéniennes sur la citoyenneté et la division des sexes*. Paris: Découverte, (1981) 1990, pp. 75–119.

2. Nanette Funk and Magda Mueller, eds, *Gender Politics and Post-Communism: Reflections from Eastern Europe and from the Former Soviet Union*. London: Routledge, 1993.

3. Svetlana Slapšak, 'Between the Vampire Husband and the Mortal Lover: A Narrative for Feminism in Yugoslavia', in Barbara Wejnert and Meta Spencer, eds, *Women in Post-Communism: Research on Russia and Eastern Europe*, vol. II. London: Jai Press, 1996, pp. 201–25.

4. Funk and Mueller, *Gender Politics and Post-Communism*, pp. 319–22.

5. Dubravka Ugrešić, *Have a Nice Day: From the Balkan War to the American Dream*. Chicago: Northwestern University Press, 1996. The author, one of the Croatian 'witches' who left Croatia in 1993, refers often to the theme of how authors from Central and Eastern Europe try to 'please' the new Western public.

6. Funk and Mueller, *Gender Politics and Post-Communism*, pp. 303–18.

7. Claude Mossé, *La femme dans la Grèce antique*. Paris: Editions Complexe, 1991.

8. Lydia Sklevicky, *Konji, ene, ratovi* [Horses, Women, Wars]. Zagreb: Druga, 1996. This Croatian sociologist was the first one in the new generation of Yugoslav feminists to research this somehow forbidden topic.

9. Funk and Mueller, *Gender Politics and Post-Communism*, pp. 241–53.

10. Ibid., pp. 95–109, 131–8.

11. Zorica Mršević, 'War Makes Us Feminists', in Svetlana Slapšak, ed., *War Discourse, Women's Discourse: Esssays and Case Studies from Yugoslavia and Russia*. Ljubljana: ISH-ŠOU, 2000, pp. 323–43.

12. See Milan Kundera's *Life is Elsewhere* (New York: HarperPerennial, 1998) and *Farewell Waltz* (London: HarperCollins, 2000). See also John O'Brien, *Kundera & Feminism: Dangerous Intersections* (London: Palgrave Macmillan, 1996).

13. Svetlana Slapšak, 'Žensko telo u jugoslovenskom filmu' ['Woman's Body in Yugoslav Film'], in Branka Arsić, ed., *Žene, slike, izmišljaji* [Women, Images, Inventions]. Belgrade: Centar za ženske studije, 2000, pp. 121–39.

14. Journalist Bogdan Tirnanić published many articles over the years in Belgrade, denigrating and slandering women pacifists and feminism. There is a tendency among more or less nationalist intellectuals in Belgrade to attack the 'anti-war profiteers', as the group which gained from 'betraying' Serbian people to the West during the war, calling for Serbian responsibility and promoting pacifism. See Svetlana Slapšak, 'Im Innern der populistischen Maschine: Eliten, Intellektuelle, Diskurslieferanten in Serbien 1986–2001', in Wolfgang Eismann, ed., *Rechtpopulismus. Östereichische Krankheitoder europäeische Normalität*. Vienna: Czernin, 2002.

15. Julie Mostov, 'Our Women/Their Women: Symbolic Boundaries, Territorial Markers and Violence in the Balkans', in *ProFemina* 3, 1995, Belgrade, pp. 210–19.

16. Alexandra Stiglmayer, ed., *Mass Rape: The War Against Women in Bosnia-Herzegovina*. Lincoln and London: University of Nebraska Press, 1994, especially the contribution by Catharine MacKinnon, pp. 73–82.

17. Serbian media manipulation was revealed in Nebojša Popov, ed., *Kosovski cvor: rešiti ili seći* [Kosovo Knot: To Cut or to Unravel]. Podgorica, 1990.

18. Renata Salecl, *Spoils of Freedom: Psychoanalysis and Feminsim after the Fall of Socialism*. London: Routledge, 1994. 'Rape is for Muslim women an especially horrible crime' (p. 16); 'because of the lack of national identity, the aggressor tries to destroy Muslims' sexual and religious identity' (p. 17).

19. Meredith Tax, 'Five Women Who Won't Be Silenced', *The Nation*, 10 May 1993, pp. 624–5.

20. A French philosopher, Alain Finkielkraut, attacked five women authors as the beneficiaries of the former communist regime in his interviews in Croatian media in 1993–4. See Alain Finkielkraut, *Comment peut-on être croate?* Paris: Gallimard, 1992. I remember a debate on war in Yugoslavia at Yale University in 1994, in which Catharine MacKinnon attacked the Croatian women as 'five witches'.

21. Curiously enough, the first images of Sarajevo women, young, urban and self-conscious, appeared on MTV in 1994.

22. Svetlana Slapšak, 'Mémoires nomades, oubli sédentaire: le cas du Kosovo', in *Migrations et errances*. Paris: Grasset, 2000, pp. 240–48; 'What Are Women Made Of? Inventing Women in the Yugoslav Area', in Gisela Brinker-Gabler, and Sidonie Smith, eds, *Writing New Identities: Gender, Nation, and Immigration in Contemporary Europe*. Minneapolis and London: University of Minnesota Press, 1997, pp. 358–73.

23. Mikhail Bakhtin, *Rabelais and His World*. Bloomington: Indiana University Press, 1988.

24. Ana Devic, 'Women's Activism between Private and Public Spaces: The Case of the Women in Black in Serbia', in Slapšak, ed., *War Discourse, Women's Discourse*, pp. 195–211. See also note 11.

25. Marina Gržinić-Mauhler, 'Introduction', in Marina Gržinić-Mauhler and Adele Eisenstein, eds, *The Spectralization of Technology: From Elsewhere to Cyberfeminism and Back: Institutional Modes of the Cyberworld*. Maribor: MKC, 1999.

9

Identity, Subjectivity and Difference:
A Critical Genealogy

ROSI BRAIDOTTI

A feminist situated in Europe cannot avoid a confrontation with the dialectics of sameness/difference. This has as much to do with mainstream European history and thought as with the specificities of each feminist political culture within Europe itself. In European culture, history and philosophy, the notion of 'difference' is central. It functions through dualist oppositions which assert a monological system of sameness through subcategories of difference. The respective positions of being 'identical to' or 'different from' therefore mark asymmetrical power relations. This implies a built-in standard of reference that constitutes the assumed norm. Phallogocentrism as an apparatus of subjectivity works by organizing the significant/signifying differences according to a hierarchical scale that is governed by the standardized mainstream subject. Deleuze calls it 'the Majority subject' or the Molar centre of Being. Irigaray calls it 'the Same', or the hyperinflated, falsely universal 'He'.

Furthermore, in European history, this 'difference' has been predicated on relations of domination and exclusion: to be 'different from' came to mean to be 'less than'. Difference thus acquired both essentialistic and lethal connotations, which have reduced entire categories of people – branded as the 'others' – to the status of disposable bodies: slightly less human and consequently considerably more mortal. In this dialectical scheme of thought, difference or otherness is a constitutive axis which marks off the sexualized other (woman), the racialized other (the native) and the naturalized other (animals, the environment or earth). These others, however, are constitutive in that they are expected to confirm the same in His superior position. They are crucial to the assertion of the power of sameness. Post-war European feminists were quick in taking to task the epistemic violence implicit in this dialectics, which is nothing more than a metaphysical consumption of the others. Carla Lonzi's (1974) 'Let us spit on Hegel!' became the rallying cry of an entire generation.

The pejorative sense of 'difference' outlined above supported European colonialism and fascism. The fact that the notion of 'difference' as pejoration goes to the heart of the European history of philosophy and of the 'metaphysical cannibalism' (Braidotti 1991) of European thought makes it a foundational concept. Because the history of difference in Europe has been one of lethal exclusions and fatal disqualifications, it is a notion for which feminist and other critical intellectuals have made themselves accountable.

This problem has become more urgent in the context of the recent history of the European Union which has included a wave of nostalgic reassertions of local identities, producing a nationalistic, xenophobic and often racist climate. The renewed emphasis on the unification process has resulted in making 'difference' more divisive and contested than ever. In the paradox of simultaneous globalization and fragmentation, which I regard as characteristic of late postmodernity in Europe today, the notion of 'difference' has become even more antagonistic. The disintegration of the Soviet bloc and the ethnic wars that followed have also contributed to resurrecting the ghost of difference as pejoration. I want to argue consequently that one of the aims of feminist practice is to overthrow the negative, oppressive connotations that are built into the notion of difference and the dialectics of Self and Other. A critique of Hegelian ways of thinking and especially of oppositional dialectics is central to this project. Continental structuralist and poststructuralist philosophies of sexual difference are fundamentally anti-Hegelian ideas. They are historically embedded in the decline and crisis of European colonialism, but they have also been translated philosophically into the critique of Eurocentric humanism, phallogocentrism and the idea of a hegemonic European identity. Let me explain.

Structuralism and Psychoanalysis as Critical Theory

The dialectical philosophical tradition is built into Marxist thought and provides the epistemological backbone for classical structuralism. The structural anthropology of Lévi-Strauss and the linguistics of Jakobson are materialist, historically embedded accounts of how signifying structures constitute subjectivity. What is meant by 'signifying structures' is something as concrete as kinship and family structures under patriarchy, the political economy of sexuality and the constitutive role played by the exchange of women, and the primacy of language – defined not only as a tool of communication but as a political economy of meaning, or a mythology in the Lévi-Straussian sense of the term.

The long-term impact of classical structuralism was to introduce a new way of thinking about the subject in an a-personal manner – that is, in terms of structures. The focus shifts from the notion of a self, with a given and chosen identity, to that of a subject. A subject is a site of entitlements, duties and power relations which intersect with the psychological entity known as 'a self' but do not completely coincide with it. When Marx suggests that the subject is the effect of socio-economic forces and relations; when Freud argues that one is fundamentally the subject of one's unconscious; when Nietzsche stresses the multilayered genealogical structure of our received ideas about ourselves – they are introducing a hiatus, a categorial distinction between humanistic ideas of 'identity' and the structuralist notion of 'subjectivity'. Psychoanalysis, Marxism and Nietzschean genealogical thinking play a major role in this shift of perspective.

The impact of psychoanalysis has been a radical deconstruction of the subject by splitting subjectivity from the supervision of rationality. The subject is no longer identified with consciousness: 'desidero ergo sum' replaces the old cogito. In other words, the activity of thinking is enlarged to encompass a number of faculties, of which affectivity, desire and the imagination are the prime movers. Psychoanalysis and, with it, structural anthropology, emphasize the crucial importance of sexuality – of the subject's 'libidinal economy' – to an understanding of subjectivity. What matters for feminism are the implications of this notion for political practice. Politics in this framework has as much to do with the constitution and organization of affectivity, memory and desire as it has with consciousness and resistance. A political economy of desire and pleasure consequently becomes necessary. Sexuality as an institution, as a pillar of identity and as a vehicle of power forms a multilayered structural apparatus of the utmost political significance. The embodiedness of the subject is a form of bodily materiality, not only of the natural, biological kind. The body is the complex interplay of highly constructed social and symbolic forces: it is not an essence, let alone a biological substance, but a play of forces within a complex web of social and symbolic relations. The subject is a process, made of constant shifts and negotiations between different levels of power and desire, that is to say wilful choice and unconscious drives. Whatever semblance of unity there may be is embodied and performed as a choreography of many levels into one socially operational self. It implies that what sustains the entire process of becoming-subject is the will-to-know. Desire is a founding, primary, vital, necessary and therefore constitutive drive to that becoming-subject.

I want to stress the extent to which the structuralist form of materialism both rests upon and reasserts the importance of desire in the sense of the non-coincidence of the self with rational consciousness and consequently of the unconscious as the principle of nonunity of the subject. I take the unconscious as the guarantee of nonclosure in the practice of subjectivity. It undoes the stability of the unitary subject by constantly changing and redefining his/her foundations. I see it as a constant return of paradoxes, inner contradictions and internal idiosyncracies, which instil instability at the heart of the self. The subject is marked by a structural nonadherence to rules, roles and models. Taking unconscious structures into account is crucial for the whole practice of feminist subjectivity precisely because they allow for forms of disengagement and disidentification from the socio-symbolic institution of femininity. In other words the recognition of the noncoincidence of the subject with his/her consciousness need not be played back to the old familiar tune of anguish and panic at the thought of incipient psychosis or imminent implosion. If it is the case that paradoxes and contradictions are historically constructed and socially embedded in practices of power and resistance, we may accept them with less anxiety (Scott 1996).

Fantasies, desires and the pursuit of pleasure play as important and constructive a role in subjectivity as rational judgement and standard political action. I would like to try to reconnect the wilful agency required of politics with the respect that is due, both theoretically and ethically, to the affective, libidinal and therefore contradictory structures of the subject. Unconscious processes, memories, identifications and untapped affectivity are the invisible glue that sticks together that bundle of contradictions that is the subject.

Poststructuralism Revisited

The structuralist legacy and the political reading of psychoanalysis are central to the making of poststructuralist critiques of subjectivity. To understand this shift, however, some important considerations must be kept in mind. This genealogical account of my main terms of reference is necessary for two other main reasons. The first is the high level of often unfair and mostly uninformed polemics that has surrounded the reception of poststructuralist philosophies in the English-speaking world. 'French theory', and 'French feminism', have become debased terms. I consequently want to redress the balance by tracing their philosophical genealogy. The second factor concerns a sort of historical amnesia that has struck deeply at the heart of postindustrial societies, especially since 1989. The sheer lack of historical knowledge about movements of thought and ideas in Europe during the Cold War period, let alone any sense of historical perspective, combine to produce simplifications, especially about radical or critical philosophies. I want to address some of these against the platitudes engendered by the socially constructed amnesia of our times.

The events of World War II – in particular fascism, Nazism and the extermination of the European Jews – constitute nothing short of genocide for some, and the moral and intellectual suicide of Europe. Many of the best scholars, scientists and thinkers had to run for their lives. The great migration of the anti-fascist, Jewish, left-wing intellectuals towards the UK and the USA, Canada and Australia was one of the biggest 'brain-drains' ever to have occurred on the continent. The entire original psychoanalytic community was dispersed in this diaspora; Marxists did not fare much better. The books of Freud and Marx were among those the Nazis burned, in their homicidal tribute to an ethnically cleansed, philosophically uncontaminated vision of European high culture. The Frankfurt School of critical theory moved to

New York City to become the New School for Social Research. The USA emerged from the war with a respectable human capital of radical thinkers, some of whom – like Adorno and Brecht – returned to Europe, whereas others – like Arendt, Marcuse, Einstein, Hirschmann – stayed on. They represented a scientific and creative community of thinkers who would go on to make a lasting contribution to American science, technology, the film industry and critical theory. Europe, on the other hand, emerged from the war an intellectual and philosophical wasteland. Only the return of the previously exiled dissident intellectuals – mostly Marxist, Jewish, or communist – ensured the continuity of a tradition of critical thought which had been violently and forcefully truncated by fascism.

A major disruption occurred, therefore, in the history of critical theory in continental Europe, in so far as at the end of World War II Europe was deprived of those very schools of thought – notably Marxism, psychoanalysis and Nietzschean genealogy – which had been the strongest work in the earlier part of the century. Moreover, the context of the Cold War and the opposition of the two blocs, which kept Europe split and dichotomized until 1989, did not facilitate the reimplantation of those radical theories back into the continent which had cast them away with such violence and self-destruction.

The period following World War II, and the moral bankruptcy of Europe under fascism and Nazism, had seen different and often conflicting practices of critical theory, emerging mostly from the German and French schools. There was little love lost between them, of course, as has often been the case in the history of Western philosophy, but a great deal of crossfire, little cross-reference and much polemic. That mutual hostility damaged an already impoverished European philosophical landscape. It is in the context of such discontinuity and a polarized world order that the roads of a renewed European radicalism in the 1960s and 1970s led to France.

That it should have been France that acted as the motor for the regeneration of continental philosophy after the war (complemented, to a lesser degree, by the Frankfurt School; the Yugoslav schools of Marxism, of which Žižek is a representative; and the Southern European schools, especially the Italian and Spanish) had a great deal to do with the moral stature of France at the end of World War II. Again, a great deal of new scholarship has emerged since 1989, which I cannot adequately cover here. Suffice it to say that this historical 'coincidence' endowed French philosophy with an intrinsically subversive charge. This representation of 'French' as synonymous with 'radical' lasted well into the last decade of the twentieth century, and had a major impact across the Atlantic.

It is significant, for instance, that most of the authors Foucault singled out as heralding the philosophical era of critical modernity (Marx, Freud, Nietzsche, Darwin) are the very authors the Nazis condemned. I want to suggest that the links between critical theory and anti-fascism need to be explored further in the light of the current revisionist waves sweeping Europe, taking into account the opening of new archives, especially in the East, since 1989. While 'the Heidegger case' periodically resurfaces, with the usual media cacophony and great discomfort for all concerned, few thinkers today dare to display the lucid approach that Hannah Arendt showed towards the issue. Nietzsche is an altogether different case, which needs to be reassessed following the opening of the Weimar archives. The case of Nietzsche's anti-Semitic sister, Elizabeth Forster, has been amply documented (MacIntyre 1992). The work of poststructuralists like Derrida, Foucault and Deleuze has led to a serious reassessment of Nietzsche as the philosopher of the 'will to power'. This may well pave the way for a reappraisal of his critical philosophy, following the end of the Cold War.

Like the Frankfurt Critical Theory school, Louis Althusser and Jacques Lacan in the late 1960s heralded a 'return' to the materialist roots of continental philosophy, via Marxism and psychoanalysis. It was not a simple return to Marx and to Freud, of course, but a more complex phenomenon, which coincided also with a change of generation. The previous philosophical generation, that of Sartre and de Beauvoir, who had lived and worked throughout World War II, did not spare criticism of the *France des salauds* (the France of collaborators). They also skimmed over the complex, guilt-ridden depths of the issue of collaboration, resistance and the moral and political decline of Europe. Certainly, these issues received attention in their philosophies: questions of responsibility for colonialism and fascism, of reparation and resistance play a crucial role, especially in the case of de Beauvoir. De Beauvoir's feminist consciousness makes her, in my opinion, a more acute ethical thinker than Sartre was. Thematic concerns for the responsibility of European philosophy, however, do not necessarily amount to an in-depth interrogation of the role of Europe in its own and other peoples' destruction. They raise with equal importance the question of the role of philosophy, science and intellectual production, both in paving the way for fascism, rationalizing its necessity, thus banalizing its consequences and eroding the possibility of resistance.

With the existentialist generation, philosophical reason escaped unscathed from the question of its historical responsibilities in perpetuating models of exclusion. The dialectics of self/other remained dominant; 'difference' equated with inferiority and as such was considered a contaminated concept, which needed to be discarded. Both Sartre and de Beauvoir, influenced by Marxist theories of alienation and ideology, connected the triumph of reason with the might of dominant powers, thus disclosing the complicity between philosophical *ratio* and exclusion. They continued, however, to rely on a dialectical model for the resolution of the inbuilt power issues. This not only perpetuated a hegemonic model of violent appropriation and consumption of the other, but also defined the activity of philosophy as an explicitly hegemonic, intrinsically violent gesture. With Sartre and de Beauvoir, the image of the philosopher-king was built into the general picture. Philosophy thus continued to be practised as the pursuit of grand theoretical systems and overarching truths. This implies that the quest for universalism remained at the heart of Western philosophy. Like Husserl, both Sartre and de Beauvoir in some ways consider universalism as the distinctive trait of Western culture, its specific form of particularism. The implication is that the epistemic violence of the universalistic stand gets conveniently tucked away under the double headings of 'transcendence' and 'the universal'. This prevents the far more uncomfortable confrontation of philosophy with its own historical responsibilities and conceptual power.

Let me clarify this: that Hegelian dialectics is built into post-war French philosophy does not automatically make it complicitous with violence. On the contrary, critical philosophy is historically and constitutionally opposed to it. It remains the case, however, that Sartre's generation did not – and maybe historically could not – push the self-questioning about philosophical and theoretical reason to the point of implosion. The threat of fragmentation and relativism was too strong; besides, the Cold War was putting a great deal of pressure on every European thinker to conform to the Western canon. With the privilege of hindsight, of course, one can see things differently; nevertheless we have to understand those who came before us within their historical context.

I wish to emphasize my central concern, namely that critical theory in Europe after fascism and World War II, and consequently also feminist practice, could only be on and of the left, inspired by Marxism. It also could not avoid issues of European identity and the crisis of European humanism, in so far as it attempted to face up to Europe's role in colonialism, fascism and the Second World War. The first generation of post-war critical philosophers began the analysis and critique of the role of European philosophy in the demise of European identity and values with and in the wake of fascism. Sartre and de Beauvoir set a significant agenda in terms of the ethics of responsibility and commitment to freedom, but left conceptually unquestioned many issues related to the fabric of philosophical reason. The post-existentialist generations took up the philosophical discussion from there.

The reaction against these silences and omissions did come – in the form of the far more self-reflexive philosophies of the younger generation, that of May '68. This generation introduced a radical critique of the by now untouchable systems of thought that had founded and guided critical theory before, during (albeit in exile) and after European fascism – namely Marxism and psychoanalysis and their shared roots in Hegel. The scholarship on the 'return to Marx' proposed by Althusser and the 'return to Freud' promoted by Lacan is quite large; suffice it to say, therefore, that what is at stake in these 'returns' is anything but a flat repetition or gesture of loyal obedience. The radical philosophies that later became labelled 'poststructuralism' represent a moment of great theoretical creativity. They repossess Marxist and psychoanalytic texts, promoting the importance of an open-ended reinterpretation of the theories.

The return to these texts was intended primarily as a critique of the prestige and intellectual power enjoyed by the institutions that emerged from the Second World War as representatives of Marxism and psychoanalysis: respectively the Western European communist parties and the International Psychoanalytic Association. To appreciate the sources of their prestige and influence, it is necessary to historicize and contextualize. At the dawn of the third millennium it is easy to forget that before, during and after the war, the communist parties were the single largest force of anti-fascist resistance throughout Europe. In the generalized amnesia that has come to mark post-industrial and post-communist societies alike, it is important to stress the specificity of Marxist philosophies in Europe and to connect them to the events of World War II, especially the Holocaust. The fact that, subsequently, the country claiming to represent institutionalized communism, the Soviet Union, developed its own variation on the tragic themes of extermination, anti-Semitism and terror is no reason flatly to assimilate it to the horrors of fascism.

I consider the equation of fascism with communism historically incorrect and want to reassert the specificity of the (Western) European brand of Marxist and materialist philosophies as a viable alternative. The specific form this materialism took in 1968 in France, finding expression in variants of philosophical radicalism, was precisely a critique of the dogmatic authoritarianism of the French Communist Party and of its links to the Soviet Union. This included a critique of the alliance between philosophers like Sartre and the Communist Party as well as of its creed. In response to the dogma, Althusser, Lacan and later Foucault, Deleuze and their generation appealed to the subversive potential of both Marxism and psychoanalysis to recover their radical roots. Their radicalness was redefined as a critique of the humanistic implications and the political conservatism of the dominant theories. Marx's texts were used as tools to criticize Marxist dogma, much as Freud's texts were turned against the psychoanalytic institution. Both were accused of late humanistic assumptions. The focal point of this humanism was identified in their implicit theory of the subject. The rejection of humanist assumptions therefore took the form of unhingeing the notion of subjectivity, freeing it respectively from the dictatorship of a libido dominated by Oedipal jealousy, and from the linearity of a telos which had married reason to the revolution, both of them vowing violence.

The issue of European consciousness is therefore built into any discussions about radical philosophy, as in the choice of cultural leaders. The most prominent figure of May '68, for instance, now very active in the European Parliament, Dany Cohn-Bendit, is almost the embodiment of a whole – till then frozen – slab of European history: German, French, anti-fascist family background, Jewish, intellectual. The shadow of the holocaust and the events of the Second World War were noticeable in the May '68 events: 'Nous sommes tous des juifs allemands' ('We are all German Jews') chanted the students in Paris, while those in Prague put flowers into the barrels of the guns of the Soviet Red Army, which had just invaded and squashed their spring of hope and liberation.

This was Europe's equivalent to Californian flower power; this was Europe's continuing saga of structural privilege and unmentionable misery, internal divisions and endless production of pejorative differences. It was also, however, a whole new story that is waiting to be told, broken open. The political culture of the European left in the 1960s and 1970s was one of great ambivalence towards the USA. On the one hand, this generation looked towards the United States for support and inspiration, given that there neither Marxism nor psychoanalysis had been disrupted as in Europe. American post-war culture contained elements of radicalism that had been lost in Europe under fascism. On the other hand, a militant anti-Americanism was dominant. It was probably the best expression of the extent to which European critical thinkers tried to strike a middle way between the two superpowers of the Cold War. This position was particularly strong in psychoanalysis, where the slogan "Where the Ego was, the Id will be" became Lacan's answer to the sweeping conformism of US-based ego psychology. He attacked explicitly the politically conservative elements of the psychoanalytic fraternity, such as it had become in its Anglo-American format. Surviving in exile, psychoanalysis had in fact closed in upon itself, in a static obedience to Freud's original ideas. Lacking flexibility, it grew rapidly out of date; the 'return' to Freud was therefore Lacan's contribution to radicalizing psychoanalytic politics (Turkle 1984).

The issue of the social imaginary was central to the political project of this generation: how it could be analysed and harnessed to a radical critique of power emerged as a central concern for the philosophies and the practices of the '68 generation. This was the generation that chanted: 'Power to the imagination!' and made John Lennon's 'Imagine' into an anthem. Profoundly Nietzschean in inspiration, the poststructuralists were politically on the far left. They practised deconstruction, and built genealogical approaches that clashed with the dogma of historical materialism. They took the instance of the unconscious not as a black box or an obscure god of some guilt-ridden subject of lack, but as the activator of internal acts of gratuitous disobedience and external acts of joyful insurrection. The work of the philosophical generation that proclaimed the 'death of Man' led to a rejection of humanism, and also marked the critique of the notion of Europe and of the geopolitical specificity of Western scientific discourses.

Postmodernity and the Return of 'Difference'

In poststructuralist thought, the historical era of postmodernity is marked by the return of the 'others' of modernity: woman, the sexual other of man; the ethnic or native other of the Eurocentric subject; and the natural or earth other of technoculture emerge as counter-subjectivities. Given the structural importance of these 'others' as props that confirm the 'same' in its dominant subject position, their 'return' coincides with a crisis of the structures and the boundaries of classical subjectivity, which challenges its very foundations. Poststructuralist philosophers address directly this crisis of dialectics and humanism; Foucault, for instance, points out that modern philosophy and social sciences have responded to the challenge of postmodernity by developing discourses that are attuned to the emerging subjectivities of the 'others'. Thus, psychoanalysis encapsulates the instance of the unconscious, the critique of rationality and the question of the feminine or of woman's desire; anthropology and especially ethnology mirror the ethnic others; and the discourses about nature beginning with Darwin developed rapidly into a cluster of fast-growing sciences and technologies of 'life'. It is worth stressing, however, that these emerging others were far from content with being incorporated in a variety of discourses in modernity, albeit critical ones. They also produced discourses of their own and voiced their increasingly visible subjectivities. Thus feminist, post-colonial, native or black theorists produced discourses and practices of their own which challenged his master's voice. Around the notion of nature or earth a number of counter-discourses emerged, ranging from ecology and the new biological sciences of today all the way to the information technologies.

This proliferation of 'differences' can no longer be fitted into a dialectical mode of opposition. For instance the women's movement has made an indelible scar on the symbolic tissue of phallocentric culture; emergent subjectivities from the post-colonial horizon have displaced the Euro-centred world-view; various brands of fundamentalism as well as both communist and post-communist nationalism, have created powerful images of 'threatening alien others'. This process confuses the distribution of values according to self–other dichotomies. To top it all, ecological disaster spells the end of the drive towards mastery of nature, while the technological revolution makes it all the more urgent to resolve issues of access to and participation in a democracy that is threatened by the informatics of domination.

Moreover, late post-industrial societies have proved far more flexible and adaptable towards the proliferation of 'different differences' than the classical left expected. These 'differences' have been turned into and constructed as marketable, consumable and tradable 'others'. The new scattered and poly-centred power relations of post-industrialism have resulted in the marketing of pluralist differences and the commodification of the existence, the culture, and the discourses of 'others' in the mode of consumerism. Popular culture is a reliable indicator of this trend, which sells 'world music', or a savvy mixture of the exotic and the domestic, often a neo-colonial romantic appropiation of 'difference'. Although ethnicity and race continue to play a major role in organizing the consumerist appropriation of proliferating differences, the trend is so global as to leave no identity untouched.

An important implication of this situation is that in late postmodernity advanced capitalism functions as the great nomad, the organizer of the mobility of commodified products. As Deleuze and Guattari (1972, 1980) argue, a generalized sense of 'free circulation' pertains, almost exclusively to the domain of goods and commodities, regardless of their place of origin, provided they guarantee maximum profit. People do not circulate nearly as freely. It is therefore crucial to expose the logic of economic exploitation that equates nomadic flux with the profit-minded circulation of commodities. Given that technologies are so intrinsic to the social and discursive structures of post-industrial societies, they deserve special attention. Access to and participation in the new high-tech world is unevenly distributed worldwide, with gender, age and ethnicity acting as major axes of negative differentiation.

I take the spasmodic and double-sided concurrence of these phenomena as the distinctive trait of our age. The proximity and quasi-familiarity of differences have turned 'others' into objects of consumption, granting them alternately a reassuring and a threatening quality that bypasses the swinging doors of their dialectic. We have instead a zigzagging pattern of dissonant nomadic subjects. Keeping track of them is the difficult challenge faced by critical theory. Expressing the positivity of difference in the age of its commodified proliferation is a conceptual task that, however, keeps coming up against dialectical habits of thought.

The work on power, difference and the politics of location offered by post-colonial and antiracist feminist thinkers like Gayatri Spivak, Stuart Hall, Paul Gilroy, Avtar Brah, Helma Lutz, Philomena Essed, Gloria Wekker, Nira Yuval-Davis and many others who are familiar with the European situation helps us illuminate the paradoxes of the present. One of the most significant effects of late postmodernity in Europe is the phenomenon of transculturality, or cultures clashing in a pluri-ethnic or multicultural European social space. World-migration – a huge movement of population from periphery to centre, on a worldwide scale of 'scattered hegemonies' (Grewal and Kaplan 1994) – has challenged the claimed cultural homogeneity of European nation-states and the incipient European Union. Present-day Europe is struggling with multiculturalism at a time of increasing racism and technophobia. The paradoxes, power asymmetries and fragmentations of the present context rather require that we shift the political debate from the issue of differences *between* cultures to that of differences *within* the same culture. In other words, one of the features of our present condition is the shifting ground on which periphery and centre confront each other, with a new level of complexity which defies dualistic or oppositional thinking.

Feminist theory argues that if it is the case that a socio-cultural mutation is taking place in the direction of a multi-ethnic, multi-media society, then the transformation cannot affect only the pole of 'the others'. It must equally dislocate the position and the prerogative of 'the same', the former centre. In other words, what is changing is not merely the terminology or metaphorical representation of the subjects, but the very structure of subjectivity, the social relations, and the social imaginary that supports it. It is the syntax of social relations, as well as their symbolic representation, that is in upheaval. The customary standard-bearers of Eurocentric phallocentrism no longer hold in a civil society that is, *inter alia*, sexed female *and* male, multicultural and not inevitably Christian. More than ever, the question of social transformation begs that of representation: what can the male, white, Christian, monotheistic symbolic do for them? The challenges as well as the anxieties evoked by the question of emerging subjects-in-process mark patterns of becoming that require new forms of expression and representation – that is to say, socially mediated forms which need to be assessed critically. Feminist theory is a very relevant and useful navigational tool in these stormy times of locally enacted, global phenomena – that is, 'glocal' – changes.[1]

Revisiting Sexual Difference

Poststructuralist theories of sexual difference become clearer if contrasted with other brands of European feminist theory. For instance, in the high Hegelian mode of the previous generation of feminist theory, for de Beauvoir, Woman as the antithesis of the system carries a yet unrepresented value, which is misrepresented by male-dominated culture. Deconstructing the dialectical mode of representating gender through the binary masculine/feminine couple amounts to a critique of the false universalism of the masculine subject. In poststructuralism, in fact, the subject position is seen as coinciding with consciousness, universality, masculine agency and entitlement. With a dialectical opposition, Woman as the Other of this subject is deprived of all these attributes. She is thus reduced to unrepresentability within the male symbolic system, be it through lack, excess or the perennial displacement of her subject positions. Even feminine sexuality is defined, by Irigaray, as not-one, that is to say multiple and complex and ex-centric to phallic genitality. This theoretical premiss leads to a political conclusion: through the strategy of mimetic repossession of the feminine by feminist women, a political process is set up that aims at bringing the 'other of the Other' into representation. This is what I have called the 'virtual feminine' of sexual-difference feminism. In poststructuralist or sexual-difference feminism, materialism is linked both to embodiment and to sexual difference, and the link is made by the political will and determination to find a better, a more adequate, representation of female corporeal reality, not as given but as virtual, that is as a process and project. In this line of feminist thought, great care is taken to disengage the question of the embodied subject from the hold of both orthodox Lacanian psychoanalysis and Marxism. The body is then an interface, a threshold, a field of intersecting material and symbolic forces; it is a surface where multiple codes (race, sex, class, age, etc.) are inscribed; it is a cultural construction that capitalizes on energies of a heterogeneous, discontinuous and unconscious nature. The body which, for de Beauvoir, was one's primary 'situation' is now seen as a situated self, as an embodied positioning of the self. This renewed sense of complexity aims to stimulate a revision and redefinition of contemporary subjectivity. This vision of the body contains sexuality as a process and as a constitutive element.

Sexual-difference theory, far from being a reactive or critical kind of thought, is also an affirmative one in that it expresses the feminist political passion for both social change and in-depth transformations of the subject. In my vision, feminists posit themselves as female subjects, that is to say not as disembodied entities but rather as corporeal and consequently sexed beings. The female feminist subject starts with the revaluation of the bodily roots of subjectivity, rejecting any universal, neutral and consequently gender-free understanding of human embodiment. The feminism of sexual difference should be read as emphasizing the political importance of desire as opposed to the will, and of its role in the constitution of the subject – not just libidinal desire, but rather ontological desire, the desire to be, the tendency of the subject to be, the predisposition of the subject towards being.

This is a way of reasserting the positivity of difference by enabling a collective reappraisal of the singularity of each subject in his/her complexity. In other words, the subject of feminism is not *W*oman as the complementary and specular other of man but rather a complex and multilayered embodied subject that has taken her distance from the institution of femininity. 'She' no longer coincides with the disempowered reflection of a dominant subject who casts his masculinity in a universalist posture. She, in fact, may no longer be a she, but the subject of quite another story: a subject-in-process, a mutant, the other of the Other, a post-Woman embodied subject cast in female morphology who has already undergone an essential metamorphosis.

Central to sexual-difference theory is the insight that the root of the term materialism is *mater*. This implies that the material is the primary and constitutive site of *origin* of the subject, and is also the instance that expresses the specificity of the female subject. As such it needs to be systematically thought through. In the perspective of radical feminist bodily materialism, the feminine is the primary matter and the foundation stone, whose silent presence instals the master in his monologic phallogocentric mode. Feminism of sexual difference argues that women have borne, both materially and symbolically, the costs of the masculine privilege of autonomous self-definition: they have been physically and symbolically dispossessed of a place from which to speak. This is remedied by the collective feminist practice which aims at making a difference; that is to say, at turning difference into the positive, empowering affirmation of alternative subject positions for and by female feminist women. The quest for an alternative female genealogy through immersion in the maternal imaginary is crucial to this project (Irigaray 1987). For Irigaray this takes the form of an exploration of images that represent the female experience of proximity to the mother's body. The opening out of the feminine towards religious or mystical experiences is central to Irigaray's notion of the 'sensible transcendental'.

There is no sentimentality involved in this reappraisal of the maternal/material feminine. Irigaray acknowledges that motherhood is also the site of women's capture within the specular logic of the same, which makes her subservient to the masculine. Maternity, however, is a resource for women to explore carnal modes and the empathy and interconnectedness that go beyond the economy of phallogocentrism. I see this 'other' maternal feminine in Irigaray as linked to the political project of providing symbolic representation for the female feminist subject as a virtual subject position that needs to be created and activated. In other words, the sexed female feminist is both the subject around which feminists have gathered in their recognition of a general condition, and the concept that needs to be analysed critically and eventually deconstructed. This means that the quest for a point of exit from phallogocentric definitions of *W*oman requires a strategy of working through the images and representations that the (masculine) knowing subject has created of Woman as Other: the strategy of 'mimesis'. The mimetic strategy, far from being biologically deterministic, exposes and critiques the essentialism of phallogocentric discourse. It is an affirmative form of deconstruction. It amounts to a collective repossession of the images and representations of *W*oman such as they have been encoded in language, culture, science, knowledge and discourse and consequently internalized in the heart, mind, body and lived experience of women. The mimetic repetition of this imaginary and material institution of femininity is the active subversion of the phallocentric habit that consists in reducing the feminine to unrepresentability. In a reversal of dialectics, sexual-difference feminism argues that the asymmetrical position of the two sexes is simply not reversible. The female feminist subject is a sexed, thinking subject, who stands in an asymmetrical relationship to the masculine. If there is no symmetry between the sexes, it follows that the feminine as experienced and expressed by women is as yet unrepresented, having been colonized by the male imaginary. Women must therefore speak the feminine; they must think it and represent it in their own terms. What then becomes central is the political and conceptual task of creating, legitimating and representing a multicentred, internally differentiated female feminist subjectivity without falling into relativism or fragmentation. The politics of location come into play here: if it is the case that the material/maternal site is primary and constitutive of the subject, it can also be turned into a location of resistance.

Here the distinction between will and desire becomes fundamental: because the implications of the phallogocentric institutionalization of sexuality are written on/in our bodies, they are complex inasmuch as that they are enfleshed. Feminists cannot hope, therefore, merely to cast off their sexed identity like an old garment. Discursive practices, imaginary identifications or ideological beliefs are tattooed on bodies and thus are constitutive of embodied subjectivities. Thus women who yearn for change cannot shed their old skins like snakes. This kind of in-depth change requires instead great care and attention. It also needs to be timed carefully in order to become sustainable – that is to say, in order to avoid lethal shortcuts through the complexities of one's embodied self. On the question of how to achieve changes and in-depth transformations, the continental school of difference departs radically from the sociological and social psychological assumptions that have supported the sex/gender tradition in the English language. A politicized vision of the 'feminine' as a positive term is set in opposition to *W*oman as Other-than or different-from – that is to say, specularly connected to the same as its devalued Other. Sexual difference as a political practice is constructed in a non-Hegelian framework whereby identity is not postulated in dialectical opposition to a necessarily devalorized other. There is no such negation: rather, it rests upon the working through of many differences between, among and within women. I see 'differences among women' as being constitutive of the category of sexual difference and not exterior or antithetical to it (Frye 1996).

The sexual politics of this project are clear, albeit complex. For Irigaray it is about how to identify and enact points of exit from the universal mode defined by man, towards a radical version of heterosexuality, that is to say the full recognition of the specificities of each sexed subject position. More specifically, she wonders how to elaborate a site – that is, a space and a time – for the irreducibility of sexual difference to express itself, so that the masculine and feminine libidinal economies may coexist in the positive expression of their respective differences. This positivity is both horizontal/terrestrial and vertical/celestial and entails the (re)thinking through of gender-specific relations to space, time and the interval between the sexes so as to avoid polarizing oppositions. Issues of 'other differences' – notably religion, nationality, language and ethnicity – are crucial to this project and integral to the task of evolving towards the recognition of the positivity of difference. This radically hetero-sexual project, however, is not heterosexist; nor does it imply the dismissal of homosexual love. Irigaray is especially keen to prevent the assimilation of female homosexuality into a phallic mode of dialectical opposition to the other and thus of masculine identification. Nor is she a dupe to the illusion that a mere choice of another woman as object of desire is enough to allow a woman to escape from the phallic clutches. In either case (homo or hetero), Irigaray is not prescriptive; she just emphasizes women's need for a space of experimentation for their desires and specific sexual morphology. Men are called upon to do the same: to reclaim a non-phallic sexuality and resignify their desires. Sexual difference cuts both ways. The real difference, which produces the ethical passion of 'wonder' (Irigaray 1982), is the escape from sexual sameness – that is, identification with male phallicity.

I want to defend sexual difference as a theory and political practice that rests upon and exploits a number of constitutive contradictions, the answer to which can be formal in a logical sense (Frye 1996), but also practical in the sense of pointing to a solution in praxis, in 'doing'. In my reading, Irigaray's version of materialism deliberately and self-consciously addresses a number of paradoxes that are constitutive of feminist theory. Sexual-difference theory simultaneously produces and destabilizes the category 'woman'. It binds together the notions of embodiment and sexual difference; the link between the two is made by the political will and determination to find a better, a more adequate, representation of embodied female subjectivity. In this line of thought, the question of the embodied subject is disengaged from the hold of naturalistic assumptions and instead the social and discursive formation of embodied materiality is emphasized.

Feminist affirmations of sexual difference go hand in hand with the rejection not only of essentialist identities but also of the dialectics of negation as the logic of constitution of the subject. Sexual difference thus brings into representation the play of multiple differences that structure the subject: these are neither harmonious nor homogeneous, but rather internally differentiated. Therefore sexual difference forces us to think the simultaneity of potentially contradictory social, discursive and symbolic effects. These multiple 'differences within' can and must be analysed in terms of power relations; they constitute overlapping variables that cut across any monolithic understanding of the subject. This is a way of acknowledging an identity which can then be put to the task of its own emancipation. The political gesture consists, first, in situating oneself at the crest of the contradictions that are constitutive of the social and symbolic position of women; and second, in activating them towards the destabilization of the socio-symbolic system and more especially of the asymmetrical power relations that sustain it. Because of this, I see the analysis of 'differences within' as perfectly suitable for a non-unitary vision of subjectivity.

Conclusion

Sexuality and hence also sexual difference, far from being marginalized, are in this conceptual framework a central point of reference, which acts as the matrix for power relations in the broad but also most intimate sense of the term. This is the theoretical genealogy that, I claim, runs from Lévi-Strauss through to Lacan and beyond. Here sex/gender is not as relevant a distinction as sexuality/sex, and consequently also sexual difference, as a distributor and organizer of social and symbolic differences. The comparison with social-psychologically inspired gender theories is important. For poststructuralist thought, sexuality is the constitutive socio-symbolic cast in which human subjectivity is thrown. It is dynamically interrelated to cultural codes and therefore coextensive with questions of power, in both the reactive (negative) and affirmative (positive) sense.

The feminist tradition of sex/gender dates back to Simone de Beauvoir, who made significant interventions to disengage materialism from the double burden of its opposition to idealism and its dependence upon Marxist theories of historical materialism. Caught in the 'Trans-Atlantic disconnection' (Stanton

1980), De Beauvoir's work becomes framed in ways that are often contradicted by her texts (Moi 1994). De Beauvoir's work is also caught in the
debate which, since the 1980s (Duchen 1986), has opposed the neo-
materialism of Monique Wittig (1973, 1979a, 1979b) and Christine Delphy
(1975, 1984) to the strategic essentialism (Fuss 1989) of the sexual-difference
theorists Hélène Cixous (1977, 1980) and, more importantly, Luce Irigaray
(1974, 1977, 1987).

I think that a fuller, more informed discussion between European continental traditions of difference and mainstream Anglo-American traditions of
sex/gender is needed in order to create productive connections. Instead of
polemical disagreements, what is needed is a detailed and careful mapping of
the respective positions. The notion of dialectics, the Hegelian legacy and the
impact of both Marxism and psychoanalysis are, in my view, central to this
discussion. Most contemporary American gender theory descends from Gayle
Rubin's interpretation of Lévi-Strauss's theory of exogamy, which she turns
into a sexual politics of compulsory heterosexuality, also known as the
heterosexual matrix of power. In turn this affects how motherhood and the
maternal imaginary are positioned: the American gender school is deeply
anti-maternalist in its approach to the discussion of female sexuality. It also
positions heterosexuality as complicit with dominant power relations. Reference to psychoanalytic theories of desire is lacking; in their place is a renewed
dialectics of oppositional positions. Especially since the 'sex wars' of the 1990s,
the only public discourse about sexuality within US feminism concerns lesbian,
gay or queer sexualities.

Wittig builds on the classic sex/gender distinction and turns it into a
radical critique of heterosexism. She emphasizes the need to free female sexuality from its subjugation to the signifier *W*oman. In her view *W*oman as the
privileged other of the patriarchal imaginary is an idealized construction of
the same order as the Phallus: it is a man-made notion, and as such is ideologically contaminated and untrustworthy. Wittig restates the importance of
dialectics and radicalizes de Beauvoir's observation regarding the constructed
nature of femininity. She proposes that we dismiss the signifier 'woman' as
epistemologically and politically inadequate and suggests that we replace it
with the category 'Lesbian'. The lesbian is not a woman because a lesbian has
subtracted herself from identities based on the Phallus. Wittig's position, while
attractive in that it aims at empowering women, is problematic, in my view,
in that it universalizes the lesbian as a new normativity model. This leaves no
room for alternative definitions of lesbianism, such as, for instance, Rich's
idea of the lesbian continuum (Rich 1985) and Irigaray's notion of a 'female
homosexual libidinal economy' (Irigaray 1977). Moreover, it excludes *a priori*
the possibility of freely chosen or optional heterosexuality. This option is seen
as coextensive with domination, and consequently leads to voluntary servi-
tude; this position is reminiscent of the most extreme anti-sexuality wing of
US feminism.

Butler emphasizes the fact that 'gender' is not a substantive reality, but rather an activity. Inspired by Rubin, she then proceeds to reinterpret Wittig's notion of 'gender' as a performative utterance that constructs categories such as 'sex', 'women', 'men', 'nature' for the specifically political purpose of repro-ducing compulsory heterosexuality. Gender is the process by which women are marked off as 'the female sex', men are conflated with the universal, and both are subjugated to the institution, in Foucault's sense of the term (Foucault 1975a), of compulsory heterosexuality in Rich's sense (Rich 1985). Thus Butler takes her leave from poststructuralist theories of sexual difference, be-cause she does not recognize the transformative power of the feminine in subverting the representational economy of phallogocentrism. For Butler, as for Rubin, de Lauretis and others, the exclusion of the feminine is accord-ingly neither primary nor foundational. It is rather presented as an *a posteriori*, hallucinatory projection that covers the sense of loss, and this sustains the subject in the delusional quest for coherence and self-consciousness.

With Irigaray, I would argue instead that the loss of the mother's body entails for the little girl a fundamental lack of primary narcissism as the scar of the wound due to the separation. This originary loss also forecloses access to the mother as primary object of desire, thus depriving the female subject of a fundamental ontological ground for self-assurance. The little boy, on the other hand, gets 'compensated' for the loss of the mother by having his desire deferred, and displaced to another woman. He may lose the original love object, but inherits the earth in return: men draw all sorts of advantages from their position of being representatives of the phallic signifier. For the little girl, however, there is only economic and symbolic misery.

The implication of this view of the original separation is that it is the whole of female subjectivity and eroticism, the entirety of her body, that is short-circuited in the process. As Deleuze would say, the little girl's body is 'stolen' from her, as the whole of her sexuality is coerced into the phallogo-centric regime. It is important to stress here the extent to which Deleuze and Irigaray share the same conceptual matrix, and how radically it differs from the paradigm of gender in Gayle Rubin. The little girl's 'stolen body', accord-ing to Deleuze, marks her complete exclusion from symbolic representation – the 'capture' of her body by the oedipalizing vampire of phallogocentrism. Both Irigaray and Deleuze stress that it is the specific materiality of the female flesh that is erased by the phallic regime. This primordial erasure is the con-dition of possibility for the subsequent kidnapping of the symbolic order by the masculine.

Butler, on the other hand, interprets this ontological kidnapping of the little girl's erotic subjectivity exclusively in terms of the foreclosure of homo-sexuality. This is the direct and coherent implication of the theory of gender that Butler works with, one which assumes the constitutive and *a priori* eras-ure of her homosexuality by a gender system that invents (hetero)sexual normativity and imposes it on living bodies. This is, in my view, however, both a reduction of the psychoanalytic insight and an unfounded theoretical assumption about the process of the sexualization of the subject.

A last and ongoing chapter in this transatlantic dialogue concerns the work of the neo-Lacanian Slavoj Žižek. He perpetuates the economy of dialectics and lack, which runs from Hegel to Lacan, though he does so with a smug pretence at debunking. He also shows the same disregard as did Lacan for the project of empowering an alternative female subjectivity. Žižek argues that the 'illusion' of consciousness comes down to its intrinsic link, and unpayable debt, to the 'Real': the primordial libidinal matter which constructs social activity by providing the necessarily silenced foundations for what – if any-thing – can be spoken. This structuring lack is central to Lacan's ontology of negativity. The 'object' of ideology does not quite exist; it is a creative empty place and what it creates is the illusion of a coherent decisional self. The point is that ideological representations work, whether their content is 'true' or 'false'. The rate of success of ideology, therefore, has nothing to do with the truth or falsity of its representation. What matters instead is the subjective position that ideology implicitly creates in the process of enunciation. With this move, Žižek actualizes at the subjective level Lacan's brand of structural linguistics: just as there is no logical or necessary connection between the signifier and its signified content, there is no necessary relation between the content of ideology and its effect. No matter what it represents, the effect is to create a 'slot' or a place of enunciation for the subject, and for Žižek there is no escape from this infernal circular machinery. It is the more infernal as its operations are non-transparent; although Žižek attempts to define three moments of ideological production – ideology as a complex of ideas and texts, as the external materiality of the state apparatus, and as the general and widespread production of society at large and especially the media – he pushes to extremes, in my view, the banalization of the notion of ideology to cover any and all forms of representation.

Žižek argues that the 'false' element in the 'false consciousness' induced by ideology is due to a structural impossibility, the translation into human/social/public language of the underlying libidinal forces. Žižek expresses this as the notion of 'fantasy', which is simultaneously driven to seek fulfilment and necessarily fails to do so. The political implications of this infernal circularity are significant: for Žižek we are within ideological space the moment any content, be it 'true' or 'false', is functional with regard to social relations. Therefore, even attempts at stepping out of what we perceive as ideology are the very form of our enslavement to it, in that they are no less 'ideological'. Žižek quotes as examples of this circularity the rhetoric of 'humanitarian wars' in the Balkans or the self-contradictions involved in trying to beat the media at their own game. The consequence is that, in order to be effective, relations of both domination and of resistance to ideology must remain con-cealed. We can only denounce ideology from a place that must stay empty, not determined by any positive reality, otherwise we would fall back into ideology. As this special place is, for Žižek as for Lacan, that of psychoanalysis, the function of which is to make the subject accept His necessary enslavement. The political double-bind closes upon itself and the end result is a recipe for disempowerment.

In opposition to this long fall into nihilism, poststructuralist philosophers of difference like Irigaray and Deleuze propose quite a different reading of the subject. Bodily matter, sexuality and reproduction are indeed central to their way of thinking, but they are also de-essentialized. The emphasis on sexuality and filiation, or the materiality of human reproduction, lies at the heart of the discussion of both the kinship system and the social field. In this tradition of thought, issues of sexuality and filiation are so fundamental that they cannot be reduced to a sociology of gender roles. I would rather say that the difference rests on one crucial point: we need to think the co-presence of morphological and social power relations and their joint impact upon the positioning of the subject.

On the issue of the dialectics of self and other, Irigaray's radical heterosexuality postulates the need for a female homosexual nucleus – a primary homosexual bond that is required to recompose women's primary narcissism, which has been badly damaged by the phallocentric symbolic. The love of another woman is crucial to this process of laying the foundations for one's empowerment. The other woman – the other of the Other – is the site of recognition of one's effort at becoming in the sense of pursuing a process of transformation, of deeply-rooted change, of in-depth metamorphoses. This primary narcissism must not be confused with secondary narcissistic manifestations – with which women have been richly endowed under patriarchy. Vanity, the love of appearances, the dual burden of narcissism and paranoia are the signs of female objectification under the power (potestas) of the Same. Nor is it per se the prelude to a lesbian position: it simply states the structural significance of love for one's sex, for the sexual same, as a crucial building block for one's sense of self-esteem. It is important to emphasize, therefore, the importance of primary narcissism as a fundamental threshold of sustainability that allows the female subject to undertake the process of self-assertion first, and then that of transformation. Before one can undo, deconstruct, redefine, or relinquish subjectivity, one has to be a subject to begin with. The alternative is a recipe for self-annihilation.

Whether in queer or in radical heterosexual thinking and politics a subversive approach to sexual identity and to sexuality is one of the legacies of feminism. The legacy of Hegelian dialectics continues to be strong, both positively and negatively, in feminist theories of subjectivity. In other words, the object choice (homo/hetero/'perverse') or the choice of sexual lifestyle is far less important than the shifts entailed by this process in the structures of the desiring subjects. I tend to see the erotics of 'becoming-woman' as a vitalistic kind of sensuality that remains deeply attached to the embodied subject. This is in keeping with the tradition of 'enchanted materialism', to which Deleuze, Irigaray and a great deal of French and continental culture belong. That much of this tradition is close to libertine literature, the *ars erotica* that Foucault regretted had left mainstream culture, only makes it historically all the more interesting. Two key ideas are worth stressing here: first, the emphasis on the specific intelligence of the enfleshed subject; second, both the continuity and the quarrel with psychoanalysis and the project to disengage desire from lack and negativity, to think it instead as plenitude and abundance.

Feminism is thus posited in turn as a political and ethical passion, and consequently the feminist subject position not as a given but as a project, as something that some women can yearn for and work towards, for the good of all. I would call this an 'intensive' reading of feminist politics which assumes a non-unitary, nomadic subject equally opposed to classical humanism and to liberal notions of the individual. Accordingly it posits the instance of the political not merely in the wilful commitment to the basic pursuit of decency, social justice and human rights, though these remain unfulfilled and desirable aims. Politics can also be defined in terms of the passions and values that underscore it. This 'typology' of ethical passions is an approach inspired by Nietzsche, read with Deleuze. It allows us to see volitional choices not as transparent, self-evident positions, but rather as complex, contradictory multifaceted ones. A dose of suspicion towards one's own 'motivations' or intentionality does not condemn one to cynicism, nihilism or relativism. On the contrary, by injecting affectivity, self-reflexivity and joy into the political exercise, it may return political beliefs to their full inspiration.

Note

1. I owe this witty formulation to the discussions with my colleagues in the European Network ATHENA.

References

Alcoff, Linda (2000) 'Philosophy Matters: A Review of Recent Work in Feminist Philosophy', *Signs*, vol. 25, no. 3, pp. 841–82.
Ansell Pearson, Keith (1997) *Viroid Life: Perspectives on Nietzsche and the Transhuman Condition*. London and New York: Routledge.
Benhabib, Seyla (1992) *The Situated Self*. Cambridge: Polity Press.
Benhabib, Seyla (1999) 'Sexual Difference and Collective Identities: The New Global Constellation', *Signs* vol. 24, no. 2, pp. 335–62.
Benjamin, Jessica (1988) *The Bonds of Love*. New York: Pantheon.
Braidotti, Rosi (1991) *Patterns of Dissonance*. Cambridge: Polity Press.
Braidotti, Rosi (1998) 'Sexual Difference Theory', in Alison Jaggar and Iris M. Young, eds, *A Companion to Feminist Philosophy*. Oxford: Blackwell, pp. 298–306.
Brodkin, Sacks (1994) 'How Did Jews Become White Folks?', in Steven Gregory and

Roger Sanjek, eds, *Race*. New Brunswick, NJ: Rutgers University Press.

Buchanan, Ian and Claire Colebrook, eds (2000) *Deleuze and Feminist Theory*. Edinburgh: Edinburgh University Press.

Butler, Judith (1987) *Subjects of Desire: Hegelian Reflections in Twentieth Century France*. New York: Columbia University Press.

Butler, Judith (1990) *Gender Trouble*. New York: Routledge.

Cavarero, Adriana (1990) *Nonostante Platone*. Rome: Editori Riuniti.

Chanter, Tina (1995) *Ethics of Eros: Irigaray's Rewriting of the Philosophers*. New York and London: Routledge.

Cixous, Hélène (1977) 'Le sexe ou la tête', *Les Cahiers du Grif* 5, pp. 5–15.

Cixous, Hélène (1980) 'The Laugh of the Medusa', in E. Marks and I. de Courtivron, eds, *New French Feminisms*. Amherst: University of Massachussetts Press, pp. 245–64.

Clément, Catherine (1974) "Lacan, ou l'identité européenne", *Le Magazine Littéraire* 271, pp. 54–5.

Colebrook, Claire (2000) 'Is Sexual Difference a Problem?' in Ian Buchanan and Claire Colebrook, eds, *Deleuze and Feminist Theory*. Edinburgh: Edinburgh University Press, pp. 110–27.

Deleuze, Gilles and Félix Guattari (1972) *L'Anti-Oedipe: Capitalisme et schizophrénie I*. Paris: Minuit; *Anti-Oedipus: Capitalism and Schizophrenia*. trans. R. Hurley, M. Seem and H.R. Lane. New York: Viking/Richard Seaver, 1977.

Deleuze, Gilles and Félix Guattari (1980) *Mille Plateaux: Capitalisme et schizophrénie II*. Paris: Minuit; *A Thousand Plateaus: Capitalism and Schizophrenia*, trans. Brian Massumi. Minneapolis: University of Minnesota Press, 1987.

Delphy, Christine (1975) 'Pour un matérialisme feministe', *L'Arc* 61, pp. 61–7.

Delphy, Christine (1984) *Close to Home*. London: Hutchinson.

Derrida, Jacques (1980) *La carte postale de Socrate à Freud et au-delà Paris*. Paris: Flammarion.

Descombes, Vincent (1979) *Le même et l'autre*. Paris: Minuit; *Modern French Philosophy*, trans. L. Scott-Fox and J.M. Harding. Cambridge: Cambridge University Press, 1980.

Dews, Peter (1995) 'The Tremor of Reflection: Slavoj Žižek's Lacanian Dialectics', *Radical Philosophy* 72, pp. 17–29.

Duchen, Claire (1986) *Feminism in France*. London: Routledge & Kegan Paul.

Foucault, Michel (1975a) *Les mots et les choses*. Paris: Gallimard; *The Order of Things*. London: Tavistock, 1977.

Foucault, Michel (1975b) *Surveiller et punir*. Paris: Gallimard; *Discipline and Punish*. London: Allen Lane, 1977.

Frye, Marilyn (1996) 'The Necessity of Differences: Constructing a Positive Category of Women', *Signs*, vol. 21, no. 4, pp. 991–1010.

Fuss, Diane (1989) *Essentially Speaking: Feminism, Nature and Difference*. New York and London: Routledge.

Gatens, Moira and Genevieve Lloyd (1999) *Collective Imaginings: Spinoza, Past and Present*. London and New York: Routledge.

Gilroy, Paul (1993) *The Black Atlantic: Modernity and Double Consciousness*. Cambridge: MA: Harvard University Press.

Grewal, I. and Kaplan, C., eds (1994) *Scattered Hegemonies*. Minneapolis: University of Minnesota Press.

Irigaray, Luce (1974) *Speculum de l'autre femme*. Paris: Minuit; *Speculum of the Other Woman*, trans. Gillian Gill. Ithaca: Cornell University Press, 1985.

Irigaray, Luce (1977) *Ce sexe qui n'est pas un*. Paris: Minuit; *This Sex Which Is Not One*, trans. Catherine Porter. Ithaca: Cornell University Press, 1985.

Irigaray, Luce (1982) *Passions élémentaires*. Paris: Éditions de Minuit.

Irigaray, Luce (1987) 'Egales à qui?', *Critique: Revue Générale des Publications Françaises et étrangères*, vol. 43, pp. 480, 420–37.

Jagger, Alison and Iris Marion Young, eds (1998) *A Companion to Feminist Philosophy*. Malden, MA: Blackwell.

Lloyd, Genevieve (1985) *The Man of Reason*. London: Methuen.

Lonzi, Carla (1974) *Sputiamo su Hegel*. Milano: Rivolta Femminile.

Macintyre, Ben (1992) *Forgotten Fatherland: The Search for Elizabeth Nietzsche*. London: Macmillan.

Massumi, Brian (1992) *A User's Guide to Capitalism and Schizophrenia*. Boston, MA: MIT Press.

Mohanty, Chandra Talpade (1984) 'Under Western Eyes: Feminist Scholarship and Colonial Discourse', *Boundary*, vol. 2, no. 3, pp. 333–58.

Moi, Toril (1994) *Simone de Beauvoir: The Making of an Intellectual Woman*. Oxford: Blackwell.

Morrison, Toni (1993) *Playing in the Dark: Whiteness and the Literary Imagination*. New York: Vintage Books.

Rich, Adrienne (1979) *On Lies, Secrets and Silence*. New York: W.W. Norton.

Rich, Adrienne (1977) *Of Woman Born*. New York: W.W. Norton.

Rich, Adrienne (1985) *Blood, Bread and Poetry*. New York: W.W. Norton.

Scott, Joan Wallach (1996) *Only Paradoxes to Offer: French Feminism and the Rights of Man*. Cambridge. MA: Harvard University Press.

Spivak, Gayatri Chakravorty (1983) 'Displacement and the Discourse of Woman', in Mark Kupnick, ed., *Displacement: Derrida and After*. Bloomington: Indiana University Press, pp. 169–95.

Spivak, Gayatri Chakravorty (1989) *In Other Worlds*. New York: Routledge.

Spivak, Gayatri Chakravorty (1992) 'French Feminism Revisited: Ethics and Politics', in Judith Butler and Joan Scott, eds, *Feminists Theorize the Political*. New York: Routledge.

Stanton, Donna C. (1980) 'Language and Revolution: The Franco-American Disconnection', in Hester Eisenstein and Alice Jardine, eds, *The Future of Difference*. Boston, MA: G.K. Hall.

Turkle, Shirley (1984) *Psychoanalytic Politics*. New York: Basic Books.

Whitford, Margaret (1991) *Luce Irigaray: Philosophy in the Feminine*. London: Routledge.

Wittiq, Monique (1973) *Le Corps lesbien*. Paris: Minuit.

Wittiq, Monique (1979a) 'Paradigm', in G. Stambolian and E. Marks, eds, *Homosexualities and French Literatures*. Ithaca: Cornell University Press.

Wittiq, Monique (1979b) *Lesbian Peoples: Material for a Dictionary*, with Sande Zeig. New York: Avon.

Wittig, Monique (1992) *The Straight Mind and Other Essays*. Hemel Hempstead: Harvester Wheatsheaf.

Wright, Elizabeth (1992) *Feminism and Psychoanalysis: A Critical Dictionary*. Oxford: Blackwell.

Žižek, Slavoj (1992) *Enjoy your Symptom! Jacques Lacan in Hollywood and Out*. London and New York: Routledge.

PART IV

Race and Ethnicity

10

Feminism and Anti-Semitism

LILIANE KANDEL

The history of the relationship between anti-Semitism and feminisms in Europe is a complex and contradictory one. Only a few years ago, the simple juxtaposition of the terms 'feminism' and 'anti-Semitism' in an article, for example, would have seemed strange, inappropriate, and indeed incongruous to many feminist activists and scholars. Born in the wake of the antiracist movements in the United States and the movements of the left and far left in Europe, feminism sought to combat not only patriarchy, but 'all forms of oppression',[1] including racist[2] and anti-Semitic ideologies, discourses and positions. Feminism was also known to have been the direct or indirect target or victim of racism and anti-Semitism, and countless parallels were drawn between ethnic (or racist) oppression and sexist domination, and between anti-Semitic hatred and its misogynist counterpart. Between the discourse of domination or exclusion, on the one hand, and the discourse of feminist liberation and the struggles to achieve it, on the other, the only relationship imaginable was one of antagonism and conflict. No proximity, link or contamination could be envisaged.

This was one of the founding assumptions of the feminist movements of the 1970s. Gradually, however, new and disturbing debates emerged (e.g. between feminists of different ethnic origins), while historical studies revealed feminisms different from those we knew or thought we knew. The notion of 'racism' itself began to cover ever more complex and increasingly polysemous situations, some of which differed widely from anti-Semitism, and even more from 'sexism'; 'antiracist' theses were sometimes, paradoxically, taken up and used by right-wing racists, particularly in the 'new right'.[3] Meanwhile the word 'feminism' itself was increasingly being written in the plural.

Completely new and sometimes disturbing political configurations were being revealed: militant feminists who were unswerving advocates of *sexual*

equality were not necessarily hostile to theories of *racial hierarchy* and eugenicism; heroic members of the French Resistance against the German occupation and Nazism seemed almost entirely indifferent to feminist arguments,
while fascist or Nazi women's groups were adopting some of feminism's
demands; lastly (though this came as no surprise to most people) impeccable
antiracists revealed themselves to be at the same time fiercely anti-feminist
and misogynous.

These are just some of the bizarre discourses and paradoxical political
phenomena that I shall try to describe here. I shall do so principally by
examining the peak moment of Western anti-Semitism: the Nazi period and
its systematic attempt to eradicate the European Jews, its echoes in contemporary feminist movements, the various readings and interpretations it has
given rise to, and their accompanying debates.

Traces, Echoes and Returns: Anti-Semitism and Contemporary Feminist Movements

Discomfort among Jewish feminists

Is the feminist movement free of any manifestations of exclusion, discrimination or ethnic prejudice? In the early 1970s we thought so, and knew that
'sisterhood is powerful'; however, it was not long before we discovered the
limits of that power and that sisterhood. The first dissonant voices were those
of women of colour and women from other marginalized groups, all of
whom voiced the discomfort they sometimes felt in militant feminist groups.

Later it was the turn of Jewish feminists to identify apparently anodyne
discourses, articles, words or books that they felt to be either overtly or
insidiously anti-Semitic.[4] They noted the various occurrences of disguised
Judeophobic phrases in feminist groups or writings, showing how Jewish
women were rendered invisible and how anti-Semitism was continually ignored
or denied; they pointed out instances of indifference towards the Shoah and
its victims, the stereotyped images of Jews and Jewish history (Jews greedy for
money and power; arrogant, ambitious Jewish women; JAPs), and so on. In
the United States 1982 was the year of 'coming out': the public and often
stormy exploration of this aspect of the movement which had hitherto remained underground or had been mentioned only discreetly. The first 'Jewish
feminist conference', which took place in San Francisco from 29 to 31 May
1982, brought together around six hundred participants;[5] the June issue of *Ms*
contained a long article by Letty C. Pogrebin (one of the journal's founders)
on 'Anti-Semitism in the Feminist Movement'; a little earlier E.T. Beck had
published *Nice Jewish Girls: A Lesbian Anthology* (1988) in which several articles
– hitherto disseminated to a limited readership only – expressed the authors'
discomfort when faced with manifestations of anti-Semitism (and particularly
their denial) in feminist and/or lesbian collectives.

However, the bitterest debates emerged around a completely different subject: the problem of the Middle East and the very recent Libyan war. In the UK *Spare Rib* published a series of unusually violent (and one-sided) texts and interviews, the first one asserting that anti-Zionism was a necessary aspect of feminism. 'If a woman calls herself feminist she should consciously call herself anti-Zionist.' For around a year the journal refused to publish any of the numerous letters of protest it received, including those from Israeli feminists who were critical of their own government. 'As a collective', declared *Spare Rib*, 'we are united in a pro-Palestinian position' (*Spare Rib* 131, June 1983: 4). Meanwhile the letters page included statements such as, 'Feminists must give full support to the Palestinians and the struggle to smash the state of Israel. Anything else is a wet liberal cop-out' (*Spare Rib* 123, July 1983: 5). The *London Women's Liberation Newsletter* included flyers from Palestinian groups of women stating: 'Israel's "Final Solution" to the Palestinian Problem – GENO-CIDE.' The feeling expressed by many readers that these articles were not only 'anti-Zionist' but also, implicitly, anti-Semitic, was rejected out of hand (which, as one article noted, would never have happened in the case of a racist text). Only in 1983 were some responses published in *Spare Rib*. More often they appeared in other journals.[6]

It was at this time that a number of militant Jewish feminists decided to found their own journal, *Shifra*, in order to explore and analyse their positions without being censured or continually subject to suspicion, criticism and attack (Seidel 1986).

The same debates occurred in the US feminist press – but there the different theses were always presented in an equal and balanced manner. In July 1982 *Off Our Backs* published a violently anti-Israeli article which challenged the state's very right to exist (Women against Imperialism 1982); it was, nevertheless, alongside a response from Di Vilde Chayes, a Jewish lesbian collective (Di Vilde Chayes 1982). These articles were followed by many others: Zionist and anti-Zionist feminists, Jewish, Israeli, Palestinian. These women expressed their opinions abundantly, and without restriction or censorship. Whatever their position on the situation, most of these contributions reflected the founding feminist utopias as well as the political climate of the far left groups of the 1970s. In this context, the feminist, anticolonial, anti-imperialist, antiracist and anti-Zionist struggles all seemed to unite against one ideal enemy: the state of Israel represented all these sins rolled into one.

The same debates occurred at the time of the Gulf War, particularly in Germany and Austria (Kohn-Ley 1994). However, here the slippage, ambiguities and amalgamations between anti-Zionism and anti-Semitism were less obvious. In the meantime many analyses of the dangers of such discourses had been disseminated:[7] the confusion between Jews/Israelis/Zionists had become more visible, and therefore more quickly identifiable and so open to challenge. Furthermore, while it was still easy for feminists (as for all movements of the left) to criticize Israeli and/or American imperialism, it was rather harder for them, as feminists, to defend Saddam Hussein, particularly after some of his measures of particular detriment to women had been publicized.[8]

However, the problem of the situation in the Middle East and its some-times Judeophobic reverberations[9] resurfaced regularly in feminist movements, as reflected in, among other things, the recent controversy between the *Nouvelles questions féministes* collective and a group of French feminist academics led by Rita Thalmann.[10]

Lastly, on another level, we should mention the many debates, notably in the United States, around the way Jewish culture and history are ignored and systematically rendered invisible in most 'multicultural' courses, conferences and study manuals, particularly within the field of Women's Studies.[11]

Feminist theology and the 'deicidal people'

Another series of debates surrounded certain trends in feminist theology, in their most characteristic aspect: the association between a form of feminine (or feminist) millenarianism with explicit, violently judeophobic ideas and/or the (surreptitious) legitimization of the genocide of the Jews. These currents, which to my knowledge[12] are not really present in France, though they flourished in the Anglo-Saxon countries and in Germany during the late 1970s, are worthy of a more extensive analysis, which I can only outline here. Let us say in summary that they are mainly characterized by a virulent – and completely new – criticism of the Jewish 'patriarchy', which is accused of having sounded the death knell of the era of mother-goddesses,[13] or of having murdered Christ out of macho resentment. Indeed, for these theologians, who claim to identify with feminism,[14] Christ is an essentially androgynous, not to say feminine, figure – or at the very least favourable to women. The position held by these authors is at great variance with Vatican II, which they ignore – and in fact openly condemn (Decke 1988).

The old theme of the 'deicidal people' has been given a modern makeover here, and not by overt anti-Semites but by radical feminist academics. Once again the Jews are guilty of murder. This time the victim is the mother-goddess (Plaskow 1980), or the woman-Christ (Daum 1980). Thus once again the Jews are guilty of nothing less than the *establishment of patriarchy*[15] – and consequentially (in a dizzy leap across twenty centuries of history) of the 'Nazi patriarchy'. It is thus no longer forbidden to think that the latter, having turned against its own 'initiators', made them pay the proper price. Or rather, as Mulack stated, that while the Christians were not responsible for the Nazi genocide, the Jews were the victims of their own religion.

It is impossible not to acknowledge in these currents some new (feminine) variant on the grand themes we thought had disappeared: in other words, the old theologies of rejection and, above all, substitution – in this case, *substitution of the victims* – and/or the possibility of a *new alliance*, this time with the people of women. We can also see that, under these conditions, the critical work being done by Jewish women (whether theologians or not) on their own patriarchal traditions (see Heschel 1988) is to all intents and purposes silenced.

These theses provoked a great many strong reactions, first in Germany and then in the United States. The debate, which began in the late 1980s, has raged for a long time, notably in *Schlangenbrut*, the German journal of feminist theology, in many articles and books written by Protestant, Catholic and Jewish women theologians, and by militant feminists with an interest in questions of history, memory and/or feminist theories.[16] Particular attention has been paid in these discussions to conflations of Judaism and/or Nazism with patriarchy: in other words, of the masculine domination of women with the genocide of the Jews by the Nazis.

This is an important issue, particularly for feminist theologians and theoreticians. Thus L. Siegele-Wenschkewitz (1997: 245) wonders whether the need felt by some theologians to 'try at any cost to establish an analogy between the suffering of women and that of the Jews' is not ultimately the proof that 'it is in some way impossible for feminists to condemn anti-Semitism in itself'.

Feminist Readings of Nazism and Anti-Semitism

These are the most visible and explicit forms of the debate on anti-Semitism in the feminist movement. There is, however, another quite separate series of manifestations that are more complex and harder to identify, yet also more widespread and more controversial (nor are they in any way specific to feminist circles). Clearly in Western countries today, particularly in movements of the left, and even more so in feminist circles, it would never occur to anyone to cry 'Send the Jews to the gas chamber!' (nor would they have the desire or even fantasy of doing so). The memory of the war and the Shoah is present in family memories and in school lessons; the media regularly take it on themselves to disseminate – with varying degrees of efficiency – its main elements; and, last but not least, the overt expression of racial hatred is an offence that can be tried by the courts. However, while no one would cry 'Death to the Jews!',[17] there is a whole group of discourses which, one way or another, suggest that perhaps the Jews after all did not really die; more precisely, that they did not die in the conditions in which they are said to have died, nor in such large numbers; or that after all their death was not as appalling as all that, nor so different from that of many other groups who have been discriminated against, oppressed or exploited at other times in history, elsewhere, in other countries or on other continents. Here we see the essential aspects of negationist and revisionist theses seeking to deny, banalize, relativize or minimize the importance of the Nazi undertaking to destroy the

Jews of Europe. It is well known that their authors often declare – and believe – themselves to be sincerely antiracist and entirely lacking in any Judeophobic feeling whatsoever. But we also know that, for many analysts,[18] negationism and revisionism are precisely the *contemporary forms of anti-Semitism* – at least in Western countries[19] – which are most frequently not identified or recognized as such by their own authors.[20]

These discourses, which are a long way from the anti-Semitism of the 1930s, are common not only in the restricted circles of the right or extreme right, but also, in only slightly different forms, in certain elements of the classic left, the far left and, again in only slightly different forms, in feminist movements. In the latter, particularly in Germany and more recently in France, they have given rise to an abundant literature, which I shall try to summarize here, concentrating my attention on the feminist historiography of the Third Reich. For it is here that the fundamental elements of feminist debates around Nazism, anti-Semitism and the Shoah are located. So it is hardly surprising that this field contains, with a few minor differences, all the variations of what Habermas, during the *Historikerstreit,* called the 'apologetic tendencies' of the Third Reich, notably:

1. Simple *omission* or occultation: the problem of the Shoah and anti-Semitism – i.e. that of the victims of Nazism as of its agents – is neither addressed nor even mentioned.
2. *Relativization*: the issue is mentioned, but among many other aspects of the Nazi period – starting with misogyny – as a kind of *detail* of that period (this was for a long time the most frequently adopted and bitterly disputed position).
3. Surreptitious (and of course guilty) *legitimization*: these are extreme but significant cases, of which the feminist theology described above is an eloquent example.

Nazism without the Shoah

The later years of the 1970s saw the emergence, particularly in Germany, of a vast array of studies on the history of women during the Nazi period. A two-volume collection entitled W*omen under German Fascism*[21] was published, full of documents and information that had hitherto been little known or understood. However, the most surprising thing about these two volumes was what did not appear within them. Devoted to 'the history of German women' under Nazism, they made almost no mention of those equally German women whom the Nazis persecuted: disabled or 'antisocial' women, women suffering from mental illness and prostitutes; still less did they deal with the Jewish and gypsy women who were deported and exterminated in the camps.

This was not an isolated case. Nicole Gabriel (1983, 1986) has shown that more or less the same silence reigned in a number of books, all published in the early 1980s, not to mention the countless articles and personal accounts of the experiences of women during the last war.[22]

So, for a long period the 'history of women' under Nazism was confined to that of *German, Aryan women, who more or less conformed to Nazi norms and ideals.* This history almost entirely omitted the existence of those women who were victims of the regime, its murders, its camps and the Shoah: it was, in its own way, *Judenrein.* This made it all the easier to detail all the forms of discrimination exerted against German (Aryan) women and to present them all as victims not only of patriarchy but also of German 'fascism' – avoiding, at the same time, any investigation of their participation in or possible support for the Nazi project.

This aspect was noted by Strobl (1985) in a fiercely polemical article on the abundant feminist literature at that time devoted to the sufferings and heroism of the *Trümmerfrauen.*[23]

> 'It is not my intention,' she said, 'to minimise the sufferings of these women.... But nor can I keep myself from asking: so what were you doing *before?*... Did you start being afraid when *you* had to run into the shelters in the middle of the night with your children in your arms? So what did you think when the woman next door was taken away in the middle of the night by the SS, with her children in her arms? When all those unoccupied homes suddenly appeared in your area – unoccupied by the Jews [who had been living there until then]? (1985: 28–9)

A great many feminist historians and theoreticians later spoke out in a similar vein against this soothing vision of German women under the Third Reich.

An 'apologetic' history; or, the innocence of the oppressed

For many years the question of women's participation in the Nazi project (or, on the contrary, of their lack of compromise with it, their 'innocence') lay at the heart of debates among feminist historians. Relegated to a separate social 'sphere' (the women's *Lebensraum*),[24] were they all, in the same way, victims of a misogynous, macho regime? Were they all cut off from the 'masculine' world – the world of war, of brutality, of slaughter and massacres, of mass extermination? Or did they in fact agree with the ideology of racial hierarchy, of 'lives unworthy to be lived'? Had they, one way or another, been implicated in the policies of stigmatization, discrimination, persecution and indeed extermination of 'undesirable' elements? Was anti-Semitism, as the psychoanalyst Mitscherlich (1983) claimed, just 'a man's illness', from which women were miraculously preserved?

There were countless discussions around these questions, of which the debate between Claudia Koonz and Gisela Bock is almost certainly the paradigmatic example.[25] According to Bock (1986) the Nazi regime was, contrary to widespread belief, an essentially anti-natalist regime, which not only carried out the forced sterilization of nearly 200,000 German women judged to be

'below standard'[26] but also maintained a constant threat for all women without exception, in their capacity as at least potential mothers. Furthermore,
according to Bock, women who were fully involved in anti-Semitic ideology
and were participants in the Nazi regime (such as concentration camp guards)
were neither mothers nor housewives, but simply 'childless working women',
victims in practice of the masculine ideology of competition and careers
(Bock 1986: 139). 'Real women' (mothers, wives) were thus above suspicion.
Lastly, she asserts, the difference between continuing to live after being stigmatized by sterilization or being condemned to die in a gas chamber because
of who one was born as (such as Jews and gypsies) 'was entirely relative'
(1986: 381).[27] All these men and women were equally stigmatized; equally
persecuted.

Koonz's work (1987) was radically opposed to this analysis, demonstrating
the various ways in which German women co-operated with the regime.
Thus she notes, without even mentioning the more fanatical activists, that
women participated in the Nazi project in different ways and at different
levels:

> mothers boycotted shops run by Jews, founded eugenicist schools ...; it was the
> women who denounced any suspicious strangers in the neighbourhood and closed
> their doors to any person regarded as dangerous. (46)

Above all, however, and in contrast to Bock, Koonz stresses the vital role of
the 'feminine sphere' (and thus that of mothers and housewives) in the functioning of the Nazi system as a whole:

> Nazi women were careful to make the world inhabited by members of their own
> community more pleasant. At the same time they made it unbearable for 'undesirable'
> citizens. They resolutely ignored attacks against socialists, Jews, religious opponents,
> the disabled or the degenerate, concentrating on their 'Aryan' families. [They] made
> an essential contribution to Nazism, preserving the illusion of love in an environment of hate.
> (46; my emphasis)

In other words, and this is her main thesis, the women's *Lebensraum* (i.e. the
specific fields of activity reserved for women and mothers) was in no way
'elsewhere', untouched by 'masculine' policy; nor was it the antidote to that
policy. On the contrary, it constituted an element, or rather an essential part
of its implementation, including its most destructive, murderous aspects:

> Women organised motherhood in a way that made the world appear normal and
> virtuous to the ordinary German citizen as to the most murderous member of the
> SS.... *They co-operated with the war, the genocide and the terror by ignoring them*, and
> helped to create an image of absolute normality. (46; my emphasis)

Other scholars have also sought to study the different ways in which women
participated in the Nazi regime, whether passively (through indifference or

simple submission to the regime) or directly, actively and deliberately, through denunciations, surveillance, betrayal, looting and involvement in the various organizations of the genocidal system, including as members of the SS or workers in the extermination camps.[28] It was therefore appropriate, according to the philosopher Walzer-Windaus, to reject the illusion, widespread among many feminist activists, of the 'grace of birth as a woman' (*Gnade der weiblichen Geburt*) and to examine the specifically feminine forms of anti-Semitism and Nazism.[29]

The issues at stake in this debate were of considerable importance: by showing that German women had not only submitted (if unwillingly) to the Nazi regime but had also, often, been its full agents, these scholars took it upon themselves to confront all their 'negative heritage' (in the words of Gravenhorst 1990) – notably the anti-Semitism of the preceding generation – and overtly refused to take one of the detours of the German historical debate as described by Rita Thalmann (1987): 'through *the banalization of the notion of victim, the banalization of genocide*'.

A matter of historical 'detail'

The issue of victims was also linked to another, and probably the most widespread, form of relativization of the Nazi period and the genocide of the Jews. On the basis of the evident continuity, permanence and universality of masculine domination, many feminists tried to show that, beyond the apparent differences in historical, sociological or political conditions, the position of women under Nazism did not, all things considered, differ radically and was no worse than that of women in other periods or other countries. They supported this idea by reference, in no particular order, to the disappearance of the mother-goddesses, witchhunts,[30] restrictions on women's right to work, family policy, eugenicism, macho violence of all kinds and, quite simply, all the disasters of war. Thus we can read, from the pen of a feminist academic, that for women everything was already so bad under Weimar that after 1933 'everything went on as before'.[31] Or that for women where family policy was concerned, there was no difference between the Third Reich and its neighbouring European countries: 'A real ideological mechanism was established in Italy, France and Germany during the 1930s in order to send women back into the home and keep them out of paid work' (Del Re 1994: 231).

Once again, we might wonder which women are being referred to in these texts. For, to support their assertions, one of these authors was obliged to forget all the women (and men) whose lives were definitively destroyed in 1933 and for whom precisely nothing at all continued as before, while the other had to keep silent on the fate of those women who, far from being sent back, were dragged away from their homes and families: women internees, deportees, women who were sterilized or murdered – in other words, the far more radical face of *the same 'demographic policy'*, which alone enables light to be shed on the Nazi slogans of the 'return to the home'. If we discount these forgotten elements, perhaps there was indeed no 'noteworthy difference' between the three countries of Italy, France and Germany.

Examples of this kind are legion, all one way or another implying the primacy (or anteriority, or pre-eminence) of gender domination over war and mass extermination. Among the more extreme, we shall cite Mary Daly, who, failing to recognize the specificity and centrality of Nazi anti-Semitism, sees it as a simple variation (or consequence) of gynophobia: 'all [Nazi victims] were cast in the victim role modeled on that of the victims of patriarchal gynocide, which is the root and paradigm for genocide' (Daly 1978: 298). She goes on: 'The paradigm and context for genocide is trite, everyday, banalized gynocide' (1978: 312).[32] (Strange as it may seem, we find the same presuppositions implicit in some more recent attempts to 'genderize' the Shoah: to prove that even the most extreme and undifferentiated situations of brutality and cruelty are simply yet more illustrations of the universality of the oppression of women and of the thousand-year-old patriarchy.[33])

There are several points to be made here. On the one hand we can observe in the history of all Western countries various and continuous forms of patriarchal mechanism (as well as continuities of capitalist mechanisms). The essential contribution of feminist studies was to make these continuities visible, to analyse and deepen our understanding of them. However, once this investigation starts to render impossible any distinction between dictatorship, terror and 'democracy',[34] or prevents (as happens in some of the studies cited) any consideration of events or extreme situations in their singularity, we can legitimately wonder whether such an analysis constitutes a proper viewpoint from which to approach and understand the Third Reich, Nazi anti-Semitism and the genocide of the Jews and gypsies, any more than the oppression of women and masculine domination.[35]

Another difficulty is that by proceeding in this way, Nazism (and genocidal anti-Semitism) can always be seen as a simple variation, an *avatar* (at best an extreme stage) *of patriarchy*; just as, for other authors before, it was an avatar of capitalism for example, or of a hundred-year-old German anti-Semitism, or of forced modernization, and so on: in other words, precisely as a *matter of detail*. It is here that the discourse of Jean-Marie Le Pen[36] parallels that of some left-wing militants and scholars. This lies in the refusal (by the former), the inability (for the latter) to conceive of historical singularities – moments of upheaval, rupture or disaster.

Lastly, it is important to note that the arguments I have (very sketchily) described up until now cannot be regarded as 'anti-Semitic' in the classical sense of the word, and their authors[37] even less so: at the most they demonstrate the difficulty, the discomfort and, above all, the *theoretical obstacles* faced by an entire generation of feminists in conceiving of their own relationship to the history of anti-Semitism and the Shoah. Nevertheless, as Gerstenberger (1987) and Nolan (1988) have shown, many of these studies, for example in social history or *Alltagsgeschichte*, often carried out by young, left-wing or feminist historians, were quickly adopted and readily used in the most conservative of circles.[38] Schmidt (1987) lists a number of paradoxical convergences and 'embarrassing similarities' (*peinliche Verwandschaften*) between feminist theses and certain ultra-conservative 'masculine' discourses, from which their authors thought themselves radically distanced. Thus she notes that the image of the women victims of Nazism unfailingly recalls that upheld, notably since Bitburg,[39] by the most conservative right:

> For conservatives, what matters are 'good Germans' in general, who are no longer ashamed of their past; for feminist academics it is 'oppressed women' in general, who must recognise their past and current role as objects for patriarchal policy.

The variations on the theme of the innocence of the oppressed (working class, civil populations, women), which were dominant at the time, simply conceal the fact that some of those oppressed were keen collaborators with the regime, and sometimes in its most bloody manifestations.

The 1930s: From 'Ordinary' Anti-Semitism to 'National Feminism'

Until now I have referred to the debates around the involvement (or not) in Nazism of 'ordinary', non-politicized, non-militant – or at least not particularly feminist – German women. Other studies have investigated the attitudes, writings and positions of feminist militants and feminist organizations before and during the Nazi period.

A certain number of studies have concentrated on anti-Semitism in the 'historical' feminist movement, from the late nineteenth century to the establishment of the Nazi regime. As might be expected, examples of public (or private) speeches, of declarations and decisions that were overtly or implicitly anti-Semitic, were neither rare nor very hard to find:[40] despite some commonality of views and unbroken collaboration with the JFB, many members of the BDF[41] subscribed, to varying degrees, to a whole series of anti-Semitic representations, attitudes and feelings current in German society at the time. The refusal to allow a Jewish activist to be the spokeswoman for one section of the BDF, attacks (on various pretexts) against this or that JFB executive, the accusation that the latter were trying to seize power, the passing over of Alice Salomon, historic leader of the BDF, as a candidate for president of the movement,[42] and Bäumer's declared indifference to anti-Semitic incidents in the BDF are just some indicators of this diffuse yet widespread *Weltanschauung*, which Volkov (2000) calls 'anti-Semitism as a cultural code'.[43]

Yet clearly it was during the 1920s and, still more, following the establishment of the Nazi regime that the question of the choices to be made in relation to the open, virulent and institutionalized anti-Semitism of the new leaders became an acute problem for the feminist movements.

Marion Kaplan (1979, 1984) has described the ambiguous reactions of German feminists during the rise and subsequent rule of the Nazis towards Jewish women who had been their fellow activists over many years. In her view an initial discomfort, followed by embarrassment, growing distance and increasing avoidance, and often the complete and brutal severing of relations, reflect the limits of sisterhood in a society increasingly dominated by anti-Semitism. Ottilie Schönwald, last president of the JFB, wrote: 'Where were German women then? If, shortly after the 9th of November 1933, they had found the same words for me that are in their letters to-day [1955] they would have meant so much to me' (in Kaplan 1979: 190). Many individual accounts confirm this description: like the rest of the population, German feminists made no effort to help; nor did they show the slightest solidarity with or compassion for their former friends, who were now ostracized and persecuted.

In June 1933 the BDF decided to dissolve as an organization rather than accept the requirements of the regime (expulsion of Jewish members, the election of National Socialists to the governing committee, integration into the *Frauenfront*, the umbrella organization of 'co-ordinated' women's organizations), which it considered incompatible with the political neutrality enshrined in its constitution. However, many BDF leaders, including President Gertrud Bäumer herself, had argued in favour of accepting the imposed conditions and the *Gleichschaltung*.[44] Some days before, and 'with deep regret', the BDF had accepted the resignation from its ranks of the federation of Jewish feminist organizations.

Certainly the BDF was itself divided: while some women had espoused anti-Semitic prejudice from the outset, others were reticent and tried in their own way to struggle against it. Between 1930 and 1932 some BDF groups and the newly elected president, A. von Zahn-Harnack, co-operated with the JFB in a campaign of conferences intended to combat the anti-Semitism that was increasing in non-Jewish circles. Meanwhile others (or perhaps the same ones?) were inviting to their debates guest speakers who were members of overtly anti-Semitic parties, and even of the NSDAP.[45]

It is also well known that a few courageous networks for mutual help existed. These were not the work of feminists (and those women who were involved in them were not acting specifically as women[46]). It was primarily the international feminist movements that gave support and, often, practical help to militant Jewish women in danger (Thalmann 1982).

Lastly, many studies have examined the paradoxical trajectories and speeches of a number of women who were sympathetic to Nazi arguments and were sometimes active militants themselves, and who also argued (or had argued at some time or another) in favour of women's rights, or at least some rights for some women. This position, for which Liliane Crips has coined the apt term 'National Feminist', was that of, for example, Käthe Schirmacher. Schirmacher had been active in the movement for women's rights since the late nineteenth century and was a fervent participant in all the big international conferences before 1914. She was the author of many feminist books expressing views quite heterodox for the time, continually restating the importance of the domestic work provided by women (Crips 1995). Gradually won over to nationalist and 'Nordist' arguments, she later defended the 'Germanic tradition of the rightful equality of the sexes' against Christianity ('an eastern Jewish conception of the inferiority, and thus the submission of Woman'), and eventually devoted herself to an implacable fight against 'internationalists', 'reds' and 'Jews'. Also worthy of mention is the case of A. Bluhm, an internationally renowned doctor and biologist, who was a wholehearted supporter of both Nazi eugenicist policy (particularly where sterilization was concerned) and the defence of the 'Germanic race' and, at the same time, of the rights of the women who belonged to that race, in particular women doctors (Crips 1997).

But the most explicit illustration of this 'National Feminist' current is provided by the journal *Die deutsche Kämpferin* and its editor Sophie Rogge-Börner. This journal advanced three main themes: virulent xenophobia, exacerbated (anti-Semitic) racism, and an elitist 'feminism' which demanded free access for 'Nordic' women to the key functions of the Nazi state. *Die deutsche Kämpferin* was thus absolutely (and publicly) opposed to the theses of the other Nazi women's groups, rejecting the cult of the woman-mother, challenging the masculine–feminine dichotomy, and calling on the new rulers to grant political and social parity to 'Nordic' men and women:

> The best men and women should share out the leadership of the Nation between them. All leadership functions should be carried out by men and women.... There should be sufficient numbers of capable women of value in all the assemblies.[47]

She also described the 'Versailles Diktat' as 'the pure expression of masculine politics'.[48] Rogge-Börner remained faithful to her *völkisch*, nationalist and anti-Semitic positions – and also, despite the many pressures to which she was subjected, to her vehement support for (Nordic) women's rights. It was for the latter position that her journal was banned in 1938 (Crips 1990).

For post-war generations, or indeed for those who lived through the war, the positions I have just described could clearly not be termed 'feminist'. Today's feminism seeks to be a universalist and egalitarian vision of the world and of society, opposed to any form of theoretical or political discrimination between different human groups. It is therefore obvious that the 'National Feminism' described above is to feminism what National Socialism was to socialism. However, this was not the case in the 1920s and 1930s. At that time many militant feminists were seduced by eugenicist theories, by the conception of the dual (masculine and feminine) social sphere, by the mystique of motherhood, and sometimes by the ambient anti-Semitism. The contradictions between these approaches seem flagrant to us today, but at the time the lines between the various discourses were fuzzy; the slippages between one position and another, the mutual encroachments and confusion of analyses and political choices were innumerable – and not only in Nazi and pre-Nazi Germany.

The Austrian Völkische Frauenbewegung (Gehmacher 1995 and 1998) or the group Aspiraciones in Spain (Bussy-Genevois 1994), to mention only two, provide illustrations of the paradoxical convergences, juxtapositions and co-habitations of the discourses of *racial hierarchy* and those of *sexual equality*.[49]

The situation was noticeably different for French feminists (Bard 1995, 1997), whose important role in the inter-war pacifist movement as a whole is well known. Indeed, we can identify every variation of opposition to the war in the various French feminist currents, from 'integral pacifism', fiercely opposed to Nazism but at the same time prepared to defend peace at all costs, to unconditional support for the Munich accords. This reflects a specifically feminine political culture of nonviolence as much as the positions dominating the overall public debate in France. Yet, whether due to some quasi-mystical attachment to the maternal (thus 'peace-loving') role of women or through active involvement in the political fight against fascism (often close to the positions of the French Communist Party), not a single group or militant feminist gave any support of any kind whatsoever to Nazi theories or the Nazi regime.

Strangely, however, the issue of Nazism aroused little interest in the feminist press and the regime was more criticized for its racism and anti-feminism than for its anti-Semitism. Like the left in general, the feminists failed to grasp the singularity of Hitler's project in this regard. Their critiques of Nazism were generally aimed at three aspects: the suppression of fundamental freedoms, the denial of women's right to work, and the Nazi conception of mother-hood and the family. It was only after 1939 that many of them were driven, out of patriotism and support for democracy, to become involved in the overt struggle against the Nazi regime: 'The defence of women's rights must now give way to that of the country.' Many feminists joined the Resistance.[50] A few others chose to collaborate. However, as Bard (1997: 160) notes, 'in either case it is clear that feminist convictions were only a marginal element in their motivations.'

Conclusions

What conclusions can we draw at the end of this brief overview? Some feminists fought against the fascist and Nazi regimes in the 1930s; others accepted and indeed joined them. In both cases, as we have seen, these choices were only distantly influenced by their involvement in feminism or their feminist beliefs.

Similarly, in the 1970s militant feminists supported (or accepted without any obvious difficulty, and sometimes themselves developed) arguments which, however unintentionally, contributed to the discourses of the banalization or minimization of anti-Semitism and the genocide of Jews. By contrast, others denounced and fought against these discourses, although it should be noted that they never did so *as feminists*; that is, in the name and with the help of the very theories that we had all helped to develop and to establish.

How do we account for these contradictions? Rather than investigate the 'resistance' of militant feminists to confronting certain problems,[51] should we not turn our attention to the massive effects of the *resistance of theory*, its difficulties or incapacities in taking account of social breakdown, of extreme phenomena, of exceptions, once these no longer concern the division of humanity along gender lines? We might then ask ourselves whether thinking in terms of the continuity, universality and centrality of gender domination[52] does not come up against its own limitations when required to deal with certain behaviours, situations and moments of breakdown, extreme violence and massive attack against (this time ungendered) humanity. Are we dealing with 'anti-Semitism' proper here? I doubt it – although many feminists often experience it as such – even though many covert anti-Semitic discourses can often, and easily, be accommodated within the approach I have described.

Perhaps the real issue lies elsewhere. As we now know, Nazi anti-Semitism was not a subcategory of racism – at least not of *discriminatory or exploitative racism* (the analysis of which proved so useful in its day for the understanding of patriarchal domination: 'anti-woman racism'). It was in a completely different category: that of *exterminationist racism* (of which the Rwandan conflict has given us a recent, appalling example).[53] To conceptualize the latter and achieve a precise measure of the historical upheavals it brought about, its effects and echoes for us, will almost certainly require different theoretical approaches from those that have long presided over feminist analyses. However, this conceptualization is also the necessary condition that will enable us to understand phenomena such as historical anti-Semitism, its developments and its contemporary modalities.

Translated from French by Trista Selous

Notes

1. Slogan of the Women's Liberation Movement (MLF) in France, 1973.
2. Of which sexism was said to be a privileged illustration.
3. Dhavernas and Kandel 1983; Thalmann 1985–98; Kandel 1993; Taguieff 1987, 1993.
4. See in particular Daum 1980; Plaskow 1980; Klepfisz 1981; London Jewish Lesbian Feminist Group 1982; Pogrebin 1982, 1991; Bulkin 1984; Kunstenaar 1988; Morris 1990.
5. The August–September 1982 issue of *Off Our Backs* (vol. 12, no. 8) is largely devoted to this conference.
6. Thus Dena Attar (1983) wondered whether 'feminist' support for the 'destruction of the Jewish state' signified unconditional support for terrorist acts such as the Munich bombing. With the *Spare Rib* collective in mind, she added, 'you, the women of colour cannot dismiss anti-Semitism as "a white women's issue" and refuse to discuss it'.
7. Taguieff 1989 in France, for example.

8. There were a few rare exceptions, however (Michel 1993), usually arguing in the name of 'pacifism', but a pacifism with an anti-American (or anti-Western), pro-Arab and anti-Israeli bias. Schulze (1991) provides a critique of the ambiguous positions adopted during this period by both the German left and some feminists, such as Alice Schwarzer, editor of the magazine *Emma*.

9. These have nothing to do with reasoned, legitimate and acceptable criticisms of the policies of the various Israeli governments.

10. See 'Les féministes face à l'antisémitisme et au racisme', *Bulletin de l'ANEF*, supplement to no. 26, Spring–Summer 1998, and the 'right to reply' exchanges in nos 27 and 28. I do not examine here the texts on the new Intifada (since October 2000); at the moment the situation is in a state of flux, as are the positions adopted.

11. Cf. Beck 1991a, 1991b; Biale et al. 1998.

12. The strong lay tradition, particularly in political movements, probably has something to do with it.

13. A prototype of this argument can already be seen in E.G. Davis (1971) and Merlin Stone (1976).

14. In particular the theologians Gerda Weiler (1984), and Christa Mulack (1987).

15. And thus of all its disasters: wars, witchhunts, all kinds of violence, etc.

16. Cf. in particular Decke 1988; Fischer 1996a, 1996b; Heine 1994; Heschel 1988; von Kellenbach 1994; Schaumberger 1987; Siegele-Wenskewitz 1988, 1997.

17. The notable exception would be the demonstrations in support of the Intifada by some antiracist movements in France in the autumn of 2000, whose organizers were swamped by many anti-Jewish slogans of that kind.

18. Cf. among many others, Vidal-Naquet 1987; Lipstadt 1993; Seidel 1986.

19. Of course there are also far more traditional, and indeed archaic forms, as demonstrated for example by the success of the *Protocols of the Elders of Zion* throughout all the countries of the Middle East and also in Russia and Japan, or the resurgence of the extreme right, with its xenophobia and virulent anti-Semitism, in many post-Communist countries.

20. It should be stressed that France is one of the few countries where negationism as a phenomenon emerged mainly from the radical far left of the 1970s. As a result, identifying it has been an even harder, slower process.

21. See Kuhn and Röthe 1982. The very use of the term 'fascism' rather than 'Nazism' was itself significant of the difficulty, commonly felt at the time, of grasping the specific characteristics of the latter.

22. Cf. Klinksieck 1982; *Courage* 1980; *Mutterkreuz und Arbeitsbuch* 1981.

23. *Trümmerfrauen* (literally 'women of the rubble') who, in the last months of the war, were subjected to extreme poverty, famine and bombing, followed by the arrival of the occupying troops, after which they immediately, and without external help, cleared the country of ruins, thereby allowing Germany to be reconstructed – and its recent past to be forgotten.

24. On the different (Christian, feminist and then Nazi) discourses on women's *Lebensraum*, see Koonz 1987; and Kandel 1990.

25. Cf. Bock 1989; Koonz 1987; Grossmann 1991.

26. And almost as many men – however, according to Bock sterilization was not equally serious in both cases.

27. More recently Bock (1992) has considerably modified her statements and analyses.

28. Ebbinghaus 1987; Scheiger 1992; Schwarz 1997a, 1997b, 1998; among many others.

29. Windaus-Walzer 1988, 1997. On the same theme, see also Gehmacher 1994, and the article by the 'Frauen gegen Antisemitismus' 1993.

30. The idea of a 'holocaust of witches' has been advanced several times by feminists, most recently by F. D'Eaubonne (1999).

31. See Stoehr 1983, and the response to this article in Brenner 1983.

32. It is surprising that only Bulkin has expressed her reservations in relation to this text of Daly; however, it should be noted that she waited many years before making up her mind to publish them (Bulkin 1984).

33. For example, Ringelheim 1985, 1993. A more detailed discussion of this research orientation can be found in Kandel 1996.

34. Which, as Michelle Perrot notes, radically deprives us of any possibility of *understanding and defending the latter* even today.

35. From this point of view, notions such as 'gynocide', the 'final solution for women' (in relation to the new reproductive technologies), of the 'holocaust' or 'sexicide of the witches' clearly do nothing to assist analysis of the Nazi genocide, nor of patriarchal oppression. (On the use of metaphor in feminist discourse, notably metaphors borrowed from the Nazi period, cf. in particular the studies by Lessellier and Dhavernas in Kandel 1997.)

36. We know that the leader of the French extreme right, a specialist of anti-Semitic 'slips', has twice been convicted of declaring the Shoah to be a 'detail' of the Second World War.

37. Including some of Jewish origins.

38. These studies (often based on oral history) of the daily lives of the civil populations under the Third Reich almost all portray, through their very methods, an image of *normality* in that period (and in those who participated in it), almost entirely ignoring its criminal, exceptional or extreme aspects. This type of image was also seen, for example, in the television series *Heimat*.

39. During the official commemoration of the defeat of Nazism in May 1985, and despite concerted protests, President Reagan took time out at the German military cemetery in Bitburg, last resting place of not only Wehrmacht soldiers but also many SS (Hartmann 1986).

40. Cf., among others, Kaplan 1979, 1984; Dürkop 1984; Fassmann 1996; Bereswill and Wagner 1998; Wavrzyn 1999. All these studies examine the 'bourgeois' feminist movement and its continuations. It is regrettable that no similar studies were made (at least to my knowledge) of the social-democratic and socialist women's movements.

41. JFB: the Jüdische Frauenbund, founded in 1904 by the militant Jewish feminist Bertha Pappenheim. BDF: the Bund Deutscher Frauenvereinigungen, founded in 1894, was a very broad umbrella group of bourgeois feminist organizations.

42. Salomon had converted to Protestantism a few years earlier, in 1914, fearing that her manifestly Jewish name would harm the movement's image.

43. This was not confined to Germany. We know that anti-Semitic discourse was even more virulent in France (Volkov 1985), that it was present in the movements of both right and left (Sternhell 1983) and also, as early as the Dreyfus affair, in many feminist currents (Blum 1998).

44. G. Bäumer remained editor of her journal *Die Frau*, which did not cease publication until June 1944.

45. And sent letters of excuse to the JFB (Kaplan 1984: 188).

46. Cf. Koonz 1987; Kaplan 1998; Schad 2001.

47. Memorandum of 18 February 1933 addressed to Chancellor Adolph Hitler (cited in Crips 1990: 173–4).

48. *Liberalismus*, September 1933.

49. Conversely, the feminist journal *Cultura integral y feminina*, which had demonstrated admirable alertness and lucidity in relation to Nazism, which it never ceased to denounce throughout its existence (1933–36), almost entirely ignored Spanish internal politics and the uprising of 1934 (Bussy-Genevois 1990).

50. However, they were not representative of the majority of women in the Resistance, who had little interest in feminism (Bard 1995: 445).

51. Clearly this does exist. German academics in particular have often stressed the impact of generational and transgenerational issues on the left-wing and feminist militants of the 1970s and 1980s (see also, for France, Auron 1998). But the problem extends far beyond the problems of individuals, or even of generations.

52. Like, in a different register, that of class domination.

53. For an analysis of the different modalities of racism(s), cf. Dhavernas and Kandel 1983; Taguieff 1987; Thalmann 1985–98.

References

Attar, Dena (1983) 'An Open Letter on Anti-Semitism and Racism', *Trouble and Strife*, Winter, pp. 13–16.

Auron, Y. (1998) *Les juifs d'extrême-gauche en Mai 68: une génération révolutionnaire marquée par la Shoah*. Paris: Albin Michel.

Bard, C. (1995) *Les filles de Marianne: Histoire des féminismes 1914–1940*. Paris: Fayard.

Bard, C. (1997) 'Le dilemme des féministes françaises face au nazisme', in L. Kandel, ed, *Féminismes et nazisme: colloque en hommage à Rita Thalmann*. Paris: Publications de l'Université Paris VII – Denis Diderot, pp. 148–61.

Beck, E. T., ed. (1988) *Nice Jewish Girls: A Lesbian Anthology*. Watertown, MA: Persephone Press.

Beck, Evelyn Torton (1991a) 'The Politics of Jewish Invisibility in Women's Studies', in J. Butler and J. Walter, eds, *Transforming the Curriculum: Ethnic Studies and Women's Studies*. Albany, NY: SUNY Press.

Beck, Evelyn Torton (1991b) 'Multiculturalism in the University and Beyond: How "Multi"? Whose "Cultures" and Why?', in *Carrying it on: Proceedings of a National Conference Organizing against Anti-Semitism, New Jewish Agenda*. Seattle: Bridges, pp. 8–12.

Bereswill, Mechthild and Leonie Wagner, eds (1998) *Bürgerliche Frauenbewegung und Antisemitismus*. Tübingen: Edition Diskord.

Biale, David, Michael Galchinsky and Susannah Heschel (1998) *Insider/Outsider: American Jews and Multiculturalism*. San Francisco: University of California Press.

Blum, Françoise (1998) 'Itinéraires féministes à la lumière de l'Affaire', in M. Leymarie, ed., *La postérité de l'affaire Dreyfus*. Villeneuve d'Ascq: Presses Universitaires du Septentrion.

Bock, G. (1986) *Zwangssterilisation im Nationalsozialismus. Studien zur Rassenpolitik und Frauenpolitik*. Zentralinstitut für sozial-wissenschaftliche Forschung der Freien Universität Berlin, Opladen: Westdeutscher Verlag.

Bock, G. (1989) 'Die Frauen unter dem Nationalsozialismus: Bemerkungen zu einem Buch von Claudia Koonz', *Geschichte und Gesellschaft* 4, pp. 563–79.

Bock, G. (1992) 'Le nazisme. Politiques sexuées et vies des femmes en Allemagne', in G. Duby and M. Perrot, eds, *Histoire des femmes en Occident*, vol. 5, *Le XXè siècle*. Paris: Plon, pp. 143–67.

Brenner, H. (1983) '"Es ging alles so weiter 1933" – Aber für wen?' *Die Schwarze Botin* 20, September.

Bridenthal, R., A. Grossmann and M. Kaplan, eds (1984) *When Biology Became Destiny*. New York: Monthly Review Press.

Bulkin, E. (1984) 'Hard Ground: Jewish Identity, Racism, and Anti-Semitism', in E. Bulkin, M.B. Pratt and B. Smith, *Yours in Struggle: Three Feminist Perspectives on Anti-Semitism and Racism*. New York: Firebrand Books, pp. 89–229.

Bussy-Genevois, D. (1990) 'Les espagnoles ou le pacifisme de l'entre-trois-guerres', in R. Thalmann, ed., *La tentation nationaliste*, Paris: Tierce, pp. 115–35.

Bussy-Genevois, D. (1994) 'Féminisme et antisémitisme dans l'Espagne des années 30', in L. Crips et al., eds, *Nationalismes, féminismes, exclusions. Mélanges en l'honneur de Rita Thalmann.* Frankfurt-am-Main: Peter Lang, pp. 99–112.

Courage (1980) Special issue no. 3, Alltag im 2. Weltkrieg.

Crips, L. (1990) 'Une revue "national-féministe": *Die deutsche Kämpferin*', in R. Thalmann, ed., *La tentation nationaliste.* Paris: Tierce, pp. 167–82.

Crips, L. (1995) 'Comment passer du libéralisme au nationalisme *völkisch*, tout en restant féministe? L'itinéraire de Käthe Schirmacher (1865–1930)', in M.-C. Hoock-Demarle, ed., *Femmes, Nations, Europe. Nationalismes et internationalismes dans les mouvements de femmes en Europe.* Paris: Publications de l'Université Paris VII – Denis Diderot, pp. 67–77.

Crips, L. (1997) 'Biologisme et "national-féminisme": le cas d'Agnès Bluhm (1862–1943)', in L. Kandel, ed., *Féminismes et nazisme: colloque en hommage à Rita Thalmann.* Paris: Publications de l'Université Paris VII – Denis Diderot, pp. 96–108.

Daly, M. (1978) *Gyn/ecology: The Metaethics of Radical Feminism.* Boston: Beacon Press.

Daum, A. (1980) 'Blaming Jews for the Death of the Goddess', *Lilith* 1980; reprinted in E. T. Beck, ed., *Nice Jewish Girls: A Lesbian Anthology.* Watertown, MA: Persephone Press, 1988.

Daum, A. (1983) 'Anti-Semitism in the Women's movement', *Pioneer Women*, September–October.

Davis, E. Gould (1971) *The First Sex.* New York: Putnam.

D'Eaubonne, F. (1999) *Le sexocide des sorcières.* Paris: l'Esprit Frappeur.

Decke, B. (1988) 'Christlicher Antijudaismus und Feminismus', in *Kongress gegen Antisemitismus.* Frankfurt: Die Grünen im Bundestag, pp. 61–78.

Del Re, A. (1994) *Les femmes et l'Etat-Providence. Les politiques sociales en France dans les années trente.* Paris: L'Harmattan.

Dhavernas, M.-J. and L. Kandel (1983) 'Le sexisme comme réalité et comme représentation', *Les Temps Modernes*, July, pp. 3–30.

Dhavernas, M.-J. (1997) 'Féminisme, eugénisme, nazisme. La confusion des langues', in L. Kandel, ed., *Féminismes et nazisme: colloque en hommage à Rita Thalmann.* Paris: Publications de l'Université Paris VII – Denis Diderot, pp. 272–87.

Di Vilde Chayes (1982) 'An Open Letter to the Women's Movement', *Off Our Backs*, July, p. 21.

Dürkop, Marlis (1984) 'Erscheinungsformen des Antisemitismus im Bund Deutscher Frauenvereine', *Feministische Studien* 3, pp. 140–49.

Ebbinghaus, A. (1987) *Opfer und Täterinnen, Frauenbiographien des Nationalsozialismus.* Hamburg: Delphi.

Fassmann, I. M. (1996) *Jüdinnen in der deutschen Frauenbewegung 1865–1919*, Hildesheim/Zürich/New York: Peter Lang.

Fischer, E. (1996a) 'Es gab auch willige Vollstreckerinnen', *TAZ*, vol. 15, no. 11.

Fischer, E. (1996b) 'War Jesus Jude oder feminist?', *TAZ*, vol. 15, no. 11.

Frauen Gegen Antisemitismus (1993), 'Der Nationalsozialismus als Extremform des Patriarchats. Zur Leugnung des Täterschaft von Frauen und zur Tabuisierung des Antisemitismus in der Auseinandersetzung mit den NS', *Beiträge zur Feministischen theorie und praxis*, vol. 16, no. 35, pp. 77–89.

Gabriel, N. (1983) 'Allemandes, si vous saviez', *La Revue d'en Face* 14, Autumn, pp. 57–64.

Gabriel, N. (1986) 'Un corps à corps avec l'histoire: les féministes allemandes face au passé nazi', in R. Thalmann, ed., *La tentation nationaliste.* Paris: Tierce, pp. 219–32.

Gehmacher, Johanna (1994) 'Feministische Geschichtsforschung und die Frage nach Antisemitismus von Frauen', in Charlotte Kohn-Ley and Ilse Korotin, eds, *Der feministische Sündenfall? Antisemitische Vorurteile in der Frauenbewegung.* Vienna: Picus Verlag.

Gehmacher, Johanna (1995) 'Le nationalisme allemand des femmes autrichiennes et l'idéologie de "communauté ethnique"', in M.-C. Hoock-Demarle, ed., *Femmes, Nations, Europe. Nationalismes et internationalismes dans les mouvements de femmes en Europe.* Paris: Publications de l'Université Paris VII – Denis Diderot, pp. 95–106.

Gehmacher, Johanna (1998) *Völkische Frauenbewegung. Deutschnationale und national-sozialistische Geschlechterpolitik in Österreich.* Vienna: Döcker Verlag.

Gerstenberger, H. (1987) 'Alltagforschung und Fascismustheorie', in H. Gerstenberger and D. Schmidt, *Normalität oder Normalisierung? Geschichtswerkstätte und Faschismus-analyse.* Münster: Westphälisches Dampfboot, pp. 35–49.

Gerstenberger H., and D. Schmidt (1987) *Normalität oder Normalisierung? Geschichts-werkstätte und Faschismusanalyse.* Münster: Westphälisches Dampfboot.

Gravenhorst, L. (1990) 'Nehmen wir Nationalsozialismus und Auschwitz als unser negatives Eigentum in Anspruch?', in Gravenhorst and Tatschmurat, eds, *Töchterfragen: NS-Frauen Geschichte.* Kore.

Grossmann, A. (1991) 'Feminist Debates about Women and National Socialism', *Gender and History*, vol. 3, no. 3, August.

Hartmann, G., ed. (1986) *Bitburg in Moral and Political Perspective.* Bloomington: Indiana University Press.

Heine, Susanne (1994) 'Die feministische Diffamierung von Juden', in Charlotte Kohn-Ley and Ilse Korotin, eds, *Der feministische Sündenfall? Antisemitische Vorurteile in der Frauenbewegung.* Vienna: Picus Verlag.

Heschel, S. (1988) 'Haben die Juden die Göttin ermordert?', *Emma*, December.

Hoock-Demarle, Marie-Claire, ed. (1995) *Femmes, nations, Europe. Nationalismes et internationalismes. dans les mouvements de femmes en Europe.* Paris: Publications de l'Université Paris VII – Denis Diderot.

Kandel, L. (1990) 'Le mouvement féministe aujourd'hui et le national-socialisme', *Les Temps Modernes* 524, March.

Kandel, L. (1993) 'Sexisme et racisme: vingt ans après…', *Cahiers du CEDREF* 3.

Kandel, L. (1996) 'Une pensée empêchée: des usages du genre et de quelques-unes de ses limites', *Les Temps Modernes* 587, special issue, '50 ans', pp. 220–48.

Kandel, L., ed. (1997) *Féminismes et nazisme: colloque en hommage à Rita Thalmann.* Paris: Publications de l'Université Paris VII – Denis Diderot.

Kaplan, Marion A. (1979) *The Jewish Feminist Movement in Germany: The Campaigns of the Jüdischer Frauenbund, 1904–1938.* Westport, CT and London: Greenwood Press.

Kaplan, Marion A. (1984) 'Sisterhood under Siege: Feminism and Anti-Semitism in Germany, 1904–1938', in R. Bridenthal, A. Grossmann and M. Kaplan, eds, *When Biology Became Destiny.* New York: Monthly Review Press, pp. 174–96.

Kaplan, Marion A. (1998) *Between Dignity and Despair: Jewish Life in Nazi Germany.* New York, Oxford: Oxford University Press.

von Kellenbach, Katharina (1994) *Anti-Judaism in Feminist Religious Writings.* Atlanta: American Academy of Religion/Scholars Press.

Klepfisz, I. (1981) 'Anti-Semitism in the Lesbian-Feminist Movement', *Womanews*; re-printed in E.T. Beck, ed., *Nice Jewish Girls: A Lesbian Anthology.* Watertown, MA: Persephone Press, 1988, pp. 45–54.

Klinksieck, D. (1982) *Die Frau im NS Staat.* Stuttgart: Deutsche Verlagsamstalt.

Kohn-Ley, Charlotte (1994) 'Antisemitische Mütter – Anti-zionistische Töchter?', in Charlotte Kohn-Ley and Ilse Korotin, eds, *Der feministische Sündenfall? Antisemitische Vorurteile in der Frauenbewegung.* Vienna: Picus Verlag.

Koonz, C. (1987) *Mothers in the Fatherland: Women, the Family and Nazi Politics.* New York, St. Martins Press.

Kuhn, A., and V. Röthe (1982) *Frauen im deutschen Faschismus.* Düsseldorf: Schwann-Bagel.

Kunstenaar, C. (1988) 'Sois juive et tais-toi', *Paris-Féministes* 59, February, pp. 18–19.

Lipstadt, D. (1993), *Denying the Holocaust: The Growing Assault on Truth and Memory.* New York: Free Press.

Lesselier, Claudie (1997) 'La représentation du "fascisme" dans les discours féministes radicaux contemporains en France', in L. Kandel, ed, *Féminismes et nazisme: Colloque en hommage à Rita Thalmann.* Paris: Publications de l'Université Paris VII – Denis Diderot, pp. 260–72.

London Jewish Lesbian Feminist Group (1982), 'About Anti-Semitism', *Spare Rib* 123, October, pp. 20–21.

Michel, A. (1993) 'De Berlin à Bagdad: les femmes et la guerre du Golfe', *Nouvelles questions féministes*, vol. 15 no. 3, August, pp. 5–15.

Mitscherlich, M. (1983) 'Antisemitismus, eine Männerkrankheit?', *Psyche* 1, pp. 41–54.

Morris, B. (1990) 'Anti-Semitism in the Women's Movement: A Jewish Lesbian Speaks', *Off Our Backs*, December.

Mulack, Christa (1987) *Jesus der Gesalbte der Frauen: Weiblichkeit als Grundlage Christilicher Ethik.* Stuttgart: Klett Verlag.

Mutterkreuz und Arbeitsbuch (1981) Frankfurt: Fischer.

Nolan, M. (1988) 'The *Historikerstreit* and Social History', *New German Critique* 44, pp. 51–80.

Off Our Backs (1982) *A Women's News Journal*, vol. 11, no. 8, August–September, Jewish feminist conference.

Plaskow, J. (1980) 'Blaming the Jews for the Birth of Patriarchy', *Lilith* 7; reprinted in E.T. Beck, ed., *Nice Jewish Girls: A Lesbian Anthology.* Watertown, MA: Persephone Press, 1988.

Pogrebin, L.C. (1982) 'Anti-Semitism in the Women's Movement', *MS*, June.

Pogrebin, L.C. (1991) *Deborah, Golda and Me: Being Female and Jewish in America.* New York: Crown Publishers.

Ringelheim, J. (1985) 'Women and the Holocaust: A Reevaluation of Research', *Signs*, vol. 10, no. 4, pp. 741–61; reprinted in C. Rittner and J.K. Roth, eds, *Different Voices: Women and the Holocaust.* New York: Paragon House, 1993, pp. 373–420.

Schad, Martha (2001) *Frauen gegen Hitler. Schicksale im Nationalsozialismus.* Munich: Heyne.

Schaumberger, Christine, ed. (1987) *Weil wir nicht vergessen wollen... Zu einer Feministischen Theologie im deutschen Kontext.* Münster: Morgana Frauenbuchverlag.

Scheiger, Brigitte (1992) 'Ich bitte um baldige Arisierung der Wohnung', in T. Wobbe, ed., *Nach Osten. Verdeckten Spuren nationalsozialistischer Verbrechen.* Frankfurt-am-Main: Verlag Neue Kritik, pp. 175–95.

Schmidt, D. (1987) 'Die peinliche Verwandschaften – Frauenforschung zum National-sozialismus', in H. Gerstenberger and D. Schmidt, *Normalität oder Normalisierung? Geschichtswerkstätte und Faschismusanalyse*, Münster: Westphälisches Dampfboot, pp. 50–65.

Schulze, Bodo (1991) 'Ce mouvement pacifiste en Allemagne', *Temps critiques* 3, Spring.

Schwarz, Gudrun (1997a) *Eine Frau an seiner Seite. Die Ehefrauen in der SS-Sippen-gemeinschaft*, Hamburger Edition. Göttingen: Wallstein.

Schwarz, Gudrun (1997b) 'Les femmes SS – 1939–1945', in L. Kandel, ed, *Féminismes et nazisme: colloque en hommage à Rita Thalmann.* Paris: Publications de l'Université Paris VII – Denis Diderot, pp. 86–95.

Schwarz, Gudrun (1998) 'Frauen in Konzentrationslagern – Täterinnen und Zuschauer-innen', in Ulrich Herbert, ed., *Die nationalsozialistischen Konzentrationslager. Entwicklung und Struktur.* Göttingen: Wallstein.

Seidel, G. (1986) *The Holocaust Denial: Antisemitism, Racism and the New Right.* Leeds: Beyond the Pale Collective.

Siegele-Wenschkewitz, L. (1988) *Verdrängte Vergangenheit die uns bedrängt.* Munich: Kaiser Verlag.

Siegele-Wenschkewitz, Leonore (1997) 'Tendances de la théologie féministe au sein des

Eglises protestantes d'Allemagne', in L. Kandel, ed, *Féminismes et nazisme: colloque en hommage à Rita Thalmann*. Paris: Publications de l'Université Paris VII – Denis Diderot, pp. 236–49.

Sternhell, Z. (1983) *Ni droite ni gauche: L'idéologie fasciste en France*. Paris: Seuil; *Neither Right nor Left*. Berkeley: University of California Press, 1991.

Stoehr, I. (1983) 'Machtergriffen? Deutsche Frauenbewegung 1933', *Courage,* February.

Stone, Merlin (1976) *When God Was a Woman*. New York: Harcourt, Brace, Jovanovich.

Strobl, I. (1985) 'Ich könnte heulen vor Wut', *Emma*, May, pp. 28–9.

Taguieff, P.-A. (1987) *La force du préjugé. Essai sur le racisme et ses doubles*. Paris: La Découverte; *The Force of Prejudice: On Racism and Its Doubles*. Minneapolis: University of Minnesota Press, 2001.

Taguieff, P.-A. (1989) 'La nouvelle judéophobie: antisionisme, antiracisme, anti-impérialisme', *Les Temps modernes*, November, pp. 1–80.

Taguieff, P.-A. (1993) *Sur la nouvelle Droite*. Paris: Descartes et Cie.

Thalmann, R. (1982) *Etre femme sous le Troisième Reich*. Paris: Laffont.

Thalmann, R. (1987) 'La normalisation du passé? La RFA et le problème juif', in *Vingtième siècle, Revue d'histoire* 16, October–December, pp. 55–65.

Thalmann, R., ed. (1990) *La tentation nationaliste*. Paris: Tierce.

Thalmann, R., ed (1985–1998) *Sexe et race. Discours et formes nouvelles d'exclusion du 19è au 20è siècle*. Paris: Université Paris VII – Denis Diderot.

Vidal-Naquet, P. (1987) *Les assassins de la mémoire*, Paris: La Découverte; *Assassins of Memory: Essays on The Denial of the Holocaust*. New York: Columbia University Press, 1992.

Volkov, Shulamit (1985) 'Le texte et la parole. De l'anti-sémitisme d'avant 1914 à l'anti-sémitisme nazi', in *L'Allemagne nazie et le génocide juif*, Colloque EHESS. Paris: Hautes Etudes/Gallimard/Seuil, pp. 76–98.

Volkov, Shulamit (1990) 'Antisemitismus als kultureller Code', in *Jüdisches Leben und anti-Semitismus im 19. und 20. Jahrhundert*, Munich: Verlag C.H. Beck.

Wavrzyn, Heidemarie (1999) *Vaterland statt Menschenrecht. Formen der Judenfeindschaft in den Frauenbewegungen des Deutschen Kaiserreiches*. Marburg: Diagonal.

Weiler, Gerda (1984) *Ich verwerfe im Land die Kriege*. Munich: Kaiser Verlag.

Walzer-Windaus, K. (1988) 'Gnade der weiblichen Geburt', *Feministische Studien* 1, pp. 102–15.

Walzer-Windaus, K. (1997) 'La "grâce de la naissance féminine": un bilan', in L. Kandel, ed, *Féminismes et nazisme: colloque en hommage à Rita Thalmann*. Paris: Publications de l'Université Paris VII – Denis Diderot, pp. 225–35.

Women against Imperialism (1982) 'Taking Our Stands against Zionism and White Supremacy', *Off Our Backs,* July, p. 20.

Yuval-Davis, N. (1984) 'Anti-Semitism, Anti-Zionism and the Struggle against Racism', *Spare Rib*, April.

Ziege, E.M. (1995) 'Femmes antisémites et images de l'"autre" juif', in M.-C. Hoock-Demarle, ed. *Femmes, Nations, Europe. Nationalismes et internationalismes dans les mouvements de femmes en Europe*. Paris: Publications de l'Université Paris VII – Denis Diderot, pp. 78–94.

11

Diasporic Subjects and Migration

SANDRA PONZANESI

Migration has always represented the most unsettling and yet enriching force of human civilization. It has redesigned geopolitical boundaries, economic structures and cultural identities. The uneven growth of the world population has increased the pressures of migration. The World Bank predicts that migration will become one of the most important determining forces of the twenty-first century. The UNHCR (United Nations High Commission for Refugees) attributes this phenomenon to new 'push factors' such as easily accessible information about other places, cheaper forms of transportation, and the emergence of a professional body of 'migration agents' who arrange the journeys and the necessary documents. Even though Asia is the mostly densely populated continent, the fastest population growth remains in the region surrounding the European basin: the Middle East and Africa. Globalization in the form of the information revolution and trade liberalization complicates this scenario further. The world has become smaller but also more polarized. The gap between rich and poor, online and offline, order and chaos, integration and fragmentation has expanded structurally.

Western Europe today is the destination for many international migrants, voluntary and forced. With slow or zero population growth in Western European countries, governments have encouraged the temporary migration of workers. Perhaps the most publicized case has been Germany, which has a large population of "guest workers" from Turkey. Within Europe, migration from the peripheral countries such as Ireland, Portugal, Spain, Southern Italy, Greece, along with migration from Eastern Europe (particularly the former Yugoslavia) and North Africa, to the core regions of Western Europe, has changed the make-up of local populations. France has received more than one million migrants from North Africa while Germany has invited between two and three million guest workers. In the early 1990s many countries expressed fear over the possibility of Eastern Europeans beginning to migrate voluntarily to Western Europe in search of better economic opportunities. While estimates placed the possible number as high as ten million, the actual number of migrants has been considerably lower, and with the toughening of entry requirements for immigration many applicants have been turned away.

It needs to be reiterated that migration is certainly not new to Europe, since migrations to, within and from Europe have been an integral part of the national formations and their transformations. What is new are the modalities with which new migrations are pressing against the borders of the newly defined Fortress Europe, as specified above, and how they qualify and magnify the altered histories of a colonial legacy and of global intersections. This shows that in Europe migration has shifted from an outward to a centripetal phenomenon. Whereas during the nineteenth century and the first half of the twentieth century migration to the Americas represented a great incentive and the solution to internal economic stagnation, and later an escape from the advent of fascist forces, the migration of the second half of the twentieth century consisted instead of a strong absorption of people from what has been defined as the end of empire. Those colonial peripheries – which, with the demise of the great European empires (British, French, Dutch, Portuguese and Italian), came to crowd the old metropolitan centres and question national identities – have been strongly voiced within the post-colonial debate of the last decade.

It is therefore important to recognize the specificity of European fluxes of migration as quite distinct from the North American melting-pot credo. Few studies have focused in a systematic way on diasporic cultural practices in contemporary Europe. Yet Western Europe offers a privileged site for an analysis of this kind, for its historical relationship with former colonies and spheres of influence has attracted growing concentrations of immigrant minorities. With the demise of empire the periphery came to coexist with the centre; the synchronicity of different historical backgrounds came to be lumped together with the flat diachronicity of the old metropolitan centres. It is in this transition from there to here, from 'us' and 'them', from colonial past to post-colonial present, that the migrant subject must be located in his/her multiple inter-sections and negotiation of identity. And it is through the idea of an imperial centre and its many ends that Europe has constructed its own homogeneous image, in opposition to those peripheral colonial histories which were an integral part of the European project of modernity.

However, not all migrant flows express trajectories from the former colonies to the former European centres. The impact of globalization and transnational capitalism associated with the difficult process of nationalization and economic development of many 'post-colonial countries' has blurred the lines of origin and destination of so many and diverse strands of migration. That has also caused great confusion for the labelling and characterization of these strands, and has made the analysis of gender and ethnic relations within communities of origin and of arrival even more complicated. This is due to the fact that migrancy empowers women and ethnic minorities, by emphasizing shifting identities and cultural negotiations, as much as it disenfranchises them, by enforcing processes of integration and homologation.

The migrant as a 'material subject' moving from one continent to the other, fleeing civil wars, famine, political persecutions or just in search of better opportunities, must be distinguished from the notion of the migrant as a symbolic category. The latter expresses migrant subjectivity as crossing the boundaries of hegemonic discourses, and of imposed categories of identity formation. Refugees, transnational workers, the exiled, expatriates, diasporic people, transnational operators or cosmopolitan intellectuals are often jumbled under the same heading – that of displaced people – despite the significant differences of their backgrounds. The fascination with people whose identities do not fit with any geography is not new to our society. What is however new and highly emphasized, to the extent of becoming overinflated, is the critical intensity with which cosmopolitan subjects, post-colonial people and globetrotters are celebrated as the new gurus, as people whose in-betweenness, cross-culturality or liminality in some respects more accurately embodies our contemporary condition.

This second notion has acquired a certain cachet in recent poststructuralist debates, since the migrant figuration allows the envisioning of trespassing disciplinary boundaries, epistemological categories and nationalistic dogmas. Most important, from a feminist standpoint, the migrant trope helps to envision the intersection of sex, class, race, age and lifestyle as fundamental axes of differentiation. Various theories of nomadism and cosmopolitanism have tried to encapsulate the notion of the migrant as an embodiment of the contemporary condition of dislocation, not only in spatial terms but as crossing existing categories, of gender restrictions and bodily limitations. Notions such as diaspora (Brah, Hall, Gilroy, Smadar, Swedenborg, Barkan), borderlands (Anzaldua), edges (hooks), eccentric subject (De Lauretis), margins (Spivak), in-betweenness (Bhabha), rhizome (Deleuze), exile (Said), nomadic subject (Braidotti), cyborg (Haraway), transversal politics (Yuval-Davies), borders (Balibar), multiple geographies (Stanford-Freeman) all emphasize theories of space as a way of describing the postmodern condition as encapsulating multiple variables of female subjectivity.

Though highly interlocked, these two readings of the migrant condition should not be conflated. An inflated migrant rhetoric will rob actual dispossessed people of their language of suffering and loss. Kevathi Krishnaswamy pleads for a political relocation of such concepts, in which the experiences of political exiles, economic refugees and migrant labourers do not become histories that designate a wide range of cross-cultural phenomena. He asks:

> What part has the 'cosmopolitan', 'Third World Intellectual' played in the manufacture of the 'diasporic consciousness'? How have metropolitan discourses framed contemporary conceptions of hybridity and migrancy? Has the mythology of migrancy

provided a productive site for post-colonial resistance or has it become complicit
with the hegemonic postmodern theoreticisation of power and identity?
(Krishnaswamy 1995: 128)

For this purpose it is important to distinguish a diasporic sensibility from a
migrant predicament. Even though the diasporic imagination stems from
concrete and historically positioned routes of dispersion and scattering, it has
nowadays acquired a great figurative flexibility which mostly refers to practices of transgression and hybridization.

The original notion of diaspora refers, in fact, to a collective trauma, of
the banishment and exile of Jewish communities. In a second stage, diaspora
also came to signify the dispersal and genocide of Armenians and the coercive
uprooting of African people for the purposes of slavery. There are also other
forms of diaspora such as imperial diasporas (the indentured labour of Indian
people), trade diasporas and cultural diasporas such as in the case of the
Caribbean (Cohen 1997). At present diasporas evoke globalized and transnational forces of the world economy, international migrations, and diasporic
intellectuals who can account for multiple subject positions such as Homi
Bhabha and Avtar Brah. They define the task of the intellectual who articulates his/her difference.

The migrant subject, by contrast, remains more closely linked to the
geographical process of uprooting and resettling. S/he has a culture of origin
and of destination and a trajectory often motivated by economic reasons,
though not necessarily. S/he posits serious questions of integration, assimilation and segregation, and the revision of citizenship criteria on the part of the
hosting nations, all issues and problematics which have been gathered under
the banner of multicultural policies. These issues have promoted debates not
only at the cultural surface but mostly within the political and economic
subtext. The debates held within the cultural arena address the paradox of
alternative cultural traditions and national identities having come to coexist
with universal values of Western democracies. The migrant experience has
abandoned its private realm of family traditions and entered public life,
reframing the old issue of migration as an interactive process and not as a
unilateral problematic.

For the sake of clarity I will stick to the notion of migration as referring
to that broad spectrum of phenomena which are usually associated with spatial
dislocation, both in its sociological component (demographic and urban shifts,
the relocation of labour force, the reassessment of citizenship and nationality),
and in its cultural implications (the questioning of Western aesthetic paradigms
and canon formations, the defence of linguistic pluralism and literary innovation, the promulgation of cultural and gender difference). In order not to
evade its problematic or to escape into a self-referential jargon that celebrates
migration as a free-floating and empowering condition, it is important to
address the wider issues at stake and to evaluate migration both in its rhizomatic
historical formations and in its contemporary geographical interchanges. The

challenge is indeed to put the category of 'migration' under fire and yet validate its utility for highlighting asymmetric relationships of power and representation.

Europe and the Lost Empire: Nationalism, Migration and the Post-colonial Predicament

People from the former colonies made, and are still making, the journey to metropolitan centres, where, together with new immigrants, asylum seekers and migrant workers, they profoundly destabilize 'older, more global imperial identities' (Schwarz 1992: 206). As Gisela Brinkler-Gabler and Sidonie Smith write, 'Now post/colonial encounters take place "at home" in the metropolitan centres, with profound effects for the imagining of the national identity' (1997: 8).

People migrating to the heart of the old empire represent the famous flux of return, the inversion of the colonial journey from centre to periphery. The patterns of absorption of these new strands are very much based on colonial policy. The British colonial policy of indirect rule, for example, is still reflected in British immigration policy, which allows certain immigrant communities to enter 'Britain' so long as they rely on their own community of origin. No claim should be made to an effective integration, since, as Paul Gilroy so poignantly illustrated in his influential *There Ain't No Black in the Union Jack: The Cultural Politics of Race and Nation*, the notions of British identity and of blackness were considered to be mutually exclusive (see also Gilroy 2000). People born in Britain or of mixed parentage created a shift in the notion of the old metropolitan centre, bringing to the fore all those submerged ethnicities which created the discrepancy between the proposed model of national cohesion and the new diversification from within. As Gilroy states, the pattern of cultural pluralism is a euphemism for a non-modifiable national purity.

These issues had already been addressed during the 1984 Essex Conference entitled 'Europe and Its Others' (Barker 1985), in which the most prominent critics of colonial discourse analyses gathered (Edward Said, Homi Bhabha, Gayatri Spivak, Benita Parry, Lata Mani, Sneja Gunew and others) in order to focus on representations of colonial and imperial power. Spivak was critical of the conference's title because it implicitly consolidated Europe as a sovereign subject by defining its colonies as the 'others' and not as constitutive subjects. To use the Third World as a convenient signifier, argued Spivak, offers 'an entire privileged discursive *field* within metropolitan radical criticism. In that field, "The Third World *Woman*" is a particular hollowed signifier' (in Barker 1985: 128).

Spivak contributed to a shift in the focus from colonial towards post-colonial discourse analyses by deconstructing the rigid opposition between

Europe and its others. These are not given entities but a web of complex power relationships which have not stopped with the end of the empires but have continued into the new world relocation of culture. Crucial for the post-colonial discourse is, in fact, the notion that the ends of empire have been brought home and have made visible the racial nature of the old national identities by highlighting the multicultural rupture of the new.

Furthermore, it was necessary to augment colonial discourse analyses with a feminist agenda. Gender relations had played a crucial role in the operation of colonization and also in the rise of nationalist movements, through the use of the strategic role of women as upholders of collective traditional values, on the one hand (therefore oppressed within their patriarchal society), and as emancipated individualized selves (obviously suggested by the colonizer's model of liberation), on the other. Frantz Fanon has broadly discussed the image of the woman as a site of controversy, as an object of control more than as a locatable agency, within the conflictual policy of empire. However, with de-colonization and the pronounced phenomenon of migration towards Europe the issue has been resuscitated with some verve.

As Nira Yuval-Davies (1997) points out, this is due to the contradictory relationship between women and culture when it comes to notions of nation, diaspora and global multiculturalism. Women are usually marginalized within ethnic projects, even though they are used as a site of interaction between hegemonic and minority cultures, in order to give content to what authenticity and tradition mean. Women, writes Yuval-Davies, are in fact the site of struggle among conflicting identities, and are often called on to

> be the intergenerational transmitters of cultural tradition, customs, songs, cuisine, and, of course the mother tongue [*sic*]. This is especially true in minority situations in which the school and the public sphere present different hegemonic cultural models to that of the home. (Yuval-Davies 1999: 115)

Multiculturalism and post-colonial homogenization can therefore have detrimental effects on women, in particular when different cultural traditions – often defined in terms of culturally specific gender relations – are used to reproduce ethnic boundaries. This clash becomes obvious in multiculturalism and post-colonial critique when the attention is shifted from the cultural domain to the legal system. Practices which are ethnically and gender encoded – such as the wearing of the veil, clitoridectomy, polygamy, child marriages – may contrast with the legal system of the host country based on secular models. Here the limits of multicultural diversity become more tangible and pressing. At the same time the dominant culture, which interferes with the religious traditions of minority groups in order to emancipate women, participates in the sex industry, marriage bureaux and the exploitation of domestic servants, profiting from the vulnerable and subordinate role that women in migration have both within their own societies and within the host ones.

Ian Chambers and Lidia Curti's *The Postcolonial Question* (1996) is one of the first volumes to present an analysis of the post-colonial condition within Europe, analysing the specificities of Southern Europe and contesting post-colonial dogmas, which are mainly held within the North American academy. Usually migration literature is seen as an extension of the post-colonial literary debate. However, migration literature and post-colonial literature in general hardly focus on the internal differences present within Europe.

The post-colonial debate tends to be dominated by the English language as it rotates around the axis Britain/India, re-proposing the old dichotomy of empire while claiming to voice subaltern histories and marginal positions. This is a highly asymmetrical scenario; for this reason various recent studies have focused on the different heritages of empire within Europe (Portuguese, French, Dutch, Italian, German) in order to analyse more effectively the condition and process of multiculturalization within Europe, but also the new strands of migration and their interconnectedness with past and modern legacies.[1]

Both post-colonial and multicultural practices, usually inflected by American models, must be deconstructed and contextualized within the specificities of the European case, significant for its own multilingual and colonial legacies.

Multiculturalisms and Politics of Identity in Europe: Case Studies

So far most of the parameters used for addressing and exposing the identity trouble brought about by immigration are premissed upon the seemingly successful American model of the 'melting pot'. These parameters are, how-ever, strongly inadequate for the mapping of the European situation in its historical and geopolitical specificity.

The United States is a nation with a strong democratic authority, capable of absorbing, and being remoulded by, the innumerable and vast transnational streams of immigrants that have been conspicuous from the moment of the foundation of the nation, a nation with a strong settler identity, supposedly made by an internal plurality that is capable of silently coexisting with the higher credo of the American dream of the self-made man. This model of the self-made man often erases the violent forms of internal colonization, such as that of the Native Americans, and the project of modernity undertaken on the back of slavery.

The American model cannot easily be applied to the situation in Europe, where migration has not only been mostly outwards, as specified above, but also historically discontinuous, uneven among the different national states, dictated both by colonial legacies (therefore an integral part of European modern history, as Gilroy claims) and divergent economic factors (dependent on global interactions but also on the internal economic policy followed by the EU). It is therefore pertinent to ask whether European society is ready for the permanent phenomenon of immigration.

The differences with the United States are obvious. The USA has space, a dynamic economy and a national identity which is not based exclusively on ethno-cultural origin, but on respect for the constitution and the Bill of Rights. Europe has no space, less economic dynamism and does not view itself as possessing an immigration culture. The European Union consists pre-dominantly of welfare states which have reached a reasonable level of social harmony; furthermore, they are nation-states that from an ethnic and cultural point of view are much more homogeneous than the United States. Europe is also the continent where the distinction between civilization and barbarism was invented. The fear of the stranger is strongly rooted in the European mentality. The scientific construction of racial taxonomies at the height of the European empires is one of the most damaging and protracted manifestations of the colonizing mission. The invention of new borders and the shifting symbolism of old boundaries make evident that not all multicultural processes and not all post-colonial strategies are the same.

In order to show how the politics of multiculturalization in Europe are very much linked to the legacy of the different colonial empires, though strongly influenced by the international redistribution of the labour force caused by transnational capital, I will make a brief excursion into the different patterns of multiculturalism which occur within the different European states.

According to Umberto Melotti (1997), the British approach, based on its colonial policy of divide and rule, is relaxed about the formation of ethnic minorities but is not committed to equality of membership in the national community, as France is. Following a long tradition of egalitarianism, France aims at extending full citizenship to immigrants on the basis of assimilation, as was done in colonial times. However, this egalitarian model refuses cultural loyalties that may compete with loyalties to the French Republic.

In *Immigration and Identity in Beur Fiction: Voices from the North African Community in France* Alec Hargreaves (1997a) emphasizes the importance of 'alternative voices', *beurs* or writing of other descendance in France, as a necessary stage to problematise the French assimilationist credo. This credo is based on the Enlightenment model of 'equality', which does not leave space for the cultural and political differences claimed by non-Western communities. Migrant identification, or post-colonial discourses, have therefore an important role to fulfil in contesting from within the ethnocentric assumptions hidden behind a supposedly progressive agenda.

The German approach to the multicultural trouble is different again, based on the ethnic principle that German blood means German nationality. For decades Germany denied its status as a host immigrant country. Incoming ethnic Germans were not considered immigrants, regardless of where in the world they were coming from. They were viewed as rediscovered members of the German nation and automatically granted citizenship. Other incomers, such as Turks, were not considered immigrants because they were seen as 'guest workers', therefore subject to repatriation and not integration (Horrocks and Kolinsky 1996).

These three European nations, Britain, France and Germany, have offered multicultural models of integration and transformation very different from the US one, because they are inserted into different democratic and colonial traditions. Within the 'dominant' Northern European model of multicultural-ization the southern front is neglected, even though countries such as Portugal, Spain, Italy and Greece have been subjected to a constant stream of immigra-tion from outside the EU. The 'EU-phoria'[2] in this region was very short-lived when confronted with the high level of anxiety shown in respect of the new stretchable borders. The policy of the countries facing the Mediterranean is of great importance for the rest of Europe. Italy as a gateway to Europe is far from being just a suggestive visual metaphor. Due to its position in the Mediterranean and because of its kilometres of barely controllable coasts, Italy is confronted with newcomers daily. Through narrative accounts of their ex-periences in Italy several migrants have attempted to engage in a dialogue with public opinion. In *Mediterranean Crossroads: Migration Literature in Italy*, Graziella Parati (1999) offers a 'limited but eloquent' selection of narrative voices which document the uniqueness of the Italian case within the larger scenario of the migration of cultures.

Donna Gabaccia's *Italy's Many Diasporas* (2000) offers a similar account. The plurals in the title refer less to the global destinations of Italians and more to two different considerations: that Italians left their country as Veneti, Siciliani, Neapolitans rather than as 'Italians'; and that a distinct feature was the varied character of their dispersion – trade diaspora, cultural diaspora, nationalist diaspora and mass diaspora. The formation of the modern Italian nation often seemed to find form more easily outside of Italy than within. Gabaccia argues: 'for a country with a long history of sending emigrants abroad, Italy experienced considerable distress in welcoming migrants onto its national territory' (2000: 170), and adds that 'a nation accustomed to thinking of its migrants as subject to racist and capitalist oppression abroad suddenly looked into the mirror to see itself as the oppressor' (2000: 172). This might have to do with the fact that Italy, unlike the United Kingdom, France, or Germany, has not developed a clear understanding of how its history of migration has defined its national identity.

However, even the 'processes of emancipation' piloted by the central governments of countries following a more advanced multicultural policy have their drawbacks. The institution of affirmative action and positive dis-crimination policies have the paradoxical function of empowering minorities only if they fit into the essentialized and fixed categories provided by multi-cultural state policy. Against this vision Tariq Modood and Pnina Werbner claim, in their preface to *The Politics of Multiculturalism in the New Europe*, that multiculturalism is not simply a novel project of social engineering, devised for the twenty-first century by well-meaning liberals or communitarians. They demonstrate that multiculturalism is the

> outcome of ongoing power struggles and collective negotiations of cultural, ethnic and racial differences. These are currently reshaping the public sphere and civil societies of the new Europe. Consequently multiculturalisms are multiple, fluid and continuously contested – a negotiation and transcendence of difference and otherness at different scales, from the communal and local to the national and supranational. (1997: vii)

The fall of the Berlin Wall in 1989 was a major turning point in European history which strongly marks Europe's specific tackling of the Cold War problematic and the highly charged symbolism of political frontiers (such as that expressed by the Wall). The notion of borders within Europe is profoundly different from that in the United States, where the Mexican frontier has come to embody a global division between developed capitalist countries and the rest. Within Europe the proximity between what used to be defined as the First and the Second Worlds has created – with the collapse of the Soviet regime – a hazy 'transit zone' (Eastern Europe going Western), a vacillation of the very notion of border (Balibar). The Eastern frontier has become the site of a recycled workforce for the expansion of the Western economy, but also a receptacle of lost histories and identities that claim their centrality in the shaping of European identity.

However, the Maastricht Treaty and the Schengen Accords have shown their limitations when faced with the drama of the Dover affair, where more than fifty illegal Chinese immigrants were stifled to death in the back of a lorry supposedly transporting tomatoes from the Netherlands to the United Kingdom. The shifting of responsibility for the frontier from country to country, with Britain blaming the Netherlands for their careless controls at the borders, is symptomatic of the vanity of political regulations when faced with the urgency of economic imbalances created by the connection between capital and metropolis. Furthermore the proto-European model of integration and cohesion is a fiction, an invention made to counterbalance bigger empires such as the American one but, as Nuruddin Farah (2000) writes in his *Yesterday, Tomorrow: Voices from the Somali Diaspora*, the European Union is another empire of a more sophisticated order, which has taken the role of negotiating away the imperial responsibilities of countries such as Britain, France, Portugal, the Netherlands and Italy. The people of this new empire are barricading themselves behind the empty rhetoric of fear and helplessness. But, as Balibar so poignantly remarks, borders are vacillating:

> This means that they are no longer localizable in an unequivocal fashion. It also means that they no longer allow a superimposition of the set of functions of sovereignty, administration, cultural control, taxation, and so on, and consequently a conferral on the territory, or better, on the duo of territory and population, of a simultaneously englobing and univocal signification of 'presupposition' for all other

social relations. Further, it means that they do not work in the same way for 'things' or 'people' – not to speak of what is neither thing or person: viruses, information, ideas – and thus repeatedly pose, sometimes in a violent way, the question of whether people transport, send and receive things, or whether things transport, send and receive people: what can in general be called the empirico-transcendental question of *luggage*. Finally it means that they do not work in the same way, 'equally', for all people, and notably not for those who come from different parts of the world, who (this is more or less the same thing) do not have the same social status, the same relation to the appropriation and exchange of idioms. (1998: 219–20)

Balibar's leitmotif 'borders are vacillating' has the advantage of showing us the significations that are at work in every tracing of a border, beyond the immediate, apparently factual determination of language, religion, ideology and power relations. This does not mean that borders are disappearing. Less than ever is the contemporary world a 'world without borders'. On the contrary, borders are being multiplied and reduced in their localization and their function; they are being thinned out and doubled, becoming border zones, regions or countries where one can reside and live.

Migrant Figurations

Nomadic subjects

Taking up the issue of the imaginary yet material presence of the borders referred to by Balibar, this section will focus on migration as part of the symbolic production of cultural practices within Europe as dictated by the specificities of European intellectual consciousness.

To understand migration as a symbolic representation has had an enormous impact within disciplinary fields such as Women's Studies. One of the most recent figurations has been offered by Rosi Braidotti (1994). Her nomadic subject is a feminist figuration whose task it is to subvert conventional representations and modes of thought. It criticizes gender-blindness by claiming that nomadic cartographies need to be continuously redrafted in order to activate a process of countermemory, 'a form of resisting assimilation or homologation into dominant ways of representing the self' (1994: 25). It refers to an engagement with the rethinking of the bodily roots of subjectivity, in which embodiment must be understood as an overlapping point between the physical, symbolic and sociological. The nomadic subject envisioned by Braidotti is not just the deterritorialized traveller (the literal nomad as much as the itinerant in cyberspace) but, in the main, a figuration that entails the situated, differentiated and multiply located feminist subject:

> though the image of 'nomadic subjects' is inspired by experience of peoples of cultures that are literally nomadic, the nomadism in question here refers to a kind of critical consciousness that resists settling into socially coded modes of thought and behaviour. Not all nomads are world travellers; some of the greatest trips can take place without physically moving from one's habitat. It is the subversion of a set

of conventions that defines the nomadic state, not the literal act of travelling. (Braidotti 1994: 5)

Though linked to the personal experience of geographical, linguistic and disciplinary nomadism (Braidotti is an Italian immigrant to Australia, educated in Paris, and working on European networks of Women's Studies from the Netherlands), Braidotti's feminist concept, inspired by Gilles Deleuze's nomadic epistemology, has had a great impact on the possibility of envisioning female agency within revised epistemological categories. Braidotti constructs one of the most inspirational metaphors of the nomad as the creator of powerful new tropes and visions that aim at engendering transformations and at subverting dominant patterns of thought. It is an intellectual style, a process to increase critical consciousness. Nomadism here is not about being homeless but about developing skills that allow a home to be re-created, as heterogeneous, transmobile and polyvalent.

Braidotti is very careful not to conflate the epistemological position with the material condition of migrants who have a clear destination and very clear purposes for moving from one space to another. She declares that 'not all diasporas are equal, though they get homogenized by the gaze of the colonial observer' (Braidotti 1994: 10). Migration to Europe has affected both the 'white women and the domestic foreigners' (22), women whose role as holders of traditional values and of the original home culture is often in conflict with the national ideology of the host country and of international feminist issues.

The nomadic subject has, therefore, the function of envisioning a feminist multiple subject positioning that is in constant renegotiation and transformation in order to unsettle patriarchal patterns of domination but also gender processes of hierarchical relocation, such as white women versus Third World women. It is in the fluidity and performativity of the nomadic figuration that women enter the realm of migration as an empowering notion in which fragmentation, dislocation and multiaxiality come to be signifying practices for self-representation.

Cartographies of diaspora

Another valuable migrant figuration has been theorized by Avtar Brah, a UK resident of Indian origin, born in Uganda. Diaspora is both a material condition of dislocation and a postmodern notion which expresses an intellectualization of existential dispersion. In both cases it indicates a post-national space where 'multiple subject positions are juxtaposed, contested, proclaimed or disavowed; where the permitted and the prohibited perpetually interrogate; and where the accepted and the transgressive imperceptibly mingle even while these syncretic forms may be disclaimed in the name of purity and tradition' (Brah 1996: 208). Diasporic spaces enable the representation of those who straddle two or more cultures, languages and ethnicities and offer a way of rethinking post-colonialism as blurring the lines of national enclaves.

However, the notion of diaspora does not do away with gender inequalities. On the contrary, it makes them more acute and urgent since women must negotiate with conflicting politics: of home and abroad, tradition and emancipation, ethnic belonging and metropolitan fusion. The itinerary of women is therefore, as Paul Gilroy writes, both 'rooted and routed' (1993: 3), and it indicates a myriad processes of cultural fissure and fusion that must be constantly situated and embodied.

Brah inflects the question of diaspora with a multiaxial slant. She investigates questions of 'difference' and 'identity' through a focus on the intersections of ethnicity, racism, gender, sexuality and class. One major area of her research is concerned with youth, diaspora and cultural change. She fuses empirical and theoretical material to map issues such as 'diversity', 'difference' and 'commonality' as relational concepts. Particular attention is paid to South Asian Muslim women in Britain and how they deal with gendered and racialized discourses. The concept of diaspora space is central to the framework of analysis Brah proposes, since it marks the simultaneous articulation of migration, race, ethnicity and class. Brah explores how the power relations which are produced by these intersections work as both inclusive and exclusive in contemporary conditions of transnationalism. For example, minorities are positioned not only in relation to majorities but also with respect to one another. Brah argues that individual subjects may occupy minority and majority positions simultaneously; this has important implications for the formation of subjectivity.

The Black Atlantic

Paul Gilroy, a second-generation British immigrant himself, who has collaborated with the Birmingham Centre for Contemporary Cultural Studies established by Stuart Hall, provides a corrective to the ethnocentric dimension of cultural studies. Gilroy points out how notions of Blackness and Britishness are mutually exclusive not only in the political symbolism of the nation but also in the cultural realm of identity construction. This is because 'the marginalisation of race and racism has persisted even where cultural studies have identified themselves with socialist and feminist political aspirations' (Gilroy 1993: 12).

The British formula of ethnic pluralism only determines the areas of tolerated vicinity without addressing the possible zones of interaction, contamination and transformation that are not only present among different ethnic groups within the British metropolitan centres – *par excellence* the areas of fusion and syncretism, the reflection of the global within the national parameter – but were already established at the beginning of modernity, through the very first moments of expansion and colonization. This reading shows that the other ends of empire are not liminal, separated, but intrinsic to the national construction of Britishness and with it to the gender model propelled within British feminism.

Gilroy is troubled by the very notion of migration, regardless of its creative or sociological component. Migration to Europe implies the vision of a 'white Europe' engrossed in its post-colonial melancholia, an essence in itself that reactively works against those 'racialized' groups which are already within, and not at the other end of, history. Migration functions as a dangerous tool of multicultural myopia, an instrument that makes of diversity a 'culturalism' and erases the still dominant political and economic materiality of racism and prejudicial representations.

Gilroy's major contribution to the debate on migration is his claim that there cannot be a debate on migration without addressing the historical source and presence of today's racism in contemporary Europe. The exploration of racial taxonomies created at the other end of the empire and protracted through fascist forces needs to be addressed and contested within the cultural contexts of Western metropolitan culture in order to understand how race-thinking is intrinsic and not external to the European project of modernity. It must be added that the racial taxonomies of the empire were highly gendered and based on the objectification of the female body (Black Venus, The Hottentot woman, women and harem, the representation of *sati*), which has enormous consequences for the politics of representation in today's Europe. This refers to the use of cultural images, from billboards to films, to photography and museum exhibitions, that are still permeated by the same racial and gender bias – about black inferiority and oversexed but victimized female natives – which characterized colonial discourse.

Gilroy's major trope of migration is that of the Black Atlantic. The image of a connected black culture travelling across the Atlantic, transmitting ideas and cultural forms is Gilroy's powerful contestation of the priority attributed to national cultures, and to the idea that diaspora necessarily equals separation and cultural fragmentation. Gilroy recognizes that there exists a double consciousness in the black flesh; that is, the black sees his own image through the 'other'. Gilroy emphasizes the interconnectedness between discourses around race, class, gender and sexuality and their impact on the black and transglobal communities. He does not want to minimize the impact of diaspora. However, he regards the notion of the Black Atlantic as a way to break out of constraining categories such as the nation, culture or ethnicity.

Conclusion

The texts discussed in this chapter offer a panoramic view of European migration as a force and of diasporic subjectivity as a gendered and ethnic category. These interrelate with the different strands of material immigration within Europe itself, as originating from the diverse forms of European colonialisms and post-colonial aftermaths and the multicultural policies followed by the different national states. Migration is thus not a spontaneous and self-contained process but is dictated by the push and pull of globalization and by other contemporary factors that often endanger and destabilize local survival.

Several critics oppose the use of 'migration' as a meaningful category at the local level, as is the case with Gilroy and other post-colonial critics who read migration as a form of ghettoization of non-Western cultures. Parati (1999) views the category of 'migration' as necessary for pedagogical purposes, in order to broaden the curriculum and give visibility to voices and experiences which get easily stifled by a conservative and traditional canon such as the Italian one, still holding on to Benedetto Croce's definitions of genre and aesthetic achievements.

As illustrated in the various approaches to the category of 'migration', it remains fruitful and often necessary despite it obfuscatory and contestatory nature. It helps to visualize and voice experiences that would otherwise be submerged by the wider dominant parameter. However, sketching these 'alternative' trajectories (by forming subcanons, new traditions and enabling alternative figurations) should not be a point of arrival but a 'testing ground', a 'provocative manoeuvre' that unsettles the self-fulfilling prophecy of a 'global world' modelled on old colonial paradigms. To address migration as a site of transition and transformation between received and appropriated categories, norms and patterns is the best way to envision a pluralistic and syncretic future.

Notes

1. For a critical study on the Maghrebis in France, see Hargreaves 1997a, 1997b; for a study of the emergence of a Italian post-colonial strand, see Ponzanesi 1999; and for a panorama on Lusophone traditions, see Chabal et al. 1996.
2. I borrow this term from Katrina Irving's article 'EU-phoria? Irish National Identity, European Union and the Crying Game' (in Brinker-Gabler and Smith, 1997: 295–314).

References

Balibar, Etienne (1998) 'The Borders of Europe', in Pheng Cheah and Bruce Robbins, eds, *Cosmopolitics: Thinking and Feeling Beyond the Nation*. Minneapolis: University of Minnesota Press, pp. 216–29.

Barker, Francis, ed. (1985) *Europe and Its Others: Essex Sociology of Literature Conference*. Colchester: University of Essex.

Brah, Avtar (1996) *Cartographies of Diaspora: Contesting Identities*. London and New York: Routledge.

Braidotti, Rosi (1994) *Nomadic Subjects: Embodiment and Sexual Difference in Contemporary Feminist Theory*. New York: Columbia University Press.

Brinkler-Gabler, Gisela and Sidonie Smith (1997) *Writing New Identities: Gender, Nation and Immigration in the New Europe*. Minneapolis: University of Minnesota Press.

Chabal, Patrick, with Moema Parents et al. (1996) *The Postcolonial Literature of Lusophone*

Africa. London: Hurst.

Chambers, Iain and Lidia Curti (1996) *The Post-colonial Question: Common Skies, Divided Horizons*. London and New York: Routledge.

Cohen, Robin (1997) *Global Diasporas: An Introduction*. London: UCL Press.

Farah, Nuruddin (2000) *Yesterday, Tomorrow: Voices from the Somali Diaspora*. London and New York: Cassell Academic.

Gabaccia, Donna R. (2000) *Italy's Many Diasporas*. London: UCL Press.

Gilroy, Paul (1993) *The Black Atlantic: Modernity and Double Consciousness*. London: Verso.

Gilroy, Paul (2000) *Against Race: Imagining Political Culture Beyond the Color Line*. Cambridge, MA: Harvard University Press.

Hargreaves, Alec (1997a) *Immigration and Identity in Beur Fiction: Voices from the North African Community in France*. Oxford: Berg.

Hargreaves, Alec (1997b) *Post-colonial Cultures in France*. London and New York: Routledge.

Horrocks, David, and Eva Kolinsky, eds (1996) *Turkish Culture in German Society Today*. London and New York: Routledge.

Krishnaswamy, Kevathi (1995) 'Mythologies of Migrancy: Postcolonialism, Postmodernism and the Politics of (Dis)location', *ARIEL. A Review of International English Literature*, vol. 26, no. 1, January, pp. 125–46.

Parati, Graziella, ed. (1999) *Mediterranean Crossroads: Migration Literature in Italy*. Madison: Fairleigh Dickinson University Press.

Melotti, Umberto (1997) 'International Migration in Europe: Social Projects and Political Cultures', in Tariq Modood and Pnina Werbner, *The Politics of Multiculturalism in the New Europe: Racism, Identity and Community*. London: Zed Books, pp. 73–92.

Modood, Tariq and Pnina Werbner (1997) *The Politics of Multiculturalism in the New Europe: Racism, Identity and Community*. London: Zed Books, 1997.

Ponzanesi, Sandra (1999) 'Paradoxes of Postcolonial Culture. Feminism and Diaspora in South-Asian and Afro-Italian Narratives'. Utrecht: unpublished PhD dissertation.

Schwartz, Bill (1992) 'England in Europe: Reflections on National Identity and Cultural Theory', *Cultural Studies*, vol. 6, no. 2, May, pp. 198–206.

Yuval-Davies, Nira (1997) *Gender and Nation*. London: Sage Publications.

Yuval-Davies, Nira (1999) 'Ethnicity, Gender Relation and Multiculturalism', in Rodolfo Torres, Louis Miron and Jonathan Xavier Inda, eds, *Race, Identity, and Citizenship: A Reader*. Oxford: Blackwell, pp. 112–25.

12

Whiteness and European Situatedness

GABRIELE GRIFFIN

WITH ROSI BRAIDOTTI

The Emergence of Whiteness

Whiteness as a critiqued and critical concept of racialized positions has a seemingly relatively recent history. During the 1990s black American feminists such as Toni Morrison, in her now celebrated William E. Massey Sr Lecture in the History of American Civilization entitled *Playing in the Dark: Whiteness and the Literary Imagination* (1992), and bell hooks in 'Representations of Whiteness' (in hooks 1992), began to raise the spectre of whiteness and its racialized and racializing meanings. This had immediate counterparts in British publications such as Robert Young's *White Mythologies* (1990), Vron Ware's *Beyond the Pale: White Women, Racism and History* (1992), and Richard Dyer's *White* (1997). Whiteness continued to be analysed in the United States with volumes such as Ruth Frankenberg's *White Woman, Race Matters* (1993) and Mike Hill's *Whiteness: A Critical Reader* (1997). Indeed, the first half of the 1990s in particular was a key moment in the establishment of whiteness as a racialized category. The texts published during that period also set the agenda for the discussion of whiteness in very particular ways, by focusing the discussion on relations between 'black' and 'white' people; between people of Afro-Caribbean descent, on the one hand, and those deemed 'white' or, as the United States would have it, 'Caucasian', on the other.

Whiteness and 'Difference'

The impetus for this agenda came from the prior emergence of a number of critical positions that enabled the formulation of a new kind of race-critical perspective. Chief of these – and this is evidenced in the number of black feminists who participated in the establishment of the 1990s' critiques of whiteness – was the surfacing of 'difference' as the second critical phase in feminist thinking in the late 1970s and 1980s. The move in feminism from notions of universal sisterhood and equality of oppressedness within patri- archy, to an understanding of the role that differences among women play in the formation and maintenance of power structures and inequality that affect women differentially, was *inter alia* spearheaded by black American feminists. They challenged the models of women's oppression offered by white middle- class women as inadequate and not representative of the experiences of those women who did not share the relatively privileged position white middle- class feminists enjoyed. Once difference became established as the key concept through which privileged signifiers might be critiqued, that concept became transportable into other terrains in which difference had been utilized in the service of oppression and exclusion. It thus opened up the possibility of investigating differences where these had previously not been named or ana- lysed as such. It is important to recognize that the emergence of difference as a critical concept in feminism was closely aligned with issues of race, racialized positions and the relation between 'black' and 'white' feminists, for it is this context that to some extent set the agenda for the whiteness debates that then flared up in the 1990s.

In the USA, in particular, the emergence of difference was accompanied by another raced and gendered struggle, that of African-American feminists such as Alice Walker, Ntozake Shange and Michele Wallace (see her *Black Macho and the Myth of the Superwoman*, 1990, as one exemplary text of that struggle) with African-American men. The latter accused the former of be- traying black men through their often negative portrayal of black male char- acters. Black feminists were exhorted to set their racial allegiances above their gendered grievances and to stop seemingly siding with white people against black men. This struggle had some significance in highlighting interracial tensions and intraracial struggles, and thus contributed to the emergence of the whiteness debate.

Whiteness and 'the Gaze'

A further, very important aspect of the rise of the whiteness debate was the, again relatively recent, emergence of the critical concept of the gaze, again initiated from within feminism and inaugurated by Laura Mulvey's fertile essay 'Visual Pleasure and Narrative Cinema' (1973; in Mulvey 1989), which be- came the founding text for the recovery of scopophilia at the basis of Western culture, and of the notion of 'the gaze' as critical to power relations. One central aspect of Mulvey's work was the foregrounding of visuality as a key element in regimes of power, an element simultaneously recovered by Michel Foucault in his analysis of surveillance regimes as part of the formation and structuration of modern society. 'Representation', and not just in its political but, more significantly, in its cultural sense, became a key issue and it is significant that many texts, such as Morrison's, dealing with 'whiteness' focused on its cultural manifestations in literature, film and other cultural forms.

Black feminists' intervention in the universalizing feminist projects of the 1960s and 1970s had paved the way for opposition within resistance, the inscription of difference into the feminist project. Oppositionality was also a key paradigm in the feminist analysis of the gaze and of scopophilic regimes in Western culture. The possibility of appropriating 'the gaze' and of producing an oppositional gaze, of looking back or claiming the visual field, rather than looking down or being the object of visual inspection, became one of the points of debate of the 1980s and 1990s, generating texts such as bell hooks' 'The Oppositional Gaze' (in hooks 1992). 'Difference' and 'the gaze' or 'the look' became central building blocks in the critiques of whiteness of the 1990s, and it is not surprising that many of the texts dealing with this issue focused on a visually articulated difference, skin colour, presented as 'black', and 'white', and offered a reverse discourse in the sense of setting out to problematize 'white' where it had previously been 'black' which had been set up as the category of interrogation and site of difference. This was, in part, of course, a function of the histories of slavery in the USA, on the one hand, and of the history of European colonial empires in Africa, Asia and Latin America, on the other. These had in both their own and different ways produced and perpetuated colour binarisms as inherent aspects of their oppressive regimentation. Driven, then, by black American feminists and taken up by British feminists and others interrogating British positions, the 'whiteness' debates of the 1990s were powerfully visually focused and sought to intervene in the seeming absence of whiteness as a racialized position and in the need for the articulation of black perspectives on whiteness, hitherto denied or erased. As hooks put it:

> Searching the critical work of post-colonial critics, I found much writing that bespeaks the continued fascination with the way white minds, particularly the colonial imperialist traveler, perceive blackness, and very little expressed interest in representations of whiteness in the black imagination. (1992: 166)

Resituating Whiteness in Europe

When the whiteness debate emerged, it was greeted with much enthusiasm both by black and by white theorists, who viewed it as an opportunity to revision relations between blacks and whites and to encourage 'white' people to engage in debates about the meaning of their colour. At the time it seemed as if whiteness was something new, an only just discovered problematic category which needed to be deconstructed and invested with its proper meanings. It also initially seemed to be very much an Anglo-American issue. However, not only had Frantz Fanon's *Black Skin, White Masks* (1967) somewhat earlier already begun a debate about interracial relations and power structures that entailed a critique of whiteness; when discussing 'whiteness'

Morrison (1992) prefaced her lecture with a discussion of an autobiographical novel by the late French feminist writer Marie Cardinal, *The Words to Say It* (1975). Morrison analyses Cardinal's representation of her illness and the need to find the words to articulate that illness so as to effect a break from her malady as a function of Cardinal's relation to Algeria and the way Algeria figures in Cardinal's imaginary. Morrison's discussion, as much as Fanon's earlier *Black Skin, White Masks* – significantly a text taught more in the USA than in the UK – locates the issue of whiteness in its contradictory relation to the North African 'other', in Europe's colonial history and its legacies, and makes these a literal as well as a literary precursor of her discussion of whiteness as it figures in black American critical discourses.

Embracing the Whiteness Debate in Europe

Europe, then, became a founding space for the articulation of racialized positions, including that of whiteness, and a history of discourses on whiteness was revealed that stretches back way beyond the surfacing of whiteness as an issue in the 1990s. To what, then, do we owe the 'happy embrace' of the whiteness debate in some European countries during the 1990s and what are the issues that arise from that embrace? We would suggest that there were three problematic reasons why the whiteness debate of the 1990s was welcomed in some European countries. The first of these was that it problematized whiteness per se, at a time when the politics of difference among feminists was in full swing, with the concomitant understanding that many women were – for diverse reasons – excluded from feminist politics because of its (previous) homogenizing stance. The debate thus fed into a sense of unease among white women about their positioning within feminist politics and constituted, simultaneously, a form of empowerment for black women, who could use that debate to ask for the acknowledgement of white women's racialized perspective and for the politicization of their position. As Helen (charles), a black British feminist put it: 'The political colouring of a skin-tone which is not independently colourized ('white' = 'non') or politicized, makes a statement in the multi-inter-cultural society of contemporary Britain.' (1991: 29) In her article, (charles) also repeatedly emphasizes the seeming novelty of the debate, and, although she is able to point – via the work of Hazel V. Carby – to a black American woman from the nineteenth century who asserted that white women needed to 'revolutionize their thinking and practices' (1991: 31), it is clear that these antecedents of the whiteness debate had been forgotten or had never been known by many/most. A sense of novelty therefore attached to the notion of politicizing whiteness. In sum, then, the whiteness debate appeared as a new intervention at a time when black women were searching for ways of empowering themselves vis-à-vis white women, and when white women were being made/becoming aware of

the untenability of certain homogenizing feminist positions. It is worth pointing out that the whiteness debate found more resonance in terms of published
interventions in European countries with colonial histories in Africa than in
others, possibly because of the specific 'colouring' of the debate.

The second problematic reason why the whiteness debate took off in
Europe in the early 1990s was that much of it was formulated both in terms
of cultural representation (i.e. what happens in literature, film, etc.) and in
terms of a black-and-white dynamic which linked the debate, especially in
terms of how it was articulated by writers in the USA and by men in the
UK, on the one hand to the American history of slavery and racial segregation, and on the other to the history of European colonial empires. All three
were effectively forms of distanciation, displacements of a problematic into
another sphere (culture), space (the USA) and time (history as opposed to
lived reality), which detracted effectively from the race politics happening
right under our European noses. And it is worth remembering that by the
early 1990s we had moved into the post-communist era, which had begun to
inaugurate its own wave of racialized violence, not least against asylum seekers.
It is significant and telling, by way of an analogy, that black women's writing
courses, as routinely taught in some European countries during the 1980s and
1990s, always centred on certain African-American women writers such as
Alice Walker, Toni Morrison and Maya Angelou. The focus on their work
over that of writing by black women living and working in European countries
helped to obscure the intermittently flaring race relations in the European
countries. The specificity of the whiteness debate, then, as it was conducted
in the first half of the 1990s, enabled Europeans to participate in it without
in some respects needing to engage with the whiteness issues that were
pertinent to their own actual race-political situation.

This leads directly to the third and final problematic reason why we think
the whiteness debate of the 1990s took off in some European countries. The
colour casting of the debate, its specificity in analysing a black–white dynamic,
spoke to a certain set of race relations and racialized positions but left un-
acknowledged those racialized positions which could not be drawn in such
stark terms, where the issues were not 'black' and 'white' as seemingly
suggested by the debate. Discussing issues of race and gender in the Netherlands, Gloria Wekker, for instance, highlights 'the many branches to the tree
of the denial of racism' (1995: 71) in the Dutch context. Dissociation and
distantiation were thus not specifically British phenomena but occurred in a
number of European countries in diverse but identifiable ways.

'Whiteness' and Race Issues in Europe

One consequence of the taking on of the whiteness debate as it emerged in
the 1990s was the obliteration within European feminist race politics of the
reality of racialized issues faced by women in Europe. These were dealt with

under different headings, such as those of 'ethnic cleansing' and the war in Bosnia, or the problematic of lone women being viewed as the equivalent of single young black mothers in the UK, or trafficking in women for sexual and economic exploitative purposes. But no specific link was made between this treatment of diverse groups of women and the issue of race as it had inhabited the Europe of the last two hundred years. It remains without question the case that when we deal with issues of race we find it easier to contemplate them as they occur elsewhere than as they come to the surface within Europe itself. The reasons for this lie in the twin historical phenomena of eugenics, the mock-scientific biological basis for European racism, ethnicism and colonialism, and the Holocaust, European racism's most appalling manifestation in the twentieth century. The culturally constructed and biologically seemingly validated racism which has informed, at least intermittently, the politics of most, if not all, European countries over the past two hundred years is an issue which we as Europeans have not even begun to address adequately. We would argue that it is this failure which continues to lead to what are described as 'ethnic conflicts' and 'racial tensions' in Europe, the fire-bombing of asylum seekers' hostels in Germany, the killing of asylum seekers on so-called 'sink estates' in the UK, the abuse of female domestic workers, illegally imported from outside Europe, the violence against Algerian and Senegalese migrants in France, and so on.

Eugenics, Anti-Semitism and the Construction of Whiteness

One of the key issues in analysing the meaning of whiteness within a European context is to understand the role eugenics and anti-Semitism have played in the construction of whiteness as it is understood in Europe. For with the rise of the European colonial empires came the rise of a 'science' designed to underwrite that empiric intent, to justify its validity by pointing, unambiguously and – at the time – unashamedly, to 'objective' science as the reason for subjugating 'others'. These others, deemed biologically inferior, encompassed not just others who were visibly different but also others who were other not by virtue of their skin colour but by virtue of some other trait, now (newly) culturally[1] loaded as designating inferiority. Inferiority thus pertained not only to those described as being of other races but also to (certain) women, people from the lower classes, certain ethnic groups. Through a complex process of classification and categorization eugenics produced a hierarchy of the racially and ethnically desirable, described in Nazi Germany as 'Aryans', and validated in their superiority biologically by their skin colour, 'white'. However, whiteness in and of itself was not a sufficient or determining factor, for if it had been why send communists, homosexuals, gypsies and Ashkenazi Jews to the gas chambers? It is at this point that the whiteness debate as it occurred in the 1990s becomes insufficient to the task of addressing race and ethnicity in

Europe, since the black-and-white dynamic, whilst offering a symbolic opportunity to analyse power relations determined by biological markers, leaves untouched the whole issue of diversity among groups seemingly of one colour, the intra-group differences that account for many of the most serious racial and ethnicized conflicts in Europe. It also leaves untouched the extent to which biology is culture, and must be read as such.

The homogenization effect which the whiteness debate entailed reproduced colour codings and castings also prevalent in Europe today, but it did not engage sufficiently with the intra-group diversities, raised above, which are at the heart of the European problematic surrounding whiteness. For whiteness is not just about the relation between 'black' and 'white' but about the definition of 'white' as such. Washing powders advertised in Europe frequently present slogans such as 'washes whiter than white'. Rock fans will remember 'A Whiter Shade of Pale'. But is there such a thing as 'whiter than white'? Does 'white' actually stand for the colour white or is it invested with meanings that do not impinge on colour so much as on what one might term ethnic or cultural differences? Diversity is not merely or exclusively about colour. This is what European anti-Semitism demonstrated. There are black and white scenarios where colour is key but in many instances of discrimination and oppression colour is not the (only) determining factor. It is this complexity that the whiteness debate in Europe needs to address.

Biology or Culture?

Whichever way one chooses to look at it, Europe's history of dealing with intra-group diversity is one of discrimination and oppression. In this context being 'white' does not signify being safe from either such discrimination or such oppression. This is what Nazi ideology proved beyond doubt. Sexual identity, religious affiliation, political persuasion and ethnic identity – under the Nazi regime all of these could and did serve as indicators of a diversity that was to be eliminated in favour of a homogenized race, a 'racism of extermination' as Liliane Kandel describes it in her chapter in this volume. Within this context biology was gestured towards through the assertion that the *Herrenvolk* should consist of pure-bred Aryans only, their racial purity being a function of a specific genealogy. The biological argument, underscored by evolutionary theories (here understood as narrative formations rather than absolute truths) served as the 'scientific' basis for the discrimination and oppression exercised as part of the anti-Semitic strategy of the elimination of Jews in Nazi Germany. The complex biological, and therefore seemingly essential, classifications which eugenics provided enabled the racialization of cultural differences and personal choices, which has been at the root of all nationalist European movements of the last two hundred years. It is this which fuelled the unrest in the Balkans and which will continue to haunt

Europe unless it can address its continuing history of the racialization of difference.

That racialization is only too evident when we consider something like the way in which census data were collected in the UK in 2001. One of the questions asked was 'What is your ethnic group?' Similar questions are commonly found on the equal opportunities forms many employers require job applicants to fill in. In the 2001 census people were offered five choices with subcategories, with the explanation 'Choose ONE section from A to E, then tick the appropriate box to indicate your *cultural* background' (emphasis added).

Table 12.1

A White	British	Irish	Any other white background	
B Mixed	White and Black Caribbean	White and Black African	White and Asian	Any other Mixed background
C Asian or Asian British	Indian	Pakistani	Bangladeshi background	Any other Asian
D Black or Black British	Caribbean	African background	Any other Black	
E Chinese or other ethnic group	Chinese	Any other		

Source: 2001 Census questionnaire.

There are many things to comment on here, but for the purposes of this chapter we simply want to point out that what is described as 'ethnic group' and 'cultural background' ultimately turns out to revolve around skin colour, for the named categories such as 'White and Black Caribbean' or 'Indian' – reproducing, of course, a map of the empire and its migratory patterns – are all concerned not with culture but with a specific range of skin tones, mediated only by the option 'any other...'. The racialization of culture, its biologization, is here replayed in ways that perpetuate the divisions that have led to persistent so-called racial tensions in the UK. The UK is, of course, not alone in this. To give a couple of other concrete examples, Gloria Wekker reports the case of a popular Indonesian-born singing duo who have lived in the Netherlands for over forty years being asked questions on a talk show that made clear that 'no matter how long they had lived in the Netherlands, they would forever remain "foreign"' (1995: 78). Valerie Mason-John, a black British writer and performer, describes how her mother thought of her: 'I am my biological mother's worst nightmare. A white English child inside a coal black skin. She tries to beat the white out of me. She sadistically tortures and abuses me.... Aged 12 and a half, I am taken back into care' (1999: 9). Such conflictual relations to one's identity based on appearance are a product of the dichotomous racialized thinking we inhabit in Europe, and which perpetuates a destructive 'them' and 'us' mentality.

A second issue that emerges from the census data is the conflation between ethnicity, culture and national identity, which has also haunted the European imaginary, taking at the beginning of the twenty-first century various forms such as the articulation of the desire for a Greater Serbian empire full of Serbs only; continuing debates about the porosity of the European borders and the problematic of asylum seekers; and, finally, discussions at national and at European level about who should and who should not be part of Europe as the European Union seeks to extend its sphere of influence whilst some nation-states that are part of Europe try to preserve theirs.

Women as Bearers of Nationalistic Ideology

It is, *inter alia*, in this context that the question of gender becomes an important issue because of the common construction of women as the symbolic bearers of national identity. Helma Lutz, Ann Phoenix and Nira Yuval-Davis have pointed to the ways in which 'women's symbolic role in nationalist and racialized narratives' (1995: 9) frequently place women in positions where they mark the boundaries between different groups, and their bodies become the territories on and through which different groups seek to signal their identity. Writing about 'affective nationalism' in the former Yugoslavia, Djurdja Knezevic highlights 'the publicly declared strategy of the Serbian warlords, that rape is a strategy of humiliation and contamination of the nation' and that 'the nation is a female body or a woman. Women are not considered as "only women" but as the personification of and symbol for the nation.... Phrases such as "mother nation" or "mother homeland" are examples of this point of view' (1997: 65).

The enlistment of women in nationalist projects has a long history. In Germany, which talks of the 'fatherland' rather than the 'motherland', the 'mother's cross', an honour of varying degrees bestowed on German women for bearing x number of children for the 'fatherland', is well remembered and was one way in which the Nazis rewarded female submission to the ideal of a nationalistic identity. Women are thus placed in a vulnerable and precarious position. As bearers of nationalistic cultures, they become attackable as such. Haleh Afshar has made the point that in the flexible, changing context of Europe, 'women's identities are the most transient' (1994: 127). Subsumed by the nexus of the social relations which continue to be the primary signifiers of their identity as daughters, wives and mothers, women's identities – always in relation – are predominantly structured around their relations to men. In consequence the policies which aim to regulate identities and migration, for example, tend to police males, and men in turn are expected to, and expect to, regulate women. Many women's lives and experiences are thus privatized and domesticated, enabling their exploitation and objectification.

Homogenization as a Racialized Strategy

One of the ways the census in the UK and other similar forms of data collection, including, for instance, ethnically based research, deal with diversity in Europe is by seeking to constitute particular groups and categories of people. Much research on issues of race, ethnicity, migration and gender, for example, focuses on groups of people from supposedly specific and thereby homogenized racial or ethnic backgrounds. As Turks are homogenized in Germany, Arabs in Sweden, Algerians in France, and Malaysians in the Netherlands, so Asians are categorized in monolithic terms in the UK. Research on particular 'ethnic' groups or subgroups, whether it be on black single mothers, or on illiteracy among gypsies, or issues of caring in Asian families, is often driven by identity politics and a sense that the needs of a particular minority group have to be recognized and dealt with. This is both understandable and necessary. Many people think and feel, without question, that they belong to a particular and identifiable group. But the cost of such homogenization is high, and often particularly high for women. Virginia Woolf's dictum 'As a woman I have no country' suggests both the invisibilization of women within (nationalist) politics and the appropriation and objectification of women for such politics. Under the mantle of homogenization women thus experience their subjection and their vulnerability.

One of the costs of this homogenization is the maintenance of the 'them' and 'us' mentality already referred to. A model of identity based on homogenization does not, for example, sufficiently address *intra-group* differences. For differences between groups may also serve to highlight differences within a group. In an increasingly mobile Europe migration involves adaptation and thus necessitates change. Haleh Afshar's research on Muslim women in West Yorkshire in the UK, for example, indicates the ways in which cross-generational differences, that is differences between mothers and daughters, promoted through migration to the West and the influence of Western culture on Muslim girls born and/or raised in the West, impact on women's sense of self within the Muslim community. Afshar's research focuses on one ethnically specific group which, from a 'Western' point of view, can easily be classified as different. But a degree of homogenization persists here, too. Southall Black Sisters, a feminist black activist group in London, have a long history of campaigning against violence against women in Asian and black communities in contexts where those communities are not invariably supportive of women, enabling women to escape from abusive domestic scenarios. The point is that migration, moving across and between cultures, has an impact on those who migrate, creating choices and opportunities, particularly for women, which are a function of different socio-cultural norms and economic opportunities in diverse countries and communities. Part of the problem of the 'them' and 'us' mentality is that it promotes a static model of two different homogenized groups; but, as Avtar Brah has rightly pointed out, 'diaspora space is "inhabited", not only by those who have migrated and their descendants, but equally by those who are constructed and represented as indigenous' (1996: 209). Both migrants and indigenous people are subjects and objects of change in this process. The 'them' and 'us' position seeks to deny that impact and the resultant inevitability of change. However, in the Europe of the twenty-first century people do not divide neatly into black and white. Many second- and third-generation migrants identify either partly or wholly with the country they inhabit rather than with the place(s) from where their families migrated, or their parents' version of their culture. Additionally, increasing numbers of mixed-race people in Europe also raise questions of identity and identification.

Revisiting Difference: Understanding the Affective Economies of Racialized Politics

One of the key issues, then, for dealing with issues of race and ethnicity in Europe is a review of how we conceptualize and deal with difference. In the whiteness debates of the 1990s, the discussion of whiteness centred on the need to mark that colour, to make it visible as a colour and to begin the process of establishing whiteness as a racialized position. In Europe that racialized position needs to be revisited to take full account of intra-group differences, to understand that identifying with one colour does not automatically and on its own determine your socio-cultural position. The women who were raped in Bosnia were not visibly different from their neighbours; neither were the Jews whom the Nazis sent to their deaths. Skin colour in and of itself is not a necessary or sufficient explanation for some of the kinds of racism that have wreaked such havoc in Europe.

It is in this context that the theoretical positions coming from France and Italy which stress affective economies and the importance of the emotions and the passions are valuable, for they offer an explanation of the irrational in public life, or for an understanding of the particular logic applied whenever a nationalist project raises its head seeking simultaneously to include and exclude or even destroy particular groups of people. It is worth noting that these poststructuralist perspectives found significant resonances in the USA in the work of both gender theorists and political/social scientists seeking to explain the (new) proliferation of gender positions, on the one hand, and the decline of democracy, on the other. To take in the insight of psychoanalytic politics, namely that the subject can only change if his/her desire is activated, is central to this, not least because it is the activation of that desire which accounts for the inter-ethnic wars, tensions and abuses of the last two hundred years in Europe. Michel Foucault, Gilles Deleuze and Luce Irigaray have emphasized the crucial importance of sexuality, of the 'libinal economy', to an understanding of contemporary subjects. This is evident not least when we consider the sexual abuse and the sexualized procreative position of women within nationalistic projects. Foucault, Deleuze and Irigaray propose an ethics of respect for affectivity, desire and memories which invests in the politics of the social imaginary. Historical memory is especially important here, in so far as it keeps alive the historical consciousness of both struggle and resistance. Its interrogation should take into account the affective impulses which come into play in the public sphere. This type of politically activating/activated memory might be described as the desire to 'forget to forget'.

Moving beyond the Black-and-White Binary

There needs to be a critique of power, in terms of the deconstruction of binary opposites and dualisms. If we take, for instance, the idea of 'national identity', a postmodernist critical perspective – inspired by Homi Bhaba or Edward Said – can make us aware of the fact that common ideas of 'nation' are to a large extent imaginary tales, which project a reassuring but nonetheless illusory sense of unity over the disjointed, fragmented and often incoherent range of internal regional and cultural differences that make up a nation-state. Moreover, a feminist knows to what extent the legitimating tales of nation-hood in the West have been constructed over the body of women, as well as in the crucible of imperial and colonial masculinity.

The fact that these allegedly universal or all-encompassing ideas of 'nation' or 'national identity' are flawed and internally incoherent does not make them any less effective; nor does it prevent them from exercising hegemonic power. But the awareness of the instability, the lack of coherence, consistency and inner rationality of the fundamental categories of political and philosophical analysis (Lyotard's 'master-narratives'), far from giving way to a suspension of belief in the permanence of power, results in a renewed need to elaborate forms of political resistance that are suited to the specific paradoxes of our historical condition. More specifically, a postmodernist political priority con- sists in dislodging the belief in the natural foundations and consequently the fixed nature of any system of values, meanings or belief. Two quite different and contradictory approaches to Europe exist, then, categorically different both at the level of content and in terms of the kind of scholarship produced. One of these is concerned with supplanting the nation-states that make up Europe with a Europe that functions like a nation-state; the other is con- cerned with regarding the European Union as an opportunity to move to- wards a post-nationalist Europe that is no longer nostalgically and detrimentally invested in the kinds of nationalisms which have marred European life for so long. As a project, then, the European Union has to do with the rejection of the false universalism that historically has made Europe into the home of nationalism, colonialism and fascism. This is an attempt to come to terms with the paradoxes and internal cntradictions of our own historical predicament as 'post-Europe Europeans', much as gender theory has had to deal with the fragments, the deconstruction and reconstruction of the 'post-Woman women' in the feminist process of transformation.

Activating the Politics of Location: The New Post-nationalist European Project

The European Union project has to do with the sobering experience of taking stock of our specific location and, following the feminist politics of location, adopting embedded and embodied perspectives. It's about engaging our collective memory in the service of a new political and ethical project which is forward-looking and not nostalgic. We have to start from where we are. We need both political strategies and imaginary figurations that are adequate to our historicity. These are all the more important in an age when advances in gene and stem-cell therapy, and biotechnologies, yet again raise the spectre of a eugenic policy ready to affirm the superiority of certain gene pools over others.

This is, however, only one side of the paradoxical coin of European deconstruction in the age of the European Union. The other side, simultaneously true and yet absolutely contradictory, is the danger of recreating a sovereign centre through the new European federation. That the two are simultaneously the case makes European identity into one of the most contested areas of political and social philosophy in our world at the moment. The reactive tendency towards a sovereign sense of the Union is also known as the 'Fortress Europe' syndrome, which has been extensively criticized by feminists and antiracists such as Helma Lutz, Nira Yuval-Davis, Avtar Brah, Floya Anthias and Philomena Essed. They warn us against the danger of replacing the former Eurocentrism with a new 'Europ-ism' – that is, the belief in an ethnically pure Europe. The question of ethnic purity is crucial and is, of course, the germ of Eurofascism. That it would result in the Balkanization of the entire region leaves little doubt, especially after the events in the former Yugoslavia.

Second, we also want to emphasize another crucial issue: the historical correlation between the crisis of postmodernity, exemplified in the crisis of European identity, the decline of European nation-states and the critical deconstruction of *whiteness*. For people inhabiting the European region, the 'post'-condition translates concretely into the end of the myth of cultural homogeneity. This is the foundational political myth in Europe, much as multiculturalism is the central myth in the United States. Of course, European history at any point in time provides ample evidence to the contrary: waves of migrations from the East and the South make mockery of any claim to ethnic or cultural homogeneity in Europe, while the persistent presence of Jewish and Muslim citizens challenges the identification of Europe with Christianity. Nonetheless, the *myth* of cultural homogeneity is crucial to the tale of European nationalism.

In our era, these myths are being exposed and broken down into questions related to entitlement and agency. Thus the European Union is faced with the issue, can one be European *and* Black or Muslim? Paul Gilroy's work on being a black British subject is indicative of the problem of European citizenship emerging as a contested issue. The need to disinvest in nationalistic projects simultaneously raises the issue of whiteness. One of the radical implications of the project of the European Union is the possibility of giving a specific location, and consequently historical embeddedness or memory, to anti-racist whites. It can, finally, racialize our location, which is quite a feat because until recently in Europe only white supremacists, Nazi skins and other fascists actually had a theory about white people. Like all fascists, they are biological and cultural essentialists.

In his analysis of the representation of whiteness as an ethnic category in mainstream films, Richard Dyer defines it as 'an emptiness, absence, denial or even a kind of death' (1993). Being the norm, it is invisible, as if natural, inevitable or the ordinary way to do things. The source of the representational power of white is the propensity to be everything and nothing, whereas black, of course, is always marked off as *a* colour. The effect of this structured invisibility and of the process of naturalization of whiteness is that it masks itself off into a 'colourless multicoloured-ness'. White seemingly *contains* all other colours, which is what makes its analysis so difficult. But, as Deleuze argued, the centre is dead and void; there is no becoming there. The action is at the city gates. By learning to view our subject positions as racialized white people, we can work towards antiracist forms of whiteness, or at least antiracist strategies to rework whiteness. All other historical and demographic differences notwithstanding, we would want to argue that this is one of the key issues at stake in the European integration project and the one most likely to go wrong.

One political strategy is to support the claim of European identity as an open and multilayered project, not as a fixed or given essence. A cultural identity of this kind is a space of historical contradictions which can be turned into spaces of critical resistance to hegemonic identities of all kinds. To rework whiteness in the twenty-first century means first to situate it, in the geo-historical space of Europe and within the political project of the European Union. This amounts to historicizing it and demystifying its allegedly 'natural' locations. It means understanding biology as culture, and whiteness as a differentiated as well as discriminating position.

Since issues of whiteness have been linked so closely and disastrously to the idea of nation-states in Europe, the new European project has to be one of developing a post-nationalist understanding of European identity and of flexible citizenship forms. This constitutes a great historical chance for Europeans to become more intelligent about our own history and more self-critical in a productive sense. Friedrich Nietzsche argued earlier on this century that many Europeans no longer feel at home in Europe. At the beginning of the twenty-first century many would want to argue that those who do not identify with Europe in the sense of the centre – the dominant and heroic reading of Europe – are ideally suited to the task of reframing Europe by making it accountable for a history in which fascism, imperialism and domination played a central role.

To become accountable for such a history requires means of revisiting it, acknowledging it, and understanding the complicity between 'difference' and 'exclusion' in the European mind-set. Repetitions are the road to creating positive redefinitions, in a progress of creative deconstruction. The focus must consequently fall on the dialectics of self and other and the violent, appropriative manner in which the One has historically been brought into relation with his (the gender is not coincidental) others. Difference must be dislodged from this disastrous history, and made to sever its links with power and domination.

Note

1. We understand culture as encompassing science and science as being an expression of a culture at a given point in time.

References

Afshar, Haleh and Mary Maynard, eds (1994) *The Dynamics of Race and Gender.* London: Taylor & Francis.

Brah, Avtar (1996) *Cartographies of Diaspora: Contesting Identities.* London: Routledge.

Braidotti, Rosi (2002) 'Gender, Identity and Multiculturalism in Europe', First Ursula Hirshmann Annual Lecture on 'Gender and Europe', Robert Schuman Centre for Advanced Study, European University Institute, 10 May.

(charles), Helen (1991) 'Whiteness – The Relevance of Politically Colouring the "Non"', in H. Hinds, A. Phoenix and J. Stacey, eds, *Working Out: New Directions for Women's Studies.* Brighton: Falmer Press.

Cardinal, Marie (1975) *Les Mots Pour Le Dire*, Paris: Grasset et Fasquelle; *The Words to Say It.* London: Picador.

Dyer, Richard (1997) *White.* London: Routledge.

Fanon, Frantz (1967) *Black Skin, White Masks.* New York: Grove Weidenfeld.

Frankenberg, Ruth (1993) *White Woman, Race Matters.* London: Routledge.

Hill, Mike (1993) *Whiteness: A Critical Reader.* New York: New York University Press.

Hirschmann, Ursula (1993) *Noi senza patria.* Bologna: Il Mulino.

hooks, bell (1992) *Black Looks: Race and Representation.* London: Turnaround.

Knezevic, Djurdja (1997) 'Affective Nationalism', in J.W. Scott, C. Kaplan and D. Keates, eds, *Transitions, Environments, Translations: Feminisms in International Politics.* London: Routledge, pp. 65–78.

Lutz, Helma, Ann Phoenix and Nira Yuval-Davis, eds (1995) *Crossfires: Nationalism, Racism and Gender in Europe*. London: Pluto.

Morrison, Toni (1992) *Playing in the Dark: Whiteness and the Literary Imagination*. London: Picador.

Mason-John, Valerie (1999) *Brown Girl in the Ring*. London: Get a Grip Publishers.

Mulvey, Laura (1989) *Visual and Other Pleasures*. London: Macmillan.

Wallace, Michele (1990) *Black Macho and the Myth of the Superwoman*. London: Verso.

Ware, Vron (1992) *Beyond the Pale: White Women, Racism and History*. London: Verso.

Wekker, Gloria (1995) "After the Last Sky, Where do the Birds Fly?' What Can European Women Learn from Anti-racist Struggles in the United States?' In Lutz et al, eds, *Crossfires: Nationalism, Racism and Gender in Europe*. London: Pluto, pp. 65–87.

Young, Robert (1990) *White Mythologies: Writing History and the West*. London: Routledge.

PART V

Violence against Women:
European Perspectives

13

Violence against Women in the European Context: Histories, Prevalences, Theories

CAROL HAGEMANN-WHITE

This chapter discusses the two areas of violence against women – sexual violation and domestic assault – that have arguably most profoundly affected our understanding of the meaning of gender in everyday life. It sketches the emergence of an overarching European perspective on the problem, closely related to the transnational development of feminist activism and practical change, within which there are also many significant differences by country and culture. There follows an overview of the state of knowledge and practice for each of the two fields. In the second half of the chapter, research aimed at measuring the extent of the problem in different European countries is summarized. It will be seen that prevalence studies have a primary focus on violence by male partners, but increasingly sexual violence is included. Finally, some issues around interpreting data are raised and questions for future research discussed.

The Emerging European Perspective

Uncovering, naming and challenging men's ability to use violence against women with impunity was not only central to the rise of late-twentieth-century feminism; more than any other, this issue has captured the attention of a broader public, focused a consensus on the imperative to overcome gender inequality, and found a place on the political agenda of local, national and transnational organizations and authorities. Despite controversy both within the movement against gender-based violence and between these and other social actors, despite struggles and many a defeat, the effort to secure women's safety, establish services, and improve women's rights and redress has made progress in much of Europe. A commitment to address and overcome violence against women is now expected of every country in the European

Union and every member state of the Council of Europe. Important milestones in the 1990s were:

- the Declaration adopted in Rome in October 1993 by the European Ministerial Conference on equality between women and men, stating that 'Violence against women constitutes an infringement of the right to life, security, liberty and dignity of the victim and, consequently, a hindrance to the functioning of a democratic society, based on the rule of law';
- a comprehensive Plan of Action published by the Council of Europe in 1997;
- the 'International Year Against Violence Against Women' declared by the European Parliament from March 1998 to March 1999, including a series of conferences where the European Commission promoted dialogue among governments, experts, and dedicated NGOs on how to proceed more effectively against all forms of domestic and sexual violence.

Overall, there has been a great increase in awareness during the last quarter of the twentieth century; a wide range of services and women's advocacy projects have been established in many (by no means all) European countries; the legal rights of women have been extended and improved, and new approaches to redress and security within both civil and criminal law are being developed. More recently, imaginative whole-community projects based on inter-agency co-operation have emerged, linking prevention and intervention, support for women and calling men to account, and creating an atmosphere of 'zero tolerance' (keyword of the 1992 Edinburgh campaign) for male violence against women (see Hagemann-White et al. 1997; Hanmer and Itzin 2000). While there are many national and cultural differences in the extent of social and legal change, it seems clear that in the European context, sexual and domestic violence is today understood as an issue both of human rights and of gender relations. This contrasts with North American debates, in which the family is often centre stage for both research and policy.

Our knowledge about the extent of violence against women, the types and circumstances of its occurrence, the perpetrators, and the risk factors influencing when and where it may be more frequent, depends very much on the existence of support, resources and redress. Where these are scarce or inaccessible, women will rarely speak out. Breaking the silence is a process of political and social change over decades, if not longer (see Klein 1998; Elman 1996). In its course, violations and injuries that have happened for generations are gradually reframed: instead of an unlucky fate, women are able to think of and then to speak about them as wrong, and perhaps even as a crime. Thus, changes in the law, in police and court treatment of women after rape, and in public discourse on women's right to sexual self-determination and respect may lead to an increase in both the number and the types of rapes reported to authorities (Gregory and Lees 1999). In this area, where shame and isolation have often kept women from speaking about the violation of their bodies and souls, a rising level of reported violent crimes does not mean that they happen more often, but that women are no longer silent. When this has been achieved, and only then, a sinking rate of reported crimes may indicate that they are becoming truly less frequent.

Since the developments addressing violence against women have differed very much within Europe, we cannot yet estimate where the real prevalence may be. This is also true within countries, since no European country today has a homogeneous population. Women from ethnic minorities and women in migration have less access to support, services and protection by police and justice; they may face harassment, discrimination or the risk of deportation when they report to statutory authorities. Data collection on the national level has often failed to include these groups in their survey. Increasingly, however, voluntary organizations and feminist researchers are turning their attention to the impact of class, race and citizenship status (see Hanmer and Itzin 2000).

Even where the women's movement raised the issue early, there are differing patterns in the emergence of awareness (Hanmer, in Elman 1996: 133). In the Netherlands, Great Britain and Germany, the first issue to be taken up was battering and abuse of women in their homes by husbands and live-in boyfriends; in France and Sweden, on the other hand, it was sexual violence, in particular rape, that generated active feminist protests. However, while activists in the former countries soon built networks of shelters where battered women might seek safety and tell their stories, thus establishing the topic in the public eye and keeping it on the agenda, the feminist movements in France and Sweden did not follow a comparable pattern for sexual violence. Christine Delphy reports (in Elman 1996: 149) that there has never been a single rape crisis centre in all of France. The Swedish 'women's centres' (*Kvinnojouren*), founded after a passionate debate on the 1976 proposal to define rape as a minor offence and eliminate all penalties for incest, won acceptance as shelters for battered women (see Eliasson 1997). Only after the establishment of the National Centre for raped and battered women in 1994 was it possible to translate knowledge about sexualized violence into high-visibility practice. Overall in Europe, sexual violence has been more difficult to address effectively than domestic violence.

Concepts

The varying success of activists in addressing issues has contributed to much controversy over the use of concepts (Kelly, in Dobash and Dobash 1998). The broader view locates violence within gender relations and keeps the interaction between sexuality, power and entitlements in focus. For research and policy purposes, distinctions are often needed: are we talking about adult women or children, sexual violation or physical assault, harassment and threats or actual intrusive acts and injuries? Yet the line is always difficult to draw, and there is much overlap in reality; some authors are concerned that using distinct concepts will blind us to the links between apparently separate phenomena. Many, probably most, battered women are also sexually abused and/or raped; sexual abuse of children is more frequent in households where the mother is assaulted; and women with extensive experience of sexual violence may tolerate a battering partner rather than live alone. Furthermore, concepts differ by country: in Scandinavia, the concept 'sexualized violence' is widely used to denote the entire field, whereas this term in Germany usually refers to the sexual abuse of girls and boys. Since this chapter aims to introduce readers to the varying states of knowledge and practice, the term 'sexual violence' will be used for hurtful and intrusive acts that are recognizably sexual in content, including threats and harassment; 'battering' and 'domestic violence' refer to the physical abuse of women within an intimate relationship, including stalking and attacks after the woman tries to end the relationship. 'Sexual abuse' will be used here to refer to all forms of sexualized interaction initiated or made use of by an adult in a position of power, authority or trust relative to a girl or boy.

Sexual Violence

Sexual violence takes many forms. Where this has been studied, research regularly finds that rape is not typically an attack by a complete stranger, but more often takes place in the context of relationships, although the acquaintanceship may be short and have even been struck up with the intention of arranging the rape. However, since women have traditionally been blamed for rape, if they were believed at all, and because this crime is intensely humiliating, in all countries the majority do not report being victimized, so that official statistics tell us little about its actual prevalence. Social science surveys face the same problem, if in a different way: whether women give information about an intimate and very painful experience depends on how the questions are asked, on the opportunities available to women for coping with and thus being able to recall such events, and on the ways in which dominant discourse permits defining what has happened (Hagemann-White 2000). It is notable that most surveys on violence against women, and even specifically on sexual violence, have either used a narrow legal definition of rape, or remained vague: women are asked whether someone used coercion to make them 'have sex', or whether they were forced to participate in 'intercourse or other sexual activities', or whether an abusive husband also 'made you do things you didn't want to sexually', or 'used pornography in a way repugnant to you'. As a result, even where survey data on sexual violence exist, it is nearly impossible to draw comparisons and describe trends. As long as research remains shackled to the notion that sexual violations cannot be talked about in plain language or in public, it will be difficult to discuss incidence or prevalence quantitatively. At present, as Kelly points out, in studies 'far more women report experiencing specific behaviours than define themselves as having been sexually harassed' (in Dobash and Dobash 1998: 61), and the same is true of rape.

Much sexual violence takes place in a framework of what is considered 'normal'. Römkens (1992, 1997) found that, of the women in her study, 7 per cent said that their husband or a partner had raped them, but 21 per cent said he had used force to make them have sex. In the Finnish survey (Heiskanen and Piispa 1998), 6 per cent of women said that their current partner had attempted rape or used sexual violence, but of those who had a previous relationship 19 per cent confirmed that the man had been sexually violent. It seems clear from these and other surveys that women find it much more difficult to name their experiences with a current partner as sexually violent, and even more so to use emotionally loaded terms such as 'rape'. Many people still share the view that a man is somehow entitled to have his wife co-operate when he feels the desire to have sex. In some countries, such as Spain and Italy, forcing a woman to submit to sexual acts within marriage is legally not rape, and other countries, such as Germany, have only recently changed their laws to penalize marital rape. This tradition extends to situations in which women are thought to raise a man's expectations of a sexual relationship, so that even women who are very brutally raped may question themselves as to their own possible guilt.

Despite all progress towards recognition of gender equality in principle, sexual violence continues to be widespread among young people. A 1990 study in England and Wales found that 21 per cent of young women (and 7 per cent of young men) had experienced sexually violent incidents of an abusive nature, excluding more impersonal forms of harassment such as flashing. A German study in 1999 with young people 17 to 20 years old found that 25 per cent of the women had unwanted sexual contacts that meet criteria for a criminal offence; when the deliberate use of alcohol or drugs was included, the percentage rose to over 50 per cent. Although young men rarely reported using force, almost a third of them said they had tried to get a young woman drunk or given her drugs to get her to have sex. Neither study was strictly representative, but both put considerable effort into recruiting a large and diverse population. This may be the best research can do, since it is doubtful whether a random sample approached in the usual ways (often in the parents' home) would get honest answers to such sensitive questions. At the very least, these studies suggest that in modernized and individualized urban environments today, where young people are expected to experiment and find partners, the use of force, pressure and intoxication to gain young women's compliance with male sexual demands is widespread (recent research in Sweden has similar findings). Little is being done to support girls and educate boys in the search for genuine sexual self-determination.

Domestic Violence

Public awareness, discussion of practical measures of intervention and research all seem to come easier when the issue is physical violence by a man against his wife or a woman with whom he is living. This has been called men's violence to known women, wife battering, woman abuse or domestic violence, and, although the naming has been hotly debated, the contours of the problem are now fairly clear. Many men repeatedly beat, humiliate, threaten and hurt the women they live with and with whom they have children; innumerable children suffer the trauma of seeing their mothers, upon whom their earliest sense of security and well-being has depended, abused and injured by their father or a father figure (Eliasson 1997; Hester, in Hanmer and Itzin 2000). The silence on these facts was broken by feminist projects providing women with safe houses and refuges where they could stay. An avalanche of stories, of women and their children seeking safety, broke loose wherever the movement gained a foothold: refuge after refuge was overfilled soon after it opened, and joined in the call for more effective measures against the widespread problem. The first refuges, some beginning as 'squats' in condemned or vacant buildings, opened in Great Britain and Amsterdam; other countries soon followed (Egger et al. 1995). In Germany, with a population of 82 million, there are some 400 refuges, and it is estimated that 40,000 battered women seek shelter and counselling each year, many of them only briefly. Spain now has 243 refuges, even though the difficulties for women are great, since they cannot depend on social welfare payments to substitute for the husband's income, and women's unemployment is severe. The documentation and research emerging from this work cast the first light on how many women suffer violence in their homes, on the wide range of social circumstances and economic and educational backgrounds of the violent men, and the dynamics of violence (e.g. Brückner 1998; Fawcett et al. 1996; Egger et al. 1995).

Within varying cultural traditions, there is a common expectation that a woman will enter into an intimate relationship with a man who is defined as her protector and provider, whether this relationship be formal marriage or engagement, cohabiting, or 'going with' a specific male friend on a steady basis. She is understood to be 'his woman', obligating other men to show restraint and a certain deference, as long as the man in question commands some basic respect (Godenzi 1993; Sørensen 1998). Rules vary on what women must do to justify his protection and economic support, but always this code centres on what she must refrain from doing, thus limiting her sphere of action. In some subcultures and legal systems, she may not go out to work without his consent, in others she may be active economically or is even obliged to do so, but should not go out for any recreational purpose without her man; she is expected to avoid sexual intimacy with any other man. If she is judged to transgress against such restrictions, she becomes doubly vulnerable: other men feel free to violate and use her, and her husband or boyfriend may claim the right to chastise or to repudiate her (Lundgren 1990, 1995; Hearn 1998). None of these restrictions applies to men in the same sense. The man's misbehaviour does not make him vulnerable to abuse by other women, nor give his wife the right to discipline him: at most, she is expected to remonstrate or show moral abhorrence, and in today's world if she cannot accept his behaviour, it is up to her to leave him.

Measuring the Extent of the Problem

Linked to the work of refuges, a considerable body of qualitative research has described women's experiences, their difficulties in escaping a violent man, the impact on their children and other dimensions of the problem (see Brückner 1998; Eliasson 1997; Lundgren 1990, 1995). Prevalence research – the attempt to define the frequency of battering in the population at large – made significant progress during the last decade of the twentieth century. It must be noted, however, that until very recently there was no effort to arrive at comparable data within Europe, and existing studies differ in their framework, in their methods, and even in their statistical categories, so that it is not yet possible to describe patterns within or between countries or possible changes over time. However, national studies in the late 1990s have begun to build a database that could allow such comparison, possibly identifying risk factors, or allowing us to trace the impact of policy efforts (Hagemann-White 2000).

A first prevalence study in Europe in 1986 by Renée Römkens (1992, 1997) in the Netherlands used a combination of qualitative and quantitative methods. Römkens was able to present an empirically derived measure of severity of violence and distinguish whether it was unilateral or mutual within the couple. Her approach, using specifically trained interviewers with prior knowledge of the problem, was to offer women the opportunity to describe experiences in their own words, subsequently structuring and coding each event with the women, and (based on interview notes) afterwards. Equally innovative was the North London survey carried out by Jayne Mooney (in Hanmer and Itzin 2000) in 1993. Again, a combination of quantitative and qualitative methods was used for a random sample of 1,000 women and men. With an interviewer-administered questionnaire open-ended questions allowed respondents to describe their experiences freely; 'vignettes' of conflict situations were also used. A supplementary drop-off questionnaire offered women the opportunity to record experiences of domestic violence in complete confidentiality. In data analysis, a composite item was constructed based on women's own definitions of domestic violence. Both studies thus used multiple measures and tried to derive a measure of violence that reflects women's own evaluation. Both studies asked women whether they had ever in their lifetime experienced

violence from a partner, to arrive at an estimate of prevalence – the proportion of individuals within the population who are victimized. Mooney also
tried to capture incidence – the number of incidents of violence occurring
within a given time span. However, women who suffer domestic violence
repeatedly can rarely give precise numbers of incidents; they respond to categories such as 'six to ten times' or 'more than twenty times'. Thus, it is not
possible to calculate a total number of violent acts per year (incidence); rather,
surveys provide, at best, figures for the prevalence of repeat victimization.

This pioneer work towards measuring the extent of domestic violence did
not have visible impact on other European studies until considerably later;
like much theoretical writing, empirical research looked to North American
models. Since 1994, however, this has changed. National prevalence studies
on 'women's safety' or explicitly on 'violence against women' have been published in Ireland (Kelleher et al. 1995), Portugal (Lourenco et al. 1997),
Switzerland (Gillioz et al. 1997), Finland (Heiskanen and Piispa 1998), and
England and Wales (Mirrlees-Black 1999). Data for similar surveys were
gathered in Sweden and France in 2000 (see Lundgren 2001; Jaspard 2001).
All of these surveys have used standardized questionnaires, building on insights from qualitative study and practice.

It is striking that in Finland and Sweden, a postal questionnaire of some
length, requiring the recipient to fill it out and mail it back, had a response
rate of over 70 per cent, double what experts normally expect of postal
surveys. This indicates that women in these countries now see violence within
intimate relationships as a legitimate subject of public inquiry. The high level
of violence actually reported suggests that women no longer see this as a
shameful secret, although many said that they had never talked to anyone
about it.

All national surveys on the continent have addressed women only. This
doubtless made it easier to phrase many questions in gender-appropriate ways,
referring, for example, to sexual or gender role pressures in everyday language. Earlier gender-neutral surveys in Denmark (Christensen and Koch-
Nielsen 1992) and Iceland (Dóms- og kirkjumálaráðuneytið 1997) established
that men experience a great deal of violence, but most of this is outside the
home, often in connection with drinking or in the streets. It is also clear from
men's studies that they experience pressure to perform sexually and to fulfil
gender-role expectations. Yet by the nature of complementary and hierarchical
gender norms, these pressures affect men differently from women (see Fawcett
et al. 1996). Men are almost never expected to submit passively to a woman's
sexual desire; they risk rape primarily in all-male institutions such as prisons,
and it is highly unlikely that a man will be beaten by his wife because there
is dust on the mantelpiece. Violence, like sexuality, is very intimate, very often
physical and highly gendered. Research in this area must be gender-based and
aware of how experiences (and how they are named) are shaped by being a
man or a woman. Although ideally a survey on gender-related experience of

violence would include both spheres, in practice considerations of cost and of political urgency – the need to eliminate egregious discrimination against women – have decided the priority.

In prevalence research, it has become standard to offer women fine-grained lists of acts that they might have experienced, as well as going on to ask about the impact of these events on their health, personal sense of safety, to whom they turned for help, and further aspects. Either women are asked whether a current or a former partner has ever done any of the following things (Switzerland, Finland), or in the reverse approach they are asked if any of these things ever happened to them, and if so by whom (Portugal, France). The former sets a focus on safety and violence within couple relationships and seems well suited to explore this central area in multiple dimensions; the latter is better able to include lifetime experiences of violence, placing the couple relationship in context and avoiding a premature narrowing of the issue of violence to marriage and the family.

Comparison of the data shows that crime surveys, even with improved technology and special modules for addressing domestic violence, yield a substantially lower level of reported violence than the dedicated surveys speaking to women. Crime surveys focus initially on the household, placing crime in the outside world (robbery, break-in, street crime). The shift to a woman's experience of attack by a household member is not easy, and many women, although they think of domestic violence as wrong, do not categorize it as a crime (Walby and Myhill 2001). As Mirrlees-Black (1999) has shown, these perceptions do not prevent significant numbers of women from reporting assaults by a partner, but it seems probable that many others do not immediately recall or willingly report on their experiences in such a context. As a German crime survey found in 1992, comparing the data from different types of question within the same survey, some women are better able to report severe domestic violence in response to a general screening question, rather than neatly sorted into single injurious acts. With these restrictions, the British Crime Survey found that 4 per cent of women had experienced physical assault by their husband or live-in boyfriend in the past year, and 23 per cent had this happen to them at some time in their lives. Of these, less than half (11 per cent of all) described intermittent or occasional attacks, whereas the majority, and 12 per cent of all women, had been subject to repeated or chronic assaults by a partner.

Within the series of surveys since 1994, the proportion of the female population reporting physical violence by a male partner has been rising. Comparison is not easy, as some surveys explicitly seek out women who have actually lived in a couple relationship, and others ask all women about their experiences. The best estimate of prevalence would probably refer figures only to those women who have had a male partner; countries and cultural regions differ considerably in the likelihood that a woman might not have had such a relationship. Put differently: in some regions and social groups, almost every woman has had a male boyfriend by the time she is 20, and in others there are women who enter such relationships much later or never. In the following summary, percentages are given (where possible) as the proportion of those women who have been part of a heterosexual couple.

The 1995 survey in Ireland – a brief questionnaire in the context of a consumer survey – found that 10 per cent of all women who had had a partner said he had been physically violent, and almost all of them qualified this as 'extremely bad', suggesting that they were not reporting minor incidents. The Swiss study in 1994 found that 13 per cent of currently married or cohabiting women had experienced physical violence by a male partner at some time, and 6 per cent had been assaulted in the past 12 months. In the 1995 Portuguese survey, the numbers are calculated only with regard to the total survey group; here, 3 per cent reported physical abuse by the husband in the previous year and 14 per cent in the past.

The Finnish study found a higher level of violence overall. Of all women living with a man at the time, 22 per cent said he had been violent physically at some time (and 9 per cent confirmed this for the past twelve months). Of all women who had lived with a partner previously, fully 45 per cent said he had been physically violent. The violence did not terminate upon separation; 36 per cent faced continued threats, stalking and attacks, and for 4 per cent the violence began at that point. Although it may be hypothesized that women are more likely to divorce a man who has become violent, the much higher rate by comparison with present partners – found in all surveys – probably signifies a greater inner and outer freedom to recognize and name violence as such. Women in shelters say, as research has consistently shown, that they could not have described or even mentally confronted the full extent of the violence so long as they were living with the man. Some degree of denial, or at least forgetting, seems essential to coping with the anxiety and pain of such a situation.

Interpreting the Figures in a European Framework

It is not yet clear whether these figures represent an overall increasing readiness to speak about violence, or differences in different countries and regions. Several studies have also looked at 'psychological violence', including such items as name-calling, hurtful and demeaning comments, chronic jealousy and possessiveness, attempting to prevent the woman from seeing her relatives (items in the Finnish study), or controlling her correspondence, cutting off the telephone, verbal humiliation (Portuguese study). In almost all of the studies that have asked, the levels of psychological violence are higher – up to 40 per cent of Swiss women with a partner report this. The Finnish study describes a strong correlation between specific psychological pressure and physical attacks: 40 per cent of the men violent within the last year demand to know where the woman goes, with whom, and when she will return. As

Jeff Hearn (1998) has emphasized, men who use physical violence also employ other means of control and intimidation; this is not a case of resorting to the physical when other techniques of control are not available. Indeed, the Swiss study also constructed an 'index of dominance' from several questions about decision-making in the family and found a strong correlation between the man's dominance and his use of violence.

Other hypotheses about risk factors and conditions that might make violence more likely have not been clearly confirmed. None of the studies has demonstrated that more alcohol or drugs are present with violence than is usual in that community, although some do find a higher level of consumption among the more violent men. The Swiss study looked for links between economic or social factors and violence and found none: the woman's actual economic contribution to the family income, her relative level of professional training and the division of housework in the home had no influence on the presence or absence of violence. In the Finnish study, younger women who are cohabiting are more likely to experience violence than married women. Some British research suggests that they also employ physical aggression more readily themselves; both findings might relate to a lower level of commitment. Single mothers with children under the age of 7 are highly vulnerable and twice as likely to have suffered violence from a current partner within the past twelve months. And a significant proportion of women are beaten during pregnancy (one-third in the Irish and 15 per cent in the Finnish study); biographical studies suggest that battering sometimes begins in a woman's first pregnancy, which presumably threatens a man's view of the marriage as totally centred on his needs. To date, all such correlations and clusterings of data are singular phenomena waiting to be confirmed or explored in further research.

A major obstacle to interpreting the data now becoming available is the question of when 'hitting' is defined as 'violence'. A number of studies have tried to define levels of severity based on the probability of injury resulting from a certain act. Culturally, women in Europe are not totally prohibited from expressing anger physically, and there are theories, world-views and subcultures that consider it healthy, 'normal' or simply unavoidable to show anger physically, as opposed to, for example, prolonged icy silence or cutting insults. Overall, Western European culture in its expansive history and competitive capitalist economy probably generates a great deal of aggressive emotion and does relatively little to cultivate skills and teach constructive and satisfying ways to express and come to terms with such feelings without doing harm to self or others. Within such a cultural sphere, it seems unrealistic to count every physical act as 'violent', but it is methodologically very tricky to define 'psychological violence' in any reliable way.

The survey research on violence against women is only beginning to consider these issues. Using factor analysis, Römkens was able to describe different patterns: while 26 per cent of the Dutch women had experienced physical aggression by a husband or partner, the majority described violence that was incidental and mild; it happened on infrequent occasions, did not increase over time and only rarely resulted in injuries. For about 5 per cent of the women, physical aggression was both mild, or incidental, and bilateral – that is, both the man and the woman occasionally resorted to hitting, but without serious impact. By contrast, 11 per cent of her total sample experienced moderate to severe or very severe violence, which was repeated, unilateral, and in almost all cases was liable to cause physical injuries. It is this smaller group – somewhat more than one woman in ten of the population – whom Römkens described as battered women. This suggests, as do Mooney's data on women's definitions, that the proportion of women in couple relationships who experience what they themselves, even in retrospect, would categorize as 'violence' may be lower than the numbers who confirm some physical act on a checklist. Now that the debate on eliminating violence against women has become truly global, it seems problematic to proclaim that levels of violence against women are more or less the same everywhere: women from countries where the economic, social and legal situation of women is dramatically worse than in the European Union find such a claim incomprehensible.

Sexual violence and domestic violence are still widespread in all EU countries, their impact is devastating, and they are embedded in the normality of gender relations. At the same time, it is important that research describe a reality recognizable to those whose lives it represents, and it has always been a core element of feminist research to describe social injustices in ways that highlight the possibility of change. Qualitative studies connected to shelters have done this with respect to women's individual lives; quantitative studies need to develop tools that can do this for the entire society and for Europe as a whole.

References

Brückner, M. (1998) *Wege aus der Gewalt gegen Frauen und Mädchen*. Frankfurt am Main: Fachhochschul-Verlag.

Christensen, E. and I. Koch-Nielsen (1992) *Vold ude og hjemme: En undersøgelse af fysisk vold mod kvoinder og maend*. Copenhagen: Socialforskningsinstituttet.

Dobash, R.E. and R.P. Dobash, eds (1998) *Rethinking Violence against Women*. London: Sage.

Dóms- og kirkjumálaráduneytid (1997) *Skyrsla, dómsmálarádherra um orsakir, umfang og afleidingar heimilisofbeldis og annars ofbeldis gegn konum og börnum*. Reykjavik.

Egger, R., E. Fröschl, L. Lercher, R. Logar and H. Sieder (1995) *Gewalt gegen Frauen in der Familie*. Vienna: Verlag für Gesellschaftskritik.

Eliasson, M. (1997) *Mäns våld mot kvinnor: misshandel, våldtäkt, dominans, kontroll*. Stockholm: Natur och Kultur.

Elman, R.A., ed. (1996) *Sexual Politics and the European Union: The New Feminist Challenge*. Providence, RI: Berghahn Books.

Fawcett, B., B. Featherstone, J. Hearn and C. Toft, eds (1996) *Violence and Gender Relations: Theories and Interventions*. London: Sage.

Gillioz, L., J. de Puy, and V. Ducret (1997) *Domination et violence envers la femme dans le couple*. Lausanne: Editions Payot.

Godenzi, A. (1993) *Gewalt im sozialen Nahraum*. Basel: Helbing & Lichtenhahn.

Gregory, J. and S. Lees (1999) *Policing Sexual Assault*. London: Routledge.

Hagemann-White, C., B. Kavemann and D. Ohl (1997) *Parteilichkeit und Solidarität*. Bielefeld: Kleine.

Hagemann-White, C. (2000) 'Male Violence and Control: Constructing a Comparative European Perspective', in S.S. Duncan and B. Pfau-Effinger, eds, *Gender, Work and Culture in the EU*. London: UCL/Routledge, pp. 171–207.

Hanmer, J. and C. Itzen, eds (2000) *Home Truths about Domestic Violence: Feminist Influences on Policy and Practice*. London: Routledge.

Hearn, J. (1998) *The Violences of Men: How Men Talk about and How Agencies Respond to Men's Violence to Women*. London: Sage.

Heiskanen, M. and M. Piispa (1998) *Faith, Hope, Battering: A Survey of Men's Violence Against Women in Finland*. Helsinki: Statistics Finland.

Jaspard, M., E. Brown, S. Condon et al. (2001) *Les violences envers les femmes au quotidien. Rapport final Juin 2001. Enquête nationale sur les violences envers les femmes*. ENVEA Envef, Institut de Démographie de l'Université de Paris I.

Kelleher and Associates with O'Connor, M. (1995) *Making the Links: Towards an Integrated Strategy for the Elimination of Violence against Women in Intimate Relationships with Men*. Dublin: Women's Aid.

Klein, R.C.A., ed. (1998) *Multidisciplinary Perspectives on Family Violence*. London: Routledge.

Lourenco, N., M. Lisboa and E. Pais (1997) *Violência contra as mulheres*, Cedernos Condicão Feminina No. 48. Lisboa: Comissão para a igualdade e para os direitos das mulheres.

Lundgren, E. (1990) *Gud og hver mann – seksualisert vold som kulturell arena for å skape kjønn*. Oslo: J.W. Kappelens Forlag A.S.

Lundgren, E. (1995) *Feminist Theory and Violent Empiricism*. London: Avebury.

Lundgren, E., G. Heimer, J. Westerstrand and A.M. Kalliokosi (2001) *Slagen dam: Mäns våld mot kvinnor i jämställda sverige – en omfångsundersökring*. Umea: Åmströms tryckeri AJ.

Mirrlees-Black, C. (1999) *Domestic Violence: Findings from a New British Crime Survey Self-completion Questionnaire*. London: Home Office.

Römkens, R. (1992) *Gewoon geweld?* Amsterdam: Swets & Zeitlinger.

Römkens, R. (1997) 'Prevalence of Wife Abuse in the Netherlands: Combining Quantitative and Qualitative Methods in Survey Research', *Journal of Interpersonal Violence* 12, pp. 99–125.

Sørensen, Bo Wagner (1998) 'Explanations for Wife Beating in Greenland', in R.A.Klein, ed., *Multidisciplinary Perspectives on Family Violence*. London: Routledge.

Walby, S. and A. Myhill (2001) 'New Survey Methodologies in Researching Violence against Women', *British Journal of Criminology* 41, pp. 502–22.

14

Sexual Violence and Ethnic Cleansing: Attacking the Family

LISA PRICE

Where there is war there is war rape – widespread, sometimes systematic sexual violation committed by soldiers and related personnel, mainly against 'enemy' women, both military and civilian. It is not a phenomenon unique to the recent conflicts in the former Yugoslavia and Rwanda. Rather, war rape is pan-historical and cross-cultural.[1] What has singled out the former Yugoslavia and, to a lesser extent, Rwanda is the attention paid to war rape, for, as Natalie Nenadic notes, it happened at a time when feminism exists to recognize it (1996: 462).

As a constituent act of genocide, rape functions to destroy bonds of family, community and society. On the one hand, female victims often experience a sense of defilement (Wing and Merchán 1993: 29–30). Fearing rejection by their family and community, they may withdraw from familial and social roles, and attempt to keep silent about what was done to them. Their fear is well grounded, for in many cultures ostracism is the common fate of survivors of sexual violence. On the other hand, men who have witnessed or otherwise learn of sexual violence committed against female family members by enemy troops often experience a sense of emasculation (Wing and Merchán 1993: 32–4) deriving from a feeling of having failed in their masculine duty to protect 'their' women. Such a sense of failure can prompt these men to abandon their families and to withdraw from their traditional role in the community.

Widespread rape is genocidal as well when it regularly results in death. This was the fate of Jewish and Polish and Russian non-Jewish women sexually abused in Nazi concentration camps, the fate of an estimated two-thirds of the 'comfort women' held by the Japanese army (Lentin 1997: 10), and the fate of an unknown number of Bosnian Muslim and Croatian women held in the so-called rape/death camps run by Serbian and Bosnian Serb militaries.

Finally, rape is genocidal when its purpose is forced miscegenation. In Bangladesh in 1971 over a nine-month period an estimated 250,000 to 400,000 Bengali women were raped by Pakistani soldiers, resulting in approximately 25,000 pregnancies (Swiss and Giller 1993: 612, citing International Planned Parenthood). The children born of these rapes may display mixed Pakistani and Bengali physical characteristics, leading at least one eyewitness, Indian novelist Mulk Raj Amand, to suggest that the Pakistani army had adopted a deliberate policy to 'create a new race', and so dilute Bengali nationalism (quoted in Brownmiller 1975: 85).

Underlying all of these functions are issues of misogyny, sexuality and male power. In relation to these, war rape is indistinguishable from 'domestic' or 'peace time' rape. As Tompkins summarizes, 'Rape is a gender-motivated crime; a one-way street where the risk factor is being female' (1995: 852). Whatever national, ethnic or geopolitical forces may be at play, the baseline reality of sexual violence in war is that *women* are raped by *men* such that 'tortured female bodies [are] translated into male power' (Seifert 1996: 41).

This chapter looks at war rape specifically as an attack on the family. It considers the intersectionality of gender hatred and ethnic hatred, the rise of European nationalism, the construction of gender in nationalism, sexual violence as a tactic of ethnic cleansing, and finally the effects on families of the sexual targeting of women in war. Most of the material is drawn from the conflicts in the former Yugoslavia: Croatia, Bosnia-Herzegovina and Kosovo.

Intersectionality and Synergism

Rape is, among other things, an expression and outgrowth of sexism. Ethnic cleansing is, among other things, an expression and outgrowth of racism.[2] Where sexism and racism meet, multiple intersectional harms are inflicted. A woman is raped not just because she is a woman but also because she is Muslim or Tutsi or whatever is the targeted group. In other words she embodies gender and race simultaneously and is attacked simultaneously on both axes. In ethnic rape sexism and racism interact synergistically to produce violence as a complex fusion in which the two elements cannot be separated. Such violence may be of an intensity far in excess of the additive value of the two elements and, just as importantly, may be qualitatively different from single-axis oppression or violence.

In examining how culture is gendered and gender is culturalized, a number of feminist writers look at the content of pornography, seeing in it motifs of the sexualization of race. Andrea Dworkin and Catharine MacKinnon, for example, discuss pornography's role in the perpetuation of racism:

> Pornography sexualizes racist hatred. It uses racially motivated violations, torture and murder as sex acts that lead to orgasm. We believe that racist pornography is

one source of the violence against Black and other minorities that is on-going in this society. We believe that this is a *dynamic* source of racist violence. (1993: 92)

When it comes to ethnic rape, the particularity of the intersection of sexism and racism leads to specific forms of violence. In Bosnia Muslim women were forced to drink alcohol, eat pork or make the sign of the cross as part of the sexual assault. In Rwanda Tutsi women had their noses and ears – features said to define Tutsi beauty – cut off. In short, in ethnic rape as in pornography, what is done to women is often specific to their ethnic identity. This specificity applies not only to the acts and intentions of the perpetrator but also to the experience of the victim. Her sense of violation extends beyond her physical and sexual integrity to her membership of a community.

The Rise of European Nationalism

Cynthia Enloe defines 'nation' as 'a collection of people who have come to believe that they have been shaped by a common past and are destined to share a common future. That belief is usually nurtured by a common language and a sense of otherness from groups around them' (1989: 45). More than mere habits of association, then, binds members of a nation. Conscious allegiance requires belief that of the multitude of experiences and traits of an individual, some are clustered as shared by others in the group but not shared by even proximal neighbours. In some contexts this belonging can take precedence over all other identities. Family, occupation, sexuality all may be subsumed and/or rendered irrelevant in the presence of national belonging: I am me because I am Serb; other Serbs are like me; non-Serbs are not like me.

Fundamentally, then, nationality is a *representational practice* which relies more on belief than on historical or genealogical fact. Additionally, an integral part of the process of both ethnic and national self-definition is what Sheila Allen refers to as 'selective remembering' (1994: 89). Today Serbian nationalists 'remember' the Battle of Kosovo in 1389, in which the Ottoman Turks defeated the medieval Serbian empire. Five hundred years after the fact, avenging that defeat is seen as just cause to murder Muslims. These ethnic nationalists do not 'remember' the common root of all Slavic peoples; still less do they remember the past fifty years of co-operation, intermingling and intermarriage among Serbs, Croats and Bosnian Muslims. As Michael Ignatieff puts it, 'it is not how the past dictates to the present but how the present manipulates the past which is decisive in the Balkans' (1994: 14).

If nationality is a belief in both commonality and distinctiveness, nationalism is a political ideology which both encourages such belief and pursues a programme of national self-determination. As a doctrine, nationalism has its origins in the European Romantic movement of the eighteenth century. In France its greatest proponent was Jean-Jacques Rousseau, while in Germany it was Johann Gottfried von Herder. The idea was that a nation or people should have sovereignty over its territory to the exclusion of foreign occu-

piers. By the nineteenth century writers such as the social Darwinist Ernst
Haeckel were advocating a nationalism not only in opposition to other peoples
in other states but also within state boundaries. According to Gisela Kaplan,
Haeckel 'seriously proposed the active elimination of groups of people and of
anyone whose life somehow polluted, threatened, or unbalanced the national
"gene pool"' (1997: 11). This doctrine was later given effect in the bio-
policies of the Nazis. As Daniel Goldhagen notes:

> Historically, the expression of nationalism, particularly in Germany, has gone hand
> in hand with the expression of antisemitism, since the nation was in part defined in
> contradistinction to the Jews. In Germany, and elsewhere, nationalism and antisemitism
> were interwoven ideologies, fitting hand in glove. (1997: 45)

In Europe the difficulty with the doctrine of nationalism is that it rests on
the mistaken assumption of the coincidence of state boundaries and national
or ethnic boundaries. In fact, all European states hold within their borders
significant minority populations. In Spain there are the Basques, in France the
Huguenots, and in every European state there are the Jews and the Roma.
These groups have traditionally inhabited land and been subjects, if not always
citizens, of the state. In times of economic stress, their presence has led to
scapegoating. Additionally, particularly since World War II, there has been
significant migration of non-Europeans into European states. These groups
also have been subject to scapegoating. Thus in the 1970s and 1980s in France
there were race riots targeting Algerians and Senegalese. More recently in
Germany right-wing nationalists have attacked hostels housing Turkish guest
workers. The point to be stressed is that Europe is made up of many small
states with disparate populations. In times of social upheaval, as for example
the Great Depression and the demise of the communist states of Eastern
Europe, nationalist sentiments are easily manipulated so that the presence of
'others' is blamed for such social and economic ills as unemployment, falling
bank rates and crime.

In Europe at least, too often it seems that nationalism leads to xenophobia
and thence to racism or ethnocentrism, to imperialism and to genocide. From
Lebensraum and *Herrenvolk* to ethnic cleansing, the history of twentieth-century
nationalism is frequently murderous.

Woman, Family, Nation

In most nationalist ideologies the family plays a central role. Indeed, Julie
Mertus refers to the family as 'the imagined mini-nation designed to advance
a political agenda' (1994: 22). The family reproduces the nation both physically and ideologically and is also a resource for both the nation and the state.
It should come as little surprise, then, that under the sway of nationalism,
particularly ethnic nationalism, gender roles within the family are sharply
delineated and rigidly enforced.

The Manichaeism of ethnic nationalism, based on a radical bifurcation of 'us' and 'them', requires a corresponding division of 'Our Women' versus 'Their Women' where 'Our Women' are perceived as virtuous, pure and in need of protection and 'Their Women' are seen as evil, defiled and defilable. The only commonality shared by 'Our Women' and 'Their Women' is instrumentality. That is, women are not political actors in their own right. Rather, they are symbols to be used in the competing nationalist projects of men.

'Our Women' are variously reproducers of the nation, transmitters of culture, and symbols of the nation and of its actual or threatened defilement. Particularly when nationalism is militarized, reproduction becomes a matter of national security. This is easily demonstrated by examining the status of reproductive rights in the republics of the former Yugoslavia pre- and post-independence. Needing to draw on women's labour power, the old Federal Republic of Yugoslavia guaranteed rights to free birth control and access to abortion. The state also provided childcare facilities to encourage women's participation in the workforce. The rise of nationalism brought a shift in priorities away from women's labour power and towards reproductive power. This shift was first seen in the late 1980s in Kosovo. Concerned that the 'wrong' people were reproducing – the fertility rate among Serbs was 1.8 while for Albanians it was 4.3 (Mertus 1993: 113) – Serb nationalists proposed legislation which would encourage Serbian women to have more children while discouraging Albanian women. Militarization, and eventually war, increased the pressure on Serbian women to have more babies. By 1993 a Serbian Member of Parliament was quoted as saying: 'I call upon all Serbian women to give birth to one more son in order to carry out their national debt' (quoted in Korac 1996: 137). Here instrumentality extends not just to women but also to children, valued not in their own right but simply as another crop of military fodder.

Inasmuch as Croatian national identity is linked to Roman Catholicism, the role of women as reproducers of the nation has added imperative. Since independence in 1991, abortion has been outlawed in Croatia, even for women raped in the course of ethnic cleansing. The ruling nationalist party, HDZ, frequently uses the image of the 'fruitful virgin-mother'; childless women are branded 'unpatriotic', even 'dangerous' (Mertus 1994: 15). By 1993 nationalist legislation aimed at the 'Renewal of the Republic of Croatia' was put forward to enforce maternity. The most chilling proposal was called 'Fighting Non-Womanhood':

> The demographic situation is aggravated by a further evil: late marriages between the ages of 35 and 50 whereby one child or even no child at all is born in these marriages. The new tax policy of Croatia will not support this Non-Womanhood; it will stimulate the family and couples with children. (quoted in Enloe 1993: 242)

Milica Antic points out that in both Slovenia and Croatia 'the family is a constitutional subject with its own rights.' In contrast, women are mentioned 'only as mothers, and motherhood is protected by the state' (quoted in Corrin 1996: 89); that is, as long as it takes place only within the confines of the traditional patriarchal family – working mothers, childless women, one-parent families, and lesbian relationships are actively discouraged, if not yet criminalized.

Having borne children, women in nationalist ideology then become transmitters of culture. It is not enough to be a mother; one must be a 'good' mother, the proof of which is a generation of children inculcated with nationalist values and possessing knowledge and pride in whatever cultural attributes the particular nationalist ideology emphasizes: language, custom, religion, (selective) history. Thus, the above-cited proposals for the Renewal of the Republic of Croatia included this proclamation: 'The Republic of Croatia must draft legislation and safeguard conditions which will ensure that the highest profession in the Republic will be that of the mother as educator of children' (Enloe 1993: 242).

As symbols of the nation 'Our Women' may be Mother, Matriarch, Protector, Warrior, Victim and Martyr. These symbolic roles may coexist. Milic describes a photograph published at the height of the 1980s conflict between Serbs and Albanians in Kosovo. It depicted a Serbian woman patrolling a road, holding a child in one arm and a gun in the other. Milic comments:

> It brought together and symbolized all the salient aspects of national identity and what threatened it: the nation's sense of jeopardy was clearly depicted by the mother and child defending themselves, by her readiness to defend her identity by means of arms but also her readiness to persevere as perhaps the last member of the nation. (1993: 115)

In the history of twentieth-century nationalism, women's vulnerability to men's sexual violence as symbolic of national vulnerability is common iconography. In World War I it was the 'Hun' raping Belgium, in World War II the Rape of Nanking. A photograph taken at a mass rally in Berlin in 1935 shows a banner warning: 'Women and Girls, the Jews Are Your Ruin' (reprinted in Goldhagen 1997: 96). These symbols have nothing to do with the actual experiences of women raped in a context of nationalist conflict. Their function is to manufacture a sense of external threat, of actual or imminent national defilement. Thus, in Kosovo in the early 1980s, reports of Serbian and Montenegrin women raped by Albanian men were exploited by state-controlled media to increase both paranoia and aggressiveness among Serbs. The actual rate of rape in Kosovo at the time was lower than in other regions of Yugoslavia, and only a small percentage involved Albanian perpetrators and Serbian victims (Mertus 1996: 264), but these facts had little bearing on either media reporting or popular perception in Serbia. Milic suggests that in the context of ethnic nationalism and patriarchal ideology, woman as sex object 'becomes the property of the national collective, and hence its sacred, inviolable borders. Violation of this common property by rape meant symbolically trespassing upon the enemy's territory and brutally destroying its physical integrity' (1993: 115). In these reports the victim is not only a Serbian woman but the Serbian (male) nation.

At the same time that women are revalued as transmitters of culture whose vulnerability requires protection, they are also seen as susceptible to outside influence, to assimilation or co-option by the Other. Accordingly, they are potential traitors. In the former Yugoslavia women who resist militarization and who attempt to maintain links with other women across ethnic-national divides are obvious targets for accusations of treason. So too are women who, while not politically active, nevertheless do not conform to the nationalist construction of femininity: divorced, childless and lesbian women. Perhaps the most often targeted traitors, though, are women who have married outside the ethnic-national clan, for they have used their reproductive power to betray the nation. Their children too are at least suspect, a potential danger to the nation. Vojislav Seselij, a Serbian ultranationalist MP and paramilitary leader, has described children of mixed marriages — that is, those with Serbian and Croatian parents — as 'illegitimate' and claims they should be 'eliminated' (testimony of M.K., Human Rights Watch 1992: 83).

Because 'Our Women' are vulnerable, men need to be protectors. Because 'Our Women' are potentially traitorous, men need to be controllers. Sometimes, though, protection requires control 'for your own good'. Women are protected by having their movements and associations limited whether by curfews or veils or driving bans or other means, enforced by the state, male members of the family or both. In the nationalist cosmology, however, 'Our Women' also represent a fifth column of internal threat. Accordingly, control is not simply protective but also preemptive. As Enloe puts it, 'it is precisely because sexuality, reproduction, and child-rearing acquire such strategic importance with the rise of nationalism that many nationalist men become newly aware of their need to exert control over the women. Controlling girls and women becomes a man's way of protecting or reviving the nation' (1993: 238–9).

Because 'Their Women' are evil and defilable, men need to be defilers. The masculine roles of protector, controller and defiler are inexorably linked. Stories of sexual violence committed against 'Our Women' by enemy men inflame heroic passions. 'Our Women', and by extension our feminized nation, are imagined to be entreating salvation which only decisive, violent action by men can provide. Finally, the role of defiler may be an extension of the protector taken in the spirit of an avenger. In former Yugoslavia some survivors have reported that Serbian rapists justify their actions with the self-serving claim, 'Your guys are doing the same thing.' Tompkins describes a sort of 'tit for tat' vengeance: 'If war is a game for and between men, then women's bodies are their scorecards. The acts of rape, sexual mutilation, sexual slavery, enforced pregnancy, and murder, in turn, make up the tally' (1995: 877). 'Stylized masculinity' (Niarchos 1995: 671) created under militarized state nationalism makes it possible for men to view sexual violence as simply an extension of their heroic soldierly duty. It is at once valorized and naturalized. As one Serbian paramilitary put it, the most interesting parts of being a soldier are 'shooting and fucking' (quoted in Korac 1996: 137).

The instrumentality inherent in the construction of both 'Our Women' and 'Their Women' at times assumes a certain materiality. Women become not just property but territory, 'blood and soil', as Seifert, citing Vlasta Jalusic, puts it (1996: 41). I think this is sometimes taken literally. When Serbian men describe forced impregnation of Bosnian Muslim women as 'planting the seeds of Serbia', it really does seem that for them rape is not simply a means of accomplishing territorial conquest but actually *is* territorial conquest; women's bodies are no different from farm fields. So too when the rape of 'Our Women' is construed as violation of national territory, the breaching of national boundaries.

Sexual Violence as a Tactic of Ethnic Cleansing

Ethnic cleansing has as its purpose rendering an area ethnically homogeneous by driving out people of other ethnic identities. To effect this purpose a range of tactics may be employed to terrorize a population: indiscriminate killing, torture, destruction of personal and cultural property, attacks on hospitals, among other things. These tactics have in common not only unwarranted violence and brutality but also the capacity to cause civilians of the targeted group to flee from their home communities and render them unable to return.

Rape and other forms of sexual violence are also effective means of instilling terror. Consider, for example, the five patterns of rape identified by the United Nations Commission of Experts in the former Yugoslavia. In the first pattern, rapes occurred prior to the outbreak of widespread fighting in an area, generally in conjunction with looting and intimidation of the targeted ethnic group. They were frequently gang rapes. Whether single or multiple, 'there is often a gang atmosphere where the abuses are part of the same event and all the attackers participate even if they do not sexually assault the victims' (Commission of Experts 1994: para. 245).

Two features of this pattern are especially pertinent in relation to war rape as a terroristic act. The first is that the women were assaulted in their homes, locations normally experienced as havens of domesticity, of safety and intimacy.[3] Equally important, the assaults often took place in the presence of family members, particularly husbands, fathers and children. Survivors' accounts suggest this was more than coincidental:

> My husband had to watch while I was raped. I have a four-year-old daughter; she saw the rape. There was no way I could avoid it; he would have killed both of us. He just said, 'Your husband has to watch.' (Human Rights Watch 1993: 169)

A key witness was detained with his family in Kula Butmir, Sarajevo. He was forced to watch while groups of guards raped and sadistically tortured his wife and two daughters (aged eight and thirteen years old). This occurred daily until on the fourth day the younger daughter's throat was cut in front of him. The witness was chained at the legs and guards beat him to force him to watch, breaking both his legs. On the sixth day his elder daughter's throat was cut. His wife survived until the thirteenth day, when her throat was cut. The man committed suicide by hanging himself on 7 April 1994. (Commission of Experts 1994: Annex IX.A, para. 115)

Forcing men to witness the sexual violation of their wives and daughters serves two purposes. First, it underlines to those men that their defeat is total, that they are powerless to act to protect those closest to them. Second and more long term, it disrupts bonds of kinship by negating the familial pact of female chastity in exchange for male protection. To the extent that the nation rests on the strength of the family, destroying those bonds becomes an act of cultural genocide.

Finally, the rapists were sometimes explicit in their intention to use rape as a means of driving civilians into exile. For example, in Trebinje a Muslim woman reported that four Serbian military police broke into her home and raped her. 'As they left, they warned her that if she did not leave, then twelve men would come the next time' (Commission of Experts 1994: Annex IX, para. 232). As refugees in many conflicts throughout the world testify, flight often brings with it both the break-up of families and the loss of cultural identity.

The second pattern identified by the Commission is a development of the first. Individuals or small groups commit sexual assaults in conjunction with fighting in an area. When a town or village is occupied, some women are raped in their homes. Others are 'selected after the roundup and raped publicly' (Commission of Experts 1994: para. 246). In the latter case there is a significant element of public spectacle in which both shame and humiliation are heightened, even more so than for victims raped in front of only family members. Furthermore, the boundaries of private and public are transgressed such that what should be the most private, intimate of acts is instead placed on public display. Such violation goes beyond rape, becoming pornography, the memory of which will last for both the victim and the onlookers. Public sexual abuse also acts to instil terror in the reluctant onlookers, particularly when the women selected are identified as community leaders. Additionally, just as in the first pattern, home ceases to represent a place of safety, so in the second pattern familiar locales of village square, police station, school are transformed into places of torture. It may be especially relevant in a campaign of ethnic cleansing where the point is to make the memory and experience of a place so horror-ridden that home becomes hell, to be fled both in fact and in memory. If it is true that the power of nation is at least in part embedded in ties of territory, then it may be possible to unmake a nation by dislocating it psychically as well as actually.

The third and fourth patterns are rapes in detention. Gang rapes are common and generally are accompanied by beatings and torture such as sexual violation with foreign objects. It would appear that the Commission's distinction between these patterns is that in the former case women were raped coincidental to being detained; whereas in the latter case women were detained *in order* to be raped, sometimes with the express purpose of enforced pregnancy. As in the first pattern, the rapists are sometimes explicit in using sexual violence as a tactic of ethnic cleansing:

> They said they wanted to drive us out, that there shouldn't be any more Muslims in Europe. (Stiglmayer 1994: 121)

> They told us we were going to give birth to Serbian children and that they would do everything they could so we wouldn't ever dare think of coming back again. (Stiglmayer 1994: 109)

The fifth pattern is that of sexual slavery. Interestingly, the Commission seemed to view this pattern as apolitical. It stated that women were detained 'for the sole purpose of sexually entertaining soldiers, *rather than causing a reaction in the women*' (1994: para. 249; emphasis added). Regardless of the purpose, the effect of sexual slavery is no less terrifying than the other patterns:

> But Pero E. is no saint. He brought twelve-year-old girls from Kalinovik to a brothel in Miljevina. They're still there; he keeps them there as his playmates. (Stiglmayer 1994: 107)

> I asked him if he knew anything about Alma [aged 12], and he told me she had been in the brothel in Miljevina and slit her wrists there. (Stiglmayer 1994: 108)

Additionally, as the Commission itself noted, the women held in sexual slavery 'are reportedly more often killed than exchanged, unlike women in other camps' (1994: para. 249). Thus, we may conclude that this pattern also contributes to the policy of ethnic cleansing, regardless of whether that is its primary purpose.

Whatever the setting of sexual violation, the effects for the victim are both immediate and ongoing. Those effects include physical suffering and sometimes permanent damage and/or pregnancy; psychological trauma manifesting as fear, insecurity, guilt and shame; loss of family stability and loss of community identity. Even under the best of circumstances she may require the care of physicians and psychosocial therapists to help her to recover. In the midst of a war zone or in flight these resources often are not available. Traditional sources of support such as family and community also may be unavailable to her either through dislocation or through social stigma. When, as in the former Yugoslavia, sexual violence is widespread and systematic, victims numbering in the thousands, trauma ripples from the individual victims, to their extended families, to local communities, to the nation as a whole. Like individual victims, families, communities and nation may require external support to recover. As with individual victims, such support may not be available during and immediately after the armed conflict. Until recently most international aid agencies considered reconstruction only in terms of roads and houses and wells. Little thought was given to reconstructing intangible yet vital bonds of family and community. Yet that work is essential if the individual, and ultimately the nation, is to survive beyond the violence.

Attacking the Family

Here is a tragic story from the 1999 conflict in Kosovo. A 22-year-old woman, married for four months, was taken by Serb forces, held in a police station for a day, beaten and threatened with death. She said she was not raped. Her husband does not believe her denial: 'I am one hundred per cent certain that they raped her. I know that when women get in their hands, there is no chance to escape.' Explaining his wife's denial, the husband said: 'She doesn't dare tell that kind of story ... I would ask for a divorce – even if I had twenty children.' He added, 'I don't hate her, but the story is before my eyes. I feel very cold towards her.' He described kissing his wife as 'like kissing a dead body.' Though young and married only a short time, the husband views the future with his wife as grim. Everything is 'black'. 'I have no will', he said, 'to have children' (all quotations from Bumiller 1999: 1).

In this account it does not matter whether the woman was actually raped. What matters is the husband's perception. His belief becomes the only reality. By his own words we can see that he cannot believe her because he knows the consequences of admitting victimization. To him lying is the logical response. We may further ask why he is so sure she has been raped. Perhaps he knows that as a man, were he in the aggressor's position he would rape 'enemy' women. Perhaps he believes that all Serb men are rapists. Perhaps he suspects that out of his sight his wife cannot be trusted. We cannot know with any certainty. What is certain, though, is the accuracy of his assessment of the marriage's future. After only four months things do indeed look grim.

It is not uncommon for rape victims to be shunned or even blamed by their partners. Many feminist commentators have recorded such experiences among individual victims in North America and Europe. In Kosovo and in the former Yugoslavia generally, however, shaming and blaming responses have added potency for two reasons. First, the rapes were ethnicized. Victimization brings shame not just to the individual woman but to her nation as a whole. Second, in Muslim communities family honour, resting largely on the chasteness and sexual fidelity of female members, is prized. Wing and Merchán state: 'For many Muslims the honour of the family is of paramount concern and the chastity and purity of women is central to that honour. If female chastity and purity are not maintained, great dishonour falls upon the entire family' (1993: 21).

Let us assume for a moment that the young woman in the foregoing account was indeed raped. Given her husband's response her denial is understandable. But remaining silent about victimization has a price. For many women it requires withdrawal from familial and social roles as they attempt to deal alone with the consequences of what was done to them. Withdrawal may also be a reaction among the fathers and husbands of rape victims or perceived victims. Not only has their family honour suffered; their masculine pride has taken a blow, for they have failed in their manly duty to protect 'their' women. Whole communities come to be affected by the rape of women. On Bosnia, Wing and Merchán write:

> The systematic rape of Muslim women in Bosnia could potentially result in the complete destruction of the Muslim social fabric. Because of the centrality of the concept of honour, the rape of one female member of the family can bring shame and disgrace to not only her immediate family, but also to the entire extended family. Thus, that family will not command the same position of respect in the community. This change in one family's social position will then affect the social ordering of that community, as another family may step into the vacuum left by the family of the rape victim. As a consequence, the systematic violation of Muslim women will destabilize the social ordering in Bosnia to the extent that the population will be fragmented and diminished, allowing for easy manipulation of the remaining inhabitants. (1993: 24)

Community breakdown can be most effectively achieved through selective targeting. During the war in Bosnia a clear pattern emerged of Serbian rapists targeting women of the intelligentsia or otherwise seen as community leaders. For example, when Serbian troops took control of the village of Grabska, the villagers were assembled: 'According to B., the Serbian soldiers had lists from which they called out women's names; they directed these women to board buses' (Human Rights Watch 1993: 216). B.'s name was on the list, possibly because she and her husband had helped found the local Party of Democratic Action. She was held in a rape camp for twenty-eight days. There, too, women were sometimes selected by name to be raped.

Documents exposed by the Italian journalist Giuseppe Zaccaria reveal that even before the outbreak of fighting in Bosnia-Herzegovina and Croatia, attacking women was a deliberate strategy within a policy of ethnic cleansing. He quotes from minutes of a 1991 Serb military strategy meeting:

> Our analysis of the behaviour of the Muslim communities demonstrates that the morale, will, and bellicose nature of their groups can be undermined *only if we aim our action at the point where the religious and social structure is most fragile. We refer to the women, especially adolescents, and to the children.* Decisive intervention on these social figures would spread confusion among the communities, thus causing first of all fear and then panic, leading to a probable [Muslim] retreat from the territories involved in war activity.
>
> In this case, we must add a wide propaganda campaign to our well-organized, incisive actions so that panic will increase. We have determined that the co-ordination

between decisive interventions and a well-planned information campaign can pro-
voke the spontaneous flight of many communities. (Zaccaria 1994: 127–9, quoted
in Allen 1996: 57; emphasis added)

It would seem that these military strategists were well aware of the nexus
of women, family and community and were willing to prey upon the place
of greatest vulnerability. Rape ceases to be an individual act – one man
attacking one woman – and becomes a national one. The object of the attack
is less the woman herself than the community she represents. The message of
ethnic rape is spoken to the men of her community. Her body is merely the
delivery system.

The effects of ethnic rape, for the victim, her family and community, are
all the more profound when pregnancy results. Evidence suggests that in the
former Yugoslavia Serbian men raped Muslim and Croat women with the
express purpose of forcing them to 'give birth to little Chetniks'. Women
were held in camps and raped repeatedly until they became pregnant. They
were questioned and searched for contraceptive devices. They were not released until their pregnancies were too far advanced to abort safely. It should
be noted that unlike the Jewish tradition, for Christians and Muslims ethnicity is held to follow the patriline. The children born of these rapes are considered Serb even though they were born of Muslim women and may be
raised in a Muslim community. Their place in the family and community can
only be that of an outsider and a symbol of the woman's shame and her
family's dishonour. Small wonder, then, that many of these children are abandoned by their mothers at birth.

Conclusion

In the former Yugoslavia countless young women have been rendered unmarriageable having been raped in the war. Among other things, being
unmarriageable means they will not have children. It is not too much to say
that these women and the children they will not bear represent the nation's
future. The harm of ethnic war rape goes beyond the individual and beyond
the five years of the war, becoming an intergenerational attack. It is common
for nations to experience an upswing in its birth rate in the immediate aftermath of armed conflict, but that cannot happen if large numbers of women
of childbearing age are shunned by their families and communities.

In the former Yugoslavia individual victims of war rape are rebuilding their
lives. Some aid agencies are providing culturally sensitive support and assistance to these women. In some cases the programme's name masks its purpose
so that the women attending are not further stigmatized. Families and communities are reuniting. Yet, as the account from Kosovo shows, as long as
female victimization is seen as a mark of dishonour, fragmentation, including
suspicion, within the family will remain. Woman, family, community and
nation all continue to suffer long after the last soldier has gone home.

Notes

1. For a historical overview of rape in war, see Brownmiller 1975, and Tompkins 1995.

2. As examples from India, Yugoslavia, Rwanda and elsewhere show, communitarian violence and hatred are not restricted to colour racism.

3. That is, safety in relation to outsiders though not necessarily to husbands and fathers.

References

Allen, Beverly (1996) *Rape Warfare: The Hidden Genocide in Bosnia-Herzegovina and Croatia*. Minneapolis: University of Minnesota Press.

Allen, Sheila (1994) 'Race, Ethnicity and Nationality: Some Questions of Identity', in Haleh Afshar and Mary Maynard, eds, *The Dynamics of 'Race' and Gender: Some Feminist Interventions*. London: Taylor & Francis, pp. 85–105.

Brownmiller, Susan (1975) *Against Our Will: Men, Women and Rape*. Harmondsworth: Penguin.

Bumiller, Elizabeth (1999) 'Kosovo Victims Must Choose to Deny Rape or Be Hated', *New York Times*, 22 June, p. 1.

Corrin, Chris (1996) 'Introduction: Feminist Campaigns and Networking', in Chris Corrin, ed., *Women in a Violent World: Feminist Analyses and Resistance Across 'Europe'*. Edinburgh: Edinburgh University Press, pp. 79–93.

Commission of Experts (1994) Final Report of the Commission of Experts Established Pursuant to Security Council Resolution 780 (1992), submitted 27 May. UNDOC S/1994/674. Accessed on War Crimes Tribunals: www.igc.apc.org/tribunal.

Dworkin, Andrea and Catharine MacKinnon (1993) 'Questions and Answers', in D. Russell, ed., *Making Violence Sexy: Feminist Views on Pornography*. Milton Keynes: Open University Press, pp. 78–96.

Enloe, Cynthia (1989) *Bananas, Beaches and Bases: Making Feminist Sense of International Politics*. London: Pandora.

Enloe, Cynthia (1993) *The Morning After: Sexual Politics at the End of the Cold War*. Berkeley: University of California Press.

Goldhagen, Daniel Jonah (1997) *Hitler's Willing Executioners: Ordinary Germans and the Holocaust*. New York: Vintage Books.

Human Rights Watch (1992) *War Crimes in Bosnia-Hercegovina*, Vol. I. New York: Human Rights Watch.

Human Rights Watch (1993) *War Crimes in Bosnia-Hercegovina*, Vol. II. New York: Human Rights Watch.

Ignatieff, Michael (1994) *Blood and Belonging: Journeys into the New Nationalism*. London: Vintage.

Kaplan, Gisela (1997) 'Feminism and Nationalism: The European Case', in Lois A. West, ed., *Feminist Nationalism*. London: Routledge, pp. 3–40.

Korac, Maja (1996) 'Understanding Ethnic-National Identity and Its Meaning: Questions from Women's Experience', *Women's Studies International Forum*, vol. 19, no. 1/2, pp. 133–43.

Lentin, Ronit (1997) '(En)gendering Genocides', in R. Lentin, ed., *Gender and Catastrophe*. London: Zed Books, pp. 2-17.

Mertus, Julie (1994) '"Woman" in the Service of National Identity', *Hastings Women's Law Journal*, vol. 5, no. 1, Winter, pp. 5–23.

Mertus, Julie (1996) 'Gender in the Service of Nation: Female Citizenship in Kosovar Society', *Social Politics*, vol. 3, no. 2–3, pp. 261–79.

Milic, Andjelka (1993) 'Women and Nationalism in the Former Yugoslavia', in Nanette Funk and Magda Mueller, eds, *Gender Politics and Post-Communism: Reflections from Eastern Europe and the Former Soviet Union*. London: Routledge, pp. 109–22.

Nenadic, Natalie (1996) 'Femicide: A Framework for Understanding Genocide', in Diane Belle and Renate Klein, eds, *Radically Speaking: Feminism Reclaimed*. London: Zed Books, pp. 456–64.

Niarchos, Catherine N. (1995) 'Women, War and Rape: Challenges Facing the International Tribunal for the Former Yugoslavia', *Human Rights Quarterly* 17, pp. 649–90.

Seifert, Ruth (1996) 'The Second Front: The Logic of Sexual Violence in Wars', *Women's Studies International Forum*, vol. 19, no. 1/2, pp. 35–43.

Stiglmayer, Alexandra (1994) 'The Rapes in Bosnia-Herzegovina', in Alexandra Stiglmayer, ed., *Mass Rape: The War against Women in Bosnia-Herzegovina*. Lincoln: University of Nebraska Press, pp. 82–169.

Swiss, Shana and Joan Giller (1993) 'Rape as a Crime of War: A Medical Perspective', *Journal of the American Medical Association*, vol. 270, no. 5, 4 August, pp. 612–15.

Tompkins, Tamara L. (1995) 'Prosecuting Rape as a War Crime: Speaking the Unspeakable', *Notre Dame Law Review*, vol. 70, no. 4, pp. 845–90.

Wing, Adrien Katherine and Sylke Merchán (1993) 'Rape, Ethnicity and Culture: Spirit Injury from Bosnia to Black America', *Columbia Human Rights Law Review*, vol. 25, no. 1, pp. 1–48.

Zaccaria, Guiseppe (1994) *Noi, criminali de guerra: storie vere della ex-Jugoslavia*. Milan: Baldini & Castoldi.

15

Violence, Militarism and War

JALNA HANMER

Consciousness and Questions

The field we now call Women's Studies owes a debt to women's movements throughout the world, as they allowed alternative conceptions to develop and enabled researchers to approach old problems – though they were not recognized as such – in new ways. Research on violence has been, and remains, a major theme in Women's Studies for the past thirty years. This chapter is an attempt to consider what contributes to and what restricts an expanded understanding of violence against women by focusing on some of the moments when gender-visible accounts became possible, and on the relevance of context.

For many of us living in Europe the recent events in the former Yugoslavia were a watershed, necessitating consideration of social, economic and political stability and instability as factors in the increase or containment of domestic and other forms of violence against women.[1] Thirty years ago, when women's liberation movements and their responses to violence became a force in European and other nation-states, there existed relatively high levels of social stability; in this context it was possible for women to reorient public understanding successfully, and to make demands on the state and for the state to respond positively, if slowly. War and its aftermath in the former Yugoslavia demonstrate empirically the impact on women of militarism and of the resulting social, economic and political instability, including an increase in violence from male partners.

Under conditions of social instability, the prevalence of domestic violence and its incidence over time cease to be a largely historical question and become one of immense practical importance to women; for experience suggests that disruption to civil society results in an increase in all forms of gendered violence, and this could happen in any nation. Those of us engaged in research on violence in Europe, who have lived and worked in relatively stable societies since the mid-1940s,[2] must reverse the equation and think of stability as unusual and instability as the norm. To do so raises the questions of why, how and what kinds of violence increase with social, economic and political instability. It is much easier to answer the 'what' than the 'why' here. Full answers require an analysis of the role of the military and its related industries and organizations, including science, and of the government and state, as well as of Western imperialist ventures of various types involving military, political and global economic interventions. Within this process of conceptual revision are questions about gender: who does what to whom, how violence is organized, carried out, and to what ends.[3]

This chapter raises questions and suggests areas for future research. What characterizes women's recognition of violence by men to women and conversely its disappearance from consciousness? What are the characteristics of gendered social relations that make this everyday behaviour invisible – reduced, at best, to a personal problem or deflected from the individual man onto an external problem, such as employment or alcoholism? How do social movements construct knowledge based on increasing the visibility of gendered social relations? What are the contextual factors that lead to the making of connections by women between private and public violence – that is, between domestic violence and war? If recognized, what are the factors that lead women to overcome political and other differences to form alliances[4] in order to provide services that improve the lives of women and their children and make demands on their behalf on the state? How do women influence organizations and social institutions dominated largely by men, who are responsible for the use of violence and for its containment? How do oppositional forces respond conceptually and practically? In Europe we are confronted by numerous examples of these largely unexplored social processes.

Making Connections across Violences

If the aim is to understand violence committed by men against women, its origins and how it is sustained socially, and ultimately what can be done about it, then focusing solely on domestically located violence in stable societies is unproductive. The possibilities for analysis are reduced not just by the focus on individuals, but also by the sharp distinction made between private and public violence. This serves to close off analysis of how various ideologies and organizational forms are able to mobilize men for collective violence against women and civil society in general.[5] Women who write on war from experience, in protest, or as fiction go beyond the form of the crimes against women, and women's own participation in violence, to examine the way men group together and organize in order to extend violence against women and their children.

This is not to suggest that the writing of the early women's movement on domestically located violence did not raise such issues, but simply to observe that over time these broader analyses have moved from the mainstream to the fringe as politicians and public services responded in more woman-centred ways to domestically located violence. Even research on political struggles and activism focused on the experiences of individual women in stable societies.

Recognizing Domestic and Private Violence

In Europe the acknowledgement of violence against women by known men in the home[6] began as a local issue and then became national in the 1970s. The timing differed from country to country, but during the last thirty years European women have recognized the persistent phenomenon of violence against women as a major factor in the personal and collective oppression of women. An understanding of why it became visible during this period must begin with an exploration of the connection between changes in individual and collective consciousness and of social processes in all their diversity.

The spreading of knowledge is an obvious partial explanation because the focus was on the need for change in the social context in which women lived. Domestic violence, as it is now called, was never considered an international issue in the same way as, for example, war or genocide, even when it was acknowledged throughout the world and discussed in international meetings and activities. For example, the first international conference on violence, the International Tribunal on Crimes Against Women, was held in Brussels in 1976. Women were asked to organize and to address major issues facing women in their country. The British group raised the issue of violence against women in their homes. One Scottish and two English women as well as a Dutch woman gave testimony on this issue. In this way knowledge of the problem and of the existence of women's refuges were passed on to women from many countries (Russell and Van de Ven 1976). The social conditions in the Netherlands and in Britain that gave rise to the independent rediscovery of violence against women by men with whom they live are yet to be fully explored.

In Britain the women's liberation movement – an outgrowth of left, anti-imperialist and student politics that had been led primarily by men and male theoreticians – began the process of uncovering the patterns of violence against women and girls in the four countries that make up the UK. In the first phase, rediscovery and activist response were to violence perpetuated against women in their homes; this saw the establishment of refuges in 1971,[7] followed by rape crisis centres in 1976, and in 1980 incest survivor groups, interventions against sexual harassment at work, and legal and illegal activities against pornography. While these issues were connected to the lives of individual women, they were responded to separately in terms of action and research.

Women who uncovered home-based violence initially believed they were the first to do so, so circumscribed was women's knowledge of their history. Such violence, well known to previous generations and marked by spirited defences of women,[8] became progressively culturally suppressed knowledge during the course of the twentieth century. By 1970 knowledge of violence against women was largely confined to social and welfare professionals, who understood it to be a small problem affecting a few women whose behaviour was questionable – that is, women were likely to have brought it upon themselves. The question had become: 'What did she do to make him respond like that?' The responsibility for violence was individualized and the remedy confined to changing the behaviour of the recipient.

In Europe women's movements and activists had first to establish that violence against women in their homes was not only a private sorrow, but also a public issue. For example, Celia Valiente (1996) describes the situation in Spain where improvements in women's legal position were required along with developing legislation, policies, guidelines and other strategies for implementation. She explains that in implementing policies, the work of 'street level bureaucrats', both male and female professionals and workers, was the most difficult part of the process as discretion favours obstruction. Such difficulties have been experienced throughout Europe since the early 1970s. Making gender visible when analysing and attempting to solve problems, especially when both men and women constitute front-line workers, if not the decision-makers, is a complex issue, which remains relatively unexplored.

Conceptualizing Men and Alliances between Women

The British example illustrates that once it is recognized, however partially, violence poses for women the problem of how to conceptualize men; this in turn influences how women organize and around which issues. It demonstrates the complexity of relating to and influencing organizations and social institutions dominated by men, including the media.

The development of women's ideas and politics on violence against women in their homes from known men drew its inspiration from the women's liberation movement's (WLM) challenges to beliefs about the family, marriage and women's role, and the ways in which these were being supported by the state and civil society. The insistence that the personal is political was a rejection of theory, both revolutionary and mainstream, that marginalized women by denying the force of a gendered analysis, and led to women exploring new ways of relating to men and to each other (see Rowbotham 2000 for an experiential account). The demand that the ideology of the family (where the family is characterized by respect for mothers as well as fathers, for wives as well as husbands, and perceived as the bedrock of society and a haven of love and kindness) be upheld by deeds not just words led to a somewhat oblique attack on male social power and domination.[9]

Violence was theorized as an independent dimension of male dominance and control, in that any woman could be victimized by any man irrespective of social class and other differences, and that all women are oppressed by male violence. Research focused not on variations in the type and extent of violence and abuse of different groups of women, but on how the state responded to women, including women from different ethnic and class backgrounds.[10] There were several political reasons for this that remain widely accepted today. First, the alliance of women from differing political backgrounds could agree on treating the state as the culprit. Second, pandering to a commonly held belief that domestic violence was, for example, class- or ethnicity-dependent would provide the state with a justification for further undermining support for women. The 'problem' would then become one for this or that group and not a social problem affecting all women. One agreed approach in stable societies is to analyse how social institutions and the state interact to protect male dominance. For example, Ailbhe Smyth uses her experience in Ireland to explore the connection between feminist actions and state and institutional resistances in order to render men's violence to women visible (1996).

Experience in different European countries shows that in conditions of political, economic and social stability women can make an impact both on the cultural understandings of violence and on the provider of services and/ or funding – that is, the state. This also affects how those who protest conceptualise the state. In the 1970s in the UK, for example, despite a constant refrain not to reify the state, this was not always easy, as decision-makers seemed 'way up there' above movement women, activists and researchers. The space between us is now not so great.[11] There is growing agreement on the importance of curtailing violence against women and how advances can be achieved, if not on the aims or on the reasons for doing so. Whereas the British government wants to spearhead family reform in order to bolster and sustain the heterosexual, nuclear family, women assisting other women want to support independence and safety for women and their children. Summarizing a review of research in Europe on violence against women, Carol Hagemann-White concludes, 'Violence deals with a dimension of patriarchal social relations that is independent of other structures of social, economic and political inequality, even as it interacts with them' (2000).

Three Phases in Confronting Men

In the UK there were three phases in the response to violence against women from known men in the home. Resisting the taboo on discussing intra-family violence, or moving domestically located violence from the socially invisible to the visible, was the first step to linking activism with research theory and practice. Phase 1, then, was to render domestic violence visible as a social problem. The shift from private pain to public issue, in the sense of state recognition, was achieved in the UK between 1971 and 1975, the year the Parliamentary Select Committee published its report on *Violence in Marriage*. This was followed by an increase in research and in services for women and children in the voluntary sector. This watershed date does not mark a uniform acceptance of domestic and other forms of violence against women from known men as a social, rather than an individual, problem. Achieving universal recognition of this shift in definition and perception is a task for the future; some individuals and communities remain resistant to change. Research and improvements in service provision continue to play an important role in the process of reorientation. While states may be unified, communities are not.

Phase 2 is a national project where the state progressively takes on more responsibility for controlling the violence of men in the home and ensuring safety for women and children. This, too, is ongoing and the practices in state agencies vary in their effectiveness and in the consistency of service delivery to the women and children in need. Historically, there has been a very slow response to the demands from women, made since 1971, for improvements in state services; consequently the process will drag on for many years to come – provided women continue to press for change. In the UK the focus is slowly turning to men rejected or in danger of rejection by women because of their behaviour. As divorce rates and cohabitation increase, the question is becoming: 'What did he do to make her behave like that?'

Phase 3 seems to be gaining momentum. In the overworked phrase of the UK's Blair government, 'joined-up thinking' is being applied to violence of different types; this includes international perspectives and analyses of domestic violence. Theoretically linking racism, sexist violence and the feminization of genocide with domestic violence will draw on and contribute to activism and fully confront the issues of men, the ways in which they are organized, and gendered social relations. Examining the changing relations between civil society, social instability and the state is pivotal. When the power of the state is dissipated, the role of paramilitaries in the oppression of women may become significant. For example, in Northern Ireland paramilitary challenges to the state have made it more difficult than in England, Scotland and Wales to make men's violence to women socially visibile, and to generate an effective response.

Gendering Sexuality and Public Violence: Conceptualizing Men

This chapter can only touch on a few issues concerned with conceptualizing gendered violence and the gendering of political action. To turn to an analysis of fiction, Evelyne Accad, writing on the war in Lebanon, examines male motivations and the consequences for women.[12] Relatively underdeveloped social science accounts, along with a lack of agreement among women on the importance of (hetero)sexuality and male domination of women as a basis for understanding male violence, led Accad to examine novels on the war in the Lebanon for their treatment of gender. The six novels she writes about (three by women and three by men) all foreground men's relations to women as cause and consequence of a war where young men – motivated by heroism, revenge and violence-as-catharsis; high on drugs – destroy the city of Beirut, a feminine symbol, and the women within it. Their desired transformation of society is to be achieved through destruction. Diversity in all its forms is to be eliminated in order to achieve male honour. Accad centrally locates violence and war in gendered social relations, in 'badly lived sexuality conceived within a tribal system based on honour, virginity, possession, jealousy and the exclusive propriety of women' (1990: 167).

As part of her wide-ranging analysis, incorporating as it does consideration of Arab history, patriarchy, nationalism, culture, ethnicity, religion, colonialism, globalization, revolution and the state, Accad describes the process whereby women in the Lebanon respond to a political analysis of (hetero)sexuality. Their voices echo views expressed in the UK regarding violence against women in their homes by men with whom they live: primacy is given to loyalty to men or to the ideology of mixed-gender political groups or parties, thereby 'hiding the sexual source of their conflicts' (1990: 23). Accad argues that in the Middle East the meaning and importance given to a military weapon and to the sexual 'weapon' are equal, and that both are used to conquer, control and possess. This links domestic and territorial violence, as rape has always been used in war and at home to control and possess, to establish ownership.

Accad concludes that the Lebanon is not unique, but 'carries the code of honour, and masculine–macho values as well as the concomitant condition of women's oppression to their farthest limits' (38). An even more extreme example of this was Taliban-controlled Afghanistan. In the Taliban's 'transformed and purified society', women who had no man to provide for them faced starvation, as they were not allowed to work outside the home. The Taliban effectively pronounced a death sentence on women whose only crime was that their husbands, sons and other male relatives had been killed in the war, 'purifying' society of women not under the direct control of men.[13]

The theme of control is pursued in women's responses to the wars in the former Yugoslavia. Lepa Mladjenovic and Divna Matijasevic (1996), for example, explore politics and power, private and public violence by men, and feminist resistance and activism. Moving from the effects on women to those on men, Lt. Col. Dave Grossman (1995), writing on preparing men to kill, killing, and its psychological costs, explains that the point of rape as a military order and by groups of men is to bond those who rape with their leadership – empowerment and bonding go hand in hand. Ensuring that the men commit atrocities links them inextricably to the fate of their leader; only total victory or total defeat are possible outcomes. Grossman observes that throughout history women are probably the largest single group of victims of this empowerment process.

War is an extreme expression of a male-dominated social structure where civil and externally promoted violence against women share common threads. In the former Yugoslavia, war crimes against women were both a form of ethnic cleansing and violence against gender. Rada Boric and Mica Mladineo Desnica (1996) raise the same issue as Accad, namely the need for women to recognize and oppose male dominant structures that do not respect diversity or, as they express it, 'care for Others'. The 'Others' to whom they refer include women as a group or social category. This accounts for the failure of individual men and women to bind together to support each other when societies become unstable and for why men increase their domestic attacks on women.

Women's experience indicates that war reduces not just women's security and living standards, but contributes to their undervaluation by the state and its agencies. Evidence of the escalation of domestic violence with war is not statistically available, but women-centred agencies, for example in Croatia, report that it increases in intensity and extent (Boric and Desnica 1996). Women's roles in peace processes, in social and material reconstruction, in support for the displaced and refugees, are not recognized; nor do women have a voice in decision-making or peace negotiations. When the smallest breakthrough is achieved – for example, the election to the peace negotiations of the Northern Ireland Women's Party after hasty organizing and a six-week campaign – the men whose right, they believe, it is to wage war, to settle disputes, and to determine the fate of women and children, are outraged. In Northern Ireland men duly had to put up with the presence of women at the peace negotiations – although it should be borne in mind that this was not a full-scale war and that therefore the power of men was not absolute.

The integration of women into peace negotiations and recognition of their public role in post-conflict development are called for by the United Nations in the form of resolutions, declarations, the Beijing Platform for Action, UNIFEM and other such United Nations activities (Karam 2001), although real progress has yet to be made.

'Badly Lived (Hetero)sexuality' and Alliances

Examples from nations characterized by social instability facilitate an understanding of violence against women as 'badly lived (hetero)sexuality' even though this is not easy for women to accept and can be even more strenuously denied by men.[14] Economic instability within Europe has seen the introduction of other forms of violence against women, in particular sexual violence through prostitution and the trafficking of women. This, too, is linked with militarism more generally, as a service industry for peacekeeping troops, not just for paramilitaries and military invaders. It is particularly difficult for women to analyse and reach a consensus on this form of male violence and domination, given the connection between sexual libertarianism and revolutionary activity or women's liberation. We are caught between competing explanations and political beliefs, from the perception that prostitution is simply a 'job like any other' to the debate as to whether the occupation is 'forced or freely chosen', to the view that totally rejects the social validity of male heterosexual demands as punters and pimps, in and out of uniform. Experience in England indicates that moves against local punters and pimps result in organized opposition by groups of both women and men, including organizations funded by the state.[15] There are various initiatives across Europe to curb the trafficking of women for sexual exploitation. Sweden has gone further than other countries in attempting to curb prostitution by a law that penalizes men. Nevertheless, everywhere in Europe there is substantial opposition to efforts aimed at restricting men's sexual exploitation of women's bodies.

Men and women do not necessarily hold the same views on trafficking or prostitution or support prostitution for the same reason. Women are more likely to understand that the estimated half million Eastern European women transported by traffickers annually into the European Union are driven by economic need to take chances that may result in their prostitution in a European Union country than are the men who police these activities. For women, they remain women or underage girls; for men they are likely to be simply prostitutes whatever their mode of entry into the racket, to be repatriated as soon as possible and without the need for prosecution. There is implicit support for traffickers and local prostitution businesses in EU countries, even though the European Union has called on its members to focus on the criminal gangs that organize trafficking and to respond to women as potential witnesses in need of protection.

There has been some progress in the recognition and condemnation of locally based sexual crime, especially against children in the family, but even here public anger, from both men and women, is reserved primarily for attacks by strangers. For example, the recent attacks on men identified as paedophiles begun by a newspaper in the UK following the murder of a young girl was community based, apparently led by women against neighbours and strangers who had been rehoused in their communities, sometimes after prison. The aim was to protect their children from specifically identified men, demonized by the term 'paedophile'. Sexual crime in the family against women when identified as rape, on the other hand, remains somewhat hidden under the term 'domestic violence' and, judging by the conviction rate, receives little sympathy from juries, on which both men and women serve.

Divisions between women, by continent, by colour and race, slow the development of alliances. However, one of the recent successes of European and international women's alliances has been to shift the status of rape in wartime from a non-prosecutable (non-crime) to a prosecutable (crime) offence. This is a major victory for the women who led the campaigns, which involved forming alliances with professional and political women. Men, too, were involved. Nevertheless, their presence was not central to the political alliances forged on this issue, which were between women worldwide.

The Military and 'Badly Lived (Hetero)sexuality'

Accounts of military violence against women in peacetime derive primarily from countries with a US military presence in the Asia–Pacific region, where there is a very high incidence of prostitution, trafficking and violence against women. Catherine Euler and Daniel Welzer-Lang (2000), in their research into violence against women living near a base in northern England and women living close to the Castelnaudary Foreign Legion base near Toulouse, describe some of the relationships near the bases as at least superficially similar to those in the vicinity of any military base in the world. Their research report focuses on military wives and cohabitees, who spoke not only of domestic violence but also of their marginalized position in relation to the military and the communities in which they live. Because men are posted elsewhere and can always return to barracks, these women are more marginalized and disempowered than women with civilian male partners. In the case of the English base, although sexual exploitation is evident – defined as under-age sex and unmarried women with children by soldiers – almost all the local residents interviewed blamed the women and girls for loose morals rather than the military system or the men involved in it.

The situation in the UK has much in common with that of the (better researched) US bases in Asia: reports of rape coupled with low conviction rates; short-term relationships involving some resource exchange; high populations of single mothers outside the base; hopes for marriage or travel or better housing; a high incidence of under-age sex; an imbalance in the local sex ratio coupled with higher soldier wages compared to those of local men; relative poverty among women compared to the soldiers; no skilled work possibilities for the women. The differences noted included the fact that in the UK there was less frequent, much less extreme violence; no official red light district or local trafficking for the purposes of prostitution; less overt racial/ethnic othering than outside the bases in Asia; more extensive, and more complex policing arrangements to control violence (Euler and Welzer-Lang 2000: 80).

In contrast, foreign legionnaires return to France with women from countries that are poor and where the women occupy a precarious position. Each French foreign base is an anchor point for a migratory chain of women. Their migration to the Foreign Legion bases abroad is often illegal; once there they work in the sex trade. A few are chosen by a legionnaire to be taken to metropolitan France; once at the Castelnaudary base, though, a woman and any children who have accompanied her exist in a state of extreme emotional and financial dependence on the legionnaire. Violence is common-place and access to services for women in the town is minimal. The relation-ship between the Foreign Legion and the population of Castelnaudary, which profits from the presence of the Legion and the women who accompany it, is described by Euler and Welzer-Lang as symbiotic. Women are silenced.

The two European countries discussed above, the UK and France, are relatively stable; it follows that, as with domestic violence generally, when there is concerted action it is possible to achieve improvements in responses to women. Euler and Welzer-Lang's research concludes that the military in stable European countries do not want attention drawn to violence against women: in Castelnaudary French women are relatively well protected; in the UK base commanders are prepared to co-operate to control domestic violence, and indeed any other forms of behaviour that may not bear public scrutiny.

There are other ways in which the militarization of societies presents a further challenge to the security of women in Europe. The world is becoming a smaller place inasmuch as it is now more difficult to prevent harm in one region spilling over into another. Daniel Volman (1998) summarizes the mili-tarization of Africa, which began with the Cold War arming of various fac-tions and states by Western countries, and continues today, albeit to a lesser degree, augmented by multinational corporations involved in light-weapons trade, illegal arms dealers and so on. Militarization and the resulting wars and civil unrest have created pervasive insecurity, and ignited an escalating level of violence, much of which is specifically directed against women. Women and children, too, are also largely those affected by famine and mass starvation, and most likely to have refugee and displaced-person status as a result of war. Volman makes a connection between economic and political instability through military organization and activities. He describes warfare as a dominant mode of production and a significant sector of the economy, as it is used to obtain and sustain control over food and related supplies now that the economies of some African countries are destroyed. He explains that the continued mili-rization of Africa is not just an African concern, as the

> consequences of the growth and spread of conflict and crime in Africa ... produced a growing demand for humanitarian assistance from the international community, ignited massive refugee migrations, facilitated the flow of drugs and other illegal products around the globe, prompted acts of terrorism, complicated efforts to monitor and control the spread of disease, and accelerated environmental degradation. (1998: 161)

He concludes that violence in Africa will escalate if the West is unwilling to confront its continuing militarization of Africa (and elsewhere) and the social instabilities it has done so much to create.

Is war changing everywhere? Mary Kaldor (1999), in a gender-free analysis, examines old and new wars, with Bosnia–Herzegovina a case study of a new war. New wars, facilitated by globalization, arise out of identity politics rather than geopolitical or ideological goals, as with old wars. The mode of warfare has shifted to control of the population through violence rather than territory. The formal economy collapses, to be replaced by plunder, illegal markets and external assistance. The aim of new wars is the destruction of communities, of civil society, through an increase in fear and hate. Reconstruction requires the restoration of state legitimacy through the control of organized violence by local, national or international public authorities. Incorporating gender into this and similar analyses would reveal the actors and processes of globalization, and facilitate the making of connections between types of violence, their prevalence and incidence.

Researching Gendered Violence

While academic language when considering violence and protest has moved away from the categories 'women' and 'men' to more abstract formulations, such as 'patriarchy' and 'gender', this does not resolve the imbalance in the giving and receiving of violence or in its organization; nor does it clarify the analysis.[16] Of course, not all men are violent and not all women are non-violent or support other women; researching violence is not about biology, but about social relations within a social context (Hanmer and Hearn 1999). If it were about biology, women would never band together at particular historical moments to oppose violence against women or take up arms, and men would never resist being violent to women. That violence and its organization are gendered is an empirical reality, and therefore the terms 'men' and 'women' remain useful. While differences based on gender are not always obvious in research, we should continue to look for these, as men and women can engage in the same struggles, the same activities, and have the same aims with very different motivations and gendered outcomes.

The transformation of society is a goal for women as well as for men, but their aims and actions can be very different from those of organized groups of warring men (Cockburn 1998). In the final analysis the elimination of violence against women is a demand for the end of male domination, as is a call for the acceptance of national identities based on cultural, religious, ethnic and other diversities. To give meaning to the demand, the recognition of women's rights as human rights also requires the end of male domination. To propose public post-conflict roles for women is a strategy to alter the unequal power relations between men and women in society. The gendered implications of these demands need not be overt to establish their centrality for research yet to be pursued.

Notes

1. This is not to say that the specificities of gendered violence as part of an attack on racial, ethnic and national populations have not occurred elsewhere in the world and become catalysts for new analyses and concepts by women. See, for example, Lentin 1997; Turshen and Twagiramariya 1998.

2. This statement is not meant to deny that social stability is experienced differently by women from the various communities that make up specific nations, e.g. differences arising out of social class, ethnicity, citizenship status, etc.

3. As Yayori Matsui points out (1999), the early 1990s were a time when women were making the connection between armed conflict and mass rape and other forms of sexual violence, for example the 'comfort women' enslaved to service Japanese soldiers sexually in the Second World War, current sexual violence by US soldiers in Okinawa, mass rape and other sexualized torture in Rwanda as well as in the former Yugoslavia.

4. The term 'alliance' is used throughout this chapter, rather than the term 'united front'. 'United front' is a political term developed to describe joint action by different groups against a common enemy, e.g. fascism. The term 'alliance' is more fluid and therefore, in terms of the actions described in this chapter, more appropriate, as women came together either primarily as individuals to offer services to other women or as individuals where their political group allegiances were not fully visible; e.g. block voting at women's liberation movement meetings was conducted clandestinely.

5. While men, too, may be victimized and women may participate in violence against others, the neutral term 'gender relations' does not adequately describe the gendered involvement in violence of victims, of aggressors, of organizers and controllers of the violent responses of others.

6. This rather long descriptor identifies and genders who does what to whom, i.e. violence against women by known men; the nature of the relationship between them, i.e. known men; and the location, i.e. the home. 'Domestic violence', a police term now widely adopted, only partially accomplishes these aims.

7. The women's liberation movement began in Britain with consciousness-raising groups and the opening of centres for women. Women's Aid began at one of these centres through one woman's account of her experience of violence at home, her safety jeopardized by the lack of alternative accommodation. The women at the centre said, if it is that bad, she should move into the centre. Once one woman and her children had been taken in, there was no reason not to admit others who defined their problems in the same way. Word spread quickly through the women's liberation movement, and a pattern of practical aid expanded throughout the four countries of England, Northern Ireland, Scotland and Wales.

8. For example, Frances Power Cobbe, 'Wife Torture in England', *Contemporary Review,* 1879.

9. The Women's Aid movement in the four countries of the UK theorized the problem as being located in the social position of women in society. Seen as politically radical by the state and society in general, this formulation neatly sidestepped the use of the term 'men', while making a demand for change that would positively impact on the lives of all women. This formulation resulted from an alliance between women who perceived men in different ways, at the most extreme either as comrades or as the enemy. There were few head-on collisions between the women who held these different positions within Women's Aid for what were initially termed battered women and their children; these tended to be reserved for the wider political clashes within the women's liberation movement (see Jalna 1977; Weir 1977).

10. One of the first research studies was conducted by Binney, Harknell and Nixon 1981.

11. Researchers and other women who began in Women's Aid when it was an oppositional movement are now involved in activities such as state-funded research, evaluations of crime reduction projects for the Home Office, preparing questionnaires for crime surveys, serving on a wide range of government committees.

12. Another example, this time non-fiction, is provided by Theweleit (1987), who explores the image of woman in the unconscious of the fascist officers in the post-World War I Freikorps. He explores how the dread of women was linked to their racism and anti-communism.

13. For further information, see www.rawa.org and www.afghan-women.com.

14. Nawal el Saadawi, in *Woman at Point Zero*, a novel based on an extended interview with a woman facing the death penalty for killing a pimp, explores how a radical shift in consciousness leads not only to the death of a man, but to the decision to die on the part of the woman, as she does not want to continue to live now that she knows retaliation is not only possible but easy. Could this story offer an insight into why it is so difficult for women to focus on men and their responsibility for violence to women? (Saadawi 1983).

15. The introduction of the kerb-crawlers re-education programme in West Yorkshire, a day school for men reported by the police for trawling for sex among women working on the street, led to the setting up of a national network composed of organizations, groups and individuals to oppose this local initiative.

16. See, for example, Roseneil 1995.

References

Accad, Evelyne (1990) *Sexuality and War: Literary Masks of the Middle East*. New York and London: New York University Press.

Binney, Val, Gina Harknell and Judy Nixon (1981) *Leaving Violent Men: A Study of Refuges and Housing for Battered Women*. Leeds: Women's Aid Federation.

Boric, Rada and Mica Mladineo Desnica (1996) 'Croatia: Three Years After', in Chris Corrin, ed., *Women in a Violent World: Feminist Analyses and Resistance across 'Europe'*. Edinburgh: Edinburgh University Press.

Cockburn, Cynthia (1998) *The Space Between Us: Negotiating Gender and National Identities in Conflict*. London: Zed Books.

Corrin, Chris, ed. (1996) *Women in a Violent World: Feminist Analyses and Resistance across 'Europe'*. Edinburgh: Edinburgh University Press.

Euler, Catherine and Daniel Welzer-Lang (2000) *Developing Best Professional Practice of Reducing Sexual Abuse, Domestic Violence and Trafficking in Militarised Areas of Peacetime Europe*. Geneva: Women's International League for Peace and Freedom (French and English editions).

Grossman, Lt. Col. Dave (1995) *On Killing: The Psychological Cost of Learning to Kill in War and Society*. Boston: Little Brown.

Hagemann-White, Carol (2000) 'Male Violence and Control: Constructing a Comparative European Perspective', in S. Duncan and B. Pfau-Effinger, eds, *Gender, Economy and Culture in the EU*. London: UCL/Routledge, pp. 171–207.

Hanmer, Jalna (1977) 'Community Action, Women's Aid and the Women's Liberation Movement', in Marjorie Mayo, ed., *Women in the Community*. London, Routledge & Kegan Paul.

Hanmer, Jalna and Jeff Hearn (1999) 'Gender and Welfare Research', in Fiona Williams, Jennie Popay, and Ann Oakley, eds, *Welfare Research: A Critical Review*. London: UCL Press.

Kaldor, Mary (1999) *New and Old Wars: Organised Violence in a Global Era*. Cambridge: Polity Press.

Karam, Azza (2001) 'Women in War and Peace-building', *International Feminist Journal of Politics*, vol. 3, no. 1, pp. 2–25.

Lentin, Ronit, ed. (1997) *Gender and Catastrophe*. London: Zed Books.

Matsui, Yayori (1999) 'Women's International War Crimes Tribunal on Japan's Military Sexual Slavery (December 2000 Tokyo)', in *Women's Asia: Voices from Japan: Men and Prostitution*, no. 5. Tokyo: Asia–Japan Women's Resource Center.

Mladjenovic, Lepa and Divna Matijasevic (1996) 'SOS Belgrade July 1993–1995: Dirty Streets', in Chris Corrin, ed., *Women in a Violent World: Feminist Analyses and Resistance across 'Europe'*. Edinburgh: Edinburgh University Press.

Roseneil, Sasha (1995) *Disarming Patriarchy: Feminism and Political Action at Greenham*. Buckingham: Open University Press.

Rowbotham, Sheila (2000) *Promise of a Dream*. London: Allan Lane.

Russell, Diana and Nicole Van de Ven, eds (1976) *The Proceedings of the International Tribunal on Crimes against Women*. Millbrae, CA: Les Femmes.

Saadawi, Nawal el (1983) *Woman at Point Zero*. London: Zed Books.

Smyth, Ailbhe (1996) 'Seeing Red: Men's Violence against Women in Ireland', in Chris Corrin, ed., *Women in a Violent World: Feminist Analyses and Resistance across 'Europe'*. Edinburgh: Edinburgh University Press.

Theweleit, Klaus (1987) *Male Fantasies*, Vol. 1, *Women, Floods, Bodies, History*. Minneapolis: University of Minnesota Press.

Turshen, Meredith and Clotilde Twagiramariya, eds (1998) *What Women Do in Wartime: Gender and Conflict in Africa*. London: Zed Books.

Valiente, Celia (1996) 'Partial Achievements of Central-State Public Policies against Violence against Women in Post-Authoritarian Spain (1975–1995)', in Chris Corrin, ed., *Women in a Violent World: Feminist Analyses and Resistance across 'Europe'*. Edinburgh: Edinburgh University Press, pp. 166–85.

Volman, Daniel (1998) 'The Militarization of Africa', in Meredith Turshen and Clotilde Twagiramariya, eds, *What Women Do in Wartime: Gender and Conflict in Africa*. London: Zed Books.

Weir, Angela (1977) 'Battered Women: Some Perspectives and Problems', in Marjorie Mayo, ed., *Women in the Community*. London: Routledge & Kegan Paul.

PART VI

Sex/Gender Terminology and Its Implications

16

The Uses and Abuses of the Sex/Gender Distinction in European Feminist Practices

ROSI BRAIDOTTI

As stated in the introduction to this volume, one of the starting points for European co-operative work has been the recognition that both the terminology and the bulk of the scholarship in Women's Studies have been generated in English-speaking cultures and traditions. 'Women's Studies' is in fact a North American term; it was readily adopted by the Anglo-Saxon world because of the strong cultural ties between the two geopolitical areas. Northern Europe followed suit. Whether the concept can be applied systematically right across Latin, Catholic, Southern and especially Eastern European countries, however, is open to question. The doubt arises through a respect for the great cultural variety of European feminist cultures, which is shared by all. There exists a consensus, therefore, that it is important to be alert to the differences in culture, religion, politics and educational practices which mark the different European cultures, which make the American-based model of Women's Studies one that is not necessarily universally applicable. Since their beginnings in the late 1980s, the European co-operative projects, joint activities, exchanges and networks in academic Women's Studies have had to confront this complex reality. The whole field of Women's Studies has been marked by a series of debates and questioning about the aims and scopes of its practice. This encompasses, not least, an important linguistic dimension.

Terminology

Even the simple and apparently straightforward term 'Women's Studies' does not strike a note of adequate simplicity. Some groups prefer the more explicitly political 'feminist studies'; others go for 'sex-role' or 'gender studies', which aim at greater objectivity by suggesting a higher level of scientific precision – or, as in the Scandinavian countries, for example, an emphasis on equality between the sexes, therefore pointing to women as well as men through the term 'gender'. The slightly older term 'female studies' may sound neutral but is far too limiting in political scope; 'feminine studies', used in France, will probably please the Lacanians but it does beg the question. 'Feminology' was suggested, and recently the term 'clitoral hermeneutics' has been proposed. More than anything else, this semantic euphoria stresses that the term 'Women's Studies' was never more than a compromise solution, revealing the depths of hesitation surrounding the very signifier 'woman'.

The instability of the category 'woman' has been emphasized over the last ten years by the so-called poststructuralist wave of feminist theory as well as by radical lesbian theorists such as Monique Wittig and Marilyn Frye; it is complex enough to deserve a better treatment than I can give it here. Suffice it to say that the question remains: how do we define the referent 'woman' and what epistemological value do we attribute to it in developing a field of study called 'Women's Studies'? What does a female knowing subject study when she undertakes Women's Studies? In dealing with these issues different cultural traditions play a very large role.

Definitions of Gender

Gender research at the international (Harding and McGregor 1995) and the European (Directorate General XII 1999) levels has undergone considerable and significant developments in the last ten years (Hanmer et al. 1994). Most of these are the result of systematic and intense networking on the part of different social actors, both male and female, within a variety of institutions in Europe. The final report of the evaluation of Women's Studies activities in Europe (Braidotti, de Dreu and Rammrath 1995) states as the main aim of gender research and education the pursuit of the political, cultural, economic, scientific and intellectual concerns in the struggle for the emancipation of women. Gender research challenges scientific thought and aims at enlarging the meaning and practice of scientific research so as to reflect further the changes in the status of women. Gender research is trans- or multi-disciplinary and it engages in a constructive dialogue with a number of established academic disciplines and scientific practices.

Those unfamiliar with gender research tend to assume that this field constitutes a unified framework for analysis. This is partly true, in so far as 'gender' plays the role of a constitutive concept. It does not, however, provide one monolithic framework of analysis. Rather, it caters for a variety of different methods that can be accounted for and evaluated with reference to specific theoretical traditions. The working definition of gender I want to present is the following: the concept of gender refers to the many and complex ways in which social differences between the sexes acquire a meaning and become structural factors in the organization of social life. Gender is a cultural and historical product, as opposed to an essentialist definition of the physical differences between the sexes. A gender approach in research focuses on:

- the study of the social construction of these differences;
- their consequences for the division of power, influence, social status and access to economic resources between men and women;
- the impact of socially induced differences upon the production of knowledge, science and technology and the extent to which these differences control access to and participation in the production of knowledge, science and technology.

According to this definition gender refers primarily but not exclusively to women. Not only does it include men but it also defines 'women' as a very broad and internally differentiated category that includes differences of class, ethnicity, religion, sexual orientation and age. All these variables are highly relevant to gender research.

Gender, being a multilayered concept, needs to be investigated on three levels, according to the useful classification system provided by the feminist epistemologist Sandra Harding (1986, 1987, 1991):

1. Gender as a dimension of personal identity. On this level gender is investigated as an interpersonal process of self-consciousness, and as the dynamic relation of self-images to individual and collective identity.
2. Gender as a principle of organization of social structure. On this level, gender is investigated as the foundation of social institutions ranging from family and kinship structures to the division of labour in social, economic, political and cultural life.
3. Gender as the basis for normative values. On this level, gender is investigated as a system that produces socially enacted meanings, representations of masculinity and femininity which are shot through with issues of ethnicity, nationality and religion. These identity-giving values are organized in a binary scheme of oppositions that also act as principles for the distribution of power.

In short, gender research aims at providing methodological and theoretical tools that study the visible and invisible power mechanisms that influence women's access to posts of responsibility in social, economic, political, religious, intellectual and cultural life. Gender research emphasizes issues such as culture, sexuality, family, gender identity and the power of representation and language. It gives high priority to women's experience and women's access to and participation in democratic processes, with special emphasis on decision-making mechanisms. It aims at revealing the full extent of women's lives, which has been hidden because men have been the predominant subjects and objects of knowledge. Most importantly, gender research aims at improving the status of women in society.

On the basic of this methodological infrastructure, the experience built up over the years of inter-European teaching and research exchanges has allowed the members of the network to reach a common definition of Women's Studies. Women's Studies is a field of scientific and pedagogical activity devoted to improving the status of women and to finding forms of representation of women's experiences which are dignified and empowering and which reflect the range of women's contributions to cultural, economic, social and scientific development. Women's Studies is a critical project in so far as it examines how science perpetuates forms of discrimination and even of exclusion, but it is also a creative field in that it opens up alternative spaces for women's self-representation and intellectual self-determination.

The issue of cultural diversity is built into the very practice of 'gender' and as such cannot fail to reference the complex linguistic diversity which exists across the different European feminist cultures. As a mixture of critique and creativity lies at the heart of the Women's Studies project, a transcultural and transdisciplinary enterprise, this extends to the languages we use to describe and operate Women's Studies. Accordingly, the focus of this chapter is on the cultural differences as they become manifest in our own theoretical practices. As an example, do we think that the Anglo-Saxon idea of 'gender' has an equivalent in, say, French or Italian culture? Conversely, is the idea of sexual difference or *difference sexuelle* translatable in a meaningful manner into other cultural and linguistic contexts? Instead of taking shelter behind a facile sort of cultural relativism, we want to take seriously the conceptual challenge raised by these questions. We want to ask whether Women's Studies, feminist theory or the women's movement as a whole possess a common language: are we talking about the same sort of project? As the case studies, detailed below, of how different European countries use the terms 'sex' and 'gender' show, 'gender' and 'sex' may diversely account for three different dimensions, which have varying prominence and inflections in the different European languages. The three different dimensions relate to the use of 'gender'/'sex' to denote grammatical, biological and/or social differentiations, respectively. As will become clear, how 'sex'/'gender' figures in a given language has important ideological implications that need to be considered when dealing with these terms.

The Case Studies

When comparing the meanings of sex/gender in a number of European languages, it is – in the experience of most participants in the ATHENA project – very difficult, if not downright impossible, to separate sex from gender. In most cases this is due to the fact that both meanings tend to be covered by a single term. Where the two terms are distinct, this occurs along dividing lines that hardly coincide with those operative in English.

Thus Eva Bahovec (2000) argues that in the Slavic languages the words *spol* (Slovenian), *pol* (Croatian and Serbian) *pohlavie* (Slovak), *pleà* (Polish), and *pol* (Russian) cover the meaning of both 'sex' and 'gender' – the same word is used for both. Similar examples of the use of a single word for both 'sex' and 'gender' can be found in dictionaries of the Slavic languages: the strong sex as opposed to the fair sex, the beautiful sex, and so on; for example, in the Slovak language: *silne pohlavie* and *nene pohlavie*.[1]

In most Slavic languages the meaning of the word 'sex' denotes the biological characteristics of maleness or femaleness, as well as grammatical gender (i.e. genus).[2] The equivalents of the term 'gender' in the Slavic languages derive from the Old Church Slavic word *rod* (gender, generation, to engender);[3] the word is the same for the Slovenian, Croatian, Serbian, Russian and Czech languages (Snoj 1997). Furthermore, the word *rod* is related to the words 'to give birth', 'nation' (*na* + *rod*), 'relatives' (Benveniste 1969 for the latter). The etymology of the word 'sex' in diverse Slavic languages derives from the Old Slavic word (*s)pol* (meaning 'half'). It developed from (*s)pholu-*, meaning what has been cut away, cut into two.[4] This may be compared to the German *Geschlecht* (derived from *schlagen* – 'to beat'), and to the Latin *sexus* (derived from *secare* – 'to cleave/dissect') (Snoj 1997).

In the Scandinavian languages, as Kari Jegerstedt (2000) argues, the words *kjønn* (Norwegian), *køn* (Danish), and *kön* (Swedish) cover the meaning of both 'sex' and 'gender'. This is because, as the Norwegian dictionary *Bokmålsordboka* puts it, *kjønn* denotes biological or physiological differences, psychological traits and the sex of an individual. As a result, in feminist research work, the word *kjønn/køn/kön* is generally used for both sex and gender. In order to make sharper differentiations between the two, markers such as 'biological' (*biologisk kjønn*) and 'social' (*sosialt kjønn*) are added.

In a similar vein, Sandra Pereira Rolle (2000) suggests that in Spanish the use of the term *género* (from the Latin *genus*, *-eris*), as a translation of the English 'gender' to designate the distinction between the sexes, is political and not grammatical. As such it is also highly polemical and contested.[5] In Spanish the word for sex is *sexo*, which, according to the *Diccionario de la Langua Española* (1992) denotes the biological characteristics of individuals, in the sense of organic and physiological factors. In contrast to the naturalistic and biologizing connotations of *sexo* in Spanish, the term *género* functions more like a grammatical category. The question then becomes whether the terms of this distinction correspond to the English sex/gender dyad. Far from being a point of consensus, the efforts related to translating the terms led to quite a lively public debate in Spain, as we shall see in a later section of this chapter.

Working from the French language in its multicultural Belgian variation, Maria Puig de la Bellacasa (2000) argues that the direct translation of gender into French is *genre*, but this by no means covers the feminist meanings and implications of the term. This is because the French *genre* is very close to the Latin *genus*, and as such refers to grammatical gender as a classificatory category that distinguishes groups of words; it is also, however, a general taxonomical classificatory category. Moreover, because *genre* covers such a large semantic field and has a common usage it is difficult to make space for the feminist meaning of 'social sex', originally coined in Anglo-American contexts. While a word has a *genre*, a person has a *sexe*, and this is reflected in the translation that some English–French dictionaries provide for gender: the first, strictly grammatical,[6] is *genre*, the second one is *sexe*.

From a different tradition, Ulla Wischermann (2000) states that the etymological definition of gender (*Geschlecht*) in German includes several levels of meaning: it refers to grammatical gender, includes the binary classification feminine/masculine, and has connotations of sexuality and sex-specific social identities. Gender 'was originally used in a genealogical or ethnic sense' – as in descent, origin of birth, or 'people of the same descent' – as well as in the sense of a 'totality of people living in the same period of time' (*Der Grosse Duden* 1963). Drawing on the Anglo-American tradition, the sex/gender distinction is today used in Germany as a biological and socio-cultural category.

Again, however, the grafting of this linguistic implant was far from painless, as we shall see later on. This point is echoed by Theodossia-Soula Pavlidou (2000) who argues that no direct translation of 'gender' into Greek is remotely possible. The equivalent of the English 'gender', γένος [*jenos*][7], carries meanings in modern Greek such as a 'general concept in whose extension specific concepts are contained', 'a group of people with common descent', 'ethnic group'. The most prominent meaning of γένος refers to grammatical gender, that is, the grammatical category according to which nouns, pronouns, adjectives, and so on are morphologically divided in modern Greek into three declension groups – masculine, feminine, neuter. This means that, for example, the gender of any Greek noun can usually be determined on morphological grounds alone. Whenever it seems necessary to distinguish explicitly this meaning of gender from others, the phrase γραμματικό γένος [*gramatiko jenos*], 'grammatical gender', is used. Accordingly, the three types of gender are specified as αρσενικό [*arseniko*], θηλυκό [*thiliko*] and ουδέτερο [*udetero*].

In grammatical contexts, (grammatical) gender is juxtaposed with natural gender – that is, sex – which is then specified as φισικό γένος [*fisiko jenos*]. Although generally grammatical gender is considered to be arbitrary, if we restrict our attention to animate beings only, we find that nouns referring to males are usually masculine, while those referring to females are feminine. In other words, when nouns refer to animate beings, and especially to persons, there seems to be a semantic motivation for the declension classes. In addition to grammatical gender, sex specification can also be achieved in Greek through lexical marking. Moreover, as in other languages, the sex of a person can be specified by adding to a noun, which may be ambiguous as to grammatical gender, the words ανδρας [andras], 'man', or γυναικα [jineka], 'woman'.

Outside of grammatical contexts, in fact, the Greek equivalent for 'sex' is φύλο [filo]: τα δύο φύλα [ta dio fila], 'the two sexes'; αρσενικό/θηλυκό φύλο [arseniko/thiliko filo], 'masculine/feminine sex'; το ασθενες φύλο [to asthenes filo], 'the weak sex'; and Simone de Beauvoir's το δεύτερο φύλο [to deftero filo], 'the second sex'. Although φύλο has always pertained to the biological foundation (and determination) of the sexes, in the last fifteen years and within the context of feminist discussions, it has been used with the attribute 'social' to point to the social determination in the differentiation of the sexes. In other words, the equivalent of 'gender' in the feminist sense is not, as one would expect, κοινωνικό γένος [cinoniko jenos], but κοινωνικό φύλο [cinoniko filo]. Moreover, it is the word φύλο that gave rise to several noun phrases or derivatives which are important in a feminist context, e.g. κατα φύλα διαφοροπίση [kata fila djaphoropiisi], 'differentiation according to sex'; φυλετικές διακρίσεις[8] [filetices djakrisis], 'sex discrimination'; εμφυλο [emfilo], 'gendered'.

The Universalist Appeal of 'Genus'

Citing Karin Widerberg (1998), Jegerstedt suggests that in Scandinavia 'attempts at introducing the equivalent of "gender", the Latin word "genus" (also a grammatical concept), have not proven particularly successful. Here the one Scandinavian word for the English "gender" and "sex", køn, is still used and is seen as useful exactly because it does not force any distinctions between the biological and the social' (2000: 134). However, in Sweden, where the term 'genus' has acquired widespread acceptance, especially, as Anna G. Jónasdóttir (1998) points out, since the mid-1980s, it has become 'the main term indicating the whole field of women's and gender research in certain research political and bureaucratic key texts as well as being used in naming newly formed research institutions' (1998: 8).

Yvonne Hirdmann (1988), one of the leading theorists behind the use of 'genus' in Sweden, argues that the term 'genus' should be used in a distinct way which differs from the English use of 'gender'. Whereas gender, and its Scandinavian translation sosialt kjønn, highlight the split between biology and culture, 'genus' is to accentuate the manner in which the two are intertwined. Thus, 'genus can be understood as changeable figures of thought, "men" and "women" (where the biological difference is always exploited), which create representations and social practices. Hence it follows that biology can also be affected/changed – in other words, genus is a more symbiotic category than gender' (1988: 51). In Hirdmann's view genus is also more of a 'performative' category; it denotes 'masculinity' and 'femininity' as categories that are enacted, and not simply added to the biological in a manner that would also suggest that they are extricable (1988: 51).

Jegerstedt argues that nonetheless the use of the term 'genus' in Sweden is by no means uniform or unproblematic and that there has been a recent 'backlash' against it. Although she has no qualms about using 'gender' when she writes in English, Jónasdóttir (1998) reacts against what she perceives as the linguistic and structural/poststructural foundation of the term 'genus' on the grounds that it is incompatible with her way of thinking social relationships (1998: 9). In her view, there is no *sosialt kjønn*, 'only male and female bodies on the one hand and, on the other, individual human beings who can freely form themselves and change the world' (Jónasdóttir 1998: 9). A more 'academic' take on the debate can be found in issue 1 of the journal *Kvinnovetenskapelig tidskrift* (1998), which is devoted to the subject 'Sex and kön'. None of the articles specifically addresses the Swedish use of these terms, however. To a greater or lesser extent they all pertain to the Anglo-American debate, reinscribing its terms.

Finland and Iceland represent a different problematic altogether. In these countries, the Nordic Institute for Women's Studies and Gender Research (NIKK) is rendered simply as the 'Nordic Institute for Women's Studies' in their respective languages. Päivi Lappalainen suggests that the reason for the omission of the term 'gender' in the Finnish translation is the fact that the Finnish term for 'sex/gender', *sukupuoli*, is exclusively biological and associated with reproduction. Thus the Finnish term for sex/gender is highly complicit with what Adrienne Rich calls 'compulsory heterosexuality' and Judith Butler 'the heterosexual matrix' (Lappalainen 1996: 9). Lappalainen also argues against a Finnish adoption of the Swedish use of 'genus', since in Finland this word lacks the linguistic dimension as the Finnish language does not possess grammatical genders. The Finnish word for 'woman', on the other hand, has multiple meanings, pointing both to the biological distinction between 'men' and 'women' and to the social and cultural condition of 'being a woman'. Thus Lappalainen recommends the use of the term 'Women's Studies' in Finnish on the basis that it both includes research on gender (*kjønnsforskning*) and preserves the political history of women's and gender-related research (1996: 10).

A Foreign Virus?
The Transatlantic Disconnection

Considering the difficulties involved in translating and adapting the term 'gender' to the different European cultural traditions, it is not surprising that this term gave rise to very lively and at times polemical public debates. Sandra Pereira Rolle (2000), for instance, argues that the adaptation of terms from foreign languages into Spanish is usually a long and difficult process. This was also the case with *género*, meaning gender. Though from the mid-1970s the use of *género* in Spanish feminism became generalized, not as a grammatical concept but as a social and cultural one, this was not common in other realms of Spanish society. No extended debate around the term took place, perhaps because the equivalence of *género* for gender was to some extent accepted in the academy. More recently, the proliferation of an interest in gender issues in Spanish society has generated something of a 'national debate' about the term gender. In February 1999, an article by Cristina Alberdi (carrying the names of seven other feminists), entitled 'Violencia de género' ('Gender Violence'), appeared in the Spanish newspaper *El País* (28 February 1999, cited in Pereira Rolle 2000). The main subject of discussion was whether *género* should be used with the meaning of the English term 'gender', or whether Spanish terms more widely known and understood in Spanish society at large should be used. The use of *género* in the English sense of 'gender' was accused of being elitist in another article in *El País*, 'Sexo solo sexo',[9] by Camilo Valdecantos, because that usage is not popularly accessible. Valdecantos's article also provided alternatives for the phrase *violencia de género* ('gender violence') such as *violencia del varón* ('male violence') or *violencia del sexo masculino* ('male sex violence'). Vicente Molina Foix, who responded with an article, 'El género epiceno' in the same newspaper (9 March 1999), offered an interesting solution to this 'political' problem: why not place *'género'* thus between inverted commas? What this discussion points to is the difficulty of adapting an important concept like gender into a Romance language such as Spanish. *Género* is now used in the academy as equivalent to gender, and courses concerning gender issues are taught in most of the Spanish universities. As English is the lingua franca of our times, perhaps it would be easier to use the English word 'gender' and not attempt to translate it into *género*.

Reports from Portugal are similar to those from Spain. Ana Gabriela Macedo (2000) argues that in some ways 'gender' has been an unwelcome addition to Portuguese, in reaction to Simone de Beauvoir's now celebrated claim that 'one is not born, but becomes a woman' (1949) and its development by Anglo-American feminism since the 1970s. This has been quite controversial, particularly among Portuguese feminist scholars and critics. The term has, however, gradually been assimilated into common speech (in part due to the impact of the media), and often unproblematically used in different fields of knowledge. This does not make it any clearer, however, or any more accessible. In Portuguese, *género* presents a semantic ambiguity and may therefore be potentially inaccurate. In fact, besides being used to designate a grammatical category – masculine/feminine – *género* also refers in Portuguese to distinct literary modes or categories: the poetic, narrative or dramatic *género* (as the English 'genre'). For this reason and as an alternative formulation, the expression *diferença sexual* ('sexual difference') has also been used, bearing the same awareness of the mark of alterity and the social construction of identity. The term 'sex' is also used and often preferred by some critics, on the grounds of the awkward translation of the concept of 'gender' into Portuguese, allied to its imputed redundancy within feminist sex/gender politics.

The French context is notoriously the most resistant to taking in new terminology from the English language. Thus, Maria Puig de la Bellacasa (2000) states that gender – as *genre* – appeared in French-speaking academic contexts in research on/by/for women of the late 1980s. Consequently the feminist Anglo-American meaning of 'gender' and its variations did not exist in French dictionaries before then. Gender is a concept that conquered a space of its own in Anglo-American academic, institutional and public discourses, in the media and, finally, as an item exported into foreign dictionaries. According to Puig de la Bellacasa the delay in the French reception of the term was due to many factors, some of which have to do with an obvious and well-grounded cultural, political and theoretical resistance to intellectual colonization. Some material concerns also came to bear on this, in particular the fact that feminist research was less promoted and supported in French-speaking contexts (universities, institutions) during the last twenty years than in North European or Anglo-American contexts.

The debates that marked the introduction of gender into French feminism and institutions are complex and their evolutions differ from one discipline to another. For instance, French feminist historians have played an important role in spreading the concept. Feminist *genre* appears thus in French with an already charged conceptual background: as the feminist attempt to break with biological determinism, as a relational category, and as a concept with political connotations.[10] During the 1990s publications that had *genre* in the title proliferated mainly in publications from conferences and meetings using the notion of *genre* to approach the disciplines. An interdisciplinary conference (Hurtig et al. 1991) focused on the sex/gender distinction.[11] There are more articles on this topic than there are books. Words such as *sexe*, *femmes* or *rapports sexués* ('sexual relations') are preferred by editors as more attractive in book titles – *genre* is considered an unknown term among the public (Thébaud 1998). Often when *genre* appears in a book title, an introduction to its meaning is provided.

Gender is mainly used in history and in the social and political sciences. Development Studies was also seduced by *genre* in the second half of the 1990s, and *genre et développement* has replaced *femmes et développement*. Appealing to the relational character of the gender category, this replacement has been theorized as the passage from a focus on 'problems of women' to a focus on problems caused by 'relations between the genders'. However, specific research on women has also continued to be developed (Jacquet 1995). Research on *rapports sociaux de sexe* (an expression used by some sociologists to denote 'social' sex) has been developed even when *genre* is avoided (for theoretical, political or strategic reasons). There is a generational dimension to this: young researchers are more likely to use the word as part of their research vocabulary than their older colleagues.

International research networks have contributed to the spread of the use of the term 'gender'. Pluri-, multi-, or trans-disciplinary networks are also sites of conceptual contagion. Not surprisingly, feminist researchers working in more 'monodisciplinary' national frameworks have difficulties in using a notion not recognized or simply not understood by their 'peers'. During the 1990s specialized dictionaries and glossaries in France began to include the term *genre*, introduced under sections with headings such as 'gender (*genre*)' (Roudinesco and Plon 1997), 'Sexes (differentiation des)' (Mathieu 1992), or 'Féminisme' (e.g. *Dictionnaire des notions philosophiques* 1990). Only exception-ally was 'Sexe/genre' itself a heading (e.g. *Dictionnaire fondamental de la psychologie* 1997). From a feminist/Women's Studies point of view it is impor-tant to note the recent publication in France of a *Dictionnaire critique du féminisme*, which includes a 'Sexe et genre' heading as well as other headings such as 'Sciences et genre' (Hirata et al. 2000).

International and European institutions have been crucial in the spread of 'gender'. For instance, the platform of the 1995 UN Beijing women's confer-ence imposed 'gender' as an omnipresent concept. When browsing in library websites it is noticeable that a huge percentage of the titles encoded with the word *genre* (in its 'social sex' meaning) are official publications from the Eu-ropean Commission or other institutional publications (e.g. from Swiss and French Canadian institutions on equality). In the context of the European Union's institutions the use of *genre* has imposed itself (or been imposed), not without some resistance from the commission translators. This institutional success of the word is influential in the fact that non-academic feminist struc-tures (permanent education centres, associations or NGOs) – often interfacing with public institutional policymaking and research – are using *genre* and organizing meetings and seminars on related subjects. *Genre* is becoming the institutionally 'obligatory' word to refer to issues concerning women or equality between the sexes. In French, then, *genre* occupies an ambiguous position: it is still a 'minority' word that represents the difficulties of the feminist ap-proach to gain a space in the disciplines. At the same time, it is appearing as a 'dominant' word in public institutions, imposed by an internationalizing move whose language is English. *Genre* has a space in the French language, but *which* space? In Europe at large it increasingly figures as a conceptual space with political implications.

Puig de la Bellacasa (2000) concludes that the introduction of a feminist variable of the classical, universalistic French term *genre* remains a complex and contested enterprise. This is not due to simple nationalism or over-sensitivity, but to questions of identity and recognition. The obvious he-gemony of the English notion of 'gender' marginalizes local, at times ancient, traditions and thus depletes the capital of diversity and cultural variety within Europe, not to speak of the wealth of feminist cultural and traditional histories.

Wischermann (2000) agrees on this point and stresses that debates about gender have played an important role both historically and in the new German women's movement. At the turn of the century, mainstream female theorists in Germany explained gender relations in terms of natural and social differences ('women are different, but equal'). During the 1970s, the question of how gender dichotomies are constituted became central to feminist theory, in particular within history (studies on the character of gender; Hausen 1976) and social sciences (research on sex-specific socialization; Scheu 1977[12]). Feminist research in the 1980s proceeded with an eye to the ever-present danger within gender theory of creating a masculine–feminine dualism and with the realization that the search for gender differences simultaneously generates such differences. 'Gender' was increasingly understood as a category of social structure as well as a dual system of symbols. Accordingly, two dimensions of the discourse on gender relations became particularly relevant. Drawing on the notion of a 'symbolic system of gender duality' (Hagemann-White 1984), human action was characterized as 'doing gender': gender was not something that we 'have' and 'are', but something that we 'do' (Hagemann-White 1993). The concept 'double societal function' (*doppelte Vergesellschaftung*; Becker-Schmidt 1987) was developed to elaborate the social foundations of the tensions in women's life contexts. The related thesis of 'gender as a social structure category' (*Geschlecht als gesellschaftliche Strukturkategorie*) thematized patriarchal and economic structures of domination and elaborated the systemic character of women's oppression – particularly in relation to the division of labour in production and family.

Wischermann adds that the 'gender debate' took a new direction at the beginning of the 1990s. The catalyst was Judith Butler's (1990) *Gender Trouble* which appeared in Germany under the title *Das Unbehagen der Geschlechter*, generating a lively – and perhaps typical – (West) German debate about abandoning the category 'gender' altogether. Dissolving the sex/gender distinction into gender and dismissing questions of bodily materiality as a symbolic, discursively produced and constitutive fiction elicited considerable dissent. Noteworthy in the reception of Butler's notion that the two biological sexes are a product of social and discursive processes was that the reactions among feminist scholars were divided specifically along generational lines.[13] In retrospect, it also became clear that although the critique of Butler was in part legitimate, the process largely erased the theoretical and political impact of her work. Her critique of the 'heterosexual matrix' and, along with it, the impulse this gave to defining a new field of inquiry, queer theory, was an unmistakable provocation for German mainstream gender research, which had been oriented towards investigating hierarchies of gender difference.

Eva Bahovec (2000) also notes that in Slovenia there has been some public discussion over the last decade as to how to introduce feminism into the academy. On the one hand, it has been suggested by sociologists that the Slovene word for Women's Studies, *ženske študije*, should be replaced by a supposedly more progressive, up-to-date, neutral term *študije spolov* ('studies of the sexes', in direct translation – the somewhat misleading translation of the

English term 'gender studies'). On the other hand, the choice of *Journal for Women's Studies and Feminist Theory* as the subtitle for the Slovene feminist journal *Delta* has been grounded in the idea of the necessity of 'situated knowledges', 'partial perspectives', and so forth (*Delta* 1995).[14] The Serbian journal in the field is called *Ženske Studije* (Women's Studies), the Polish one *Pelnym Glosem: Periodiyk Feministyczny* (In a Loud Voice: A Feminist Journal). Several proposals have been made as to how to translate 'sex' and 'gender' into Slovenian, the most widely used equivalents being *biološki spol* (literally: biological sex) for 'sex' and *družbeni spol* (literally: social sex) for 'gender'. The Russian translators seem to be working along the same lines (Ajvazova 1999).

The Russian Case

Irina Aristarkhova (2000) supports this in her analysis of the translation of 'gender' into Russian. She offers a complex and highly articulate genealogy of the concept 'gender' in Russian culture. She stresses the huge influence of revolutionary thinking upon the usage of the term, due to the communist legacy. This problematizes the private and critiques the individualistic essence of the citizen, stressing instead the value of the collective and the communitarian. Sexual relationships, both in and outside of the family, are transformed by the communist philosophy of love. Aristarkhova argues that the category of 'woman' was employed as a tool in the governmental constitution of the 'new proletariat family', built after the destruction of the individualistic 'peasant' and 'bourgeois' family (Lenin collapsed the distinction between them to legitimize the destruction of both as one).

Polovoi vopros (The Sex Question), formulated as early as 1924, stresses a healthy, rational and realistic relationship to sexuality. It claims that human sexuality and sexual relations are fundamental to the constitution of 'all aspects of our existence, not only in physical health, but in our moods, our capacity for work, our relations with people, our social activity, our creativity', and as such goes on to advise its ordered and healthy management. '[T]he new world', they say, 'can be created only by a thoroughly healthy, strong and cheerful generation. And only a generation which orders its sexual life on a rational and healthy basis can be healthy' (L.A. and L.M. Vasilevsky, 1924, quoted in Aristarkhova 2000).

This attitude to sexuality became the distinctive trait of the Soviet Russian emancipation of women from the bourgeois family and also from the dominant idea of love. Aristarkhova stresses, however, the limitations of this otherwise novel approach to the issue. For instance, Alexandra Kollontai's (1923, in Aristarkhova 2000) attempt to engage the question of men–women relationships without reference to children, to relations of reproduction, was both naive and contrary to the Marxist notion of social instinct. However, Kollontai made it clear that, from her point of view, love emotions should be directed for the benefit of the collective; thus 'biological instinct becomes spiritualized' (Kollontai, 1923, quoted in Aristarkhova 2000). Aristarkhova concludes that the discourses about women that characterized this period seldom engaged the complex interplay of sex and gender categories but rather preferred, as a matter of governmental convenience, to collapse the distinctions between them.

Post-perestroika: gender as agenda

The most recent trends in Russian academic discourses specifically employ the term 'gender' in post-perestroika discourses about 'gender'. They have been instrumental in its 'importation' into the Russian academy, as well as into official policy discourses.

In 'The New Women's Studies' Natalia Rimashevskaya shows how the notion of 'gender' (as *zhender*) has come to be used in academic circles in Russia through her activities as a participant of a special committee with the task to cover 'the social activities of women in the contemporary world' (Rimashevskaya 1992: 118; in Aristarkhova 2000). She particularly emphasizes the reluctance of the academic community within Russia to adopt the *zhender* concept when she introduced it in her article 'How We Solve the Woman Question'. She notes that the new egalitarian approach she proposed in the earlier article was based 'on a mutual complementarity of the sexes' in opposition to the traditional assumption of the (natural) 'differentiation of role functions between the sexes' (1992: 119).

However, Rimashevskaya indicates that the concept of *zhender* received many negative responses both within the academy and from the authorities. She writes that the male majority at the top of the academy did not take ideas such as 'gender' seriously since 'public consciousness is still extremely patriarchal, especially among men' (1992: 120). She notes in conclusion that as the 'conceptual analysis of the "woman question" develops the need for praxis is increasingly pressing' (1992: 120) in a way that seems to underscore a certain anxiety about praxis vis-à-vis conceptual analysis.

A Centre for Gender Studies, she says, 'focuses on the issues of sex, as socially constructed' (1992: 121),[15] attempting also to make its work intelligible to both men and women and presenting new approaches to the 'woman question'. Then Rimashevskaya presents a list of the activities the Centre provides, ranging from the development of theoretical perspectives to organizing activities within the women's movement.

In her discussion of the women's movement in Russia, Konstantinova, another Russian academic who has been actively engaged in feminist activities, echoes the libertarian/humanist rhetoric characteristic of the early women suffragists. She bemoans the fact that 'in the Soviet period the emancipation of women was not even an issue in the ongoing debate between the Slavophiles and the Westerniser authors' who set the intellectual agenda for Russia

(Konstantinova 1992: 204, in Aristarkhova 2000). In summarizing the contemporary situation of women in post-perestroika Russia, Konstantinova claims that the resurgence of the Orthodox Church has had negative effects on women's social positions. 'Religion once more plays an increasingly important part in society. The Russian Orthodox Church is deeply conservative and patriarchal, and its repressive attitude to women has emerged unchanged by the *perestroika* reforms' (Konstantinova 1992: 204, in Aristarkhova 2000). Here she seems to be caught within what Foucault has referred to as the 'repressive hypothesis', characteristic of traditional political analyses, where power is conceived as that which represses or oppresses instead of being examined in its actual operations, which defy such easy theoretical appropriations.

'Throughout the history of the Soviet state', Konstantinova asserts, 'the position of women has been determined by state-defined demographic and economic imperatives: either women must be productive workers or they must stay at home; at other times they are expected to combine the two, but never have they been able to make their own choices or to formulate the issues themselves' (Konstantinova 1992: 204–5, in Aristarkhova 2000). In addition to drawing on largely impoverished paradigms of libertarianism and humanism, she also seems to be assuming that men had the privilege to make free choices during the Soviet period and have it today.

Yet another example of a feminist academic who operates from within the libertarian rhetoric of early suffragists is Anastasia Posadskaya, Director of the Gender Centre in Moscow, who, interestingly, seems to have been one of the first persons to have used the term 'gender' as *zhender*, in the Russian academic community. In addition to being instrumental in the formation of the Gender Centre (together with Rimashevskaya), she has remained one of Russia's foremost feminist activists, constantly organizing women's forums and workshops. In her recent book, *Women in Russia* (1994), Posadskaya has reiterated her conviction that the current situation in Russia threatens to develop into a 'renaissance of patriarchy' in so far as the rise of capitalist enterprise within Russia 'excludes' women from both the labour market and political participation.

Tatyana Mamonova, a Russian émigré writer living in the United States who has achieved great popularity within feminist circles in Australia, Canada and France, equally draws on this tradition.

> Where, then, is the moral imperative of feminism? What does feminism have to offer if it is to distinguish itself from patriarchy? What is the point of our struggle? For thousands of years men have not been not ashamed to assert their superiority, so why have we been so frightened by new alternatives that have opened up after a ten-year battle? (Mamonova 1989: 172, in Aristarkhova 2000)[16]

While showing an anxiety to 'get involved' and 'do something', Mamonova's faithful reiteration and appeal to humanist principles and liberty seem to restrict unduly the scope of feminist political engagement.

I believe in woman. A new path lies ahead of her, but the habit of enslavement that
has been instilled in her for thousands of years has not been overcome. Yet there are
in women reserves of strength, unknown to the world, and resources of energy, still
hidden, that are capable of enriching humanity. Men have already demonstrated
their possibilities, but women have yet to reveal theirs. (Mamonova 1989: 172, in
Aristarkhova 2000)

The constant reminder of the 'not-yet-unveiled' strengths of women, though
rich in suggestion and promise, cannot but remain utopian in a situation
where the articulation of women is still only with reference to their sex.
Moreover, to present the strengths as unrealized wipes out the actual achievements of many ordinary women.

The term 'gender' seems to be employed (when employed at all) in the
above mentioned discourses as a 'catch-all' term within which the general and
more specific issues about 'women' and 'sex' can be and are practically engaged
with or discussed. It seems to be used as a convenient locus around which to
set the agenda for the Centre and for women's activities. It is possible that the
urgency of the need to work actively with issues and problems that relate to
women in Russia forced the Centre and its pioneers promptly to compromise
the cultural commensurability and translational adequacy of the terms of/in
their agenda. The fact that gender served the agenda seemed enough. However, the term 'gender', as an imported term, remained semantically empty;
the discursive space it opened up within the academy and in society was filled
with the terms 'women' and 'sex'. While this made for prompt action, it may
unfortunately have blunted the possibilities for a more concerted, long-term
political engagement with regard to gender issues.

Rod as gender: rooting and uprooting

Aristarkhova reaches the conclusion, mentioned earlier, that the term 'gender'
is most appropriately translated as *rod*. In addition to having a wider cultural
currency, the term *rod* is particularly suited for a more nuanced (feminist or
otherwise) politics than that offered by the semantically empty, imported term
zhender and other translations like 'social sex' (*sotsialnii rod*).

The word *rod* has rich etymological roots in the Russian language and
culture. The *Oxford Russian Dictionary* provides an idea of the diverse meanings
that the word evokes. The word *rod* refers to the social entities of the 'family',
'kin', 'clan', 'generation'; it also means – not surprisingly, given its associations
with family and kin – 'birthing', 'origin' and 'stock'; denotes the 'genus', 'sort'
or 'kind' to which a thing belongs; and finally the grammatical category
'gender', which differentiates between 'masculine', 'feminine' and 'neuter'.

Why is *rod* a more appropriate translation of gender? First because the
term enjoys a greater cultural currency in having wider social usage and
commensurability (thus it is easily understood). The connotations that this
term evokes are multiple – especially in the cultural memories of Russian

speakers. Historically the pre-revolutionary kinship structures were destroyed in relation to private property by reference to women's social position (i.e. liberating them from the oppressive 'traditional' peasant/bourgeois family). As such, a retrieval of women's issues through/as 'gender' (*rod*) inevitably implies a simultaneous recovery and remembering of such kinship structures. Despite (and because of) the fact that *rod* draws upon the historical and etymological associations between kinship and gender, it is important to employ this term with a sensitivity to the possibility of its corruption in what Posadskaya has called a 'renaissance of patriarchy'. Posadskaya claims that the post-perestroika years have been characterized by a renewed emphasis on family and kinship relations, which represent a renewal of the patriarchal structures that oppress women.[17] Thus in employing *rod* as 'gender' one should strategically articulate its difference from and tensions with(in) kinship structures in a way that retains its *political efficacy*.

Second, the term allows for a more nuanced and politically sophisticated engagement and activism. In this sense it has greater political efficacy than a term like *zhender*. While the term 'gender' as it has been used in English does not restrictively denote women only (though some feminists would disagree), the term as it has been 'imported' into the Russian context has failed to articulate the complexity of gender relations by consistently excluding men from its discourses framed within the term 'gender'. Too often they even equate power with/as 'male', and 'gender' as (the repressed) 'female'.

Conclusion

All other differences notwithstanding, it is impossible to establish a one-to-one relationship between women and a country or national identity, not only because identifications are not one-dimensional, but also because in the multicultural societies of Europe today they are not easily classifiable in terms of 'national' versus 'international'. Under the impact of globalization and the repoliticization of religious affiliations as markers of identification, it is increasingly doubtful whether the 'nation-state' still functions as a matter of course as a major point of reference in identity formation. Nonetheless, the efforts made by the Women's Studies community in Europe to investigate critically the uses and abuses of culturally dominant terminologies are of great importance.

In this respect one of the points of consensus among Women's Studies teachers and researchers co-operating in the European networks is to maintain a very open, dialogical mode of interaction. A flair for the complexities involved in finding adequate modes of translation and adaptation from the dominant Anglo-American model is essential. It is also accompanied by an equally firm commitment to researching more adequately the historical material and sources of the many and rich different feminist cultures of Europe.

In some ways, this approach is akin to the creation of a class of transdisciplinary translators who can transpose the assumptions and methodologies of one discipline or of one cultural tradition into those of another. This taskforce of conceptual translators could well become the core of what might be called a feminist intellectual class. The work of George Steiner comes to mind here: he argues that 'the currents of energy in civilization are transmitted by translation, by the mimetic, adaptive, metamorphic interchange of discourse and codes' (1975: 202) And in so far as no translation can ever be a perfect duplication, approximations, deletions, omissions, and a vast array of subjective factors are an integral part of the process of interchange which alone makes intellectual processes possible.

Moreover, hiding the complexities of cultural differences among women under the convenient umbrella of a universal, or global, sisterhood (Morgan 1984) seems both unfair and unworkable. A critical discussion about the signifier 'woman' became necessary due to the emergence of the question of 'differences among women'. This has resulted in the rejection of the univocity of the term 'woman', especially within feminist theory. The political urge to develop this issue has come from specific sectors of the movement: first, from psychoanalytic feminism (Irigaray 1974; Melandri 1977; Molina 1986); second, in lesbian discourse, theory and practice (Rich 1981; Wittig 1973); and third, from the so-called 'post-colonial' discourse of Third World feminists (Lorde 1984; Mohanty 1992; Spivak 1988) who have analysed the way in which the category 'Third World women' has been constructed by feminist discourse.

Another argument for translation as an epistemological stance is that unless we submit our own discourses to the test of feminist transdisciplinary translation we run the risk of reinventing the wheel – of borrowing sloppily from the terminology and conceptual framework of other disciplines and cultures. This may induce a false sense of creativity; thus, an idea from sociology applied to literature may seem revolutionary, though it is absolutely commonplace in its own discourse.

The experience of setting up Women's Studies in a European perspective has proved to be a delicate exercise in cross-cultural analysis and comparison. In its daily practice, this has turned out to be a labour-intensive process of confronting the differences among women, which has only just begun: it will keep us busy for years to come. One thing that is already clear to all concerned is that the idea of 'Europe' we have in mind is critical of ethnocentrism and nationalism. Fortunately, most European feminists dissociate themselves from the legacy of European nationalism and are deeply concerned about the rebirth of xenophobia, racism and anti-Semitism on our continent. Moreover, without turning our back on our historical heritage, many of us have also voiced pertinent criticism of the increasing isolationism and protectionism fostered by the idea of a 'United' Europe (Braidotti and Franken 1991). These concerns can be put to the task of contributing actively to the construction of a genuine European community spirit, where sexism, racism and other forms of exclusion will be targeted for elimination. As Helma Lutz (Lutz, Yuval Davis and Phoenix 1996) so eloquently puts it: in the EU today, we need to put an end to that centuries-old European habit that consists in holding on to an ethnocentric centre, confining the rest of the world to the position of a necessary and necessarily underrated periphery. Lutz explores especially the condition of immigrants in the EC today as a significant case of peripheral existence within the alleged centre of this community. In other words, Women's Studies is not only education for women; it is the re-education of a whole culture, to help it move away from discriminatory practices, so that it can give the best of itself to the development of a renewed sense of a common Europe.

In order to construct effective inter-European perspectives in Women's Studies, due attention must be paid to cultural differences and to the specificity of national contexts. Noting that both the terminology and most of the existing teaching material in this field is of North American origin and consequently is available only in English, European Women's Studies scholars have been faced with a double task. On the one hand, they have had to struggle to get this new field of study accepted in their respective countries and institutions; on the other hand, they have had to develop their own instruments for teaching and research. In this regard, the support that Women's Studies academics have been able to gather from the Commission of the European Community has been and remains crucial in many different ways. Whereas countries where this field is underdeveloped have benefited from both the financial and the moral support of the EC, well-endowed programmes in other EU countries have experienced EC support as a form of international recognition and therefore of scientific legitimation. In both cases, the impact of the EC's 'stamp of approval' is enormous.

The feeling is strong among European Women's Studies academics that this field can only be genuinely 'European' if it addresses rigorously issues of ethnic identity, multiculturalism and anti-racism. The issues of cultural and gender identity are intimately interlinked and cannot easily be separated. We would even go so far as to suggest that no perspective in Women's Studies can be considered truly 'European' unless it addresses the need to produce non-exclusionary and non-ethnocentric models of knowledge and education. The new European consciousness that could emerge from the European Union can only profit from the enlarged definition of knowledge which Women's Studies implies and enacts. In this respect, many Women's Studies scholars feel very strongly that they need to strengthen and broaden the anti-racist European dimension of their work. More international exchanges and comparative research projects are needed in order to develop an in-depth understanding of the cultural diversity of Women's Studies traditions and practices in the European community today. Moreover, for this work towards a common and yet diversified definition to succeed, discussions are needed in a comparative framework with women from Eastern and Central Europe, from the United States and from developing countries. Research on gender methodologies is a top priority in our field today.

Notes

1. See Smolej 1983, 1994; see also Kozmik and Jeram 1995; Boriš 1998.
2. The examples for the words 'woman', 'female', 'man' 'masculine' seem to be telling as well (Boriš 1998; *Delta* 1998).
3. 'The human race' in Slovenian: *šlovečki rod* (i.e. the human gender).
4. From the same term the words for a 'a half of', 'one half', have been developed (Croatian *pol*, Serbian *po*, Russian *pol*, Czech *pul*, etc.).
5. The reference to 'Spanish' covers a variety of languages which are officially recognized by the Spanish state: Catalan, Basque, Galician and Castilian or Spanish.
6. Going deeper into grammar and genre it is possible to find a subdistinction between 'grammatical' and 'natural' genre (as a function derived analogically from grammatical gender). A word such as 'father' has a 'natural' masculine gender because a father is a man. The constructed character of 'natural' genres was first pointed out by the Anglo-American definitions of gender (*Grand Robert*, Paris 1989).
7. The pronouncation is given in the International Phonetic Alphabet.
8. This phrase is ambiguous, since its original meaning was 'race discrimination' with the adjective φυλετικες derived from the word φυλη, 'race', and not φυλο, 'sex'. This is the reason why some people prefer the phrase σιεστικες διακρισεις, 'sexist discrimination', instead of the ambigous φυλετικες διακρισεις.
9. www.presenciaciudadana.org.mx/articuloelpais.html.
10. I will not take up here the theoretical and political debates regarding the preferability of a 'gender 'or 'sexual difference' approach, the binarism of the sex/gender distinction, etc. These debates are, of course, very important but they are not specific to French-speaking contexts, which are the object here.
11. The resultant publication includes an influential article by Christine Delphy that was later translated into English and published in *Women's Studies International Forum*, vol. 16, no. 1, 1993.
12. Just how important this text was inside the new women's movement and beyond is illustrated by the fact that 45,000 copies were printed during the first half of 1977.
13. About the Butler debate and her reception, see Landweer and Rumpf 1993.
14. An interdisciplinary study program, introduced in 1997 at the Faculty of Arts, University of Ljubljana, has the same name.
15. It is this idea of 'socially constructed sex' which has lent legitimacy to one more alternative translation of 'gender' into Russian academic texts as *sotsialnii rod* meaning 'social sex'. See especially Per Monson, ed., *Contemporary Western Social Theories*, published in the Russian language in Moscow in 1993, wherein 'gender' is translated as 'social sex'.
16. Note that this article was written in 1986 in the wake of *perestroika*, and thus the 'ten-year battle' and 'new alternatives' were made with reference to that.
17. Valentina Konstantinova (1992) gives as an example of such patriarchal 'rationalizations' Solzhenitsyn's (1990) article 'How Are We to Structure Russia: Feasible Considerations'. In this article Solzhenitsyn expresses views common to Slavophiles – Konstantinova refers to writings by Rasputin (1990), Belov (1990), Tolstaya (1990), and Tokareva (1989) – and widely propagated that 'Today the family is the key to saving our future. The woman must be given a chance to return to the family to bring up children

and men's pay must reflect this, though with anticipated unemployment in the initial stages it will not work successfully right away; some families will be better off if the woman continues to have a job for the time being' (cited in Konstantinova 1992: 204).

References

Ajvazova, S.G. (1999) *Le Deuxième sexe en russe. Les problèmes de la transmission* [The Second Sex in Russian: The Problems of Transmission]. Cinquantenaire du deuxième sexe. Paris: Colloque International.

Alberdi, C. (1999) 'Violencia de Género', *El País*, 28 February.

Aristarkhova, Irina (2000) 'Trans-lating Gender into the Russian (Con)text', in R. Braidotti and E. Vonk, eds, *The Making of European Women's Studies: A Work-in-progress Report on Curriculum Development and Related Issues*, vol. II. ATHENA, Utrecht: Utrecht University, pp. 67–82; www.aristarkhova.com.

Bahovec, Eva (2000) 'A Short Note on the Use of "Sex" and "Gender" in Slavic Languages', in R. Braidotti and E. Vonk, eds, *The Making of European Women's Studies*, vol. I. ATHENA, Utrecht: Utrecht University, pp. 28–9.

Baker, M. (1991) *In Other Words: A Coursebook on Translation*. London: Routledge.

de Beauvoir, S. (1949) *Le deuxième sexe*. Paris: Gallimard.

Becker-Schmidt, Regina (1987) 'Die doppelte Vergesellschaftung – die doppelte Unterdrückung: Besonderheiten in der Frauenforschung in den Sozialwissenschaften', in Lilo Unterkircher and Ina Wagner, eds, *Die andere Hälfte der Gesellschaft*. Vienna: ÖGB-Verlag pp. 10–25.

Benveniste, E. (1969) *Le vocabulaire des institutions indo-europeennes*. Paris: Minuit.

Bilden, H. (1991) 'Geschlechtspezifische Sozialisation', in K. Hurrelmann and D. Ulich, eds, *Neues Handbuch der Sozialisationsforschung*, 4th edn. Weinheim-Basel: Beltz Verlag, pp. 279–301.

Bock, G. (1999) 'La Historia de las Mujeres y la Historia del Género: Aspectos de un Debate Internacional', *Historia Social* 9, Valencia: Instituto de Historia Social, UNED.

Boriš, R. (1998) *Zenski identitet u jeziku* [Female Identity in Language], 1, Trena, Croatia.

Brück, B., H. Kahlert, M. Krüll et al. (1992) *Feministische Soziologie. Eine Einführung*. Frankfurt-am-Main: Campus Verlag.

Braidotti, R. and C. Franken (1991) 'United States of Europe or United Colors of Benetton? Feminist Thoughts on the New European Space', *Differences*, vol. 2, no. 4 (Brown University), pp. 109–21.

Braidotti, R., E. de Dreu and C. Rammrath (1995) *Women's Studies in Europe. Final Report of the Evaluation of Women's Studies Activities in Europe for the SIGMA Network and Directorate General XII of the Commission of the European Union*. Utrecht: Utrecht University.

Braidotti, R. and E. Vonk, eds (2000) *The Making of European Women's Studies: A Work-in-progress Report on Curriculum Development and Related Issues*, 2 vols. ATHENA (Advanced Thematic Network in Activities in Women's Studies in Europe), Utrecht: Utrecht University.

Butler, J. (1990) *Gender Trouble*. New York and London: Routledge.

Corominas, J. and J. A. Pascual (1984) *Diccionario Crítico Etimológico Castellano e Hispánico*, vol. 3. Madrid: Ed. Gredos.

Delta. The Journal for Women's Studies and Feminist Theory (Slovenia: 1995–).

Dictionnaire des notions philosophiques (1990). Paris: Publications Universitaires de France.

Dictionnaire fondamental de la psychologie (1997). Paris: Larousse.

Diccionario de la Langua Española (1992). Madrid: Real Academia Española.

Directorate General XII (1999) *Women and Science: Proceedings of the Conference*. Brussels: Commission of the European Union.

Der Grosse Duden. Etymologie. Herkunftswörterbuch der deutschen Sprache (1963). Mannheim: Duden Verlag.

Hagemann-White, C. (1984) *Sozialisation: weiblich-männlich?* Opladen: Leske & Budrich.

Hagemann-White, C. (1993) 'Die Konstrukteure des Geschlechts auf frischer Tat ertappen? Methodische Konsequenzen einer theoretischen Einsicht', *Feministische Studien* 2.

Hanmer, J., et al., eds (1994) *Women's Studies and European Integration: A Report to the Equal Opportunities Unit.* DGV: Brussels.

Harding, S. (1986) *The Science Question in Feminism.* Ithaca: Cornell University Press.

Harding, S. (1987) *Feminism and Methodology: Social Science Issues.* Bloomington: Indiana University Press.

Harding, S. (1991) *Whose Science, Whose Knowledge?* Ithaca: Cornell University Press.

Harding, S. and E. McGregor, eds (1995) *The Gender Dimension of Science and Technology – Extract from the World Science Report.* New York: UNESCO.

Hausen, Karin (1976) 'Die Polarisierung der "Geschlechtcharaktere" – Eine Spiegelung der Dissoziation von Erwerbs- und Familienleben', in Werner Conze, ed. *Sozialgeschichte der Familie in der Neuzeit Europas.* Stuttgart: Metzler, pp. 363–93.

Hirata, H., L. Laborie, H. Le Doaré, and D. Sénotier, coordinators (2000) *Politique d'aujourd'hui.* Paris: Presses Universitaires de France.

Hirdman, Y. (1988) 'Genussystemet – reflexioner kring kvinnors sociala underordning', *Kvinnovetenskapelig tidskrift*, vol. 9, no. 3.

Hurtig, M. et al. (1991) *Sexe et genre.* Paris: CNRS.

Irigaray, Luce (1974) *Speculum de l'autre femme.* Paris, Minuit.

Irigaray, L. (1993) *Sexes and Genealogies*, trans. Gillian Gill. Ithaca: Cornell University Press.

Irigaray, L. (1994) *Je, tu, nous: Toward a Culture of Difference.* London: Routledge.

Jacquet, Isabelle (1995) *Développement au masculin/féminin. Le genre: outil d'un nouveau concept.* Paris: L'Harmattan.

Jegerstedt, K. (2000) 'A Short Introduction to the Use of "Sex" and "Gender" in the Scandinavian Languages', in R. Braidotti and E. Vonk, eds, *The Making of European Women's Studies*, vol. I. ATHENA, Utrecht: Utrecht University, pp. 24–5.

Jónasdóttir, A.G. (1998) 'Kvinnoord-i-Norden: Varför använda "genus" när "kön" finns?' *Nytt fra NIKK*, vol. 3, no. 2. Nordic Institute for Women's Studies and Gender Research.

Kollontai, A. (1923) 'Make Way for the Winged Eros', *BV1*, pp. 84–95.

Konstantinova, V. (1992) 'The Women's Movement in the USSR: A Myth or a Real Change?', in Shirin Rai, Hilary Pilkington and Annie Phizacklea, eds, *Women in the Face of Change: The Soviet Union, Eastern Europe and China.* London: Routledge.

Koster-Lossack, A. and T. Levin (1992) 'Women's Studies in Europe', *Women's Studies Quarterly*, vol. 20, nos 3 and 4.

Kozmik, V., and J. Jeram (1995) *Neseksisticna raba jezika* [Non-sexist Use of Language], Ljubljana: Bureau for Women's Politics.

Landweer, H. and R. Mechthild, eds (1993) 'Kritik der Kategorie "Geschlecht"', *Feministische Studien* 2.

Lappaläinen, P. (1996) 'Kvinna och kön är NAINEN och SUKUPUOLI på finska', in *Nytt fra NIKK* 2/1. Nordic Institute for Women's Studies and Gender Research.

Lutz, H., N. Yuval-Davis and A. Phoenix, eds (1996) *Crossfires: Nationalism, Racism and Gender in Europe.* London: Pluto Press.

Lorde, Audre (1984) *Sister Outsider.* Trumanberg, NY: Crossing Press.

Macedo, A.G. (2000) 'Gender–genero; diferenca sexual; sexo', in R. Braidotti and E. Vonk, eds, *The Making of European Women's Studies*, vol. II. ATHENA, Utrecht: Utrecht University.

Mamonova, T. (1989) *Russian Women's Studies: Essays on Sexism in Soviet Culture*. Oxford: Pergamon Press.

Melandri, L. (1977) *L'infamia originaria*. Milano: Erba Voglio.

Mohanty, C. (1992) 'Feminist Encounters: Locating the Politics of Experience', in M. Barrett and A. Philips, eds, *Destabilizing Theory: Contemporary Feminist Debates*. Cambridge: Polity Press.

Molina Foix, Vicente (1999) 'El género epiceno', *El País*, 9 March.

Molina, María (1992) *Diccionario del Uso del Español*, vol. I. Madrid: Ed. Gredos.

Morgan, Robin (1984) *Sisterhood is Global: the International Women's Movement Anthology*. Garden City, New York: Anchor Doubleday.

Pavlidou, Theodossia-Soula (2000) 'Modern Greek "gender"', in R. Braidotti and E. Vonk, eds, *The Making of European Women's Studies*, vol. I. Utrecht: ATHENA/ Utrecht University, pp. 26–7.

Pereira Rolle, Sandra (2000) 'Gender versus "genero"', in R. Braidotti and E. Vonk, eds, *The Making of European Women's Studies*, vol. II. Utrecht: ATHENA/Utrecht University, pp. 90–92.

Posadskaya, Anastasia (1994) *Women in Russia: A New Era in Russian Feminism*. London: Verso.

Puig de la Bellacasa, M. 'The Sex/Gender Distinction in French-speaking Contexts', in R. Braidotti and E. Vonk, eds, *The Making of European Women's Studies*, vol. I. ATHENA, Utrecht: Utrecht University, pp. 94–8.

Rich, A. (1981) 'Compulsory Heterosexuality and the Lesbian Experience', *Signs*, vol. 7, no. 1, pp. 158–99.

Rimashevskaya, N. (1992) 'The New Women's Studies' in M. Buckley, ed., *Perestroika and Soviet Women*. Cambridge: Cambridge University Press.

Roudinesco, E. and M. Plon (1997) *Dictionnaire de la psychanalyse*. Paris: Fayard.

Scheu, U. (1977) *Wir werden nicht als Mädchen geboren – wir werden dazu gemacht. Zur frühkindlichen Erziehung in unserer Gesellschaft*. Frankfurt: Fischer Verlag.

Smolej, V. (1983) *Slovensko-slovački slovar* [The Slovene–Slovak Dictionary]. Ljubljana: Državna založba Sovenije.

Smolej, V. (1994) *Slovar slovenskega knjižnega jezika* [The Dictionary of Standard Slovene Language]. Ljubljana: Državna založba Sovenije.

Snoj, M. (1997) *Slovenski etimološki slovar* [Slovene Etymological Dictionary]. Ljubljana: Mladinska knjiga.

Spivak, G. (1988) *In Other Worlds*. New York: Methuen.

Steiner, G. (1975) *After Babel: Aspects of Language and Translation*. Oxford: Oxford University Press.

Thébaud, F. (1998) *Ecrire l'histoire des femmes*. Fontenay/St-Cloud: Ecole Normale Supérieure Editions.

Vasilevsky, L.A. and L.M. Vasilevsky (1924) 'The Sex Life of Man', in *BVI*, pp. 112–21.

Widerberg, Karin (1998) 'Translating Gender', *NORA*, vol. 2, no. 6.

Wischermann, Ulla (2000) 'The Sex/Gender Debate in Germany', in R. Braidotti and E. Vonk, eds, *The Making of European Women's Studies*, vol. I. ATHENA, Utrecht: Utrecht University, pp. 30–31.

Wittig, M. (1973) *Le corps lesbien*. Paris: Minuit.

PART VII

The Rises and Falls of Women's Movements in Europe

Women's Movements and Feminist Research

UTE GERHARD

Everywhere on this earth women's movements have acted as a starting point and catalyst for change. They have also acted as the basis for feminist research. For both the women's movements and feminist research have the aims of contributing to women's emancipation and to eliminate social discrimination and inequalities in gender relations. The women's movements seek to do this through the mobilization of women and through the attempt to exercise political influence; feminist research seeks to realize these aims through acting as a critical forum which intends to uncover the reasons for the continuing discrimination and structural violence to which women are exposed, to introduce women's experiences and knowledges into scientific discourse, and to further the inclusion of women in research and teaching within higher education. Due to their shared aims and proximity of interests, as well as their differing institutional positionings, the relationship between women's movements and feminist research is not always straightforward. Feminist research or feminist theory cannot claim to prescribe the political practice of the women's movement; feminist research should also not serve a specific party-political position since this would compromise its critical relation to science and to general social conditions. Simultaneously it is noticeable that the women's movement became the object of feminist research only relatively recently in some countries, and that it has remained, in some counries, the domain of inquiry of a select few women. This may be due to the fact that the subject matter makes it difficult to retain a critical distance. It may also be because social movement research has to fight for recognition in the social sciences as it is viewed as being ideologically biased and lacking in scientific rigour. The latter is, of course, an argument that cannot raise more than a tired smile within the feminist critique of science.

By now the research domain of the women's movements has grown into a vast arena not only as regards historical research but also in respect of work focusing on the present. Nonetheless when one undertakes an international comparison it becomes evident that English-language-based research on women's movements and research accessible in English is given greater attention with the effect that women's movements not extensively documented in English are underestimated and sometimes bizarrely misjudged (see Chafetz, Dworkin and Swanson 1990). In addition not much research attempts to compare historical and recent waves of women's movements (see Offen 2000).

This section engages with those omissions. It cannot claim completeness regarding the charting of women's movements in Europe but it does foreground the very different developments of the women's movements in Northern and Southern Europe, and between Eastern, post-socialist and Western ones. Here both the differences and the similarities between the movements become apparent, regarding the periodization of women's movements, the structures of political opportunities into which they feed and fit, their aims and conflicts. What becomes very evident in this comparison is the damage done by National Socialism and by fascism regarding the development of feminism in Europe. The pioneering role Scandinavian countries played in the establishment of women's rights of citizenship seems to be particularly due to the shared political platform of the labour movement and the women's movement during that period. Completely new and different questions are raised by the juxtaposition of East and West. Here Western feminism cannot and should not be taken as a role model. But it would without doubt be interesting to investigate further the history of the women's movements in Eastern Europe prior to the establishment of so-called social realism. For there existed a shared international platform in these countries too, going back to the late nineteenth century.

A fundamental comparative analysis of the women's movements in Europe remains a project which would enhance the development of a European consciousness. The various brief case studies in this section contribute to this project, and offer considerable insights into the European specificities of the women's movements.

References

Chafetz, Janet, Anthony Salzmann Dworkin and Stephanie Swanson (1990) 'Social Change and Social Activisms: First Wave Women's Movements around the World', in Guida West and Rhoda Lois Blumberg, eds, *Women and Social Protest*. Oxford and New York: Oxford University Press, pp. 302–20.

Offen, Karen (2000) *European Feminisms, 1700–1945: A Political History*. Stanford: Stanford University Press.

17

The History of the Feminist Movement in France

FRANÇOISE PICQ

The women's liberation movement in France began in 1970, after the student and worker revolt of May '68. It was the time when the post-World War II baby boom generation was entering university. Traditional universities came under increasing pressure from young men and women, and a large youth population was poised to rebel.

Many of the feminists who initiated the second-wave feminist movement had previously been active in other political movements. The older ones had learned their militancy during the 1960s in campaigns against the war in Algeria, then against the war in Vietnam. Then came May '68 and the hope to 'change life'. Whilst the older feminists shared the younger generation's vision of politics and commitment to change, they rebelled against the sexism that was reproduced in the New Left organizations which arose. Women felt ignored as individuals in the revolutionary movement, their problems pushed aside and held up to ridicule. In France, as in the United States, they were fed up with playing a subordinate role. They denounced the sexual division of labour among activists where men supposedly did the thinking, formulated the theory, organized and made decisions, while women worked mimeograph machines and distributed leaflets. So they followed the example of the American feminists, breaking away from the New Left to form women-only groups. The MLF (Mouvement de libération des femmes – Women's Liberation Movement), wise to the criticisms levelled against the left, valued direct democracy, spontaneity and radicalism. Considering that it was impossible to imagine women's liberation within contemporary social and political structures, the MLF intended to destroy these, and saw reformism as a danger because partial improvements might demobilize activists.

The MLF bloomed in the leftist culture of contestation, and developed a radical critique of the leftists themselves. It highlighted the incoherence in their behaviour and the limits of their revolutionary projects. It denounced the vanguard's authority to maintain power relationships within the groups and over people. It put into question revolutionary dogmas such as the primacy of class struggle and economic changes, and the necessity of a party to lead the revolution (Picq 1993).

The First Women's Movement

The year 1970 was proclaimed 'year zero' for women's liberation (*Partisans* 1970), ignoring the long history of women's struggles in France. In fact feminist movements have developed within many social movements at various moments in France's history, demanding the same rights for women as for men, arguing with the prevailing ethos of the time and pushing its boundaries. Feminism always looked ahead of its time. French feminism first arose in the revolutionary movement of 1789, as an intellectual protest against women's exclusion from the supposedly universal principles of the revolution. It demanded equal rights for women, in the name of the Natural Rights from which women were unfairly excluded: 'Either each human individual or none has the same right.' Later, feminism re-emerged from the utopian socialism and the revolution of 1830, then during the social revolution of 1848, which brought 'universal' suffrage (excluding women once again from that 'universal'), and during the Paris Commune in 1871. When the Republic built a new society affirming the unity and solidarity of the nation, progressively forging rules and democratic behaviour, a large feminist movement developed, with numerous associations, representing various political trends, whether liberal, radical or socialist, but aiming at unity and autonomy. It discussed and formulated concrete demands in its congress and mobilizations: equal rights in civil life (reform of the Civil Code), suffrage, education, the right to work.

It was only after World War II and the victory over fascism that French women obtained the equal rights that feminists had demanded for so long. The new Republic proclaimed: 'The Law guarantees to woman, in every domain, rights equal to those of man.' The long fight of women for equal rights was at last victorious, but the feminist movement had vanished, and history did not recognize its part in this belated victory.

Continuities and Ruptures

Most of the 1970s' feminists ignored the history of feminism as it was not part of the narrative history of France. The latter told of the long and glorious struggle of the people for freedom and for social justice, ignoring the exclusion of women at every stage of this fight. The collective memory of women's struggles vanished because of the lack of a group to keep it alive. Even Simone de Beauvoir in 1949 doubted that women had ever tried to play a part in history as women. Feminism, she said, cannot be 'an autonomous movement' (de Beauvoir 1949). It was only after the revival of feminism during the 1970s that the long story of women's struggles began to emerge from the void.

Proclaiming 'women's liberation, year zero' in 1970 was not only a matter of ignorance; it did announce a new way of thinking. The new generation no longer vindicated 'women's rights' because those very rights had hardly been won, but also because equal rights no longer appeared to be the goal. Instead the new generation claimed freedom, protesting against women being dominated, exploited, locked into traditional roles. The product of May '68, women's issues as conceived of by the new generation were recast in the terms and the style of that movement.

Key Figures in the New Women's Movement

The MLF decided to be a completely spontaneous and democratic movement without any power structure or hierarchy. Regarding liberation as a self-sufficient process, it considered that no one can decide in the place of another what to do or think. It claimed that each social group has to choose its goals and ways of fighting.

May '68's conception of politics allowed women's issues to be raised in a new and subversive way. It stated that 'everything is political', aiming to redefine collective issues, to enlarge the political domain to include everyday life and privacy. It scorned the traditional view of politics as an activity monopolized by specific representatives who were elected to settle matters in the place of each citizen. The goal became deciding for oneself, taking control over one's own life. The feminist statement that 'the personal is political' was part of this new definition. It maintained that private life, sexuality, and relationships between men and women are political issues, at a time when politics was valued as the way to radical social transformation. Personal experiences and not theories were, then, the basis for understanding women's oppression. Women were the objects and subjects of their own struggle, determining the means and ends of their own liberation. Involved in the collective struggle, every woman should aim to be both an individual and a member of a collective.

Feminists who were part of the beginning of the MLF were very disparate in terms of age, social origins and familial situation. This diversity could not be explained either by leftist anti-bourgeois sentiments, or by the images of feminists offered by the media. But studies of these women (Ringart 1991; Picq 1991) show several particularities. They often came from families with a tradition of humanist, social or political engagement. They often had mothers and grandmothers who were ahead of their times, with personal independence or cultural confidence. Several came from large families of girls where gender divisions were redefined due to the composition of the family.

Comparing the social, cultural and personal trajectories of these feminists with the socio-economic trends of the period is very instructive. They heralded the democratization and feminization of the university before and after May '68. They also embodied the waning of the traditional middle class – trades-people and craftsmen – and the growth of a new group between 1954 and 1981: medium and upper wage-earning strata grew from 9 per cent to more than 20 per cent. The feminists of the period show a distinct pattern in their personal and professional choices. They were more likely to have had a university education than other women of their generation, of their social origin or even of their family. They tended to choose public-sector and intellectual professions. They were less likely to marry and more likely to divorce. If they had children, they tended to have them later than other women of that time and often out of marriage. Lesbianism was common and valued.

These tendencies are not particularly surprising. They are consistent with the aim of feminism for personal autonomy. What is most interesting, however, is not that these feminists differed in a number of respects from other women but that their differences would become a wider trend in the whole of society. Statistics show that incidence of marriage decreased in France (from 416,000 weddings in 1972 to 265,000 in 1987), that cohabitation became usual in every social group, and that birth out of marriage increased (from 6 per cent to 40 per cent). The seemingly marginal choices of the feminists of the 1970s reveal themselves, in retrospect, as announcing an evolution in family patterns, which manifest themselves in several configurations: free union with or without cohabitation, single motherhood, recombined families, homosexuality.

The MLF was not in fact a movement of 'all women'; feminists functioned as a sort of cultural vanguard. As an active minority these feminists could lead a greater number of women because what they said and did could be heard by women looking for a new way to live, especially women who had chosen to combine working and family careers, and wanted to succeed in both.

Campaigns and Networks

The term 'movement' reflects the MLF's theoretical and political diversity, and multiplication of the themes of action and reflection. At the same time the MLF shared several basic principles: male exclusion, rejection of hierarchy and leadership, group autonomy and independence from political parties (Lhomond 1991). Women's mobilization was very new and radical. It reproduced the spectacular and provocative style that had been so effective in May '68, with transgression, insolence and caustic humour to win the media's attention. There were scandalous demonstrations, such as the one when women laid a wreath of flowers under the Arc de Triomphe for the wife of the unknown soldier (even more unknown than the unknown soldier himself); effective provocations, such as 343 women signing an article in a newspaper declaring that they had had abortions; public disobedience of the law, such as charters advising women to have an abortion in more liberal countries, and even open performances of this illegal practice in France.

Key Issues/Arguments/Debates

The demand for bodily self-determination went much further than rejecting compulsory motherhood. The fight against rape, an extreme form of physical coercion to which women are subjected, was another landmark for the MLF. But its greatest victory was a new law liberalizing abortion. This issue had been one of the principal fights of the new women's movement in every Western country. In France the battle was especially heroic and mobilizing. In the end the whole of society was mobilized, and the state had to concede. This issue forced the political parties to reorganize themselves in light of the new divisions. The battle over abortion, although not articulated as such at the time, was another stage in the long conflict between 'the two Frances'; the victory of secularism over Catholicism. Republicans, democrats, liberals and modernists supported the women's fight because at that moment it was the symbol of freedom of choice and social progress over and against Catholicism's claim to be the moral arbiter of French society.

The government was challenged and in the end had to change the law. Not only did it change the laws on abortion and contraception; it also reformed the laws on other issues where feminists could obtain the support of public opinion (such as family laws, divorce, rape). Many laws that gave more freedom to women, more power and more equality (in the family, at work, and in society) were voted in.

From Women's Movement to Women's Studies

Feminist studies came directly out of the women's movement. During the mid-1970s activism turned into intellectual controversy and active research. Feminist issues such as abortion and contraception, rape, family and motherhood, women's work and exploitation, social and sexual relationships, and lesbianism became the subjects of theses. History and the social sciences were the fields for a new contest. Women challenged male-dominated disciplines, underlining women's exclusion and identifying the social construction of sexual difference. That is why it is more common in France to speak of 'feminist studies' than Women's Studies, naming an approach rather than a field of research. That is also why academic institutions often resist this new and inventive work. With the early 1980s and a new government, feminist studies began to gain a shy legitimacy in several universities and the Centre National de la Recherche Scientifique (CNRS). Courses were taught, a steady flow of conferences were held, and research programmes were established. A national feminist studies association, Association Nationale des Études Féministes (ANEF) brought together students and scholars. ANEF participates in the European Women's Studies Network (ANEF 1995).

The French Exception

What in the history of the MLF was specific to France? What was shared by all or most other feminist movements of the 1960s and 1970s? The rise of feminism was greeted enthusiastically by women everywhere. Recognizing one another, the women's movements in the 1970s had the feeling of participating in a historic global phenomenon, and easily adopted ideas and ways to organize from one movement to another. 'Women-only' groups, 'consciousness-raising', 'grassroots' movements were common everywhere. A lack of hierarchy, centralization and permanent structures emerged as the pattern to adapt, according to national situations and issues. Thirty years on, the commonalities and differences among the women's movements of the 1970s in various countries have become clearer.

We can agree, I think, that feminism was an international phenomenon that affected most occidental societies from the 1960s and 1970s onwards; that it generally arose from the New Left, in the revolutionary perspective opened by May '68, but broke away from this movement as women and their issues were unable to find their place within it. We can agree, too, that everywhere the major goal of that 'second wave' of feminism was the same (after the first wave had won 'formal rights'). Denouncing women's assignation to motherhood and the home, the movement claimed free choice for individuals. Abortion was the symbol of that fight, just as suffrage had been for the first wave, but its purpose was much larger, questioning women's roles, the relationships between the genders, and in the end women's identity. It is also the case that everywhere, following a period of victories, there was a retreat or backlash. The feminist movement went into decline before attaining its goals.

On the other hand, there were many differences among 1970s feminist movements, depending on the cultural traditions within which they arose, the historical and socio-political contexts in which they were rooted, the capacity of the political system to take women's demands into account, and the ability of the individual women's movements to find powerful allies in left parties or trade unions.

The MLF can be seen as another example of the 'French exception', the cultural tradition of confrontation which likes intellectual controversy and refuses compromise (Picq 1998). In France, revolution belongs to the political tradition. The great revolution of 1789 is imprinted in our collective memory as an archetype for history-making. It left a revolutionary style as an inheritance, one that prefers political breaks, which present themselves as a new beginning and aim at total change, demanding all or nothing.

All feminist movements have known contradictions – between radical and socialist feminism, between lesbian and heterosexual women, between universalism and particularism. Those debates are unavoidable and productive. Some may be intrinsic to feminist mobilization because women have to vindicate themselves as a specific group at the same time as demanding women's place as part of what is perceived as 'the universal'. Many feminist movements were able to manage these contradictions, letting diverse points of view quietly cohabit. Yet nowhere were the violence and divisions among political and feminist groups as absolute and destructive as in France. While the MLF proved unable to turn from utopia to reformism, and was left on the margin, some grassroots movements were able to convert and enter mainstream society, their leaders co-opted into the state machine. Being outside was the condition of a radically new thinking, but it is of course from the inside that it is most possible to influence public policy (Dahlerup 1990). The decline of feminism may not have been as brutal everywhere as it was in France, but nowhere did the 1970s' women's movement attain all its goals. The feminist revolution remained unfinished. The second wave of feminism has calmed, leaving important changes in women's representation and situation, but also both regrets and hopes for the future. Feminism is not finished. History shows that feminism is involved in a long-term battle, with an uneven course. It has never disappeared completely but was sometimes deeply repressed, not least in cultural memory. Then it sprang up again with new opportunities, defining fresh issues and new ways of expression. Each wave has focalized priorities that in that period symbolized women's exclusion from full human status; each wave has won part of the fight.

References

ANEF (1995) *Etudes féministes et études sur les femmes en France en 1995* [Feminist Studies and Women's Studies in France in 1995], supplement to *Bulletin de l'ANEF* 18, Toulouse.

Beauvoir, Simone de (1949) *Le deuxième sexe*. Paris: Gallimard.

Dahlerup, Drude (1986) *The New Women's Movement*. London: Sage.

GEF (Groupe d'études féministes, Université Paris 7) (1991), *Crises de la société, féminisme et changement* [The Crisis of Society, Feminism and Change]. Paris: Tierce–Revue d'en face.

Lhomond, Brigitte (1991) 'France: Feminism and the Women's Liberation Movement', in Helen Tierney, ed., *Women's Studies Encyclopedia*. London: Greenwood Press.

Partisans (1970) 'Libération des femmes année zéro' [Women's Liberation, Year Zero], July–October, Paris.

Picq, Françoise (1991) 'Stratégie de sexe ou destin de classe?' [Gender Strategy or Class Destiny?], in GEF, *Crises de la société, féminisme et changement*. Paris: Tierce–Revue d'en face.

Picq, Françoise (1993) *Libération des femmes. Les années mouvement* [Women's Liberation: The Movement Years]. Paris: Seuil.

Picq, Françoise (1998) 'Le MLF, exception française ou modèle?' [The MLF, French Exception or Archetype?], in Y. Cohen and F. Thébaud, eds, *Féminismes et identités nationales* [Feminisms and National Identities]. Lyon: Programme Rhône-Alpes, Recherches en sciences humaines.

Ringart, Nadja (1991) 'Quand ce n'était qu'un début… Itinéraires de femmes à Paris', [When it was just the beginning… Women's Ways in Paris], in GEF, *Crises de la société, féminisme et changement*. Paris: Tierce–Revue d'en face.

18

The Women's Movement in Germany

UTE GERHARD

It has become commonplace to describe the women's movement as proceeding in 'waves.' In fact, this metaphor can be more accurately applied to the historical ebb and flow of social movements, their inner dynamic and varied significance for society, than to the women's movement, dividing it strictly into a historical and a newer one. I would even prefer a concept of 'long waves' to underline the connections and lines of tradition tying various women's activist phases together, without, however, overstating the unity and similarities of women's movements and their aims (Gerhard 1996). Still, a historical consciousness of these continuities and a knowledge of the history of other social movements, especially when viewed from an international perspective, help us to avoid a timid and all too myopic evaluation of the present situation. In their analysis of the American women's movement between the two world wars, Leila Rupp and Verta Taylor (1990) borrowed a nautical term to evoke the cessation of feminist activity during that period. They wrote about the 'doldrums', using the word to underscore a passing phase and implying that the women's movement has not yet seen its end. The question arises as to whether this analogy can be effectively applied to the present situation of the women's movement in Germany.

The Beginnings

The history of the German women's movement begins with the *Vormärz*, the social and political movement around the revolution of 1848. Yet, instead of any continuous process of development, we have a history of repeated setbacks, halts and numerous arduous and courageous new beginnings. Even this first wave of the women's movement, which ended in 1933 with either the suspension or the Nazification (*Gleichschaltung*) of all organizations during the National Socialist regime, may be divided into different phases corresponding to various generations or cohorts of women.

In the historiography of the first women's movement itself, the 1848 beginnings are attributed generally to one particular woman, the pioneer and 'mother of the German women's movement', Louise Otto (Bäumer 1901: 22f.; Twellmann 1972: 1). Actually she was the first, as a supporter of the democratic and social movement, to raise the woman's issue consistently and in the face of the newly constituted public sphere of the *Vormärz*. Besides her accomplishments, recent feminist studies have collected a great variety of new evidence for the existence of a first movement, based on a 'collective actor' (Hummel-Haasis 1982; Lipp 1986; Paletschek 1990).

The beginnings seem rather inconspicuous: anonymous letters to editors of new journals, political poetry and novels of social critique, scandals about particular 'emancipated' women such as Louise Aston which became political issues, as well as new forms of female resistance and a discourse about women on the barricades of the revolution. The press – which from 1843 onwards increasingly and incessantly resisted political censorship – was a crucial medium of mobilization and of publication of explicit women's issues. For the first time there existed a political women's press, headed by the *Frauen-Zeitung*, edited by Louise Otto from 1849 to 1851, and other publications. The motto of Louise Otto's journal characterizes the goals and tone of that early democratic movement: 'For the realm of freedom I'll recruit female citizens' (Gerhard, Hannover-Drück, and Schmitter 1979). It was not only the public and strong participation of women in the liberal-democratic movement, but even more so the increasingly expanding network of women's organizations with political goals that provided proof of social movement organizations such as 'Democratic Women's Associations', particular female labour associations, as well as welfare organizations that supported families of victims of persecution and prisoners (Gerhard 1983: 196ff). The kindergarten movement that followed Fröbel's concept of a democratic education was also part of this female opposition (Allen 1991: 58f.).

The trigger for women organizing themselves was an experience typical for the feminists of the modern age and a paradox: on the one hand, involvement with the democratic movement and the political alliance with leftists and democrats; simultaneously, on the other, the experience and disappointment at being excluded from equal participation and universal rights, constitutional and human rights, and specifically in 1848 the fact that the constitution drawn up at the 'Paulskirche' proclaimed equal citizenship for male Germans only. The political significance of this early phase of the women's movement can at the same time be seen in the repressive state reactions after the failure of the revolution and its long-lasting consequences: the Press Laws that explicitly forbade women to edit newspapers (for example, the Saxon Press Law of 1850 known as the 'Lex Otto'); but particularly the

Vereinsgesetze (laws restricting associations), in force since 1850 in most states of the German Federation, which forbade 'women' and 'minors' to found political organizations or to take part in such gatherings (in Prussia and others in effect until 1908). This ban on political agency, which was in effect for more than two female generations, both tremendously shaped and hindered the German women's movement.

'The Insect Work of Local Organizations'[1]

The next step forward was made in 1865, when women who had been engaged around the 1848 events decided to convene 'a conference of German women from different cities and states' and founded the 'Allgemeinen Deutschen Frauenverein' (ADF; General German Women's Organization), led by Louise Otto and Auguste Schmidt (Otto-Peters 1890: 4). 'Women's days' were to be held regularly, in rotation in different cities, in order to found local women's organizations. Although patriarchal resistance and political stagnation after the founding of the German Kaiserreich in 1871 were obvious (Bussemer 1985: 119), nevertheless, this organizational new beginning remained the seed of all further initiatives and the starting point for practical self-help, such as a special newspaper, the *Neue Bahnen* (1866–1919), many petitions to the Reichstag and the governments, surveys and publications, and the founding of a network of associations.

However, in the 1870s, the paths of middle-class women and the female labour movements parted, in parallel with the separation of the labour movement and liberalism. The female labour movement was *de lege lata* oppressed in two ways, an experience that shaped the class-struggle politics specific to the German women's movement. It suffered both from the laws restricting associations and the *Sozialistengesetze* (socialist laws), 'a political battle', according to Hilde Lion (1926), 'through disturbance and prohibition and the closing of organizations, through trials against them, press prohibitions, through arrests and expulsion of leaders' (Lion 1926: 31). Characterizing this epoch of the women's movement, Twellmann wrote:

> In 1889, at the end of the epoch treated here, the middle-class women's movement had still not yet succeeded in becoming an influential factor in public life; but ha[d] been able to gain a foothold, thanks to its 'practical' activities over the decades.... However, the significance of this work should be estimated not only on the basis of scarce successes.... In the midst of an economic and social transformation process, the organizations of the women's movement thus gained significance as an 'intellectual centre of leadership', applying an ordering and planning focus that took care to remember that the 'women's question' included more than the question of earning a living, but rather touched on every aspect of human life as 'an issue of humanity'. (1972: 221–3)

The Height of the Women's Movement and its Turning Point at the beginning of the Twentieth Century

The third phase and uplift of the women's movement around 1890 owed its occurrence to a new structure of political opportunity: the dismissal of Bismarck, the abolition of the Socialist Laws, a new socio-political awareness of problems that temporarily counted on the resolution of social conflicts, and at the same time the growing contradictions between the traditional women's role and economic, industrial-capitalist development. A number of new political organizations emerged, not only within the women's movement. But the latter was well prepared for a qualitative shift forward. It had at its disposal networks, organizations and various media, and had already an advanced understanding of the factors which impacted on women's exclusion and discrimination in the public sphere. In the late 1880s, the leaders of the bourgeois and the proletarian women's activist strands simultaneously, but independently of each other, articulated what they saw as the main contexts in women's experience of injustice: education and work. These two now became the strategic basis for the bourgeois and proletarian women's groupings respectively.

In 1889, at the founding congress of the Second International in Paris, Clara Zetkin gave her great and acclaimed speech to the world at large about the necessary connection between socialism and women's issues on which socialist women's emancipation theories were based (Zetkin 1957: 1ff). Since 1889, the female worker's movement, which even after the abolition of the *Sozialistengesetze* was still judged 'political' by state offices and thus continued to be prohibited and oppressed, had also given itself a new structure under the 'era Zetkin'. It had installed so-called women's agitation commissions, which, without statutes, membership lists or chairwomen, tried to undermine the *Vereinsgesetze*. The newspaper *Die Gleichheit* (Equality), edited by Clara Zetkin from 1893, became their propaganda instrument, which Zetkin knew how to use effectively, in conditioning and indoctrinating her followers but also as a weapon in political struggles.

Helene Lange had published her so-called *Gelbe Broschüre* (Yellow brochure) in 1887, a petition to the Prussian ministry of education written as a manifesto, and pointedly and sharply criticizing Prussian educational politics, specifically educational institutions for girls. Lange justified and connected her liberal concept of emancipation – 'Knowledge is power' – as a personal right to education for women with the demand for participation in the shaping of social circumstances; it already contained the notion of a 'spiritual motherhood'. Lange went far afield in order to ground her theory of gender difference, as we would call it today: a gender philosophy that in the main followed women's true calling and the essential differences between the genders in terms of Rousseau's theory of gender roles (Lange 1928: 197ff). Yet it was based on the idea of a special cultural mission of women in modern societies

that determined the goal of the women's movement, formulated in the programme of the ADF which came into effect in 1905: 'to lead the cultural
influence of women to its fullest inner bloom and to its free social effectiveness' (Lange 1908: 121).

The road to the realization of this goal was, however, contested even
among the different currents in the bourgeois spectrum. Helene Lange and
Gertrud Bäumer represented the majority of bourgeois 'moderates', in contrast
to the so-called 'radicals' or 'left-wing' activists like Minna Cauer, Anita
Auspurg or Helene Stöcker, who combined the claim for women's suffrage
with international campaigns for peace and sexual reform. The radicals and
liberals were thus designated because they led the controversies that the turn-
of-the-century women's movement espoused: prostitution, patriarchal matri-
monial law, discrimination against illegitimate motherhood and abortion. One
of the major differences between the radicals and moderates was their different perception of legal issues and their importance in the struggle for emancipation. For the radicals the struggle for rights was not only 'a question of
pace' or of method, as was it sometimes conveyed, but rather, laws represented to them the crucial lever and starting point for their mobilization.
They agreed that the woman question was also a 'cultural issue', but saw it
primarily as a 'legal issue' to be solved politically (Gerhard 1990).

In 1894 the bourgeois spectrum of associations joined in an umbrella
organization, the Bund Deutscher Frauenvereine (BDF; German Alliance of
Women's Associations). It is worth noting that the stimulus for this came from
the outside. After three activists had visited the general assembly of the International Council of Women (ICW) held in Chicago in 1893 on the occasion
of the World's Fair, they came back with the idea to 'strengthen women's
philanthropic organizations through organized co-operation', modelled after
the American National Council. However, the BDF was tainted with a
structural defect from the very beginning: it excluded the female workers'
organizations of the social-democratic party, or rather did not invite them to
the first meeting. This was not only in response to the *Vereinsgesetze*, but it
also strengthened and reflected the class differences that dominated turn-of-
the-century society.

The historical women's movement in Germany has thus been marked by
strong differences of opinion, political struggle and, not least of all, class
distinctions. Without doubt, these clashes hindered what might otherwise
have been a successful coalition politics. Yet, at the same time, these differences exemplify the liveliness and breadth of the movement which also
mirrored a variety of social classes and factions. The three directions of the
German women's movement are briefly characterized by a chronicler as
follows: 'The social democratic women foreground the economic dependence
of women, the bourgeois left (the radicals) fight most of all against legal and
political oppression, and the right (the moderates) experience the spiritual
lack of freedom as the strongest shackle.' 'It hardly merits mention', the author

continues, 'that this comparison only provides a very rough measure of differ-entiation, and that sometimes the roles can be reversed' (Magnus–Hausen 1922: 200). These three currents were paralleled by three federations or umbrella organizations, also on the international level: the charitable and moderate organizations in the Bund Deutscher Frauenvereine, which was a member of the ICW; the separation of the more 'radical' wing, especially the suffrage organizations from 1902 on, in the Verband Fortschrittlicher Frauen-vereine (Federation of Progressive Women's Association), which was a founding member of the International Alliance of Women (IAW) from 1904 on; and the organizations of female labourers, also internationally, which built up a separate organizational structure (women's agitation commissions, confidantes, women's conferences and, from 1910 on, International Women's Days).

Only at the end of the First World War would the three wings of the German women's movement again actively join together in calling on the Reichstag to finally grant women's suffrage. However, only after military defeat and the end of the monarchy, after a new revolution and the declara-tion of the Republic by the 'Council of People's Representatives', would women, in November 1918, be granted the right to vote and in the Weimar Constitution (article 109) in principle be granted equal citizenship rights. Thus, the women's movement achieved a significant aim. The lively agitation sustained by all women's associations assured that the percentage of women elected to parliament in 1919 would be higher than in all elections to follow, even those in the Federal Republic, until 1983. At the same time, the 'basic principle' of equal civil rights continued to allow exceptions, for instance the passage of special provisions forbidding female civil service employees to marry – a regulation often invoked.

Stalemate and the End of the First Women's Movement

A change in political relationships also reshuffled the cards for the women's movement. While radical bourgeois feminists, without mandate or electoral success via party lists, increasingly dedicated themselves to pacifist and inter-national work, and socialist and social-democratic women drowned in party work, the organization of the bourgeois centre proceeded well as the BDF gained members, especially from women's professional associations as well as conservative housewives and agrarian women's groups, which, with the support of the BDF, moved visibly towards the right. Only this part of the women's movement thus managed to establish itself. By the end of the Weimar Repub-lic, it had however become inflexible, even old. The lack of younger members was attributed to generational conflicts by the older women, who did not want to understand that the new generation, the first students as well as those streaming into the new women's professions as employees, rejected the strict leadership style, overorganization and gender separation (considered super-fluous) that marked the older movement. Much too late did activists recognize the danger emanating from the National Socialist movement and its explicit anti-feminism. Nonetheless, the last board of the BDF chaired by Agnes von Zahn-Harnack, following Hitler's seizure of power in 1933, was unwilling to expel the Jewish feminist organization, preferring to dissolve itself rather than succumb to political pressure and join the National Socialist women's organization, the so-called German Women's Front.

The Silence between 1933 and the 1960s

The question arises, why did the break in German women's movement activity last so much longer than the end of National Socialism? Why were the victories and struggles of the earlier century so thoroughly forgotten that more than a generation would have to pass before a new women's movement, seemingly without knowledge of its predecessor, would appear to start from scratch towards the end of the 1960s? Even by international standards, this hiatus in, and loss of history by, the German women's movement and its generational divide stand out. One reason for the silence was the difficulty Germans in the post-war period experienced in confronting their Nazi past at all. Given the Cold War and the division of Germany, another reason was the rejection and denunciation of radical or left-wing positions, so that after 1945 people were equally indifferent both to those individuals the Nazi regime had persecuted and to those who had survived in exile. An additional reason why nothing in the revived women's movement advanced was that in both West and East Germany the constitution guaranteed equality in civil law. In the opinion of some few activists, there was therefore no longer any 'woman question' to be confronted, but only individual women's issues on their way towards reform.

The New Women's Movement

It was to be the new women's movement of the 1960s and 1970s that initiated a profound change in thinking, in many respects comprising a 'new social movement'. It was part of the civil rights and protest movements which in the 1960s opposed a restorative political climate, opposed rearmament and atomic weapons, opposed a conservative authoritarian-oriented politics of amnesia, transforming the West German democracy that had been imposed by the victorious powers into an acquired, living democracy. They thereby fundamentally changed the state and its institutions, and also civil society. The long-term effects of this process are less evident in the accomplishment of specific political aims, and more visible on the socio-cultural level. Here the women's movement played a decisive role. For, despite a similarity in political orientation with the protesting left, and especially the student movement, a separate women's movement became necessary, as repeatedly experienced by women throughout the modern period. The departure of left-wing feminists from the student movement in Western Germany was signposted by a famous 'tomato throwing' incident. Noting that male colleagues refused even to listen to Helke Sander's speech at the SDS Delegates' Assembly in Frankfurt in 1968, the women present created an uproar by throwing tomatoes at their colleagues. Ulrike Meinhof commented on this shortly afterwards in the left-wing magazine *Konkret*: 'Apparently we've got to shoot off whole stock cars full of tomatoes before the comrades get it' (cited in *Frauenjahrbuch* 1975 1: 11).

This experience led to the founding of the 'Crones' Committees' (*Weiberräte*), formed not only by students but by housewives and working women. However, it was the political debate around the issue of abortion reform, enflamed by a self-accusation campaign by prominent and other women in the magazine *Stern* in 1971, that lifted the women's protest out of the academic milieu and gave it to a broader public, signalling a clear conflict with the law. As a result, all over the country consciousness-raising groups were formed, women's centres and bookstores appeared, universities and community colleges initiated courses on women-specific themes, and women's projects launched activities viewed as a countercultural alternative to bureaucratic forms of social work and the health-care system. One of the more important long-term projects was the founding of houses for battered women, not only helping women to achieve self-sufficiency but also making the political claim that hidden violence against women should be made public and rendered impossible.

The background to all this included structural changes as well as the unveiling of social contradictions and gender-specific inequality. Despite the West German Basic Law's guarantee of equality, despite improved opportunities to enter the labour market, and due to achievements in female education and training, expectations and a sense of entitlement among women had also grown, and the sensitivity towards inequalities and limitations in life chances had increased. But the political prescriptions for mastering the assumed private duty to combine work and family were increasingly questioned by women. What Betty Friedan called 'the problem without a name' was now articulated as a societal problem, not as 'the feminine mystique' (Friedan 1963).

In many respects, this new women's protest was distinct from all previous ones: the movement, from the very beginning, was internationally oriented – that is, its launch can be clearly traced to influences from abroad. Of great importance to the feminist movement was the example given by French, Dutch and American women, whose radicalism was transmitted via the media, personal contact and soon-to-be best-selling books and publications. There was a new openness in discussing intimate aspects of sexuality and social taboos, which in this climate of alleged sexual freedom brought about a new diagnosis of gendered power relationships (see for example Millett 1970; Firestone 1970; Schwarzer 1975; Stefan 1975).

Also new was the form that political intervention now took. In contrast to the historical women's movement, the new one founded no associations or organizations, and had no leaders, but was rather composed of a loose network of groups and broader networks, projects and organized meetings which informed the public about specific issues, thereby contributing to the mobilization and spread of the movement. This relaxed structure was at once a strength and a weakness. Just as double-edged was another characteristic of the new women's movement which in West Germany would be defended with particular enthusiasm and dogmatism: the women's movement viewed itself as primarily autonomous. The concept of autonomy was deliberately brought up again and again to distance the new women's movement from the long-lived traditional women's organizations, which in the 1970s had also begun to call for reform. 'Autonomous' meant independence in two senses: self-determination for the individual as well as institutional freedom from established forms of politics. For individual women, self-determination applied to their own bodies but also implied freedom from men's tutelage, and economic independence. Yet even more provocative than this politicization of the private was the claim to autonomy for the movement of women, for the group or collective as a whole, because this represented a distancing from and refusal of all the usual means of engaging in politics: associations, parties and even parliament. It was not until the 1980s that the fronts softened and the abyss was bridged between the established women's organizations (collected under the umbrella of the German Women's Council, the Deutscher Frauenrat) and feminists, as the Greens entered parliament with several feminists and the movement achieved greater diffusion in established women's politics, including a growing influence of women in the parties, in the unions and even in the churches. At the same time, radical feminists called this process adjustment or co-option, signalling the 'end' of the autonomous movement itself. The question has yet to be answered as to whether a period of political autonomy – including coalition-building and intelligent pragmatism – impeded political agency.

Following the 1989 reunification of the two German states the West German women's movement, which stood only for Western experience, looked set to become a historical movement unless it was able to find a new platform and agenda covering the interests of both East and West German women. In 1990, attempts to influence the discussion about a new constitution, including feminists from the East and the West, represented an attempt to join both groups and to communicate women's experiences, anchoring them in the law (*Feministische Studien Extra* 1991). However, the present doldrums are clearly due to the fact that the problems occasioned by the reunification have monopolized all political and economic attention. Once more, as a society consolidates its gains, women's issues are wiped off the political agenda.

Conclusion

Despite all this, I would like to emphasize that the women's movement has achieved a remarkable transformation in gender relations, in women's plans for their lives, in their striving for autonomy and in their chances to realize their options. However, this achievement lies more in the socio-cultural realm than in politics and positions of power. In decisive areas, with regard to the central aims of the women's movement, feminists have not yet succeeded in eliminating structural social and legal discrimination. The abyss between women's self-awareness, their sensitivity towards problems in gender relationships, and the corresponding defensiveness on the part of men is still quite apparent. Conflict between the sexes has thus been sharpened, not defused. Daily life has become increasingly difficult. Thus the motto of the new women's movement, 'the personal is political', identifies the core of the problem, since it questions traditional styles of life and orientation as well as politics in a broader sense. The new definition of what counts as political touches the very foundations of the existing political order because it also challenges the private realm. In my view, the new women's movement has already displaced to a significant degree the boundary between the personal and the political, thereby initiating a transformation in values and society.

If the movement is presently taking time out to take a breath, this break means that women's and gender studies, even if only just established, remain very important bastions of the movement, with academic Women's Studies centres playing a significant role in conserving the legacy and disseminating knowledge of women's history and position in contemporary society. In addition, Women's Studies might prepare the coming generation to tread its own self-determined path into the next women's movement wave, without, however, being dictated to about which direction it might take.

Note

1. Bäumer 1901.

References

Allen, Ann Taylor (1991) *Feminism and Motherhood in Germany, 1800–1914*. New Brunswick, NJ: Rutgers University Press.

Bäumer, Gertrud (1901) 'Die Geschichte der Frauenbewegung in Deutschland', in Helene Lange and Gertrud Bäumer, eds, *Handbuch der Frauenbewegung*. Berlin: Moeser.

Bussemer, Herrad-Ulrike (1985) *Frauenemanzipation und Bildungsbürgertum. Sozialgeschichte der Frauenbewegung in der Reichsgründungszeit*. Weinheim/Basle: Beltz.

Feministische Studien Extra (1991) 'Frauen für eine neue Verfassung'. Weinheim: Beltz.

Firestone, Shulamith (1970) *The Dialectic of Sex*. New York: Morrow.

Frauenjahrbuch (1975) ed. Jahrbuchgruppe des Münchner Frauenzentrums, Münster: Tender-Verlag.

Friedan, Betty (1963) *The Feminine Mystique*. New York: Norton.

Gerhard, Ute (1983) 'Über die Anfänge der deutschen Frauenbewegung um 1848. Frauenpresse, Frauenpolitik und Frauenvereine', in Karin Hausen, ed., *Frauen suchen ihre Geschichte. Historische Studien zum 19. und 20. Jahrhundert*. Munich: Beck, pp. 196–220.

Gerhard, Ute (1990) *'Unerhört'. Die Geschichte der deutschen Frauenbewegung*. Reinbek: Rowohlt.

Gerhard, Ute (1996) 'Atempause: Die aktuelle Bedeutung der Frauenbewegung für eine zivile Gesellschaft', in *Aus Politik und Zeitgeschichte. Beilage zur Wochenzeitung Das Parlament* (B 21–22), pp. 3–14.

Gerhard, Ute, Elisabeth Hannover-Drück and Romina Schmitter, eds (1979) *'Dem Reich der Freiheit werb' ich Bürgerinnen'. Die Frauenzeitung von Louise Otto*. Frankfurt-am-Main: Syndikat.

Hummel-Haasis, Gerlinde, ed. (1982) *'Schwestern zerreißt eure Ketten'. Zeugnisse zur Geschichte der Frauen in der Revolution von 1848/49*. Munich: Deutscher Taschenbuch Verlag.

Lange, Helene (1908) *Die Frauenbewegung in ihren modernen Problemen*. Leipzig: Quelle & Meyer.

Lange, Helene (1928) *Kampfzeiten. Aufsätze und Reden aus vier Jahrzehnten*. Berlin: Herbig.

Lion, Hilde (1926) *Zur Soziologie der Frauenbewegung*. Berlin: Herbig.

Lipp, Carola, ed. (1986) *Schimpfende Weiber und patriotische Jungfrauen. Frauen im Vormärz und in der Revolution von 1848/49*. Moos: Elster.

Magnus-Hausen, Frances (1922) 'Ziel und Weg in der Deutschen Frauenbewegung des XIX. Jahrhunderts', in Paul Wentzke, ed., *Deutscher Staat und deutsche Parteien. Friedrich Meinecke zum 60. Geburtstag dargebracht*. Munich/Berlin: Oldenbourg, pp. 201–26.

Millett, Kate (1970) *Sexual Politics*. New York: Avon/Doubleday.

Otto-Peters, Louise (1890) *Das erste Vierteljahrhundert des Allgemeinen Deutschen Frauenvereins*. Leipzig: Schäfer.

Paletschek, Sylvia (1990) *Frauen und Dissens. Frauen im Deutschkatholizismus und in den freien Gemeinden 1841–1852*. Göttingen: Vandenhoeck & Ruprecht.

Rupp, Leila and Verta Taylor (1990) *Survival in the Doldrums: The American Women's Rights Movements 1945 to the 1960s*. Columbus: Ohio State University Press.

Schwarzer, Alice (1975) *Der 'kleine Unterschied' und seine großen Folgen: Frauen über sich, Beginn einer Befreiung*. Frankfurt-am-Main: Fischer.

Stefan, Verena (1975) *Häutungen*. Munich: Frauenoffensive.

Twellmann, Margrit (1972) *Die deutsche Frauenbewegung. Ihre Anfänge und erste Entwicklung 1843–1889*. Meisenheim: Hain.

Zetkin, Clara (1957) '"Für die Befreiung der Frau!" Rede auf dem Internationalen Frauenkongreß zu Paris' [19 July 1889], in C. Zetkin, *Ausgewählte Reden und Schriften*. Berlin: Dietz, pp. 1–11.

19

The Feminist Movement in Italy

ANDREINA DE CLEMENTI

The Italian feminist movement had established itself during the second half of the nineteenth century, but during the Fascist regime, from the early 1920s to the early 1940s, it was reduced to silence like all the other independent political organizations. Because of this long period of hibernation, along with the peculiar national and international conditions under which the Italian Republic was born in 1945, the feminist historical tradition was recovered only in the 1970s.

Women and the Italian Communist Party

In the period after Italy's liberation from Fascism (25 April 1945), the left-wing parties, and the Italian Communist Party (PCI) in particular, believed that the unified anti-fascist parties that had led the Resistance would be able to meld in the new republican phase. This was a miscalculation because, to put it briefly, the confirmation of the East–West divide and the beginning of the Cold War would impose choices incompatible with such a wide and indiscriminate arc of alliances. The break duly occurred in 1948 when an election campaign of unprecedented bitterness concluded with the landslide victory of the Christian Democrats and the expulsion of the left from government once and for all. It was then that forty years of Christian Democrat power began.

Not even after such a crushing defeat was the PCI willing to give up its strategy of drawing other political forces into its orbit; part of its strategy was to set up a collection of supporting bodies with no formal ties but firmly under control through the loyalty of militants and sympathizers. These bodies were distinguished from the party by the narrowness of their aims, the lesser degree of dedication required of their members, and a political spectrum open to other forms of membership and to those without a party.

These were also the principles of the Unione Donne Italiane (UDI; Union of Italian Women), where socialists, Roman Catholics and laity came together in a hybrid coalition unbalanced by the overwhelming presence of militant communists. As we shall see, independent choices would also become manifest many years later.

The PCI, driven to the wall by their opponents, eager to earn the middle-class respectability denied them, and wanting – as they claimed – to avoid alienating the large numbers of Catholics, lowered a thick curtain of silence over their more secular and modernizing aspirations and imposed a rigid observance of the more antiquated canons of family respectability on militants of both sexes, including the party's chief Palmiro Togliatti. They confined their political battles to public life alone, and passed on this model to satellite organizations. Even operating within these limits, the UDI managed to mark up several undeniable successes, especially in the protection of women workers, who, thanks to the UDI's initiative, were able, for example, to receive an equality of wages that even today has not been achieved in many Western countries. And yet Italian women continued to live as a minority group in a situation of serious inferiority, not unlike that reserved for them by the Fascist regime that had just passed.

Women and the Rule of Catholicism during the 1950s and 1960s

The Italy of the 1950s and 1960s was marked by the pervasive influence of the pontificate of Pius XII, a pope suspected of Nazi sympathies and numbered among the main authors of the electoral defeat of the left. The country was governed by narrow and reactionary legislation: the indissolubility of marriage, state-controlled prostitution, extreme indulgence towards crimes of 'honour', the punishment of abortion as an 'attack on the health of the race' (in the words of the Fascist code still in force), and severely discriminatory treatment in cases of adultery, to list just some of the most humiliating aspects of that legislation. The disqualification of women from the magistrature gives an indication of the esteem in which they were held.

If this was the legal background, the cultural picture was little different. Women moved between the folds of a hostile society, crushed by the weight of numerous duties with no corresponding rights, at the mercy of and dependent on male relations – husbands, fathers, brothers. Not even left-wing women militants – who then boasted an extremely solid and numerically strong organization – escaped these rules, even though many of them had taken an active part in the Resistance. But in the blink of an eye the political parties had eliminated even that memory. And domestic subjection was practised with equal zeal by their male comrades. In addition, the recently acquired right to vote had shown itself to be half a victory: as the women deputies never exceeded a few dozen, in reality women were almost excluded from political participation.

Beneath this inert crust, however, simmered tensions that were not long in revealing themselves. The reopening of international circuits (blocked by Fascism) of exchange, communication and information; the first signs of social well-being and the spread of mass consumption; the leaps forward in literacy and education for girls up to university level; and, lastly, intense internal migration, could only place the existing immobilism in a critical position.

The Rise of Neo-feminism

The typically Italian cleavage between the reacquired dynamism of the production sector, which reached levels defined, without too much exaggeration, as 'miraculous' in the early 1960s, and, on the other hand, a society suffocated by the alliance between two parochial cultures – Christian Democrat and Communist, which in substance were mutually supportive – acted as a detonator for youth protest.

From this collective mobilization neo-feminism arose. The fable of the sorcerer's apprentice was repeated. First the student movement, then the extraparliamentary offshoots that followed, had relegated girls to well-tried subaltern roles, but women very soon learnt their lesson, turning the challengers into the challenged and a mirror image of a male, authoritarian and self-referring universe.

Italian feminism has had an ambiguous relationship with the powerful left-wing parties that have put their stamp on a great part of Italian history, a relationship delicately poised between kinship and conflict. The left wing has often supplied an influential and reassuring cushion, but the anxieties and psychologisms raised by women have made the left-wing parties simultaneously suspicious and mistrustful, fearful of drifting away from the dogma of materialism and class struggle.

For these reasons, in both of its historical phases – that is to say, before and after the Fascist regime – Italian feminism has cultivated a dual agenda: real emancipation in the socialist-communist tradition, and thus dedicated to the position of women in social conflict, and an independence of decision-making hinging on a redefinition of identity and role that cuts across social class. This last has always gained the greatest consensus.

The First and Second Waves of Feminism in Italy

Common to both phases was a radicalism borrowed from the ideological arsenals of the different eras. The first phase of feminism moved in the wake of the alliance between anarchism and the heritage of the Risorgimento[1] in the Mazzini,[2] anti-clerical mould. Its most outstanding exponent was Anna Maria Mozzoni. In the 1960s, however, the second wave of feminism viewed itself mainly in terms of post-Freudian psychoanalysis and Franco-American theoretical feminism. Any discontinuities between the first and second feminisms should therefore be traced to aims and historical conditions far distant from one another. First and foremost, between the nineteenth and twentieth centuries, in an industrially developing country such as Italy, there were numerous ranks of unprotected female workers. The reformist leaders most linked to the Socialist Party, such as Anna Kuliscioff, worked less for general than for specific causes and succeeded in starting the first drafts of protective legislation for women workers. The most prominent struggles, however, were for the right to vote – which Italian women only obtained in 1946 – and for education. In the latter case it was necessary not only to eliminate female illiteracy, which was very much more widespread than male illiteracy, but to gain access for women to secondary and university education as well.

The outbreak of the First World War threw the ranks of Italian feminism into disorder, as it did others; an interventionist-nationalist wing of the movement had already taken shape along the lines of the Socialist divisions, and it followed in the steps of Mussolini, ending by merging into the Fascist ranks. Here Margherita Sarfatti must be mentioned; she was not only the lover and biographer of *il Duce* but also Jewish and one of the figures of major talent with whom Mussolini in his first phase surrounded himself. The cabinet crisis caused by the assassination of the Socialist member of parliament Giacomo Matteotti led to the regime's hurried completion of its dictatorial structure. In 1926 political parties were outlawed and even the moderate Consiglio Nazionale delle Donne Italiane (National Council of Italian Women), founded in 1897, was dissolved. And nothing more was said of feminism.

Spitting on Hegel: The Women's Movement from the 1960s Onwards

The first voices in the 1960s' movement were raised as much outside and against left-wing parties (the Socialists and Communists) as against the extra-parliamentary groupings that had formed during the last phase of the student protest. Several vanguard positions appeared on the horizon: the Milan group DEMAU (Anti-authoritarian demystification), inspired by the philosophy of Herbert Marcuse; then a short time afterwards, also in Milan, Anabasi (Anabasis); and, in Rome, Rivolta femminile (Female Rising), founded by the art historian Carla Lonzi, author of books whose very titles were provocative, such as *Sputiamo su Hegel. La donna vaginale e la donna clitoridea* (We Spit on Hegel: Clitoral and Vaginal Women). The topic of sexual liberation would accompany the movement for a long period of its life.

These standard-bearing groups were immediately conspicuous for their aggressiveness and challenging tone. Their rejection of Marxism led to the vindication of feminine otherness and extremist separatism. But it was the rejection of traditional roles and models, and the discovery of an autogenous feminine identity, founded on self-esteem and recognition of self, that had the disruptive effect that transformed thousands of women into mass-movement militants. The practice of the 'small consciousness-raising group' aimed at these objectives; these groups were strictly separatist, and formed on the basis of sympathies, affinities and personal friendships. Women were seized by an irresistible urge to eradicate signs of dependence, submission and indulgence and they began a journey in search of themselves without retreating before the scars and traumas they carried.

In short, the movement spread. The largest cities (Milan, Rome, Naples and Florence) became political laboratories and significant points of reference for all women who, in the South and in the North, met together in private houses or premises borrowed from more generous organizations, and steeped themselves in discussion, agonizing and pitiless confrontation, and the baring of their souls to each other so as to delve into a lost identity.

Few leaders were acknowledged as having national stature and prestige. Shared anti-individualism caused any attempt to stand out from the others to be viewed with suspicion, and 'collective' was the generic name for the more artificial groupings that followed. They proliferated almost everywhere, free from formal co-ordinating bodies but tuned into the same wavelength.

Italy was at this time experiencing one of the most difficult and disturbing times in the history of the Republic, a period of terrorism which culminated in the assassination of the Christian Democrat leader Aldo Moro (1978). Feminism, too, suffered the depressant effect of this, but did not lose its vitality.

Unlike the movement in the early years of the century, feminism could now avail itself of widespread education and culturalization, which gave it sophisticated analytical tools capable of decoding acquired social roles, driving political parties into the wings and creating a culture of independence – at first separatist, then centred on gender relationships – which competed fully with men and was capable of true epistemological revolutions.

A substantial presence of women intellectuals opposed the dominant culture in its official seats – in universities, research centres, the serious press, television and cinema – both to alleviate denied visibility, suppression of talent or confinement to the margins and lower levels of responsibility; and to deconstruct the dominant culture's professed universalism. It was a period of exciting creative explosion and the appropriation of new arenas. Publishing houses specializing in women's books were founded; women's bookshops opened – piloted by the Milan bookshop of the differentialist group that had grown up around Luisa Muraro; the Centri di Documentazione (Documentation Centres), the largest in Bologna, were created, as was 'Virginia Woolf' in Rome which was conceived as a kind of alternative university. Advice bureaux that specialized in self-help practices were set up, aimed at encouraging women in all situations into a more intimate knowledge of their own bodies and give advice and information on sexual and medical matters. The relationship with one's body was one of the most intoxicating discoveries.

A dust cloud was stirred up, of a myriad legal cases and contestations of established male power in microcosm and macrocosm. Women journalists, teachers, researchers and directors devoted themselves to translating the collectives' ideas into political questions. Combative prostitutes founded their own union to face the dangers of their profession with greater knowledge and be able to protect themselves better.

Such uneven terrain and such an effervescent atmosphere cast the preliminaries for the two most memorable battles: the referenda on divorce (1974) and abortion (1981). In both cases there was an identical starting point. Thanks to the far-distant initiative of meagre bands of courageous women, and after interminable bureaucratic procedures, parliament passed the law on divorce in 1970 with a cross-party vote. The Christian Democrat majority, defeated – though not resigned to defeat – on one of its most jealously guarded territories, the indissolubility of marriage, then promoted a referendum to repeal the law, certain of regaining lost ground. The 'No' campaign was resolutely espoused by a UDI on a collision course with the initially cautious Communist Party and saw women in the front line. In spite of more pessimistic predictions, the final response left the law intact. Some years later attention was focused on the decriminalization of abortion, which put an end to the thousands of deaths caused by recourse to more primitive methods – the alternative choice to the greed of obliging doctors, the so-called 'golden spoons'. The same scenario with the same actors was presented again – a flood of women poured into the streets, raising the flag of femininity and self-determination – and the same result was obtained.

The Achievements of Second-wave Feminism in Italy

What was achieved? Much on the legal plane. Alongside divorce and abortion, there was a new family law that abrogated women's multiple forms of subordination to men, and – the last to be established – a law on sexual violence, which transformed rape from a crime 'against morality' to a crime 'against the person' and made it actionable officially rather than dependent upon the woman involved reporting it. This last result, a harbour for age-old worn-out diatribes, was aided by the mobilization of women parliamentarians beyond party boundaries. It should be added, however, that the most militant feminism had been hostile to any unwarranted interference in women's privacy and to frequently undesirable publicity. In any event, these changes were not true victories, but rather signalled the end of bigoted and punitive laws.

Women and Power from the mid-1990s to the Present

During the centre–left governmental coalitions (1996–2001), more than in the past, women held political office and were in charge of some key ministries such as the Home Office, Health, and Social Affairs, the addition of a new office for Equal Opportunities, whose provenance is still uncertain. But in the most recent centre–right government there is only one woman, who is in charge of Public Education. And at the time of writing Naples is the only large city with a woman mayor. The most painful fact is the extremely poor presence of women in parliament: 9.2 per cent of MPs, a decline after the last elections, which has placed Italy at the bottom of the table within the whole of Europe.

As far as professional visibility and the giving of responsibility goes, almost nothing has changed. None of the large serious newspapers, no large bank, no television network is run by a woman, and no university either, where the excellence of female students and their brilliant results have not been translated into a redress of the gender balance in academic careers: when they do not find doors closed to them, young women students remain confined to the lower echelons. The only innovations seem to be coming from the business world, where an increasing accession of women to the top of small- and medium-sized companies is evident.

There has been little advance in the redefinition of women's roles, the cornerstone of the neo-feminist movement. In the last few decades the family has seen a new period of triumph, but one that has not dented the traditionalism of male–female relationships. The new critical spirit of women, applied to the subject of sexuality as well, has made more sensitive men wary and uneasy and other men more aggressive. Statistics report an increase in rapes, in part the result of a greater tendency to report the crime.

Crucial problems, such as the legal recognition of couples living together and the end of discrimination inflicted on lesbians and homosexuals, have had difficulty in making their presence felt, both because the Vatican has regained its ability to interfere and bargain politically, which had almost disappeared with the last pontificate, and because of the hostility of a pro-fascist, pro-clergy right wing, which gained members during the May 2001 general elections.

Conclusion

Despite such a thin balance sheet, neo-feminism has not been in vain. On the credit side it has irreversibly produced an awareness of a sense of self-esteem and a proud sense of gender, running parallel to a rebellious emphasis on the inequalities of which women see themselves daily victims; the whole has acted as a capillary penetration, even among women least touched by the movement and the most polemical.

The middle-class, cultured sector of the movement has itself marked the stages of reflection and research to follow. From this point of view, progression has been linear. The 1970s' militants in flowered skirts and platform shoes have adopted a more sober style of dress, but have not thrown in the towel. They have founded magazines – *DWF* (Donna, Woman, Femme), *Memoria* (Memory) – and organizations – Società Italiana delle Storiche (Italian Society of Women Historians), Società delle Letterate (Society of Women Scholars in Literature) – published books, held conferences, established university centres, research doctorates and courses on women and gender, in unceasing work that is enriching and updating the panorama of Italian Women's Studies. They have consolidated a large feminine scientific community that has branched out into almost all subjects. And they coexist without too much friction with a fundamentalist wing which would rather see a return to its original militancy.

Interaction with similar movements in other countries has blown hot and cold; the delay that preceded the Italian movement taking off facilitated loans and borrowings from others without suffocating its special characteristics. Among these, I would like to draw attention to an asymmetry that has been little considered: a marked inclination to resist the role of authority, a 'genetic' trait that has remained almost intact until now, progressing in a way similar to that of a karst river, at times subterranean, as in the case of the mobilization on the referenda, at other times coming forcefully to the surface.

Two examples are worth mentioning. First the repeal of the law on sexual violence, mentioned above. In this case even authoritative politicians believed that resorting to the courts was wrong, inasmuch as the law should not regulate situations better left to the free choice of women. However, sexual violence as a crime against the person was affirmed. Second, and notwithstanding the lamented scarcity of women members of parliament, is the still widespread aversion to any policy of positive discrimination, especially the introduction of 'quotas'. Women's arguments against it are identical to those of men: the characterizing of women as a 'protected species'.

This attitude – which, I repeat, is very popular among large numbers of women – has made Italian feminism deaf to and uninvolved in one of the most important debates of the last ten years, which has developed around the theme of 'equality'. In contrast to Italy, this debate has engaged the best intellectual energies from France and the United States.[3] Authors have confronted the problem of a sexed redefinition of democracy, attacked the chief taboos of the French Revolution, and formulated corrective hypotheses, which in part have been taken into account in changes to the French Constitution. All of this has found little resonance in Italy, and up until now there has been a lack of information regarding what is happening elsewhere.

Today, women in their twenties have an aloof attitude towards feminism. They tend to assume the movement has achieved its aims and therefore lost its function. We thus witness a generational gap, the effects of which are difficult to foresee.

Notes

1. 'Risorgimento' is the term for the historical period that prepared the Unification of Italy (1861).

2. Giuseppe Mazzini (1805–1872) was one of the leaders of the Italian Risorgimento, and the founder of the Republican Party.

3. This debate arose around the pamphlet *Au pouvoir, citoyennes: liberté, égalité, parité*, by Françoise Gaspard, Anne Le Gall, Claude Servan-Schreiber (1992). Thereafter, many other opinions were expressed by such scholars as Joan Scott, Etienne Balibar and Naomi Schor.

References

Anon. (1982) 'Gli anni cinquanta' [The Fifties]. *Memoria* 6.

Anon. (1987) 'Il movimento femminista degli anni '70' [The Feminist Movement in the 1970s], *Memoria* 19–20.

Anon. (2001) *Il Novecento delle italiane. Una storia ancora da raccontare* [The Italian Women's Twentieth Century: A Story to Tell]. Rome: Editori Riuniti.

Beccalli, B., ed. (1999) *Donne in quota* [Women and Quotas]. Milano: Feltrinelli.

De Clementi, A. (2001) 'Egalité o parité. Come ripensare la democrazia' [Rethinking Democracy], in A. Arru, ed., *La costruzione dell'identità maschile nell'età moderna e contemporanea* [The construction of Male Identity in this Modern and Contemporary Age]. Rome: Biblink.

De Giorgio, M. (1992) *Le italiane dall'Unità ad oggi. Modelli culturali e comportamenti sociali* [Italian Women from the Unification to Our Times. Cultural Patterns and Social Behaviour]. Rome and Bari: Laterza.

Gaspard, F., A. Le Gall and C. Servan-Schreiber (1992) *Au pouvoir, citoyennes. Liberté, egalité, parité.* Paris: Seuil.

Lonzi, C. (1982) *Sputiamo su Hegel. La donna clitoridea e la donna vaginale* [We Spit on Hegel: Clitoral and Vaginal Women]. Milan: Gemmalibri.

Pieroni Bortolotti, F. (1963) *Alle origini del movimento femminile in Italia* [The Origins of the Female Movement in Italy]. Turin: Einaudi.

Pieroni Bortolotti, F. (1987) *Sul movimento politico delle donne. Scritti inediti* [The Political Movement of Women: Unpublished Writings by A. Buttafuoco]. Rome: Utopia.

20

Three Waves of Feminism in Denmark

DRUDE DAHLERUP

In the year 1909, the oldest Danish feminist organization, the Danish Women's Society (Dansk Kvindesamfund, founded in 1871), published a poster with the following text: 'There is no *universal suffrage* in Denmark, when *women* don't have *political suffrage*.'[1] Today this statement seems self-evident. But the archives of the organization reveal that this poster was published only with some reluctance. This in itself tells us something about what the early feminist movement was up against. The reluctance stemmed from the fact that on 5 June every year, the first free Danish Constitution of 1849 was celebrated for, among other things, having introduced 'universal' suffrage. The fact that all women as well as male servants were excluded was ignored. This can only be explained by the existence of a contemporary hegemonic discourse in which women and servants were not considered citizens. In the construction of liberal democracy this quality belonged only to white men, often combined with property requirements. Thus in Denmark, as in most other countries, feminists had to fight for the recognition of women as individuals, persons and citizens.

The history of the feminist movement indicates that in fact suffrage should be considered one of the most important issues of *recognition* in feminist history.[2] The right to vote was not just a means to an end, but was seen as an act of justice. The many organizations involved in the suffrage campaign did not agree upon what should happen after the vote was won: should women go into politics 'just like men', or should they act as representatives of a new female force in history (Dahlerup 2002)? Everyone was convinced that gaining the vote was extremely important because it would change women's status from dependants to individual citizens. Contrary to what many believed, suffrage was not, however, one of the first feminist demands in the nineteenth century.

The Wave Metaphor

It is common to describe the history of the feminist movement in terms of 'waves'. This metaphor indicates that the feminist movement has lived through ups and downs. Periods of mobilization and lively public discussions have been followed by quieter periods. However, the image of waves rests on what I have called *the continuity thesis* – that is, the idea that it makes sense to speak of one long feminist movement in history (Dahlerup 2001).

In the Nordic countries the continuity of the feminist movement is unquestioned, and considered part of common knowledge. This is due to the fact that, contrary to the case in most other countries, the original feminist organizations that fought for women's access to education, for the legal rights of married women, and later for the suffrage still exist in the Nordic countries. The Danish Women's Society still exists. Its magazine, *Kvinden og Samfundet*, founded in 1885, claims to be the oldest feminist magazine in the world. In Sweden, Fredrika-Bremer-Förbundet started in 1884, and its magazine, *Hertha*, under different titles and published by changing organizations, can be traced back to 1859. The journal of the women's section of the Swedish Social Democratic Party, *Morgonbris*, has been published since 1904. Still active also are the Norwegian *Norsk Kvinnesaksforening*, established in 1884; the *Unionen* in Finland, dating back to 1892; and in Iceland, *Kvénrettindafélag Islands*, which was set up in 1907.

In many other countries in East and Western Europe as well as in the United States and in other parts of the world, the most prominent feminist organizations of the nineteenth century were disbanded after the vote was won. However, recent studies have shown that in many countries other than Nordic ones, some feminist organizations and groups continued their work after the vote was won, and new groups emerged (Rupp and Taylor 1987).

On what grounds do we speak of one feminist movement throughout the last 150 years? Organizational continuity cannot alone sustain the claim of one long historical feminist movement, the Nordic case being the exception. The continuity thesis rather rests on the assumption that we are able to identify a common core for all historical feminist movements. This common element must be found in feminism as an ideology. It is, however, not possible to identify a feminist utopia, common to all feminist movements. Neither can we find one Western feminism or one European feminism (Bryson 1992; Tong 1992; Evans 1995; Dahlerup 1986, 1998; Whelehan 1995). Today it is common to talk about 'feminisms' in the plural, indicating that there are many different types of feminism – which is true. But Marxist feminism, classic liberal feminism, existentialist feminism, modern liberal feminism, modern socialist feminism, and modern radical feminism, not to speak of postmodern feminism, do not share a common dream. Thus feminism should perhaps be defined by the common core of its protest, by what all feminists have been fighting against. Feminism might then be defined as an ideology, the basic goal of which is to fight against male dominance and against the discrimination and degradation of women (Dahlerup 1986: 6).

Along the same lines, and based partly on Judith Evans (1986), Imelda Whelehan states that all feminist positions are 'founded upon the belief that women suffer from systematic social injustices because of their sex and therefore any feminist is, at the very minimum, committed to some form of reappraisal of the position of women in society' (1995: 25). At the core of feminism, then, is the protest against male dominance, a dominance which implies the degradation of women and of what women do. It has been an essential problem for the feminist movement that recognition cannot be taken but only given to you by others. That is why the Danish feminists were so reluctant to publish their poster and thereby challenge the male establishment, which was to give women the vote.

Three Waves of Feminism

The new feminist movement of the 1960s–1980s is usually labelled 'second wave' feminism and seen as the 'new' feminist wave (Schenk 1983; Ryan 1992; Evans 1995). I will, however, argue that three, not just two, waves of feminism can be identified in Denmark. The first was in the last decades of the nineteenth century, and the second before and around World War I. The reason for defining two earlier feminist moments is that, contrary to conventional wisdom, suffrage was not part of the first feminist agenda during the second half of the nineteenth century, neither in Denmark nor in countries like Sweden, Germany, Russia and England. The oppression women encountered simply made this demand too radical. Consequently, the latest wave represents the third wave of Danish feminism. Between these moments, a more persistent and continuous feminist work has constantly taken place.

The First Wave

As it happens, 1871 was the founding year of both the above-mentioned Danish Women's Society and the Social Democratic Party in Denmark, and two often conflicting types of feminism were born: the liberal women's rights feminism and the feminism of working-class women. The active women, mostly middle and upper class, that formed the Danish Women's Society defined their new organization as bipartisan ('party-neutral') and as working for all women. The links to the Liberal Party and the ideas of the great Danish reformer and priest N.F.S. Grundtvig were, however, many. The first issues to be taken up by this new society was married women's legal maturity, women's access to higher education, and unmarried women's right to jobs in the public sector. The urge for recognition as equals to men was very strong.

During the first mobilization of the working class in the 1870s, women's sections were soon established within the Social Democratic Party and within the young trade-union movement, often in conflict with the men that led the movement. This conflict arose because some men in the movement did not like independent women's organizing and took exception to working-class women collaborating with bourgeois women in the feminist movement in campaigns such as the suffrage one. In 1885 a union of unskilled women workers was set up. It became a national union in 1901 under the name of the Union of Women Workers (Kvindeligt Arbejderforbund). This union still exists as an all-female trade union, one of the biggest unions in Denmark today. These women did not ask for women's 'right to work', since working-class women were already overloaded with work. Their demand was for better working conditions, shorter working hours, and women's access to and recognition as full members of the working-class movement, and, eventually, voting rights.

In Denmark and in most other countries, waves of feminism have often coincided with the simultaneous emergence of many other movements. The 1880s in Denmark were such a period of general mobilization, namely of the democratic forces against the conservative establishment. It also became a very lively period in Danish feminist history and several new feminist organizations were formed. One such new organization, the more radical Female Progressive Association (Kvindelig Fremskridtsforening), only accepted women as members, while the Danish Women's Society had well-known male politicians in its leadership. The Female Progressive Association stood between the liberal and working-class movements of that time. But in general, the feminist movement in Denmark, like in most other Western countries, was split between socialist and trade-union women on one side, and the autonomous, largely middle-class-based feminist organizations on the other – a split that became less pronounced after World War II.

The Second Wave

If one starts from the assumption that basically all women share a common destiny, then one's analytical focus on the women's movement is on the differences between various women's organizations. If, however, one takes as one's starting point that women are split by class, ethnicity, age, marital status, and so on, then the focus of one's analysis becomes: When and on what issues are women able to join together in a united front?

The fight for women's suffrage became an issue that created possibly the broadest alliance of women in Danish history. The campaign for suffrage for women developed after the turn of the nineteenth century, and in my definition represents the second wave of Danish feminism. The right to vote in and stand for public local elections had been won already in 1908, but the greatest mobilization took place around the demand for parliamentary ('political') suffrage, which was obtained in 1915. An exceptionally broad coalition of women's organizations supported the campaign, including nurses' organizations, female teachers' associations, the girl scouts, deaconesses, as well as the autonomous feminist organizations. These diverse organizations were able to co-operate with women from the trade unions and the Social Democratic Party to some extent on the issue of parliamentary suffrage. Richard Evans has noted that, in relation to the size of the population, the mobilization for suffrage in Denmark was remarkable (Evans 1977: 80).

Backlash in the Interwar Period?

In Denmark, as in other European countries, the interwar period saw a backlash against feminism. Even though only minor and insignificant fascist or Nazi groups emerged in Denmark, the general atmosphere became hostile to feminism. Married women's right to a job, for example as a teacher, was attacked during this period of high unemployment. I consider this to have been not just a consequence of the general right-wing turn, but also as a reaction to the many reforms that were introduced during the period after women had won the vote. A law on equal pay for men and women working in the public sector was passed in 1919; equal access for women to all positions except in the military and as priests was granted in 1921; and finally a very progressive reform of the marriage law came into force in 1925.

It is a matter of debate, however, whether or not the interwar period with its backlash against feminism should be called a silent period. Many new women's organizations, such as housewives' associations and women's sections within the political parties, were in fact formed in Denmark during this very period. Some courageous women managed to raise the issues of contraception and abortion as part of the political agenda. At the same time, the 1930s saw the beginning of the welfare state, which in its later extensive form became the trademark of Denmark and the other Nordic countries. Recent research has been conducted into the actual role of women's agency in developing Nordic welfare states (Siim 2000).

The progressive legislation of 1919–25 was based on inter-Nordic inspiration. It may have paved the way for what was later labelled 'Nordic exceptionalism'; that is, a society with a relatively high level of gender equality and an extended welfare state (von der Fehr et al. 1998; Bergqvist et al. 1999).

The 1940s and 1950s

Due to the general shortage of supplies, a revaluation of traditional household tasks took place during the period of the German occupation between 1940 and 1945. The election of 1943 was turned into an expression of national unity against the German forces, but the outcome came as a shock to the feminist movement because only two women were elected to the lower chamber. Consequently women's organizations began to press for more women in political life, a pressure that has been quite successful, especially during the last decades. Today women occupy 38 per cent of the seats in the Danish parliament.

It should not be forgotten that most women's organizations did not define themselves as feminist. The 1940s and 1950s in Denmark were the peak for women's organizations in the political parties as well as for the many house-wives' organizations in the countryside and in the cities. Relatively speaking, social divisions have been comparatively weak in Denmark, especially after World War II. It has therefore been possible to bring together most women's organizations in Denmark in one big umbrella association, the Women's Council in Denmark (Dansk Kvinderåd), which celebrated its hundredth birth-day in 1999. This umbrella association has managed to obtain some represen-tation in the official political committee system as the representative of 'woman'. One may conclude that when women's organizations in Denmark have been able to co-operate across dividing lines, they have constituted a relatively strong political force.

Ironically, the moderate women's organizations gradually lost their legiti-macy as representing women when the next wave of feminism emerged in the 1970–1980s. Their strength had ultimately rested on the perception of women as housewives and mothers. That changed with the growing number of (middle-class) women in the labour market. The new feminists revolted against the parliamentary strategy of the 'old' feminists and against women being seen primarily as mothers and housewives.

The Third Wave

The third wave of feminism in Denmark came with the radical and leftist Women's Liberation Movement of the 1970–80s. It was preceded by the so-called Nordic sex-role debate in the 1960s, during which traditional gender roles and the still strong patriarchal biologistic discourse were vehemently challenged.

Inspired by the new Women's Liberation Movement in the USA, the UK and the Netherlands, the new feminist protest began in Denmark in 1970. The Redstocking Movement became the core of the new feminist protest. It was named after the New York Redstockings, indicating that this new femi-nist movement defined itself as part of the New Left. In my study of the Redstocking movement I have concluded that this new feminist protest was not radical *or* left, but both. The usual distinction between radical and socialist feminism of this period may be relevant for individual authors (see Tong 1992; Bryson 1992). But when it comes to the actual movements, their very combination was the essential characteristic. The Danish Redstocking move-ment may thus be defined as a radical and leftist (anti-Soviet) feminism, with the consciousness-raising group as its main organizational base. The movement represented not only a reaction against the moderate feminism of, for example, the Danish Women's Society ('no feminism without socialism') but also a protest against the oppression which women encountered within the New Left itself ('no socialism without feminism').

It seems to be a fact that every new wave of feminist protest starts out from a trenchant critique – not just of male-dominated society, but also of previous and contemporary feminist organizations. In the beginning, the Redstockings were rather unaware of their predecessors. But soon the history of feminism became part of the common knowledge of the new activists through their intensive studies and new interpretations of their feminist foremothers. Interestingly enough, these studies concentrated on the history of their grandmothers' or great grandmothers' generation – women like Clara Zetkin, Alexandra Kollontai, Emma Goldman and other leftist feminists. Feminism in their mothers' generation was of less interest to the young Redstockings.

The Redstocking movement wanted to overturn capitalism as well as patriarchal society, nothing less. Its rhetoric was revolutionary, and the young feminists did not believe that women's liberation was possible within the framework of the present society. But at the same time they engaged in political campaigns around many specific political issues, such as free abortion on demand, better contraceptives, equal pay, opposition to Denmark joining the EEC, crisis centres, longer maternity leave, equal sharing of household tasks, establishing Women's Studies centres and many other issues. In its short history the movement developed through three stages:

1. Period of direct actions (1970–c. 1974).
2. Feminist counterculture (c. 1974–1980).
3. Specialization (1980–c.1985).

Following the many powerful direct actions which made the movement well known during the first period, the movement spread from the biggest cities to towns all over the country. In the second period, a new 'feminist counterculture' developed: women's theatres, women's art galleries, women-only bands, women's films and, not least, a huge 'women's literature' emerged which introduced the feminist message to more women than had been achieved by demos and actions. During the last period, movement activities became increasing specialized: Women's Studies emerged at the universities, a women's Folk High School was established, shelters for battered women and courses for unemployed women were created (Dahlerup 1993). Through these more permanent projects the movement survived, but it also gradually lost its character as a grassroots movement. In the mid-1980s the movement faded away, and the more moderate feminism, which had absorbed some of the Redstocking movement's radical feminist views but not its socialism, again became the dominant feminism in Denmark.

State Feminism

The anti-establishment Redstockings first and foremost directed their activities towards *women, not the state.* Analysis reveals, however, that the radical movement indirectly transmitted strength to the more moderate feminist organizations and to the increasing number of women in parliament. My own study (Dahlerup 1998) shows that even if the two wings of the feminist movement viewed each other with suspicion, the radical, leftist Women's Liberation Movement, which defined itself as anti-establishment, indirectly contributed to the development of a new 'state feminism' – an example of which was the extensive, although not always effective, equal opportunities policy. The Redstockings indirectly gave legitimacy to the more moderate feminists, and together they managed to get many new feminist issues onto the public and the formal political agendas.

Contrary to what happened in many other countries, the more moderate women's rights organizations did not manage to mobilize new women during the third wave in Denmark, nor in the other Nordic countries. A large survey of 1,300 former Redstockings indicated that the new feminist organizers were well-educated younger women in their twenties (Dahlerup 1998: chs 7 and 15). Most Danish women felt that the Redstockings were too radical and provocative, but nevertheless their message was spread to all corners of society. During the third wave, women formed 'women's groups' in the trade unions, at educational institutions, and in the political parties. Every woman and every women's group translated feminist protest according to her/their own needs. Many women would now say: 'I am not a Redstocking, but...' This important 'but' would include claims for equal pay or for equal distribution of household tasks or a demand for equal representation. One of the main successes of the Redstocking movement was that it contributed to important changes in women's individual and collective identity and to a new general discourse in society about what women can, should and will do (Dahlerup 1998).

The Amazing Silence of the 1990s

During the second half of the 1980s, the Redstocking movement and most of the many other new feminist groups gradually disappeared. From a feminist perspective, the 1990s became a quieter period. The official equal opportunities politics continued, but new discourses changed the agenda. Men's groups, demanding equal right to child custody after divorce, raised their voices effectively. The notion that equality between men and women was by now already achieved became increasingly widespread. Compared to the other Nordic countries, and especially to Sweden, the feminist movement in Denmark lost momentum in the 1990s (Bergqvist 2000).

Several factors contributed to this decrease. The general decline of the New Left was an important factor, even if the Women's Liberation Movement in fact lived on somewhat longer than most other parts of the New Left. A neoliberal discourse took over and gradually became the dominant force in the 1990s. This change was not limited to the bourgeois political parties, but also influenced the ideology and the policy of the ruling Social Democratic Party and the trade unions. In this new, more individualistic period the collective strategy of feminism became less popular. However, this individualistic trend was taken up and developed by young feminist scholars, influenced by postmodern thinking, towards the end of the 1990s.

The serious split in Danish society over the European Union has probably also contributed to the decline of the feminist movement. Between 1992 and 2000, four referenda were held in Denmark over EU questions (1992, 1993, 1998 and 2000). In each referendum the population was split almost in half. Importantly, this issue also divided and still divides the feminists, and old allies have become political enemies. This constant and unbearable split over the EU has no doubt contributed not only to the decline of the feminist movement but also to the present problems of the formerly so powerful Social Democratic Party in terms of reduced voter support and many internal divisions. Political energy has been concentrated on EU questions.

Nevertheless, inspired by the new feminist voices in Sweden and Norway, young Danish women started a new feminist debate around the turn of this century. Whether this will be restricted to a media debate or in fact lead to new feminist mobilizations remains to be seen.

Notes

1. 'Political suffrage' was the term for the right to vote in parliamentary elections. Danish women had won the right to vote in local elections in 1908 (Dahlerup 1978).

2. In fact, the urge for recognition is nothing new, but a core element of all historical feminist claims. I share Nancy Fraser's critique of the present idea of a general move from redistribution (economic distribution) towards recognition (cultural approval and political rights), but not just for political reasons. The new distinction between recognition and redistribution misses the point that even economic demands, like the claim for equal pay, always involve a symbolic claim for equal recognition.

References

Bergqvist, Christina et al. (1999) *Equal Democracies? Gender and Politics in the Nordic Countries*. Oslo: Scandinavian University Press.

Bryson, Valerie (1992) *Feminist Political Theory*. London: Macmillan.

Dahlerup, Drude (1978) 'Women's Entry into Politics: The Experience of the Danish Local and General Elections 1908–20', *Scandinavian Political Studies*, vol. 1, nos 2–3, pp. 139–62.

Dahlerup, Drude (1986) *The New Women's Movement: Feminism and Political Power in Europe and the USA*. London: Sage.

Dahlerup, Drude (1993) 'From Movement Protest to State Feminism: The Women's Liberation Movement and Unemployment Policy in Denmark', *Nora*, vol. 1, no. 1, pp. 4–20.

Dahlerup, Drude (1998) *Rødstrømperne. Den danske Rødstrømpebevægelses udvikling, nytænkning og gennemslag 1970–85* [The Redstockings: The Development, New Thinking and Impact of the Danish Redstocking Movement 1970–85], 2 vols. Oslo: Gyldendal.

Dahlerup, Drude (2002) 'Continuity and Waves in the Feminist Movement – A Challenge to Social Movement Theory', in Hilda Römer Christensen, Beatrice Halsaa and Aino Saarinen, eds, *Women's Movements: Cross-national and Global Perspectives at the Turn of the Twenty-first Century*. Odense: Odense University Press.

von der Fehr, Drude, et al. (1998) *Is There a Nordic Feminism?* London: UCL Press.

Evans, Judith (1995) *Feminist Theory Today*. London: Sage.

Evans, Richard (1977) *The Feminists*. London: Croom Helm.

Rupp, Leila and Taylor, Verta (1987) *Survival in the Doldrums: The American Women's Rights Movement 1945 to the 1960s*. Oxford: Oxford University Press.

Ryan, Barbara (1992) *Feminism and the Women's Movement*. London: Routledge.

Schenk, Herrad (1983) *Die feministische Herausforderung*. Berlin: C.H. Beck.

Siim, Birte (2000) *Gender and Citizenship: Politics and Agency in France, Britain and Denmark*. Cambridge: Cambridge University Press.

Tong, Rosemarie (1992) *Feminist Thought*. London: Routledge.

Whelehan, Imelda (1995) *Modern Feminist Thought*. Edinburgh: Edinburgh University Press.

21

The History of the Women's Movement in Norway

BEATRICE HALSAA

The Norwegian women's movement is multifarious, with varying degrees of mobilization, strategies and concerns. As women struggle to cope with the movement's tensions and ambiguities, its profile reflects the shifting, inconsistent and sometimes conflicting demands of different groups of women. The history of the Norwegian women's movement has two particularly prominent waves, with crests during the 1880s and 1970s. Both decades were periods of unusual political turmoil, during which the radicalization of the political left was conducive to women's demands. Other features added to a favourable context: Norwegian society has, for example, been small and homogeneous, almost without nobility or an upper class. The liberal constitution of 1814, ensuring independence from Denmark, cherished a relatively open political system. Numerous voluntary associations paved the way for women's organizations. Political conflicts have tended to be handled peacefully, even dramatic ones such as the introduction of parliamentary democracy in 1884 and the end of the Swedish-Norwegian Union in 1905. The Lutheran Protestant state Church generally allows for more liberal attitudes than the Catholic Church, dominant in certain other countries, and systematic attempts to construct a welfare state have benefited women.

The latter half of the nineteenth century was a period of transition from an agricultural to an industrial society, with enormous structural changes. Political and cultural conflicts came to a head during the 1880s, when the first women's rights organizations were established to promote women's civil, social and political rights: the Norwegian Women's Rights Association (NWRA), established in 1884 and still existing today; and the Women's Suffrage Association, set up in 1885. Women working in service as maids started to organize in 1886, factory workers soon followed suit, and women's trade unions affiliated to the Women's Union in the Social Democratic Party in 1901.

The most prominent issues of the first wave of feminism in Norway – sexual morality, suffrage, education and work – differed according to class and civil status. Unmarried women from the middle class gradually acquired legal majority (the right to trade) from 1845, and then demanded education in order to have decent work and an income. The university was opened to women in 1884, the right to apply to most offices in 1912. Married women from the middle class also challenged the narrow definitions of femininity of which they were the objects, and described marriage as a kind of prostitution. Working-class women had to cope with long working hours, low salaries and insupportable living conditions. Many were forced into prostitution, and the spreading of sexually transmitted diseases represented serious problems independent of class. The double standard of sexual morality among bourgeois men was exposed in a heated Scandinavian debate. A ban on public brothels as well as an end to the humiliating health inspections of prostitutes were effectively implemented from 1887 (Nagel 1995). Subsequent to men's universal suffrage in 1898, women's political rights were gradually extended. Norway was the fourth country to grant women universal franchise in 1913. A specific event facilitated the process: in 1905 almost half a million women signed a petition in favour of Norwegian independence from Sweden, concurrently protesting their exclusion from the referendum of the same year.

Camilla Collett (1813–95) is usually regarded as 'the mother' of the Norwegian women's movement, sharply criticizing women's estate in love and marriage in her writings. Aasta Hansteen (1824–1908) is well known as a harsh feminist, unbendingly exhorting the church even though she was a Christian herself. Gina Krogh (1847–1916) had an exceptional talent for organizing. She was the initiator of the NWRA, published its magazine for many years, and was a stubborn supporter of universal suffrage. Like Collett and Hansteen she was well informed about feminism internationally. Fredrikke Marie Qvam (1843–1938) was a shrewd leader of the Women's National Suffrage Association (1898). Katti Anker Møller (1868–1945) advocated women's social rights and was a leading figure of the labour women's movement. Thanks to her efforts children attained equal rights in 1915, irrespective of their parents' civil status. She also made abortion a public issue, declaring: 'We love motherhood and wish it the best, but in full liberty and under our own responsibility.' In 1924, Møller started the first Health Centre for Mothers, providing information about contraception and other reproductive issues. Marie Lous Mohr (1892–1973) was a prominent peace activist, for many years the leader of the Women's International League for Peace and Freedom (WILPF) in Norway (Vogt et al. 1985; Lønnå 1996).

The first-wave women were able to co-operate across class divisions on many issues but split on some, such as the issue of special protection for working women. Protection was not favoured by most women's rights activists, who argued principally against such protection, while working-class women tended to favour them. The equal-rights protagonists won the dispute. In fact, Norway and Denmark were the only states in Europe not to introduce special protection for women (Hageman 1990).

During the 1920s class conflicts were prominent. Working-class women formed the Federation of Housewives' Societies, mostly to support their men. Women's rights issues were not pronounced. Yet liberal reforms in the marriage law were passed in 1918 and 1927, a result of the Scandinavian Family Commission. During the 1930s, nationwide attacks on married women's rights to paid work spurred anger among women across the class divide and a radical women's movement formed. Margarete Bonnevie (1884–1970) was able to revitalise the NWRA, and her books contributed to the women's rights revival. The attacks on married women's rights to paid work were defeated by the end of the decade.

1940–45 was a dark chapter in Norwegian history. The German Nazis successfully invaded Norway in 1940, leaving the political establishment in shock and the people deeply bewildered. Little by little a resistance movement was set up, although based on a traditional gender structure (Halvorsen 1985). Women mostly played key roles as couriers, distributors and assistants of the illegal press, and were involved in helping people needing to escape from the Nazis. When the Nazis shut down political organizations or 'gave' them a Nazi leadership, the reactions were spontaneous: dissolution. Women continued to work underground, however, often effectively resisting the new regime. For instance, the Nazi decision to establish an obligatory youth service in 1942 was stopped by a clandestine campaign initiated by Helga Stene, in which 200,000–300,000 letters of protests were presented to the power holders (Wiig 1984).

Before 1940, there had been almost no support for the fascists, if measured by electoral statistics, and few women had been members of the Nazi party Nasjonal Samling (NS) before the war. By the end of the war, however, women accounted for one-third of the membership. This was partly because men had listed their family members, but also because of the NS's Women's Organization. Leading figures like Øyvor Hansen and Olga Bjoner had been able to attract 'race-conscious, self-sacrificing and patriotic' women. However, Norwegian women with German soldiers as lovers or husbands were treated very harshly when the war ended. Compared to the war trials generally, pursued according to legal regulations, they were left to the 'justice of the street', deeply humiliated in public and even subsequently deprived of their Norwegian citizenship (Wiig 1984; Lønnå 1996).

After the war, there was a fresh and optimistic reconstruction period, also concerning women's issues. Norsk Kvinneforbund (The Norwegian Women's Association), affiliated with the Women's International Democratic Federation, was established in 1948, with Mimi Sverdrup Lunden as a prominent figure. A new feminist journal was published, *Kvinner og Tiden* (1945–55). As the post-war spirit of community evaporated, and the invasion of Czechoslovakia in 1948 allowed for anti-communist attitudes to spread, the feminist journal suffered: 'We were born during the warm peace. The cold war killed us', the editors wrote.

During the 1950s, the housewife's decade, various ideological mechanisms reminded women of their 'proper place'. In spite of this, women's rights protagonists like Eva Kolstad were able to voice their concern (Kolstad was appointed as the first Gender Equality *Ombud* in 1979). The 1950s are called 'the decade of the build-up' because of the dawning critique of 'women's place'. A lecture by Åse Gruda Skard for NWRA in 1953, in which she demanded a reorganization of the family and focused on men's roles, was very influential. Traditional sex roles were ironically exposed in movies, and a Swedish production of Ibsen's play *A Doll's House*, in which Nora decides never to leave her children, called forth a heated media debate. Most important, however, was the emerging and radical Nordic sex-role debate, in which social scientists like Harriet Holter insisted on the social construction of gender. A shift in perspectives from 'women's issues' to a more relational approach, including men's share of family work, gradually took place.[1] But even the 1950s saw some material victories: the principle of equal pay was adopted in 1958, and a new taxation system for married couples weakened the male breadwinner system.

The transition from an industrial to a postindustrial society in the last half of the twentieth century was accelerated by the discovery of vast oil reserves in the North Sea in the late 1960s. The expected economic growth was dependent upon increasing labour, and married women were mobilized. This was also a period of reforms in higher education, during which thousands of women enrolled, often encouraged by their housewife mothers. Public student loans and a gender-equality rhetoric stimulated by the sex-roles debate also contributed to the realization of women's demands for economic independence. A combination of push and pull factors explains this 'silent revolution', during which married women, even mothers of young children, entered the labour market and changed society.

Two early signs of a new wave of feminism are worth mentioning. The first of these was a nationwide, cross-party campaign initiated by Birgit Wiig and the NWRA in 1967 to increase the representation of women in politics. This campaign made a significant impact, and was the beginning of regular election campaigns. Today, the proportion of women in most political institutions is well above the critical mass (30 per cent). Berit Ås's name is strongly linked to women in politics, as well as to a broad range of feminist issues from the 1970s onward: the women's anti-EEC campaign, the women's peace movement, and feminist research (Wiig 1984; Bergqvist et al. 2000). The second sign of a new wave of feminism was the Norwegian Breastfeeding Mother's Support Group, set up by Elisabet Helsing in 1968 to stop the decreasing inclination of women to breastfeed. The network of mother-to-mother support groups established then is still active, and has contributed to a radical change in the discourse on breastfeeding, in particular the issue of breastfeeding in public.

These examples illustrate shifts in the women's movement to a prouder and louder way of addressing women's problems and to a critique of the public gender equality discourse. The demand for improved conditions for women on the basis of their difference, for women's culture and women's bodies, never resulted in an extremist or essentialist celebration of femininity as it did elsewhere. In opposition to gender equality, the women's movement demanded liberation, while at the same time preserving a pragmatic orientation towards the state. Instead of turning its back on traditional political institutions, the new wave in Norway established separate institutions and integrated into old ones simultaneously. Norwegian feminism – for better and worse – developed through the concerted efforts by women in the autonomous movement, in politics, and in bureaucracy.

The 1970s saw an explosive growth in groups, networks and organizations expressing a new acceptance of feminist ideas. The new wave was part of a general radicalization in Norway, influenced by social movements abroad and some distinct Norwegian features: the referendum on membership of the European Economic Union in 1972 effected a mass mobilization of protests against the political establishment that advocated membership. As the protesters 'won', the feeling of optimism among the radical left, including the women's movement, was almost euphoric. During the same years splits among the political left, polarization and the forming of a Marxist Leninist Party, AKP-ml, further destabilized the political system. The social democrats, having lost their absolute majority during the 1960s, were desperate to attract new voters, and listened seriously to the articulation of radical feminist demands. This was possible due to Norway's remarkable tradition of peaceful integration of new political groups into the political system. The tradition of pragmatic and extensive negotiations between opposing groups was there to be applied to negotiations with the new feminists.

The feminist movement in the 1970s, however, was characterized by heated ideological disputes concerning the origin of women's oppression and how to oppose it. The new wave of activism gave rise to new organizations like the radical-feminist New Feminists (1970; not existing today) and the socialist/ Marxist/Leninist Kvinnefronten (1972–), but also embittered the movement and exposed the activists to wear and tear (Haukaa 1982). Feminists disagreed on the proposal for a Gender Equality Act, outlined in 1974. The NWRA defended pragmatic legal reforms stressing equality, whereas the new organizations wanted a ban on discrimination against women as well as preferential treatment. The general clause of the final Act (1978) was a compromise with respect to preferential treatment; the demand by many feminist organizations for more effective equal pay regulations was dismissed (Lønnå 1996).

On a more practical level women's issues were less class-divided than during the previous wave, partly because of effective social-democratic redistributive policies, and partly because of structural changes. The housewife ideology gave way to new gender-equality ideals, and the transition from one-income to two-income families generated problems. Women addressed their problems by demanding child-care facilities, a six-hour working day, equal pay, and reproductive rights. The arrival of the contraceptive pill contributed to the feeling of a sexual revolution during this period, in which women proudly broke the silence previously surrounding their sexuality, be it hetero- or homo-. 'The right to control one's own body' was a paramount issue (van der Ros 1994). The existing 'class law' was considered humiliating because women had to argue their case in front of a commission of physicians. Simultaneously, better-off women went abroad to have their abortion. Despite a vigorous counter-movement, abortion on demand was introduced in 1978. As for child-care facilities, the Norwegian government lagged behind Denmark and Sweden (Leira 1989). Thus, women had to invent private and individual solutions, resulting in extended part-time employment and a black market for child care. The demand for a six-hour day was never met, but during the 1990s the government introduced a reform to address the 'time squeeze' experienced among working parents: twelve months' parental leave, with 80 per cent of salary and effective pressure on fathers to play their part.

In spite of ideological disputes, women also joined forces to campaign, as was the case during the ultimately victorious Women's Campaign against Norwegian Membership of the EEC and the campaign for abortion on demand. Unni Rustad's lectures on the sex industry provoked debate, and the Campaign Against Pornography and Prostitution mobilized across party lines. Inspired by the International Tribunal on Violence against Women in Brussels, a helpline for raped and battered women was set up in Oslo in 1977, and domestic violence was soon considered an urgent issue. The Lesbian Movement was established in 1975, and a milestone in the struggle for gay and lesbian rights was reached in 1993 when the formal right to 'marry' (formally: partnership) was obtained.

The crest of the second wave was soon to come, expressed for instance in the overwhelming demand for the three new feminist journals *Sirene* (1973–83), *Kjerringråd* (1975–86) and *Kvinnefront* (later *Kvinnejournalen*, 1975–). Three major struggles came to an end: the EEC controversy, abortion and the Gender Equality Act. The discourse changed, and the movement was fragmented during the 1980s. A number of new issues emerged, and immigrant women began to voice their interests, disclosing the development of a less homogenous society. Today, the MiRA Resource Centre for Black, Immigrant and Refugee Women reflects a dramatic change in the ethnic composition of Norway.

One issue dominated the movement during the 1980s, triggered by NATO's new atomic strategy. A Nordic Women's Peace Movement was born in 1980, with Eva Nordland among the key leaders. Half a million protesters gathered ahead of the UN Women's Conference in Copenhagen in the same

year, and the movement arranged several international peace marches, mobilizing many thousands until Gorbachev and Reagan signed the Intermediate
Nuclear Force Treaty in 1987. The women's peace movement appealed to
women as mothers and grandmothers and may not have challenged the gender
system as radically as did the women's movement during the 1970s. It was
nevertheless a powerful political force (Skjønsberg 1998). Together with WILPF,
the Grandmothers against Atomic War, Grandmothers at Stortings Plaza still
keep the peace issues alive.

During the 1990s problems relating to the sexualization of women's bodies
became prominent. Norway had been without red light districts, but now
brothels were established in cities, soft porn spread more openly, and women's
bodies were strategically exploited in the advertising industry. Kvinnefronten
was deeply involved in these issues, but split in 1991 when Ottar was established. Ottar has taken a more restrictive position concerning brothels and
pornography, and a more activist orientation. International events also mat-
tered: the disintegration of the Soviet empire and the dominant discourse of
economic liberalism facilitated both trafficking in women and the exploitation
of women as cheap labour. In order to address the North–South and East–
West problematics more effectively, a new umbrella organization was established: Forum for Women and Development (FOKUS).

A growing interest in feminism has emerged at the turn of the twenty-first
century. Inspired by the Swedish book *Fittstim*, young Norwegian feminists
have triggered off a chain of events through their thought-provoking publications. It is too early, however, to know whether or not we are facing another
major wave of feminist activism.

It is difficult to differentiate the effects of the movement from the effects
of gender-equality policies and structural changes. Nevertheless, certain outcomes are beyond dispute. One is the new ways of thinking and 'doing
gender', including the exploration of men as fathers. Another concerns women's
access to new positions and institutions (political, religious etc.), as well as the
forming of new institutions (like women's shelters, election campaigns and
Women's Studies). Furthermore, new individual and collective rights have
been introduced, like abortion on demand and parental leave. A number of
social problems still exist, however, mainly related to work–family problematics
and sexual violence. Unequal pay, a gender-segregated labour market, lack of
child-care facilities, and tight schedules remain unsolved issues. Anorexia and
lung cancer are among new gender-related diseases;[2] there are increasing inequalities between women as welfare cutbacks hit certain groups hard.

The women's movement and Women's Studies grew out of the same social
situation in the early 1970s in Norway. They were expressions of similar
forms of feminist protest, with *liberation* and *visibility* as joint aims. For instance, when Women's Law was established at the University of Oslo in 1974
by Tove Stang Dahl and several other women, the purpose was to address
problems they had discovered through their activist Free Legal Service for

Women. Their first book was a sharp critique of the proposed Gender Equality Act, and had a serious impact (Dahl et al. 1975). On an institutional level one could say that the movement articulated political problems and mobilized for political action, whereas Women's Studies elaborated ways of understanding and documenting facts. On a personal level, feminists handled the activist and intellectual roles simultaneously, influenced by the traditions of their various fields of study.

Women's Studies had a hard time trying to integrate the disciplines and transform curricula. Few scholars were able to get permanent positions in universities and regional colleges. Women's research was more welcomed by the media, the state and the general public than by academic institutions. The state was apt to fund research because female politicians and femocrats alike needed feminist research to underpin gender-equality policies. There was a kind of mutual dependency between Women's Studies and the state, eased by the state-oriented women's movement and the woman-friendly welfare state (Hernes 1987).

Gradually processes of differentiation between the movement and women's research took place, on a personal as well as an institutional level. Theoretical perspectives and concepts developed in somewhat different directions, and the connections between academic knowledge and social change became less obvious. Women's Studies' relations to the state and the academy became more prominent. On the one hand, Women's Studies developed with its own dynamics, inspired and co-ordinated by the Secretariat for Women's Studies in the Social Sciences set up in the Research Council in 1977 (in 1982 it expanded to all fields). For instance, the original newsletter *News about Women's Research* is now a full-blown academic journal. Nevertheless, the construction of feminist knowledge in the academy was inspired by the same general ideas as the movement. This was evident in the rhetoric as well as manifest in the collective, co-operative nationwide research models, such as the project Women's Collectivities headed by the grand old lady of Norwegian Women's Studies, Harriet Holter, and in the book series *Women's Living Conditions and Life Course*, edited by Helga Hernes.[3] The movement declined, however, during the same years as Women's Studies gained strength and legitimacy. Feminist scholars gradually prioritized activism in the academy to grassroots activism in society at large.

External processes also influenced the relationship between the movement and Women's Studies. The movement was not represented on the board of the Secretariat whereas the Ministry was represented, which obviously weakened the ties. In addition a number of applied research programmes were initiated by the government during the 1980s (New Technology and Women's Employment, Research for Gender Equality, Gender and the Fisheries, Gender and Agriculture, The Battering of Women). Even though the resulting knowledge was utilized by the women's movement, the programmes also underlined the growing (financial) importance of the state compared to the movement. The relationship between Women's Studies and the state, however, was not without strains and conflicts.

During the 1990s the tensions came to a climax when the government tried in vain to unite the Secretariat and the Gender Equality Council.[4] Feminist scholars strongly protested what they interpreted as a new way of directing their research, and turned to the academy as their ally in defence of autonomy. This shift towards the academy reflects an ongoing process of institutionalization: since the mid-1980s, centres for Women's Studies have been established at universities and colleges, and Women's Studies curricula introduced on a larger scale. In addition, Women's Studies' long-running efforts to improve the conditions for basic feminist research have finally been acknowledged through programmes for foundational feminist research in social sciences, the humanities and medicine. At the same time, the influence of postmodernist theories and metatheoretical discussions did not bring the movement and Women's Studies closer. Modern feminist theories are not seen as immediately relevant to many grassroots activists, and questions of who are actually producers and users of relevant feminist knowledge are more complicated than they were in the 1970s. Sometimes grassroots activists express feelings of alienation with respect to Women's Studies, and envy its resources.

Then there is the aspect of generation. Being socialized in Women's Studies before, during or after the highly politicized 1970s makes a difference (Holst 2000). The second generation of feminist scholars has had to cope with a more or less established canon, including presuppositions of male dominance and female subordination. Norwegian women's increasing integration into politics, higher education and paid work, along with new parental roles, are only some of the fundamental social changes that now have to be considered in feminist theories of gender and power. This is reflected in the younger generation's efforts to form its own platform, symbolized in the contested name of this field of studies. For example, Women's Studies is now generally replaced in Norway by Women and Gender Studies, in order to reflect gender as a relational category and to recognize the institutionalization of Critical Studies on Men without losing the feminist ambition.

Generally speaking, Women's Studies has continually to concern itself with a triangle of dynamic relations: the women's movement, the state, and the academy. While the women's movement seemed to play the most important role during the 1970s, the state was more central during the 1980s, and now the academy is in first place. The lack of institutionalized arenas for mutual discussions with the movement is detrimental. Nevertheless, students still associate Women's Studies with politics and feminism, with 'the angry women' of the 1970s. These connections are expressed, for example, in the fact that Women's Studies also celebrates International Women's Day on 8 March, but the ties vary according to the discipline. Women's Studies also advocates the importance of transforming academic institutions, and their commitment to transmit feminist knowledge reflect their continued ties to the movement.

Notes

1. The Norwegian word *kjønn* means both sex and gender.
2. Ministry of Health and Social Affairs 1999: 13.
3. The book series, the major outcome of the first decade of Women's Studies, published seventeen books, some of them in English, including *Kvinner i fellesskap* [Women in Community] from Holter's project.
4. Arbeidsgruppe, *Om reorganisering av Likestillingsrådet, herunder en sammenslåing av Likestillingsrådets sekretariat og Sekretariat for kvinneforskning* [Reorganization of the Gender Equality Council and Secretariat for Women's Research]. Oslo: Barne- og familiedepartementet, 1996.

References

Bergqvist, Christina et al. (2000) *Equal Democracies? Gender and Politics in the Nordic Countries*. Oslo, Stockholm: Scandinavian University Press/Nordic Council of Ministers.

Dahl, Tove Stang, Kjersti Graver, Anne Hellum and Anne Robberstad (1975) *Juss og juks* [Law and Deceit]. Oslo: Pax.

Hagemann, Gro (1990) 'Forskjellighetens dilemma' [The Dilemma of Difference], *Historisk tidsskrift* 2.

Halvorsen, Terje (1985) 'Kvinnene i norsk motstandsbevegelse 1940–1945' [Women in the Norwegian Resistance Movement 1940–45], *New Women's Research* 3.

Haukaa, Runa (1982) *Bak slagordene. Den nye kvinnebevegelsen i Norge* [Behind the Slogans: The New Women's Movement in Norway]. Oslo: Pax.

Hernes, Helga M. (1987) *Welfare State and Woman Power: Essays in State Feminism*. Oslo: Norwegian University Press.

Holst, Cathrine (2000) 'Sosiologi, politikk og kvinnelighet. Norsk kvinne- og kjønnsforskning etter 1970. Generasjoner, identiteter og diskurser' [Sociology, Politics and Femininity: Norwegian Women's and Gender Research after 1970]. Bergen: Sosiologisk Institutt, Universitetet i Bergen.

Lønnå, Elisabeth (1996) *Stolthet og kvinnekamp. Norsk kvinnesaksforenings historie fra 1913* [Pride and Women's Struggle: The Norwegian Women's Rights Association from 1913]. Oslo: Gyldendal.

Ministry of Health and Social Affairs (1999) Executive summary of NOU 1999, no. 13, *Women's Health in Norway.*

Nagel, Anne-Hilde (1995) 'Politiseringen av kjønn: Et historisk perspektiv?' [The Politication of Gender: A Historical Perspective?], in Nina C. Raaum, ed., *Kjønn og politikk*. Oslo: TANO.

Skjønsberg, Else (1998) *Kvinnenes fredsbevegelse på åttitallet* [The Women's Peace Movement in the 1980s]. Oslo: Prosus.

van der Ros, Janneke (1994) 'The State and Women: A Troubled Relationship in Norway', in Barbara J. Nelson and Najma Chowdury, eds, *Women and Politics Worldwide*. New Haven: Yale University Press.

Vogt, Kari, Lie Sissel, Karin Gundersen and Jorunn Bjørgum (1985) *Kvinnenes kulturhistorie* [The Cultural History of Women], 3 vols. Oslo: Universitetsforlaget.

Wiig, Birgit (1984) *Kvinner selv* [Women Themselves]. Oslo: Cappelen.

22

The History of the Hungarian Women's Movement

ANDREA PETÖ

Political scientists often use the symbol of a red carpet for communism, covering a whole society and masking it as a homogeneous entity. The women's NGOs in communist Hungary were not visible in civil society before 1989. After the collapse of communism the red carpet was taken up and – surprise, surprise – underneath it was precisely what had been there prior to communism's advent. Very few changes had occurred, so far as the structure of civil society was concerned, in comparison to the situation immediately after the First World War and, indeed, the Second World War.

The Origins of the Hungarian Women's Movement

Women were completely excluded from party politics in Hungary until the acceptance of the first partial suffrage in 1918. It would be illusory to talk of any kind of direct parliamentary political pressure exercised by women until universal suffrage in 1945 (Petö 1997: 153–61). In the pre-suffrage period women exercised their political power through their male partners, fathers, or husbands (Balogh and Nagy 2000).

The first group of women's organizations in Hungary preceded the period of reform in the early nineteenth century – that is, it was connected to the upper strata of aristocratic women. The charitable organizations or women's clubs they started served as an example to the lower strata of society, setting the norm of activism as being associated with social issues. The aims of the charitable societies were drafted within a 'maternal frame', stressing women's maternal, family-preserving role. At the same time the women's organizations operated within a 'maternal frame' connecting their aims with the social welfare of the nation, interpreting the nation as one great family. The link between the maternal frame and the national frame thus established ensured that women's societies found a favourable reception in the strata of society which had a social voice and standing. There was a simultaneous rise in religious women's organizations. Their aim was also formulated within the 'maternal frame', but linked with a religious missionary purpose.

By the end of the nineteenth century participation in women's organizations became a prestigious activity in the upper strata of Hungarian society. This facilitated the emergence of the so-called revolutionary women's organizations: trade unions, social democrats who accepted female members within their masculine organizations but within an 'equality frame'. With the organization of Female Civil Servants (Nőtisztviselők) and then the Feminist Association (Feminista Egyesület), intellectual middle-class women's groups were established which until World War I expressed their demands alongside Hungarian progression, with the intellectual avant-garde movements of turn-of-the-century Hungary (Szapor 1984; Zimmermann 1997). The aim of the feminist women was to eliminate the laws discriminating against women in education, employment and law. But their main focus was the struggle for female suffrage. With the feminization of certain professions, demands for 'equality for difference' were made and the female representatives of the various professions formed women's organizations.

The history of female suffrage in Hungary after World War I is itself an example of how demands for female emancipation within an 'equality frame' manifest themselves also in part in the 'national frame'. The period brought changes on many fronts within women's organizations. Following a process of liberalization (from 1895 women were admitted to selected branches of higher education; in 1918 women were given a selective right to vote, etc.), 'the women's question' was discovered by national conservatism because selected women were given the right to vote. Restricted female suffrage meant that female MPs entered politics and parliament only in 1920. But Hungarian public discourse was dominated by the demand for the revision of the country's borders, which had been redrawn, with the country drastically reduced in area and population, by the Treaty of Trianon in 1920. The organization of women within the 'national frame' became the only acceptable public discourse because of defeat in the war; hence the 'maternal frame' could only attempt to realize its programme indirectly, as it were. Nevertheless, the revisionist struggle brought about the first women's mass movement, the 'maternal frame' of which made it popular within the national frame.

The 'revolutionary' organizations survived this period, but their membership decreased and they became invisible in public discourse. These 'submerged networks' were typical for the activities of both the communist and feminist organizations after 1919, following the two revolutions in Hungary. Many formerly great and influential organizations became small and unimportant. Their memberships comprised only the chosen few; this went hand in hand with the centralized organizational structure which they adopted as necessary for their survival. The activities of the 'submerged networks' were primarily restricted to cultural events.

By 1914 the majority of the female population of Hungary was participating in different types of women's movements. Trade unions, charities, professional, educational and religious associations also became an integral part of civil society. By the 1930s more than 14,000 associations had 3 million members, of which a third were women's associations. Women's specific interests were represented at the level of 'grand politics' through the fight for suffrage. The 'pre-suffrage' women's movement (before 1918) was characterized by its neglect of politics. These associations (charity, alumni, artistic, cultural, scientific) were formed with a small membership, based on a specific region, aiming first of all to support well-to-do families with individual charity. The 'post-suffrage' women's associations were different from the previous ones so far as their political aims and their mass membership were concerned. After 1919 and the fall of the Hungarian Bolshevik revolution, the 'pre-suffrage' associations continued their activity, but the new type of associations changed the social space for their activity. They built up a strong relationship with the state, acting in some cases as a 'transmission belt' between policymakers.

Yet another change after the First World War was the appearance of the 'party frame'. The renewal experiment of the National Unity Party (Nemzeti Egység Pártja) and of the Christian Women's Camp (Keresztény Nöi Tábor) was to mobilize women (Vonyó 1997). Due to the serious economic crisis the role of the state increased in the sphere of social welfare politics; the activities of civil and religious charitable societies duly decreased but were not rendered completely superfluous. Fascist women's organizations never became powerful in Hungary due to the strong women's movement organized within the maternal–national frame, which resisted fascism from a conservative–religious standpoint.

During the Second World War the women's organizations polarized according to how much they identified with the 'national frame'. The Social Democrats joined the 'submerged network' after the German invasion of Hungary in 1944, as did religious and other civil organizations. The members of the 'submerged network' co-operated in saving or protecting Jews in Hungary.

The situation after 1945 appears simple at first sight (Petö 1999a and 1999b): the Second World War had eradicated the earlier women's organizational network; with the MNDSZ (Magyar Nök Demokratikus Szövetsége – Democratic Alliance of Hungarian Women) a mass movement was established which mobilized women in the interest of communist aims (Petö 2000). The year 1945 was one of new beginnings and rebuilding; it was the golden age of the 'submerged network'. The communist women's movement was very active. It immediately issued a programme and established an organization, shaped by those women who were living as émigré communists in the West – for example, in Paris. The communist activists initially supported a hard-driven 'revolutionary-equality frame' focusing on radical transformation and

the quick mobilization of Hungarian women. The results of the first democratic election of 1945 came as a surprise: the Communist Party turned out
to be the most unpopular among women. Consequently certain elements of
the 'maternal frame' reappeared in the communist programme, particularly in
the prisoner-of-war projects. In Hungary women's political weight was ensured by women's general suffrage, which was achieved in 1945. This proved
to be more important in changing women's situation than any other single
factor.

In the case of the feminists the tactics of the 'submerged network' which
had worked so well between the wars failed to produce any results afterwards.
The general democratization of the country, including the gaining of general
suffrage for women in 1945, meant that the feminists lost ground. Generational
conflicts and the class struggle made it difficult for the Feminist Association
and the MNDSZ to cooperate, as the average age of the feminists' membership
was much higher than that of the MNDSZ. An additional conflict was due
to the fact that the leadership and the membership of these organizations came
from different social backgrounds. The mission of the submerged networks had
been to keep ideas alive and to strike when the time was again right. But the
fight was not now theirs. No one needed the feminists' experience. Yet,
because of its centralized structure, its status as an accepted submerged network, and the cultural values it upheld, the association survived for a while.

The women's association organizing within the 'maternal–national' frame
was banned in the wake of the armistice of 1945. The activities of the 'maternal
frame' organizations were reduced because the membership neither had the
time nor the means any longer for charitable works. The social prestige of
ameliorative work was reduced to a minimum as the MNDSZ, supported by
the Hungarian Communist Party (MKP), now determined this field. With
nationalization the middle and upper-middle class, and any institutional network that was somehow independent of the state, ceased to exist, including
independent schools, hospitals and public libraries.

In order to mobilize women, an atmosphere of passivity was necessary, as
was the need to establish control over the activities of Hungary's women's
organizations. This was carried out by the MNDSZ. The latter tried to co-
opt these organizations into the MNDSZ and then disband them. According
to data from 1946, and excluding the big national women's movements, several
women's organizations with more than 1,600 members applied to restart their
activities. Decree I of 1946 recognized the indisputable right of citizens to
assemble. At the same time another law placed responsibility for all organizations in the hands of the Interior Ministry, which was controlled by the
Communist Party. They gradually used this power, with the help of an increasingly influential police, to ban the organizations. With the MNDSZ an
organization emerged which mobilized and brought women out onto the
streets in the interest of political aims, as for example on 6 December 1946
when there was a celebrated protest by housewives against rising prices.

Women's emancipation in Hungary took place without the active participation of either the women's organizations or female politicians. There is no evidence in the documents of the women's secreteriats of the various parties that they exercised any political pressure for female politicians in parliament. The number of female politicians rose from 1 or 2 to 12 by the time of the 1944 Provisional National Assembly, and after the 1945 elections to 14. At the 1947 election there were 22 female MPs; by 1949 this had risen to 71 – still only 17 per cent of all MPs. In 1953 only 52 women sat in the by now completely powerless parliament, 17 per cent of the total (Balogh 1975: 57).

Between 1945 and 1947 the Hungarian judiciary decreed in unparalleled measure the very laws and regulations which the liberal feminist and social-democratic women's movements had demanded in the first years of the twentieth century. The opening of university gates to women without restriction, family law reform, pension reform, the regulation of child-care benefits, the abolition of sex discrimination in various professions – such as the pressing need for female recruitment in the police – were all demands of earlier women's movements. These legal provisions created new opportunities for women (Petö 1998, 2000). But the elimination of civil societies and the increasing sovietization of Hungary redefined these opportunities.

The Period 1951–89

The women's history of this period has not been written. Some attempts have been made to move beyond the image of the Stakhanovite worker as a symbol of 'state feminism' in Hungary, and new oral history projects have been conducted to recover this unseen part of the history of Hungarian communism. During the political, economic and social upheavals women were used as co-soldiers and helpers, but once the changes were over, women were pushed back into their 'traditional place', as happened in the 1956 Hungarian Revolution, leaving women as invisible partners (Juhász 1999). In this section I would like to illustrate, by way of two parallel life stories, the issues raised by women during this period.

Júlia Rajk, born Júlia Földes in 1914 (d. 1981), was from a lower working-class family with a strong communist tradition. Between 1945 and 1949, as the wife of the famous communist minister of the interior, Lászlóné Rajk (Mrs László Rajk), she was one of the leaders of the communist mass women's organization MNDSZ. In 1949, after the execution of her husband, she was sentenced to five years' imprisonment for supporting his so-called 'subversive policy'. After she had completed her sentence, she was released from prison as Lászlóné Györk (Mrs László Györk). Her name and that of her son were changed without any consultation, in order to consign the name of her husband to oblivion. Her appeals to the leaders of the Communist Party for an official rehabilitation were signed with both names, Rajk and Györk. She used her unquestionable and uncontested moral power as the widow of an innocently executed hero of the Hungarian communist movement to force the Communist Party leadership to rehabilitate political prisoners. Eventually, on 6 October 1956, her husband was buried with all official honours. The photo of the widow and her son taken at the funeral became known across the world, symbolizing the victims of Stalinism. Following the reburial of her husband, she regained her name as Lászlóné Rajk and her son that of László Rajk Jr. On 4 November 1956, when the Soviet Army occupied Hungary, she, together with Imre Nagy and the members of his cabinet, asked for political refuge at the Yugoslav embassy. Ms Rajk was abducted by the Soviets together with Imre Nagy and sent to Romania. She spent two years there until she was given permission to return to Hungary as Julia Rajk. After 1958 she became *the* Júlia, a real institution, who protected the weak against those who abuse their power. She negotiated with the party leadership to protect anti-communist intellectuals. She organized the first NGO in Hungary following a ban on associations in 1951: a dogshelter. She also organized signatures in support of Charter 77, and campaigned against strengthening the abortion law in 1975, the first civic action against communism. She offered the compensation she received for the loss of her husband to a fund support-ing talented university students at a time when individual charity was not officially condoned (Petö 2001).

Anna Kéthly (1889–1976), the great lady of the Hungarian and the Inter-national Social Democratic Women's Movement, was born into a poor worker family in Budapest. She was a poverty-stricken student who gained scholar-ships. Since she was not physically capable of doing manual labour, she stud-ied book-keeping and typing. She started to work at the editorial office of Tolnai Vilaglapja, and joined the National Association of Private and Com-mercial Clerks (Köz és Magántisztviselök Nemzeti Szövetsége); she was sub-sequently elected head of the Association's women's section. She also joined the Social Democratic Party. After 1919 the Hungarian social-democratic movement was beheaded; there was consequently a need for new cadres. Kéthly became the head of the women's section of the SDP, and in 1922 at the age of 33 she was elected as an MP. She served in parliament until 1944, supporting social legislation and voting against the Anti-Jewish Law. In 1945 as a Member of Parliament and as a leader of the party, she opposed the merger with the Communist Party, which took place in 1948. Kéthly used her excellent international connections to secure her presence in the inter-national social-democratic scene. She was arrested in 1950 and was kept in prison without trial for three and a half years. During her rehabilitation trial in 1954 she refused to collaborate with the communists. In 1956 she refounded the Social Democratic Party. She was on a diplomatic mission to the United Nations in New York when the Soviet Army occupied Hungary on 4 November 1956. Kéthly served as a representative of the other Hungary in the UN and settled in Brussels, which served as a centre for the emigrant social-democratic opposition. She edited *Népszava* from 1957 to 1963, and, until the 1970s, *Szocialdemokrata Szemle*. Kéthly remained active in the international socialist movement until her death, in exile, in 1976 (Kádár 2000).

Neither of these women was active in the official women's movement of Hungary after 1951. Their life stories, however, serve to indicate the differences and similarities between the struggle of Hungarian women for dignity and autonomy and that of other women on the other side of the Iron Curtain. The official women's movement itself was dominated by the mass women's organization, with its loyal and functional relationship to the Communist Party. During the period of consolidation of the Kadar regime after 1956, the occupation of Hungary by the Soviet forces was based on the depoliticization of the population and an increase in the standard of living. Meanwhile the decisive factor that influenced women's situation was their full employment. Women's employment required the building up of social-support networks of crèches and nurseries. From 1967, three-year maternity leave was introduced. This served not only to increase the number of children born but also successfully directed the female labour force back into the kitchen. In this context the gender politics of Hungary remained based on a patriarchal order and full employment did not bring emancipation (Corrin 1994).

After 1989

In 1989 the structure of women's organizations in Hungary followed the pattern established in 1947. In the pre-1989 period it was a legitimate focus of academic inquiry to research women as a separate social group. During the forty years of socialism equal opportunities had supposedly been enjoyed by all, and researches related the discrimination of women to state socialism, not to gender inequality. The rebirth of feminism in Central Europe after 1989 was generally characterized by the fragmentation of women's organizations. After the first years of freedom only those which had a relation to political parties survived; in this they mirrored the old–new political division of society after the collapse of communism.

Of the 65,000 not-for-profit organizations listed in the registry of the Central Statistical Office in 1997, 60 were labelled women's organizations (Lévai and Kiss 1997). The not-for-profit sector of Hungary is powerful; its associations own more than 30 billion forints. State subsidy as part of the income of not-for-profit organizations is growing steadily but is still very low overall. Support from local governments has, however, doubled in the last ten years to help these organizations fulfil specific tasks. Not-for-profit organizations servicing certain community needs are thus able to generate local funding. In the non-governmental sector 50,000 are employed full time and 28,000 part time, but actually only 20 per cent of the NGOs can, in fact, afford to have paid employees (Cz.G. 2000).

The list of Hungarian women's NGOs in 1999 was divided along the following lines: civil or religious, local or national, welfare-service or professional. Membership numbers are not made public because of the continuous struggle for outside funding; indeed every organization has a vital interest in keeping its membership figures secret. The structure of the organizations very much resembles the historical structure of women's mobilization in Hungary. The main division in the civil sector is still between independent organizations and those semi-civil bodies that are strongly affiliated to political parties, keeping NGO status to open up channels for other sources of funding to support their party. The women's organization of the Smallholders Party, for example, operates as an NGO but also has strong institutional and personal ties to the party. However, some recent issues seem to have mobilized Hungarian women. They include the abortion debates in 1991–92 and in 1999–2000, the reform of the pension system (raising women's retirement age), and the regulation of prostitution in 1999–2000. These measures saw women's issues become part of public discourse.

Feminism as a Mobilizing Force

The feminist movement in Hungary, banned in 1951 and then re-established after 1989, claims that notions of gender equality are tied to the desires of middle-class women. Yet, 'at the same time, a group of highly educated, self respecting, well-to-do women with a lot of leisure time, which is the basis of Scandinavian and American upper-middle-class feminism, is missing in Hungary' (Tamás 1987). This may well be true; after 1989 there were no influential interest groups outside party politics. Thus women's interests have been subordinated to a dominant parliamentary political discourse. Middle-class women seem satisfied with their political representation in the existing political system.

At present, the Hungarian feminist movement is confined to a very narrow social spectrum. It is made up predominantly of women intellectuals (sociologists, economists, journalists, and a few historians in their mid-thirties to forties) based in university departments. After 1989 women researchers were pioneering in taking up fundamental issues such as housing, employment, economic and sexual rights, women's self-perception, body image, sexuality, and media presentation from a gendered point of view. Since generations of women grew up without experiencing any real prospect of engaging in political activity, and matched their lives to the demands and expectations of state socialism, women's political activism during the first decades of the twenty-first century has to be cautious and tolerant, but persistent.

Hence, after 1989, when feminists drew attention to the lack of a feminist consciousness in Hungary, they encountered deep antipathy among other women in the former Soviet bloc. Just as in the West, most of the women involved in Women's Studies are members of the intelligentsia. The difference between Hungary and many Western countries lies in the strength of civil society in the West and the presence of a network of associations and organizations extending throughout society that can be used by female scholars and academics both as a defensive power-base and as a tool to increase social awareness. In Eastern Europe, the abolition of women's associations and the *Gleichschaltung* of the women's movements not only eliminated any prospect of institutional pressure but also led to a dearth of female politicians capable of representing women's interest in other fields. Women's political socialization took place in the victorious communist women's mass organizations, on the basis of psychological reflexes that were formed by male politicians in order to secure and maintain their political power.

In the long run, the development of the Hungarian women's NGOs is likely to go in two directions: first, creating a service sector, which is of vital importance for improving women's position in the political and economic market; second, increasing co-operation between different branches of the women's NGOs across political and strategic lines. These developments would force political parties to address women as citizens in their programmes, which in turn would produce a higher level of women's political mobilization.

One of the differences in the structure of the pre-1989 and the post-1989 women's movements is the formation of environmentalist and Romany (gypsy) groups. The majority in Hungarian society ignore the most important social and cultural problem of present-day Hungary: increasing racism and continuous discrimination against the Romany population, who are now very vulnerable. The anti-discrimination law submitted by oppositional parties was rejected by the Hungarian government in 2001. Romany women suffer double discrimination; even more than other women, without a powerful pressure group, without strong social alliances, they are very exposed. At present they remain powerless because they lack strong Romany intellectuals to support their cause. Training programmes now exist to help Romany women deal with economic and political life.

Women's representation remains largely outside of the conventional political framework. Influential pressure groups and some NGOs have not been able to overcome the gap between the 'big policymakers' and the voters. The election of 1998 ended the illusion that professional politicians might be forced to look for wider social support when addressing women's issues. The more strongly a political party represented the most traditional values in the 'maternal frame' the surer they were of receiving the vote of women. Since Hungarian electoral preferences are volatile (25 per cent of voters are 'undecided'), democratic elections may boost interest in women's issues – again from above. The political consensus among Hungarian politicians in favour of joining the European Union might still open up space for the international community to promote and organize women's issues in Hungary. The grassroots organizations may be missing, but the social needs are there. Hungarian society faces the task of building a new political system, one that acknowledges inequalities and that is able to develop a new body of social knowledge which recognizes gender distinctions as an aspect of human dignity and freedom.

References

Balogh, M., and S. Nagy Katalin, eds (2000) *Asszonysorsok a 20. században.* [Women's Lives in the 20th Century]. Budapest, BME Szociológia és Kommunikációs Tanszék, Szociális és Családvédelmi Minisztérium Nőképviseleti Titkársága. Reviewed in English in *WISE Women's News*, vol. 10, no. 1 (2000), p. 10.

Balogh, Sándor (1975) *Parlamenti és pártharcok Magyarországon 1945–47* [Parliamentary and Party Struggles in Hungary 1945–47]. Budapest: Kossuth.

Corrin, Chris (1994) *Magyar Women: Hungarian Women's Lives 1960s–1990s.* London: St. Martin's Press.

Cz.G. (2000) 'Az utóbbi években megtört a civilek lendülete' [In Recent Years the Increase of the NGOs Stopped], *Népszabadság*, 9 June, p. 4.

Juhász, Borbála (1999) 'Women in the Hungarian Revolution of 1956: The Women's Demonstration of 4th December', in A. Petö and B. Rásky, eds, *Construction and Reconstruction: Women, Family and Politics in Central Europe 1945–1998.* Program on Gender and Culture, Austrian Science and Research Liaison Office, Budapest, OSI Network Women's Program. Budapest: CEU Press, pp. 19–31.

Kádár, Zsuzsa (2000) 'Kéthly Anna', in M. Balogh and S. Nagy Katalin, eds, *Asszonysorsok a 20. században* [Women's Lives in the 20th Century]. Budapest: BME Szociológia és Kommunikációs Tanszék, Szociális és Családvédelmi Minisztérium Nőképviseleti Titkársága, pp. 239–51.

Lévai, K. and R. Kiss (1997) 'Nök a közéletben' [Women in Public], in Katalin Lévai and István György Tóth, eds, *Szerepváltozások. Jelentés a nök és a férfiak helyzetéröl* [Changing Roles: Report on Women and Men]. Budapest: TÁRKI, Munkaügyi Minisztérium.

Petö, Andrea (1997) 'Hungarian Women in Politics', in Joan Scott, Cora Kaplan and Debra Keats, eds, *Transitions, Environments, Translations: The Meanings of Feminism in Contemporary Politics.* New York: Routledge, pp. 153–61.

Petö, Andrea (1998) *Nöhistóriák. A politizáló magyar nök törtémetéböl 1945–1951* [Hungarian Women in Politics 1945–1951]. Budapest: CEU Press.

Petö, Andrea (1999a) 'Stimmen des Schweigens. Erinnerungen an Vergewaltigungen in den Haupstaedten des "ersten Opfers" (Wien) und des "letzten Verbündeten" Hitlers (Budapest)', *Zeitschrift für Geschichtswissenschaften* 10 (Berlin), pp. 892–914.

Petö, Andrea (1999b) 'Memory Unchanged. Redefinition of Identities in Post WWII Hungary', in *CEU History Department Yearbook 1997–98.* Budapest: CEU Press, pp. 135–53.

Petö, Andrea (2000) 'Women's Associations in Hungary: Mobilisation and Demobilisation, 1945–1951', in Claire Duchen and Irene Bandhauer Schöffmann, eds, *When the War Was Over: Women, War and Peace in Europe, 1940–1956.* Leicester: Leicester University Press, pp. 132–46.

Petö, Andrea (2001) *Rajk Júlia.* Budapest: Balassi.

Tamás, Pál (1987) 'Hova tûnt a magyar feminizmus?' *Élet és Irodalom*, 1 May, p. 6; quoted in Chris Corrin, *Magyar Women, Hungarian Women's Lives, 1960s–1990s.* London: St. Martin's Press, 1994, p. 211.

Szapor, Judith (1984) 'Les associations feministes en Hongrie, XIXè–XXè siècle', *Penelope pour l'histoires des femmes* 11, pp. 169–74.

Vonyó, József (1997) 'Nöi szerepek a Nemzeti Egység Pártjában (1932–1939)' [Women's Roles in the National Unity Party], in Bea Nagy, S. Sárdi and Margit Csokonai, eds, *Szerep és alkotás. Nöi szerpeka társadalomban és az alkotómüvészetben* [Role and Construction of Women's Role in Society and Arts]. Debrecen: Csokonai, pp. 279–90.

Zimmermann, Susan (1997) 'Frauenbestrebungen und Frauenbewegungen in Ungarn. Zur Organisationsgeschichte der Jahre 1848–1918', in Bea Nagy, S. Sárdi and Margit Csokonai, eds, *Szerep és alkotás. Nöi szerpeka társadalomban és az alkotómüvészetben.* Debrecen: Csokonai, pp. 171–205.

23

Lacking Integration:
The Relationship between the Women's
Movement and Gender/Women's Studies
in Transitional Slovenia

RENATA ŠRIBAR

The Slovenian sociologist and feminist Tanja Rener suggests that the relative lack of institutionalization of Women's/Gender Studies at Slovenian universities might be attributed to the non-supportive attitude of the women's/feminist movements towards this development. At the same time she regards the successful strategies for introducing Women's/Gender Studies into the university curriculum as subversive and partisan (Rener 1996: 58, 61). These strategies are reflective of both the dependency of academic Women's/Gender Studies on the individual feminist scholar and the problematic status of the studies and theories concerning women's and gender issues in universities.

The 'universal' question of the origin – that is, which was first, the women's movements or Women's Studies – has not been the object of much discussion in Slovenia. To date, the problem of whether or not scientific and theoretical work on women and gender is 'polluted' by cultural, civil and/or political interests has only been briefly addressed. Its theoretical treatment might deconstruct the question of origin.

The above-mentioned issues cannot be theoretically reflected upon without a sustained study of the history of women's movements and Women's/ Gender Studies in Slovenia from the end of the nineteenth century and into the twentieth century, including the feminisms of the 1970s, 1980s and 1990s. Some historical research has been carried out and more is in progress, but there are still some completely blank areas both as regards women's history and in the field of the 'new history'. The latter includes an analysis of the role of Slovenian women in the Second World War, the complex study of 'state feminism' (Jalušič 1993: 114) in the period of socialism, an analysis of the topics of the Slovenian–Croatian and Yugoslav feminists' endeavours of the 1970s with the Association of the Working Class as the background but in the context of the decline of 'state feminism' (Ule 1993: 121). An additional issue in the study of the relationship of the women's movement to Women's/ Gender Studies in Slovenia is the lack of an analytical approach to the relatively new concept of 'policy', which implies the reconsideration of the categories of (women's/feminist) movements and studies. In Slovenia the prevailing categorization of the women's movements in the registers of civil activism and academic studies degrades the epistemological potential of women's experiences in women's groups, and pushes the research and theoretical projects of the non-governmental feminist associations to the margins of the intellectual community of the humanities.

Vlasta Jalusic, the feminist director of the Peace Institute in Ljubljana, approached analysis of the relationship of Women's/Gender Studies and the women's movements in Slovenia by separating the theoretical from the political, and by situating the debates about the relevance and possibilities of Women's Studies in Slovenia within the field of politics (Jalušič 1993: 109). In 1997 she established a new department, the Centre for Gender and Politics, within the Peace Institute with the aim of undertaking feminist history studies, cultural studies of women, and so on. This move by one of the most influential Slovenian feminists can be interpreted as a revision of her own thinking. The close relation of the scientific and theoretical work to political interest is possible now that Western feminist epistemology and debates in the humanities have undermined the notion of disinterested scientific objectivity.

Abortion: A Case Study of the Relationship between the Women's Movement and Women's Gender Studies

When the first democratically elected government in Slovenia, which was right-wing, pledged to abolish the constitutional guarantee of the legality of abortion in 1990, the response was a huge demonstration of women's power; this resulted in the dropping of the subject from the planned parliamentary business of the day. That demonstration, along with other events, such as a meeting between representatives of women's groups, academic feminists and President Kučan, and involving other important political personalities as well as a media campaign, was vital in upholding women's right to govern their own bodies regarding reproduction, in opposition to the new conservative tendency of using the reproductive rights issue for ideological purposes. As the right to abortion had been incorporated in the constitution since 1974, it was considered a self-evident right by the women affected. When this right was put in question, the spontaneous reaction to the threat required some theoretical explanation, slogans to articulate it, and a supportive infrastructure – in other words, the campaigns to save women's right to abortion on demand needed a focal point, financial resources and appropriate management. The last was obtained through the renamed Communist Party; the first two were delivered by university women whose feminist identity was formed within

Yugoslav and foreign feminist networks, and influenced by publicly intellectuals rooted in the civil movements of the last two decades. The force produced by the uniting of these different social subjects of civil society promised
to be an intellectual and activist cradle for a few new-born feminist/women's
groups. Notwithstanding this development, the long-term effect of the
campaign has been – and remains – immobilizing.

Following this successful campaign feminists continued the restructuring
which had begun in the 1980s. New institutions at governmental level were
founded, such as the Committee for the Equality of Women and Men in
Parliament, and the Office for Women's Politics. It was intended that these
new institutions in the first few years would co-ordinate feminist interests and
try to implement – with the help and theoretical support of respected feminist intellectuals – the aims of the feminist movement. Due to the specificity
of the campaign to preserve women's right to abortion on demand, and
despite the fact that the campaign was documented and theorized in Bahovec
(1991), the campaign acquired the status of a myth, and has produced only
fragments of a now lost paradise.

One cannot resist concluding that, having won the battle for the constitutional right to abortion, the Slovenian feminist movements lost their will to
mobilize for further collective campaigns with common goals, such as the
demand for women's quotas in the representative bodies of the political parties and on election lists; the establishment of a women's information and
organization centre, in response to the impending collapse of the Women's
Programme of the Open Society Institute–Slovenia; or participation in the
Council of the Centre of the Slovenian NGO (constituted by the Slovenian
government and the Council of Europe). The difficulty in overcoming the
very real obstacles and consequent immobilization of the collective women's/
feminist movement has already been demonstrated in a case very similar to
that of abortion. In April 2001 the Slovenian parliament discussed a proposed
law on artificial insemination that would grant single women the legal right
to IVF treatment without medical grounds. The right-wing parties boycotted
the vote, but the law was passed by parliament anyway. The conservative
members of the different parties in opposition then proceeded to collect
enough support for their proposal for a referendum on the law in question.
The few intellectuals who defended the law in public used similar arguments
to those used in the abortion case. Indeed, the slogans of the campaign aimed
at the public are interchangeable with those of the pro-abortion campaign
eleven years earlier. But the organizers of the campaign were of a completely
different social pedigree. In the group of the main supporters of the 'you are
free' campaign, thirty-five in number, there were only three feminists – all
university professors. No woman from a feminist NGO was invited or helped
co-organize the campaign. One of the first sponsors to sign up was a philosopher who has publicly proclaimed the 'sanctity of life' – an important line
of argument in the pro-life movement in the abortion case. The main spokes-

woman of the 'you are free' pro-artificial insemination for single women campaign, for her part, however, associated the campaign with the 'Slovenian Spring' democratic movement of 1989 and not with the pro-abortion campaign. Besides, the central argument in favour of IVF for healthy single women should rest on egalitarian grounds, regardless of marital status (proponents of the referendum have no objection to fertility treatment for healthy woman with a partner). As it is, and as the recycled but misused slogans of the pro-abortion campaign indicate, this is a political fight that has little to do with women's rights.

Women's Studies in Slovenia

In Slovenia Women's/Gender Studies in universities is not an autonomous discipline. Women's/feminist movements lack both information and organizational focal points. Common goals are not recognized. The only integrating factors are certain individual feminists who choose to be scientists/theoreticians and simultaneously promote feminist ideas in the public arena, as well as acting as lobbyists for certain political solutions. At the same time there are women with a feminist NGO background who have feminist theoretical knowledge and abilities but no academic career in the field of Women's/Feminist Studies.

The academic subordination of Women's/Feminist Studies has led to gaps and omissions in the theoretical work and methodologies that serve to bind the studies and movements together (the politics of experience, work with a methodologically explicit political interest, etc.). Women's Studies is considered unscientific by mainstream academicians. The only exceptions are in the field of feminist social work, where the connection of theory and practice is institutionalized and canonized, and in the work of some autonomous feminist intellectuals who are part of international policy projects and programmes, and cover the domain of social policy at the state level and socio-political issues such as violence against women, refugees and prostitution. In some cases, which might have involved feminist scholars in the movement – for example the regulation of pornographic images of women in the media, the introduction of quotas in political parties and elections – positive action was either blocked by political interests in power (the campaign for quotas was compromised early on, for example, because a key feminist involved in the campaign allowed herself to be hushed up by the governing Liberal Democratic Party), or by a clash of interests among different feminisms (for example, the regulation of advertising of pornographic hotlines was not supported by a sufficient number of individual feminists and women's/feminist groups because a counter-argument for freedom of expression in printed media and freedom of speech emerged, accompanied by a fear of being labelled conservative were such advertising regulated).

On the Differential Characteristics of the
Slovenian Women's/Feminist Movements

Slovenia's relatively strong status as a first-round candidate country for integration within the European Union, combined with a traditionally stable economy, put Slovenian NGOs out of the many foreign funding schedules and international networks early on in the transition period. For many small women's/feminist groups and projects the decision of George Soros to transfer the Open Society programmes to the Peace Institute, leaving the women's programme without funds, represented the height of the crisis. Further backsliding occurred when no women's/feminist group was invited to join the founders of the Centre for Non-Governmental Organizations. Thus another access route to funds – this time national – was denied. Slovenian women's/feminist groups are consequently poorly resourced in financial and material terms.

During the socialist period Slovenian women had certain values and institutionalized rights which differentiated Slovenia from the developed Western countries, and which, due to the relatively weak influence of the Catholic Church and to the opposition of an socio-economic system of self-management, also distinguished it from the majority of other former socialist countries (Jogan 2000; Kirn 2000).

Publicly influential feminists and the promotion of certain women's groups' actions in the media transformed or confirmed public opinion on violence against women, the participation of women in politics, homosexuality, family politics, and so on. The Slovenian public space opened to so-called third-wave 'popular' feminism, which is a reaction to post-feminism and the backlash in the developed democracies. In Slovenia the popularization of some feminist concepts was also a reaction to the neo-conservative trends of the transition period. A lively interest in historical personalities who transgressed the rules of patriarchal society has surfaced since 1996, and in the last year or two a few previously uninterested journalists have begun to present feminist perspectives when covering cultural and political events. Many Slovenian women are now highly critical of the consequences of the new economic and political order, and are becoming a radical political force (Jogan 2000: 18, 19). According to Jogan, Slovenian women express the highest degree of trust in the women's movements among the transitional countries (2000: 25).

The feminist lesbian movement in Slovenia (Lilith, renamed LL) was among the first of the 1980s. Compared to the other transitional countries, Slovenian feminist lesbians have established a relatively strong public voice, speaking on behalf of homosexual rights to partnership, marriage, the adoption of children, and artificial insemination for single women, among other issues. The Slovenian women's/feminist movements are very dispersed, because they lack information and organizational centres and a common platform for actions. Yet they are highly specialized (e.g. the Association for Non-violent Communication, a telephone helpline for children and women who are victims of violence;

the Women's Counselling Room; the Association for the Promotion of Women in Culture) and competent at promoting their work and goals. This strength – along with the strong and publicly effective feminist lesbian movement – is also a point of difference from the majority of the countries in transition. Certain segments of the feminist movements, however, have been incorporated in the institutions of the state, leaving whole areas uncovered by nongovernmental organizing; this is most obvious when comparing Slovenia with the transitional country that it is closest to culturally and politically – Croatia. Croatia has strong independent feminist information and activist centres and an autonomous centre for Women's Studies. None of this exists in Slovenia.

Slovenia is excluded from the greater part of the networking and foundation building that is taking place in the transitional countries of Central and Eastern Europe. The consequences of this for existing women's/feminist NGOs have not been positive, although the moment is one of transition. In light of the relative awareness of Slovenian women, the successful incorporation of women's/feminist programmes within the institutions of the state from the early 1990s, and the Council of Europe directives on gender equality, the expected trend of development in Slovenia is not the empowerment of autonomous movements but the consolidation within institutional politics of women's/feminist perspectives, and co-operative projects involving governmental institutions and women's/feminist NGOs.

References

Bahovec, E. (1991) *Abortion – The Right to Choose?* Ljubljana: Women for Politics.

Jalušič, V. (1993) '"New Democracies" and "Women's Studies"', in E. Bahovec, ed., *From Women's Studies to Feminist Theory: The Journal for the Critique of Science, Imagination and New Anthropology*, Special Edition. Ljubljana: Students' Organization of the University of Ljubljana.

Jogan, M. (2000) 'Post-socialism and Androcentrism', in M. Jogan, ed., *Transition and Gender (In)equality. Journal of Social Science Studies* 26. Ljubljana: Slovenian Sociological Association.

Kirn, A. (2000) 'Women in Science and Science in Society', in M. Jogan, ed., *Transition and Gender (In)equality. Journal of Social Science Studies* 26. Ljubljana: Slovenian Sociological Association.

Rener, T. (1996) 'The Opening of Places: On the Situation of University Women's Studies', in L. Bogovič and Z. Skušek, eds, *Gender F.* Ljubljana: Institutum Studiorum Humanitatis; Cultural and Arts Centre France Prešeren.

Ule, M. (1993), 'The Context of Women's Studies in Slovenia', in E. Bahovec, ed., *From Women's Studies to Feminist Theory. The Journal for the Critique of Science, Imagination and New Anthropology*, Special Edition. Ljubljana: Students' Organization of the University of Ljubljana.

24

Women's Associations and Education in Spain

MARÍA S. SUÁREZ LAFUENTE

The first women's associations in Spain were established at the end of the nineteenth century, when industrial progress made women redundant at home and needed elsewhere. Backed by liberal groups such as Krausism and its Institución Libre de Enseñanza (Free Institute for Education), of key political importance in Spain, women founded a space in which to learn to argue for their right to education, to earn a salary and to advance towards full citizenship on an equal footing with men. One of the first steps was the Asociación para la Enseñanza de la Mujer (Association for the Education of Women), created in 1870, where women could learn typewriting, shorthand and all that was needed to work in an office or in public libraries and archives.

American scholars brought to Spain the idea of opening a college for women, such as existed in New England, an idea that was welcomed by some liberal families. In 1903 the Instituto Internacional para Señoritas de España (Spanish International College for Young Women) opened its doors in Madrid. It offered lay education, American pedagogy and a teaching degree. The Instituto proved a success: by 1912, 125 students were registered; sixteen years later this total had risen to 1,681, representing a spectacular annual progression.

Access to university studies was not easy for Spanish women; the isolated numbers who first entered the lecture rooms had to do so in the company of professors, and remain sitting at their desks, or disguised as men, so as not to be a source of distraction to male scholarship. But by 1915, and as a result of the many women who graduated from the International College, numbers at university had grown to such an extent that the founding of the Residencia de Señoritas de España (Residence for Spanish Young Women) became a pressing need. It is important to note that the Residencia de Estudiantes (Residence for Students – male, of course) had been opened in Madrid only five years earlier – it was the place where internationally known male artists such as Lorca, Buñuel, and Dalí first met and exchanged dreams and ideas. The International College and the Residence for Women provided an intellectual space for students that the university was still denying women. They found a place to meet, discuss and organize, a place to invite lecturers and speakers, and a well-stocked library.

Women learned fast and very soon there were several associations pursuing causes such as well-paid jobs, welfare for workers and, above all, the right to vote. It is significant that these groups also proposed internationalism and pacifism as valid bases for promoting social change in Spain. An important, if nationalistic, group was the Asociación Nacional de Mujeres Españolas (National Association of Spanish Women), founded in 1918 by María Espinosa de los Monteros, which lasted long enough to see the achievement of universal suffrage in 1931.

Spanish women won a space in the founding of the International Federation of University Women, which took place in London in 1919. María de Maeztu travelled to London as the Spanish representative for the First Conference of the Federation in 1920. Her talk, entitled 'University Education for Women', dealt with the fact that although women had never actually been barred from university, they had never been encouraged to attend either, until the twentieth century. She enumerated the subjects favoured by women (medicine, pharmacy, philosophy, and librarianship and archivism) and denounced the fact that there was only one woman lecturer in the eleven universities then existing in Spain. She also exposed the fact that better qualifications were demanded of women than men for the same jobs, and that women earned a smaller salary than men for an equal amount of work. At a conference of the International Federation in Barcelona in 1928 the rector of the University, in his welcoming words, warned women of the danger of losing both grace and virtue in entering men's domains.

María de Maeztu was one of the foremothers of the women's movements in Spain. Maeztu worked to alter the legal system to the advantage and promotion of women, aided by other distinguished women such as Clara Campoamor, founder of the Federación Internacional de Mujeres de Carreras Jurídicas (International Federation of Women in Law Studies) in 1929. Campoamor challenged the legal subordination of married women and entered a political career to fight for women's vote.

Between 1931 and 1936, during the Second Republic, Spanish women gained the right to abortion, maternity leave and full medical assistance, which made Spain one of the first countries to introduce such measures. This was the period in which women finally obtained political recognition: Federica Montseny was the first woman to become Minister of Health and Social Assistance, and writer Concha Espina was the first woman to be appointed consul in France. Victoria Kent, Clara Campoamor and Margarita Nelken sat in the parliament that finally passed, in 1931, the right to vote for all women. This was not an easy victory. Kent and Campoamor spoke on the issue from opposing political platforms. While Campoamor sought the universal vote without restrictions, Victoria Kent feared that women voting might mean the end of the Republic itself, since she believed the common proposition that 'la mujer vota con los curas y con la reacción' (women vote with the Church and the reactionaries) (Nash 1995: 256). The discussion lasted several sessions, allowing the airing of both logical arguments and atavistic simplifications on the nature of women. A representative of the Partido Republicano Federal (Federal Republican Party) 'defendió la irrisoria proposición de conceder el voto a las mujeres a partir de los cuarenta y cinco años, argumentando que hasta esa edad no estaba capacitada la "bella mitad del género humano", lo cual produjo fuertes risas en el hemiciclo' (defended the ridiculous proposition that women should vote from the age of 45, since 'the beautiful half of mankind', great laughs in the room in hearing this, was still immature before that) (VV.AA 1995: 77). An MP from the Partido Progresista Republicano (Progressive Republican Party) answered in his capacity as a medical doctor that women at 45 were most unstable of all, since their psychological balance was endangered by the loss of their physical abilities ('era precisamente en estos momentos cuando estaba en más peligro el equilibrio psíquico de la mujer que perdía serenidad con el deterioro de sus facultades'; Nash 1995: 254). Such arguments only put in official words what was obvious in all spheres of public life: that women's capacity as civic subjects was in doubt at both ends of their lifespan, before 45 and after. Against all odds, and thanks to the notorious absence of many representatives who thought the debate unimportant, the proposition of universal suffrage was passed with 161 votes in favour, and 121 votes against.

With the Second Republic, Spanish women's rights closed a period that had started with the debates on education of the last part of the nineteenth century. Women and men such as Faustina Sáez, Dolors Monserdà and Adolfo Posada are known for discussing at that time the notion of a Spanish 'feminism' different (Catholic and culturally distinct) from the British and American suffrage that was then becoming well known internationally. Posada popularized the term 'feminism' in *Feminismo*, a book he published in 1899, to explain the debates on women's social situation, and Monserdà adopted the term 'feminist' in her book *Estudi feminista* (Feminist Study) in 1909 (Nash 1994: 167).

The Spanish Civil War and Franco's regime heralded a complete regression in the social consideration of women, recognition of their rights, and the possibilities for free association. The regime readopted the legal code of 1889 and followed it to the letter so far as women were concerned. Only in 1950 did Spanish universities start some kind of resistance against Francoism, organizing a dissident movement in which women saw the opportunity to recover their ground. In 1953 the Asociación Española de Mujeres Universitarias (Spanish Association of University Women) was created to work for the development of women's profile at university and to find a path to communicate with other women outside Spain, which opened with its admission to the International Federation of University Women.

Spanish associationism came back with Justina Ruiz de Conde, former secretary to Clara Campoamor, and Pilar Lago, married to one of the leading intellectuals in Franco's time, Rafael Lapesa. They were soon joined by Soledad Ortega Spottorno, daughter of philosopher José Ortega y Gasset. The fact that these women were well-connected socially made them less suspicious both as women and as intellectuals. Nevertheless, their zeal and the many cultural events they organized soon brought them problems with official censorship, which they overcame as well as they could, disguising debates and using noms de guerre to introduce more dangerous guests. They organized lecture series on seemingly innocuous themes that were in fact pregnant with critical possibilities, such as 'education', 'the university' or 'Catholicism'. These series functioned as a forum for the dissemination of knowledge and criticism, and served to create a social conscience that was completely lacking in the street. But their most important contribution to feminism was giving scholarships to young university women to study abroad and 'see other worlds'.

In a different but parallel field, lawyer Mercedes Fórmica started a public campaign in the press in 1953, to call attention to the abuse of women within the family and women's lack of defence before the law. After five years of intense debate and outrage Fórmica succeeded in starting the reform process of the obsolete Legal Code; sixty-six articles pertaining to women were modified in 1958, making life easier for women, but not altering society's idea about women's maturity:

> [n]o varía la norma de obediencia que tiene que prestarla esposa al marido, ni la obligatoriedad de seguirle a donde quiera que fije su residencia, ni aquél deja de ser el único representante legal de su mujer. Y ello porque el proemio de la ley decía que 'el matrimonio exige una potestad de dirección que la Naturaleza, la Religión y la Historia atribuyen al marido'. [A woman still has to obey her husband and follow him wherever he wants to establish residence, and the husband is still the legal representative of his wife. This happens because the preliminaries to the law say that 'a marriage asks for a power of direction given by Nature, Religion and History to the husband'.] (Falcón: 405)

Pilar Primo de Rivera, Delegada Nacional de la Sección Femenina (National Director of the Feminine Section, the official organization managing women's affairs), took it upon herself to become the voice of Spanish women during the first twenty-five years of Franco's regime. She defined the essence of femininity, guided women in the glorious path to maternity (she who never married) and kept them shut up in the kitchen or the cell; there were no other alternatives to Primo de Rivera's essentialist conception of womanhood but *sus labores* (her natural tasks). The Catholic Church joined forces with the Feminine Section, and their common 'Crusade' caused problems and inconveniences for women of several generations; it also left a wonderful legacy of absurd situations and social caricatures, to be exploited in

later feminist research. A certain Cardenal Segura, for instance, forbade dancing
in Seville in the 1940s because it meant 'tiniebla de varones, infamia de
doncellas, alegría del diablo e histeria de los ángeles' (darkness for men, in-
famy for young women, joy for the devil and hysteria for angels). Though not
wishing to overdo it with such examples, let us just quote the director of a
Feminine Youth Penitentiary from her paper entitled 'How They Get Lost',
read in the First National Conference on Morality on Beaches and at Swim-
ming Pools, held in Valencia in May 1951:

> No hay en la conducta social de la mujer una acción más grave, más excitante al
> pecado feo, que la que realiza tranquilamente en sus baños públicos en la playa. Son
> ocasión próxima de pecado mortal. [Women's public bathing on the beach consti-
> tutes the most dangerous social behaviour a woman can perform, the most inviting
> to 'the ugly sin'. Baths are the ante-room to mortal sin.]

Author Carmen Martín Gaite describes such a world of constraints not
only in her novels but in her study *Usos amorosos de la postguerra española* (Love
Mores of the Spanish Post-War Period), where she analyses material from
magazines written for young and married women, from Primo de Rivera's
talks, and from other public sources from that time. She concludes that society
had no doubts about the education of women:

> De forma bien tajante lo había establecido Pilar Primo de Rivera en su catecismo
> particular. A las que pretendieran surcar los aires del saber con vuelo tan seguro y
> ambicioso como el del varón convenía cortarles las alas. 'Las mujeres nunca descubren
> nada: les falta desde luego el talento creador, reservado por Dios para inteligencias
> varoniles; nosotras no podemos hacer nada más que interpretar mejor o peor lo que
> los hombres han hecho'. [It was quite clear from what Primo de Rivera established
> in her particular catechism. Women trying to soar the skies of knowledge with a
> flight as sure and ambitious as that of men should have their wings clipped. 'Women
> never discover anything: they lack that creative talent that God reserved for male
> intelligence; we can only interpret, according to our lights, what men have made'.]
> (Martín Gaite: 68)

In view of such official 'representatives', it is easy to understand the difficult
but necessary task that the Asociación Española de Mujeres Universitarias
faced.

The year 1975 marked a turning point in Spanish history and in the
history of Spanish women: Franco died and with him his regime. The United
Nations declared that year 'International Women's Year'. In December of that
year Madrid saw the First Conference for the Liberation of Women, attended
by five hundred women from all over the country. This constituted the first
feminist public event in thirty-nine years. In 1979 Lidia Falcón founded the
Feminist Party, which was to be instrumental in organizing women's
vindications in the first difficult years of the political and social transition.
Gradually other groups and associations were created, but Falcón's party
remained and still runs in the general elections, more as a testimony than as

a real political option. The 1980s saw many women engage in a personal debate between feminism and other political ideologies; leftist parties were not quick enough in incorporating women's issues into their agendas, and many women opted out of established parties to fight alongside other women.

The awakening of women at university followed along the same lines. Scholarships for working-class children in the 1960s precipitated the access of women students to university in the 1970s. The numbers progressed at such a rate that today there is a higher percentage of female than male students in Spanish universities. The national rate is 52 per cent women students, the University of Islas Baleares being the most feminized with 57 per cent. It was only to be expected that in graduating from university, women were going to become lecturers. They did so in large numbers, but were detained mostly at the middle level of the university scale; higher posts and professorships are largely occupied by men, who dedicate their entire time to their university career and are pushed upwards more easily by a still patriarchal corporative system. Out of 47 Rectors, only one is a woman, elected at the newly founded Universidad Pablo de Olavide in Seville. Women professors account for no more than 10 per cent of academic staff in any faculty, and in some faculties such as engineering they account only 2.2 per cent; there are none in navigation and mining.

Female students are also differently distributed: there is a substantially higher percentage in the humanities, health and social sciences, than in engineering. In naval engineering in Madrid there are no women, which could be accounted for by the fact that female engineers were vetoed in all shipyards. Similarly, in the sciences women are way behind in numbers. Milagros Rivera analyses this fact:

> cuando en las universidades casi nadie sabía bien qué es lo que era [la ciencia] ni de dónde venía, pasó a ser patrimonio de hombres que la diseccionaron, la clasificaron y compusieron con ella diccionarios de autoridades. [when nobody knew at the university what science was really about and where it came from, it became the toy of men that played with it, classified it and wrote authorities into dictionaries.] (Hipatía 1998: 9)

That is probably why in the High Council for Scientific Research there are only 2 women out of 22 direction posts, even though 40 per cent of scientific assistants, 26 per cent of research assistants and 11 per cent of the teaching staff are women. Whenever a woman merits scientific recognition the world shows surprise and feels compelled to explain such 'an oddity'. Contemporary feminism, therefore, is working to prevent a similar process occurring with the new technologies.

Although women are now accepted within the university context, conservative sections still consider the introduction and regularization of Women's Studies a menace, loaded with ideology and politicized, but never scientific. Despite this there has been a considerable increase of such work in the 1990s;

named degree routes are very rare, but teachers apply a feminist perspective to their analyses. Nevertheless, society is demanding more feminist knowledge and analysis, and specific postgraduates programmes in Women's Studies. Such programmes run in Granada, Málaga, Madrid, Valencia, Oviedo and Cádiz; there is an inter-university programme in Andalucia for the eight universities in the region; and Barcelona has an on-line master's degree. Between 1992 and 1995, 566 MA theses on Women's Studies were submitted, as well as 262 doctoral theses.

The Women's Institute, attached to the Ministry of Culture and Social Affairs, and the different Women's Offices in the regional administrations and city councils have been backing research on women, funding scholarships for research in archives and libraries at home and abroad, and funding publication and helping to disseminate such knowledge. This institutional help has been instrumental in furthering Women's Studies at the different Spanish universities.

We cannot underestimate the impact and importance of the university women's associations that fought unbendingly through the difficult 1980s, sometimes to the detriment of their associates' hopes of a university career. Nowadays there are several such associations and research groups in practically every university; they are instrumental in collaborating with the political and social powers and in organizing debates and lecture forums for university circles and for the public at large. One result of all this activity was the establishment of a national association in the early 1990s: AUDEM (University Association for Women's Studies), which became the natural interlocutor of the national Women's Institute, advising on the needs and orientation of Women's Studies within the university.

A product of this co-operation was the research and publication of a 'white book' on the subject, which gathered information and documentation from the onset of Women's Studies in Spanish universities until 1992; there was a later updating, from 1992 to 1996. These books (Ballarin et al.; Ortiz et al.; VV.AA) are fundamental to an understanding of feminism, women at university and Women's Studies in Spain. Collective books are the main vehicle for compiling research; many associations publish the results of their debates and research or the proceedings of the conferences they organize in this way. There are in the country at least three well-known series publishing monographs on women, which come out on a regular basis: *Feminismos*, from the University of Valencia; *Colección Feminae*, from the University of Granada; and *Alternativas*, from the University of Oviedo. There are now also some well-established journals such as *Duoda*, edited in Barcelona since 1990; *Asparkía*, edited in Castellón since 1992; and *Arenal*, published in Granada since 1994.

Spanish university women, like their forerunners Meaztu or Campoamor, understand the importance of working and collaborating with their European colleagues. Thus AUDEM was present in WISE (Women's International Studies in Europe) from its foundation in 1990. AUDEM associates have also taken part in WINE (Women's Information Network Europe) since 1996; in AOIFE

(Association of Institutions for Feminist Education and Research in Europe), also since 1996; and in ATHENA (Advanced Thematic Network in Activities in Women's Studies in Europe) since 1998.

Contemporary Spanish feminism is mainly social: it demands legal reforms to balance civil rights, fights for equal job opportunites and equal salaries, and wants an equal share in power. It works for the deconstruction of secular patriarchy; it denounces sexism in language and strives to awaken gender consciousness in the use of everyday language. Spanish feminism theorizes and works to push women to be active in social and political matters, to open all spaces to women, and to denounce the lies and traps of patriarchal tradition and socialization.

Note

A version of this chapter was delivered in Casa de las Americas, Havana, in February 2001. My gratitude to historian Mary Nash who gave me valuable advice on the subject.

References

Ballarin, P., M. Gallego and I. Martinez (1995) *Los estudios de las Mujeres en las universidades españolas. 1975–1991*. Madrid: Libro Blanco, Instituto de la Mujer.

Falcón, Lidia (1996) *Mujer y sociedad*. Madrid: Vindicación Feminista Publicaciones.

Hipatía (1998) *Autoridad científica. Autoridad femenina*. Madrid: Cuadernos inacabados, Editorial Horas y Horas.

Martín Gaite, Carmen (1994) *Usos amorosos de la postguerra española*. Madrid: Compactos Anagrama.

Nash, Mary (1994) 'Experiencia y aprendizaje: la formación histórica de los feminismos en España', *Historia Social* 20, October, pp. 151–72.

Nash, Mary (1995) 'Género y ciudadanía', *Ayer* 20: 240–58.

Ortiz, T., J. Birriel and V. Marin (1998) *Universidad y feminismo en España I. Bibliografía de Estudios de las Mujeres, 1992–1996*. Colección Feminae, University of Granada.

VV.AA. (1995) *El voto femenino en España*. Madrid: Documentación del Instituto de la Mujer.

VV.AA. (1999) *Universidad y feminismo en España II. Situación de los estudios de las mujeres en los años 90*. Colección Feminae, University of Granada.

Notes on Contributors

Liana Borghi is Senior Researcher in Anglo-American Literature at the University of Florence. Her interests include women's literature and feminist theory from the late eighteenth century to the present. She is the editor of two volumes on women's comparative literature, *Passaggi: Letterature comparate al femminile* and *S/Oggetti Immaginari: Letterature comparate al femminile* (Urbino: QuattroVenti, 2000 and 1996), and the author of several essays on poetry, science fiction, and Jewish women's writing. Her several literary translations include works by Kate Chopin and Adrienne Rich. She has also translated some of Donna Haraway's essays (Milan: Feltrinelli, 1997) and her latest book, *Modest_Witness@Second_Millennium* (Milan: Feltrinelli, 2000).

Rosi Braidotti is Professor of Women's Studies and Director of the Netherlands Research School of Women's Studies at Utrecht University. Her research is in feminist philosophy, especially poststructuralism and psychoanalysis, theories of sexual difference and the history of feminist ideas. She is currently working on the politics of feminist postmodernism from a multicultural perspective, and on the history of scientific teratology. Recent publications include *Nomadic Subjects* (New York: Columbia University Press, 1994), *Patterns of Dissonance* (Cambridge: Polity Press, 1991), and many articles in journals and books. She has also edited a number of books, including, with Nina Lykke, *Between Monsters, Goddesses and Cyborgs* (London: Zed Books, 1996).

Marina Calloni is Professor of Social and Political Philosophy at the State University of Milan–Bicocca, where she directs the International Network for Research on Gender. Her main research areas are gender studies and theories of ethics, politics and justice, and democracy and cultural conflicts. Among her recent publications are *Il bene, il giusto e le differenze. Il conflitto publico–*

privato dell aborto (Rome: Donzelli, 2002); *Amelia Rosselli Pincherle: Mie Memorie*, ed. (Bologna: Il Mulino, 2001); and 'Gender, Research and Networks across Boundaries: A Different Approach to Globalization' (Copenhagen: Nordic Council of Ministries, 2001).

Andreina De Clementi lectures in contemporary history at the Istituto Universitario Orientale, Naples. Specializing in the history of emigration, she has written a number of books, including *Vivere nel latifondo. Le comunità della campagna laziale tra '700 e '800* (Milan, 1989), and has edited, among others, *La società inafferrabile. Protoindustria, città e classi sociali nell'italia liberale* (Rome 1986) and, with Maria Stella, *Viaggi di donne* (Naples, 1995). She is president of the Società Italiana delle Storiche.

Drude Dahlerup is Professor of Political Science at Stockholm University. She has published widely on women in politics, the women's movement and feminist theory. In 1998 she published *The Redstockings: The Development, New Thinking and Impact of the Women's Liberation Movement in Denmark 1970–85*, 2 vols (Copenhagen: Gyldendal). She is currently engaged in a project on Gender, Empowerment and Politics (www.i4.auc.dk/gep).

Ute Gerhard is Professor of Sociology and Director of the Cornelia Goethe Centre for Women's and Gender Studies at the University of Frankfurt. Her research fields are women's rights, social policy, the women's movements and feminist theory. Among her recent publications are: *Debating Women's Equality. Toward a Feminist Theory of Law from a European Perspective* (New Brunswick, NJ: Rutgers University Press, 2001); 'Legal Particularism and the Complexity of Women's Rights in Nineteenth-century Germany', in Willibald Steinmetz, ed., *Private Law and Social Inequality in the Industrial Age: Comparing Legal Cultures in Britain, France, Germany, and the United States* (Oxford: Oxford University Press, 2000); *Atempause. Feminismus als demokratisches Projekt* (Frankfurt: Fischer, 1999); and *Frauen in der Geschichte des Rechts. Von der Frühen Neuzeit bis zur Gegenwart* (Munich: Beck 1997).

Tuula Gordon is a Member of the Helsinki Collegium for Advanced Studies, University of Helsinki. She has published widely on education and gender. Her publications include *Feminist Mothers* (London and New York: Macmillan and New York University Press, 1990); *Single Women: On the Margins?* (London and New York: Macmillan and New York University Press, 1994); and *Making Spaces: Citizenship and Difference in Schools*, with Janet Holland and Elina Lahelma (London and New York: Macmillan and St. Martin's Press, 2000). She is director of the project 'Gender and Nationality' (Academy of Finland).

Gabriele Griffin is Professor of Gender Studies at the University of Hull. Her research interests include twentieth-century women's cultural production, feminist theory, and issues of bodies/sexualities. She is co-founding editor of the journal *Feminist Theory* (London: Sage, 2000). Her publications include *HIV/AIDS and Representation: Visibility Blue/s* (Manchester: Manchester University Press, 2000); *Straight Studies Modified: Lesbian Interventions in the Academy*, co-edited with S. Andermahr (London: Cassell, 1997); *Gender Issues in Elder Abuse*, co-authored with L. Aitken (London: Sage, 1996); *Feminist Activism in the 1990s*, ed. (London: Taylor & Francis, 1995); *Heavenly Love? Lesbian Images in 20th Century Women's Writing* (Manchester: Manchester University Press, 1993).

Carol Hagemann-White is Professor of Feminist Studies and Educational Theory at the University of Osnabrück. Over the past twenty years she has done many empirical studies as well as theoretical analysis on women's advocacy and strategies to overcome gender-based violence; she is currently evaluating community intervention models. Her numerous publications include work on gender theory, socialization, women's health issues and equality policy in a European perspective. Two of her key publications are *Sozialisation: weiblich – männlich?* (Opladen: Leske & Budrich, 1984; new edition in preparation) and *Strategien gegen Gewalt im Geschlechterverhältnis. Bestandsanalyse und Perspektiven* (Pfaffenweiler: Centaurus 1992).

Beatrice Halsaa is an Adjunct Professor at the Centre for Women and Gender Research, the Norwegian University of Science and Technology, Trondheim, and chair of the board of Kilden, Norwegian Information and Documentation Center for Women's and Gender Research. Halsaa is also one of three co-ordinators of the Nordic research network Women's Movements and Internationalization: The Third 'Wave' in the Contexts of Transnational Democratic Institutions. She has published widely on equal opportunities and gender politics, the feminist movement, feminist utopias and feminist theory, mostly in Norwegian. Among her publications are *Kvinner og politisk deltakelse* [Women and Political Participation] (Oslo: Pax 1978); *Unfinished Democracy*, co-ed. (London: Pergamon Press, 1985); *I pose og sekk. Framtidsbilder* [In Both Ways. Pictures of the Future], with Else Viestad (Oslo: Emilia 1990); and *Hun og han. Kjønn i forskning og politikk* [She and He: Gender in Research and Politics], co-ed. (Oslo: Pax, 1996). At present she is working on *Feminism as Critique*, a historiography of feminist research in Norway.

Jalna Hanmer is Professor of Women's Studies at the University of Sunderland. Her research interests are in the areas of violence, abuse and gender relations. Recent publications include: *Arresting Evidence: Domestic Violence and Repeat Victimisation* (London: Home Office 1999); *Women and Social Work: Towards a Woman-Centred Practice* (2nd edn, London: Macmillan 1999); *Women, Violence and Crime Prevention* (Aldershot: Avebury 1993).

Liliane Kandel is a sociologist, active in the feminist studies movement since its beginnings in the early 1970s. She was co-director of CEDREF (Centre d'enseignement, de documentation et de recherche pour les études féministes) at University Paris 7 – Denis Diderot until 1999. She is on the editorial committee of *Les Temps Modernes*. Her research centres mainly on relationships between gender and race issues, feminist history, and feminist theory. Among her recent publications are: *Féminismes et nazisme, colloque en hommage à Rita Thalmann* (Paris: Publications de l'Université Paris 7 – Denis Diderot, 1997); 'La question du sexisme, du racisme et de l'antisémitisme dans les recherches féministes en France' (*Cahiers du Cedref* 6, 1997); 'Is Auschwitz, then, Just an "Epiphenomenon"? Notes on a "Disquieting Familiarity"', in Goldhagen, ed., *Theory and Psychology* (vol. 8, no. 5, October 1998); and 'Sexe, nature – et amnésie', in *Le piège de la parité. Arguments pour un débat* (Paris: Hachette Littérature, 1999).

Zarana Papic, who died as this book was going to press, was Assistant Professor at the Faculty of Philosophy, University of Belgrade; co-founder and Professor at the Belgrade Women's Studies Centre and at the Alternative Academic Educational Centre (AAEN) in Belgrade. She was also an associate researcher of the Laboratoire d'anthropologie sociale, Collège de France, Paris. A long-time feminist activist/supporter of Women in Black, Women's Political Action and other women's initiatives in the region of the former Yugoslavia, she published widely in English, French and German. Her articles include 'From State Socialism to State Nationalism: The Case of Serbia in Gender Perspective', in Rada Ivekovic and Neda Pagon, eds, *Otherhood and Nation* (Ljubljana and Paris: Institutum Studiorum Humanitatis and Editions de la Maison des Sciences de l'Homme, 1998); 'Women in Serbia: Post-Communism, War and Nationalist Mutations', in Sabrina Petra Ramet, ed., *Gender Politics in the Western Balkans: Women and Society in Yugoslavia and Yugoslav Successor States* (University Park, PA: Penn State University Press, 1999).

Luisa Passerini is Professor of the History of the Twentieth Century at the European University Institute, Florence. Among her recent books are *Europe in Love, Love in Europe: Imagination and Politics in Britain between the Wars* (London: I.B. Tauris, 1999); *Identità culturale europea. Idee sentimenti relazioni*, ed. (Florence: La Nuova Italia, 1998); and *Across the Atlantic: Cultural Exchanges between Europe and the United States*, ed. (Brussels: Peter Lang, 2000).

Andrea Pető is a Hungarian feminist historian who has lectured in a number of higher educational institutions including the Central European University, Budapest, on post-World War II Central European history, oral history and women's history. She is President of the Feminist Section of the Hungarian Sociological Association. In 2001–2 she held a Jean Monet Fellowship at the European Institute in Florence. Her publications include *Nohistoriak. A politizals magyar nuk tvrtinete (1945–1951)* [Women's Stories: From a History of Hungarian Women in Politics, 1945–1951] (Budapest: Seneca, 1998); a biography of Julia Rajk (Budapest: Balassi, 2001) in the series 'Feminism and History' she edits for the Balassi Publishing House. She is now working on women and political conservatism.

Françoise Picq is an Assistant Professor at the University of Paris IX – Dauphine. Since 1970 she has been involved in the Women's Liberation Movement, MLF. She has had many roles in developing feminist studies in France since 1975. She was an organizer of the first National Conference 'Femmes, Feminisme, Recherche' (Toulouse, December 1982). She was also part of the organizing team of the International Research Conference initiated by the French mission for 4th UNO Global Conference on Women. She was one of the founders and president (now vice-president) of the National Feminist Studies Association (ANEF), and was the national contact for the European Network for Women's Studies (ENWS). Picq holds a Ph.D. in Political Science. Her writings are on anthropology and theories of maternity rights; feminism and socialism; the origin and history of the International Women's Day, the history of feminism in France; and the feminist movement in the 1970s. Her recent publications include *Libération des femmes: les Années mouvement* (Paris: Seuil 1993), and 'Le féminisme entre passé recomposé et futur incertain' (*Cités* 8, 2000).

Sandra Ponzanesi is a fellow of the University of Amsterdam. She graduated in English literature at Bologna University with a dissertation on V.S. Naipaul and has a Ph.D. from Utrecht University. Her doctorate, published as *Paradoxes of Post-colonial Culture: Feminism and Diaspora in South-Asian and Afro-Italian Women's Narratives* (Albany: State University of New York Press, 2002) is a critical approach to post-colonialism, comparative literature and Third World feminist theories. She is currently researching on issues of gender and migration in Europe with special focus on literary representations of urban space. She has also worked and studied in the United Kingdom. Her major publications focus on Italian colonial history, Women's Studies and post-colonial literary criticism. She has contributed to the *Cambridge Guide to Women's Writing in English* and to the *Routledge Companion to Contemporary Black British Culture*.

Lisa Price completed her doctorate at the Research Centre on Violence, Abuse and Gender Relations, Leeds Metropolitan University. Her research interests include rape as a war crime, the intersection of gender and ethnicity, and the construction of gender under conditions of militarized state nationalism. She has published an article entitled 'Finding the Man in the Soldier-Rapist: Some Reflections on Comprehension and Accountability' (*Women's Studies International Forum*, vol. 24, no. 2, March–April 2001).

Elena Pulcini is Professor of Social Philosophy in the Department of Philosophy at the University of Florence. Her research centres on the theory of the passions with a focus on the construction of modern identity and the formation of social bonds. Among her recent publications are: *Amour-passion et amour conjugal. Rousseau et l'origine d'un conflit moderne* (Paris: Champion-Slatkine, 1998; orig. 1990); *L'individuo senza passioni. Individualismo moderno e perdita del legame sociale* (Turin: Bollati Boringhieri, 2001); and *Filosofie della globalizzazione*, co-ed. with D. D'Andrea (Pisa: LETS 2201).

Maria Serena Sapegno is Professor of Italian Literature at the University of Rome I ('La Sapienza'). Her research interests are in the area of cultural tropes, political and historiographic writings, poetry, women's culture and politics in the twentieth century. She contributes to various reviews (*DWF, Tuttestorie, Critica del testo*) and her recent publications are *Petrarca e lo stile della poesia* (Rome, 1999) and thematic criticisism, *Costanti, varianti, 'arbitrarietà' dell'interprete. gli 'oggetti' di Orlando e la critica tematica* (Rome, 1998).

María S. Suárez Lafuente is Professor of English Literature at the University of Oviedo. She has published extensively on women's world literature, both in English and in Spanish. She is a lifelong researcher of the Faustian tradition. At present she is President of the Spanish Association for Women's Studies (AUDEM).

Renata Šribar is a writer, feminist activist and independent researcher located in Ljubljana. She founded a feminist group for the promotion of the equal status of women in public and the media and a women's reading room. She also co-founded an association of Slovenian feminist groups. She has published two books of feminist short prose. She is working on the sociology and anthropology of menstruation, and on the relationship of the female body to culture.

Harriet Silius is Professor of Women's Studies at Åbo Akademi University, Finland. Her research interests are gender and ethnicity, women's life stories, the Nordic welfare states, women in the legal profession, and issues of feminist methodologies. Recent publications include: 'Finnish Gender Contracts', in K.C. Roy, C.A. Tisdell and H.C. Blomqvist, eds, *Economic Development and Women in the World Community* (Westport, CT: Praeger 1996); 'Att var kvinna och jurist' [To be a woman and a lawyer], in Gudrun Nordborg, ed., *13 kvinnoperspektiv på rätten* (Uppsala: Iustus Förlag, 1995); 'I dialog med kvinnoliv' [In dialogue with women's lives] (Publications from the Institute of Women's Studies at Åbo Akademi University no. 11, Åbo 1998).

Svetlana Slapšak is Professor of Anthropology of Ancient Worlds and Anthropology of Gender Co-ordinator at the Institutum Studiorum Humanitatis (ISH) at the University of Ljubljana. Recent publications include: *Women's Icons of the 20th Century* (Ljubljana: UZP, 2000); *For the Anthropology of the Ancient Worlds* (Ljubljana: ISH, 2000); *War Discourse, Women's Discourse: Studies* *and Essays on Wars in Yugoslavia and Russia* (in English) (Ljubljana: ISH, 2000); *The Adventure Novel Goes East: Transformations of a Popular Genre* (Ljubljana: SH Apes, 1997); and *Wartime Candide*, essays (Belgrade: B92, 1996). She is also editor-in-chief of *ProFemina*, Belgrade, which in 1997 published an issue, in English, on modern women's literature in Serbia.

Index

Abbott, Berenice, 90
abortion, 71, 73, 129, 149, 256, 264, 318, 345, 352, 368; case study, in Slovenia, 373–5; criminalized, 71 (in France, 317); decriminalized in Italy, 337; Italian referendum on, 337; liberalized in France, 317; outlawed in Croatia, 256
Accad, Evelyne, 272–3, 274
Adorno, Theodor, 162
affective economies of racialized politics, 231–2
affectivity, women and, 98–102
Afghanistan, 273
Africa: militarization of, 277; slavery in, 208; Western blindness to, 92, 94
Afshar, Haleh, 229, 230
Agape, 101
agency of women, 26, 75, 216
Albanian women, violence against, 138
Alberdi, Cristina, 293
Allen, Sheila, 254
Allgemeiner Deutscher Frauenverein (ADF), 323, 325
alliances between women, 270–71, 274–6
Alternativas journal (Spain), 384
Althusser, Louis, 163, 164, 165
amateurs, women as, 88
Anabasi group (Italy), 335
Anderson, Margaret, 90
Angelou, Maya, 225
Anguissola, Sofonisba, 85
anorexia, as gender-related disease, 357
Anthias, Floya, 233
Anti-fascist Front of Women (AFŽ) (Yugoslavia), 149

Anti-Jewish Law (Hungary), 366
anti-racism, 303
anti-Semitism, 12, 21–2, 302; feminism and, 183–204; feminist readings of, 187–8
anti-Zionism, 185
Antic, Milica, 256
Anttonen, Anneli, 39
Anzaldua, Gloria, 207
applied arts, women's activity in, 87
Arc de Triomphe, wreath laid at, 316
Arenal journal (Spain), 384
Arendt, Hannah, 91, 100, 162, 163
Aristarkhova, Irina, 297–301
Aristotle, 66, 98–9
Arkan (Zeljko Raznatovic), 141, 142, 143
Armenians, genocide of, 208
artificial insemination, 150; in Slovenia, 374–5
Ås, Berit, 354
Asociación Española de Mujeres Universitarias (Spain), 380, 382
Asociación Nacional de Mujeres Españolas (Spain), 379
Aspiraciones group (Spain), 196
Association for Non-Violent Communication (Slovenia), 376
Association for the Promotion of Women in Culture, 377
Association Nationale des Études Féministes (ANEF) (France), 318
Association of Institutions for Feminist Education and Research in Europe (AOIFE), 385
Association of the Working Class (Yugoslavia), 372

ZED BOOKS ON WOMEN

Zed Books has a reputation as a leading publisher of critical, intellectually innovative and important books in the fields of Women's Studies. Amongst the many titles that we have published in recent years are:

Margaret Gallagher *Gender Setting: New Agendas for Media Monitoring and Advocacy*

Gabriele Griffin and Rosi Braidotti (eds) *Thinking Differently: A Reader in European Women's Studies*

Martha Gutierrez (ed.) *Macro-economics: Making Gender Matter. Concepts, Policies and Institutional Change in Developing Countries*

Wendy Harcourt (ed.) *Power, Reproduction and Gender: The Intergenerational Transfer of Knowledge*

Wendy Harcourt (ed.) *Feminist Perspectives on Sustainable Development:*

Wendy Harcourt (ed.) *Women@Internet: Creating New Cultures in Cyberspace*

Miriam Jacobs and Barbara Dinham (eds) *Silent Invaders: Pesticides, Livelihoods and Women's Health*

Susie Jacobs, Ruth Jacobson and Jennifer Marchbank (eds) *States of Conflict: Gender, Violence and Resistance*

Kumari Jayawardena and Malathi de Alwis *Embodied Violence: Communalising Female Sexuality in South Asia*

Naila Kabeer and Ramya Subrahmanian (eds) *Institutions, Relations and Outcomes: A Framework and Case Studies for Gender-aware Planning*

Karin Kapadia (ed.) *The Violence of Development: The Political Economy of Gender*

Joanna Liddle and Sachiko Nakajima *Rising Suns, Rising Daughters: Gender, Class and Power in Japan*

Yayori Matsui *Women in the New Asia: From Pain to Power*

Sheila Meintjes, Anu Pillay and Meredeth Turshen (eds) *The Aftermath: Women in Post-conflict Transformation*

Maria Mies *Patriarchy and Accumulation on a World Scale: Women in the International Division of Labour*

Maria Mies and Vandana Shiva *Ecofeminism*

Judy Mirsky and Marty Radlett (eds) *No Paradise Yet: The World's Women Face the New Century*

Haideh Moghissi *Feminism and Islamic Fundamentalism: The Limits of Postmodern Analysis*

Caroline O.N. Moser and Fiona C. Clark (eds) *Victims, Perpetrators or Actors? Gender, Armed Conflict and Political Violence*

Ranjani K. Murthy and Lakshmi Sankaran *Denial and Distress: Gender, Poverty and Human Rights in Asia*

Helen Pankhurst *Gender, Development and Identity: An Ethiopian Study*

Susan Perry and Celeste Schenck (eds) *Eye to Eye: Women Practising Development across Cultures*

Rosalind P. Petchesky and Karen Judd (eds) *Negotiating Reproductive Rights: Women's Perspectives Across Countries and Cultures*

Marilyn Porter and Ellen Judd (eds) *Feminists Doing Development: A Practical Critique*

Maryam Poya *Women, Work and Islamism: Ideology and Resistance in Iran*

Kalima Rose *Where Women are Leaders: The SEWA Movement in India*

Sheila Rowbotham and Stephanie Linkogle (eds) *Women Resist Globalization: Mobilizing for Livelihood and Rights*

Nawal El Saadawi *The Nawal El Saadawi Reader.*

Nawal El Saadawi *A Daughter of Isis: The Autobiography of Nawal El Saadawi*

Nawal El Saadawi *Walking through Fire: A Life of Nawal El Saadawi*

Nawal El Saadawi *The Hidden Face of Eve: Women in the Arab World*

Nawal El Saadawi *Woman at Point Zero*

Kriemild Saunders (ed.) *Feminist Post-Development Thought: Rethinking Modernity, Post-Colonialism and Representation*

Vandana Shiva *Staying Alive: Women, Ecology and Development*

Jael Silliman and Ynestra King (eds) *Dangerous Intersections: Feminism, Population and Environment*

Sinith Sittirak *The Daughters of Development: Women in a Changing Environment*

Torild Skard *Continent of Mothers, Continent of Hope: Understanding and Promoting Development in Africa Today*

Susanne Thorbek and Bandana Pattanaik (eds) *Transnational Prostitution: Changing Patterns in a Global Context*

Janet Townsend, Emma Zapata, Jo Rowlands, Pilar Alberti and Marta Mercado *Women and Power: Fighting Patriarchies and Poverty*

Meredeth Turshen and Clotilde Twagiramariya *What Women Do in Wartime: Gender and Conflict in Africa*

Nalini Visvanathan, Lynn Duggan, Laurie Nisonoff and Nan Wiegersma (eds) *The Women, Gender and Development Reader.*

L. Muthoni Wanyeki (ed.) *Women and Land in Africa: Culture, Religion and Realizing Women's Rights*

Sarah C. White *Arguing with the Crocodile: Gender and Class in Bangladesh*

Christa Wichterich *The Globalised Woman: Reports from a Future of Inequality*

Saskia Wieringa (ed.) *Subversive Women: Women's Movements in Africa, Asia, Latin America and the Caribbean*

Nira Yuval-Davis and Pnina Werbner (eds) *Women, Citizenship and Difference*

For full details of this list and Zed's other subject and general catalogues, please write to: The Marketing Department, Zed Books, 7 Cynthia Street, London N1 9JF, UK or email Sales@zedbooks.demon.co.uk

Visit our website at: http://www.zedbooks.demon.co.uk